L9

Praise for *Why We're Liberals* by Eric Alterman

"Alterman spends a lot of time clearing away the falsehoods spread by both right-wing and mainstream media figures, but the core of the book is a vigorous defense of liberalism as a credo—a credo, Alterman argues persuasively, that most Americans actually subscribe to in its constituent parts. Acknowledging that liberalism is notoriously difficult to define, he nonetheless provides an extensive and nuanced analysis of its substance."   —*The Atlantic Monthly*

"[A] passionate call to arms to his brethren to reclaim their nobility of purpose . . . a masterful new thesis about the distortion of the liberal agenda. . . . Writing without rancor, Alterman is boldly critical of both his adversaries and his allies. He comes off not as an extremist but a pragmatic patriot in love with his country."   —*The Star Ledger* (Newark)

"Alterman writes in a refreshingly clear and simple tone. And for a liberal, he takes a refreshingly nonideological approach. Think of his book as a tactical field manual for liberals who want to come out of the shadows."
                                                —*St. Louis Post-Dispatch*

"[Alterman] makes an enthusiastic . . . case that liberalism is poised to rise again."   —*Kirkus Reviews*

"[Alterman] admirably rebuts all the right's powerful canards about the left."
                                                      —*TimeOut New York*

"He offers some solid advice for Democrats on the construction of a bigger ideological tent."   —*The New York Sun*

Praise for Eric Alterman

"The only hope of staying sane in the lockstep stereotyped reporting was to look up Eric Alterman."   —Harold Evans, *The Wall Street Journal*

"[Eric Alterman is] the most honest and incisive media critic writing today."
                          —Raymond A. Schroth, *National Catholic Reporter*

"Eric Alterman's blog, Altercation, is easily the smartest and funniest political journal out there."   —Jon Carroll, *San Francisco Chronicle*

"Eric Alterman . . . is a one-man truth squad. If you read Alterman's book[s] and his columns you will never again fall victim to the pernicious and pervasive right-wing attempts to dominate the media."
                          —James Carville and Paul Begala, *Take It Back: Our Party, Our Country, Our Future*

PENGUIN BOOKS

WHY WE'RE LIBERALS

The author of six previous books, Eric Alterman is Distinguished Professor of English, Brooklyn College, City University of New York, and Professor of Journalism at the CUNY Graduate School of Journalism. He is also "The Liberal Media" columnist for the *Nation;* a senior fellow and Altercation weblogger for Media Matters for America (formerly at MSNBC .com) in Washington, D.C.; a senior fellow at the Center for American Progress in Washington, D.C., where he writes and edits the "Think Again" column; a senior fellow (since 1985) at the World Policy Institute in New York; a history consultant to HBO Films; and a quarterly columnist for the Jewish magazine *Moment.* Termed "the most honest and incisive media critic writing today" in the *National Catholic Reporter* and author of "the smartest and funniest political journal out there" in the *San Francisco Chronicle,* Alterman is a frequent lecturer and a contributor to numerous publications in the United States, Europe, and Latin America. In recent years, he has also been a columnist for *Worth, Rolling Stone, Mother Jones,* and the *Sunday Express* (London).

Previous works include the national bestsellers *What Liberal Media? The Truth About Bias and the News* (2003, 2004) and *The Book on Bush: How George W. (Mis)leads America* (coauthor, 2004), as well as *When Presidents Lie: A History of Official Deception and Its Consequences* (2004, 2005); *Sound and Fury: The Making of the Punditocracy* (1992, 2000), which won the 1992 George Orwell Award; *It Ain't No Sin to Be Glad You're Alive: The Promise of Bruce Springsteen* (1999, 2001), which won the 1999 Stephen Crane Literary Award; and *Who Speaks for America? Why Democracy Matters in Foreign Policy* (1998).

Alterman received his B.A. in history and government from Cornell, his M.A. in international relations from Yale, and his Ph.D. in U.S. history from Stanford. He lives with his family in Manhattan, where he is completing a history of American liberalism since 1945.

WHY WE'RE LIBERALS

A HANDBOOK FOR
RESTORING AMERICA'S MOST
IMPORTANT IDEALS

ERIC ALTERMAN

PENGUIN BOOKS

PENGUIN BOOKS

Published by the Penguin Group

Penguin Group (USA) Inc., 375 Hudson Street, New York, New York 10014, U.S.A. • Penguin Group (Canada), 90 Eglinton Avenue East, Suite 700, Toronto, Ontario, Canada M4P 2Y3 (a division of Pearson Penguin Canada Inc.) • Penguin Books Ltd, 80 Strand, London WC2R 0RL, England • Penguin Ireland, 25 St Stephen's Green, Dublin 2, Ireland (a division of Penguin Books Ltd) • Penguin Group (Australia), 250 Camberwell Road, Camberwell, Victoria 3124, Australia (a division of Pearson Australia Group Pty Ltd) • Penguin Books India Pvt Ltd, 11 Community Centre, Panchsheel Park, New Delhi – 110 017, India • Penguin Group (NZ), 67 Apollo Drive, Rosedale, North Shore 0632, New Zealand (a division of Pearson New Zealand Ltd) • Penguin Books (South Africa) (Pty) Ltd, 24 Sturdee Avenue, Rosebank, Johannesburg 2196, South Africa

Penguin Books Ltd, Registered Offices:
80 Strand, London WC2R 0RL, England

First published in the United States of America by Viking Penguin,
a member of Penguin Group (USA) Inc. 2008
Published in Penguin Books 2009

10 9 8 7 6 5 4 3 2 1

THE LIBRARY OF CONGRESS HAS CATALOGED THE HARDCOVER EDITION AS FOLLOWS:
Alterman, Eric.
Why we're liberals : a political handbook for post-Bush America / Eric Alterman.
p.   cm.
Includes bibliographical references and index.
ISBN 978-0-670-01860-4 (hc.)
ISBN 978-0-14-311522-9 (pbk.)
1. Liberalism—United States.   I. Title.
JC574.2.U6A44   2008
320.5'130973—dc22   2007048477

Printed in the United States of America
Designed by Carla Bolte • *Set in Dante*

FOR VICTOR S. NAVASKY AND EDGAR L. DOCTOROW:

FRIENDS. TEACHERS. HEROES. LIBERALS.

I'm more of a man than any liberal.

—ANN COULTER

I have to ask, like who are these parents to allow their kids to sleep with Michael Jackson?

Liberals.

—ALAN COLMES AND SEAN HANNITY

I never meant to say that the Conservatives are generally stupid. I meant to say that stupid people are generally Conservative. I believe that is so obviously and universally admitted a principle that I hardly think any gentleman will deny it.

—JOHN STUART MILL

Contents

WHY WE'RE LIBERALS

Introduction

We're living at an odd political moment in America. For the past three decades or so, those of us who answer to the name "liberal" have seen ourselves demonized by conservatives and by their conscious and unconscious allies in the media as weak, elitist, out of touch, lacking in moral fiber, unpatriotic, unwilling to stand up for ourselves, and a general pox on the body politic. All the politicians with aspirations outside of the deep blue regions of the Northeast insist that not only are they not one of those dreaded "liberals," they're not sure they've ever even *met* one—at least not that they can remember. The word *liberal* has been employed as the political equivalent of an untreatable but potentially containable social disease—the kind that could be contracted merely by going to a foreign movie or ordering a decaf latte, or worse, a glass of French wine.

Ever since Richard Nixon walloped George McGovern in the presidential election of 1972, political pundits have treated as a truism the proposition that liberals are out of step with the rest of the nation, and therefore all but unelectable outside the precincts of the Northeast—give or take a college town here or a ski resort there. During the course of every presidential election for the past forty years now, Republicans have sought to wield the word *liberal* as if it were a twelve-gauge shotgun. "Senator Kerry is rated as the most liberal member of the United States Senate, and he chose a fellow lawyer who is the fourth most liberal member of the United States Senate," President Bush joked. "Back in Massachusetts, that's what they call balancing the ticket." Asked to respond, the man from Massachusetts complained, but did not defend. "It's not real," Kerry told *USA Today* about the "Massachusetts liberal" tag; "that stuff is just old hokey that just doesn't stand up. People know it's a lot of malarkey." His running mate, North Carolina's John Edwards, was hardly more forthcoming. Asked by ABC's Ted Koppel, "Are you a liberal?" he responded, "No. I don't believe in labels, first of all. I don't think they mean anything. I think what John Kerry and I are is mainstream America."[1]

As Newt Gingrich has pointedly observed, "Kerry says labels are misleading because he understands labels are the end of his campaign."[2] Indeed, even Rush Limbaugh proved uncharacteristically accurate when he pointed out that conservatives evince no such reticence when it comes to labeling. "Somebody calls me a conservative," he teased his tongue-tied opponents, "I flex my muscles and say, 'Yeah, baby.' You want to call me a right-winger, I say, 'Hell, yes, I'm a right-winger.' But you call them liberals, they don't want any part of it. They get defensive. 'What do you mean by that? Why do you have to always say the L-word? You know that that doesn't mean anything.' Well, it does. It means a lot."[3]

As neoliberal pundit Michael Kinsley pointed out during the 2004 Democratic convention, "It's true enough that this is a moment when the Democrats are called upon to reject extreme liberalism (whatever that might be) and to embrace moderation. But that is only because every moment is such a moment." He termed this meme "one of the very safest in all of punditry," which, as the old song goes, is really saying something.[4] And yet Republicans, Kinsley noted, receive the equivalent of a free ideological pass despite the fact that their leadership was, at the time, committed to an agenda so politically extreme that it was preparing to drive the nation off several cliffs simultaneously. Not surprisingly, his prediction proved prescient, and the warnings to liberals and Democrats came fast and furious throughout the election season. Typical was ABC's Cokie Roberts's announcement as if on cue that yes, "It's a unified party, but it is a party of the left."[5] Most members of the mainstream media reinforce this notion of liberal as leper. "This is basically not a liberal country," said John F. Harris, then political editor of the *Washington Post* and now an editor of the influential tip sheet the *Politico*, in May 2005. "It's a conservative country."[6]

During the 2006 election season, the same leading lights of the pundit-ocracy rehearsed their talking points with nary a comma replaced. When political neophyte Ned Lamont defeated three-term senator Joe Lieber-man in Connecticut's Democratic primary with the help of liberal activists and the energetic participation of the liberal blogosphere, Roberts complained that Lieberman's defeat would lead to "chaos." She got no argument from her ABC News colleague George F. Will, who added, "So if the blogosphere and MoveOn.org dragged the party to the left, it will be a disaster."[7] Pundit "Dean" David Broder bemoaned that the "terrible tug" of a Lamont victory would undoubtedly presage "decisive defeats" for the party in November.[8] *Slate's* Jacob Weisberg complained that "the 2006 Connecticut primary points to the growing influence within the party of leftists unmoved by the fight against global jihad."[9] *New Republic* editor Martin Peretz denounced the "thought-enforcers of the left" in the *Wall Street Journal*.[10] In the same pages, Lieberman's friend Lanny S. Davis professed to detect a kind of "liberal McCarthyism,"[11] while over at the *Times,* neocon David Brooks lashed out at the party's "liberal inquisition."[12] This was polite compared to cable news, how-ever. CNN Headline News anchor John Roberts went so far as to label Lamont "the al-Qaida candidate," before being forced to apologize.[13] Fox News anchor John Gibson did him one better, unapologetically an-nouncing, "The Khmer Rouge wing of the Democratic Party is making a bid for a complete takeover."[14] It is worth recalling that these hysterics were directed at a businessman-turned-candidate who campaigned as a mere garden-variety liberal, whose views on Iraq and the Bush adminis-tration were shared, according to every poll published during the period, by over 60 percent of Americans.[15]

Lamont ultimately lost, but the Democrats' sweep of the House and Senate demonstrated how misguided were the pundits' predictions of doom over the presence of a liberal replacement for Lieberman for the national party. Meanwhile, many of these same journalists and pundits viewed the election as yet another opportunity to dust off some of the same hoary clichés. On the occasion of his party's smashing and surpris-ing victory party chair Howard Dean was immediately confronted by a suspicious Chris Wallace on Fox, who posited: "You've got to show that you're up to governing and, frankly, governing from the center, not from the left."[16] "Liberals Aim to Push Ideas through Congress," ran an MSNBC.com headline over an Associated Press story that quoted leaders of various liberal organizations saying exactly the opposite,[17] while *Newsweek*'s famed "Conventional Wisdom Watch" warned Americans to be on guard against what it called Nancy Pelosi's "dopey liberalism."[18]

These views, one can't help but notice, proved to be in complete contrast to those voiced when the Republicans took over Congress in 1994. Back then, a front-page analysis in the *New York Times* made the unremarkable and then largely unchallenged assertion that "the country has unmistakably moved to the right."[19] And yet if one examines the numbers of voters who switched from one party to the other, the shift to the Democrats in 2006 was actually far larger, both in real numbers and as a percentage of those voting, than that to the Republicans twelve years earlier. But when it comes to "liberal" victories in American politics, there's always some other explanation available.

It may shocking to some to discover that for much of the past century, the term *liberal* suggested, in the words of historian John Lukacs, "generosity nay, magnanimity; not only breadth of a mind but strength of soul." A liberal was someone "free from narrow prejudice," according to the *Oxford English Dictionary*. Even the enemies of liberalism sought legitimacy within it. In 1960, the *New York Times Sunday Magazine* published an article by the philosopher Charles Frankel in which he observed that it would be difficult to locate a single major figure in American politics who could not find a favorable remark or two about American liberalism. Indeed, he wrote, "Anyone who today identifies himself as an unmitigated opponent of liberalism . . . cannot aspire to influence on the national political scene." Frankel noted that even politicians who indulged in attacks on "liberals" were usually sufficiently cautious in their criticism to attach qualifiers to the word, lest they be accused of antiliberalism themselves. Southern conservatives, for instance, complained about "Northern liberals," often insisting that they themselves were liberals in matters of social welfare. Even Joe McCarthy usually restricted himself to attacking "phony liberals," leaving open the inference, as Frankel put it, "that he had nothing against genuine liberals, if only he could find one."[20] Later the same year, "Mr. Republican," Senator Robert A. Taft, claimed the liberal label for himself, stating—accurately, as it happens—that he was in reality "an old-fashioned liberal."[21] The party's successful 1952 presidential candidate, General Dwight D. Eisenhower, was also on board: "To be fully effective," Ike explained, "we need in Washington liberal and experienced members of Congress."[22] As late as 1968, voters heard this moving tribute to the virtues of liberalism: "Let me give you a definition of the word 'liberal.' . . . Franklin D. Roosevelt once said . . . It is a wonderful definition, and I agree with him. 'A liberal is a man who wants to build bridges over the chasms that separate humanity from a better life.'" The speaker? That famous liberal presidential candidate: Richard Milhous Nixon.[23]

And yet to judge merely by the titles that pop up on a search of Amazon.com, to be a self-confessed "liberal" in George W. Bush's America is to place oneself literally in the rhetorical company of pedophiles, axe murderers, and mass murderers. Titles range from Ann Coulter's *Treason: Liberal Treachery from the Cold War to the War on Terrorism*—along with pretty much every one of her other titles—to Michael Savage's *The Savage Nation: Saving America from the Liberal Assault on Our Borders, Language and Culture* and *Liberalism Is a Mental Disorder*, Mona Charen's *Useful Idiots: How Liberals Got It Wrong in the Cold War and Still Blame America First*, and Sean Hannity's *Let Freedom Ring: Winning the War of Liberty over Liberalism* and *Deliver Us from Evil: Defeating Terrorism, Despotism, and Liberalism*, among many, many others. (For conservatives in training, there's Katharine DeBrecht's *Help! Mom! There Are Liberals under My Bed!*)

One can discern few, if any, limits to the kinds of accusations prominent conservatives have made about liberals in recent years. Coulter, to whom fellow right-winger Jonah Goldberg once referred as "barely coherent," was also among liberalism's most widely quoted and publicized critics.[24] Her book *Treason* took liberalism to task for everything from allegedly "undermining victory in the Cold War" to aiming "to destroy America from the inside with their relentless attacks on morality and the truth."[25] And she does so not merely with impunity, but with widespread admiration. Coulter herself joked, after she had called Democratic presidential candidate John Edwards "a faggot" (after she was introduced by Republican presidential candidate Mitt Romney), that it turned out to be her "seventeenth allegedly career-ending moment." The "lesson," she explained, that "young right-wingers ought to draw from this is it's really not that scary to attack liberals."[26]

The continuum of relatively respectable abuse of liberals and liberalism stretches all the way to former militant left-wing Stalinist turned militant right-wing Stalinist David Horowitz, who offers this: "Here's the reason liberal has become a dirty word. . . . Because Communists, fellow-travelers, pro-terrorists, terrorist sympathizers have hijacked the word."[27] Horowitz has been eclipsed by Coulter in recent years, but beginning in the late 1980s, he became an important consultant to conservative politicians, including 1996 Republican presidential candidate Bob Dole. As we will see through the course of this book, there appears to be nothing at all that someone can say about liberals that would disqualify him or her from regular media bookings and respectful introductions and quotations from Republican presidential candidates.

Janice Rogers Brown, confirmed in June 2005 to the U.S. Court of Appeals, termed the New Deal "the triumph of our socialist revolution."[28] Former Republican House majority leader Dick Armey has written that the New Deal and the Great Society, on the one hand, and Soviet Russia's five-year plans and Communist China's Great Leap Forward, on the other, were created by "the same sort of person" separated only by differences of "power and nerve."[29] Former House majority leader Tom DeLay goes him one better, comparing "liberals" to "scoundrels like Hitler," but also noting that they are "much like communists."[30] Former Pennsylvania senator Rick Santorum, speaking as the body's third-ranking Republican, blamed the city of Boston's historic liberalism for the Roman Catholic Church's pedophile scandal. "It is no surprise," he says, "that Boston, a seat of academic, political, and cultural liberalism in America, lies at the center of the storm of the clergy sexual abuse scandal."[31] Former House Speaker Newt Gingrich went so far as to blame both the 1999 Columbine massacre and the even more horrific 2007 Virginia Tech killings on liberals, who have "created a situation ethics, essentially, zone of not being willing to talk about any of these things."[32] Rush Limbaugh, naturally, went even further, exploiting the Virginia Tech tragedy in a manner than many might have predicted, but would still have had trouble believing until he actually said it: "This guy had to be a liberal. You start railing against the rich and all this other—this guy's a liberal. He was turned into a liberal somewhere along the line. So it's a liberal that committed this act."[33]

The word *liberal* exercises such power in America's political debate that it can apparently transform even the most perceptive conservative minds to mush. The brave Islamic dissident and critic Ayaan Hirsi Ali has spoken and written with uncommon audacity and perspicacity about the values of the Enlightenment and the intellectual shortcomings of her own tradition, but after spending a few months at the American Enterprise Institute, a neoconservative Washington think tank, she answered the question of whether she was a liberal, "Yes, but not 'liberal' in the Communist sense."[34] Although the African-American scholar Shelby Steele frequently offers interesting and provocative challenges to conventional wisdom on race and affirmative action, when it comes to "liberals," he somehow finds little difference between a young man's northern California upbringing—with a gay father, which is unspoken in Steele's analysis but undoubtedly key—and training in an al-Qaeda cell. "This liberalism thrives as a subversive, winking, countercultural hipness," he writes, referring to the milieu that gave rise to "American Talib" John Walker Lindh. "Cultural liberalism serves up American self-hate to the young as idealism. . . . And when he [Lindh] turned on his country to be secure in his new faith, he followed a logic that was a part of his country's culture."[35] (Apparently, the countercultural atmosphere of California liberalism trumps free will in Steele's world—though one cannot help but wonder where all the other Marin County–born and bred Taliban fighters are hiding out these days.)

All of this raises the obvious question: If liberalism has grown so weak and ineffective, why does it evoke such alarm on the part of conservatives?

It turns out that while liberals are weak and spineless, they are also sneaky and clever, especially when it comes to the use of language. In a column appearing on the *Wall Street Journal* site opinionjournal.com, Manuel Miranda, a staffer for then Senate majority leader Dr. Bill Frist, charges that

> when liberals say "civil rights," they mean mostly lucrative trial-lawyer-driven employee grievances, the rights of convicted murderers, and the continued use of divisive racial quotas. When liberals say "women's rights," they mean that parents have no right to know when a man impregnates their minor daughter and takes her for an abortion. When liberals assail Judge Roberts about the issue of equal pay for women—which is the law—they really mean that government should dictate how much every worker is paid. When liberals speak of environmental and worker rights, they mean unlimited federal government regulatory power over local governments and the private sector.[36]

What's more, right-wingers explain, though they have been forced to relinquish the levers of political power, liberals have nevertheless managed to gain control of almost all of the country's cultural institutions for their nefarious purposes. According to Hilton Kramer, who edits the neoconservative arts journal the *New Criterion,* the American left can be said to include "almost (if not quite) everybody in the media, the academy, the arts, the literary and publishing worlds, the entertainment industry, and the Democratic party." This is dangerous, he explains, because the liberal agenda is rooted in the idea that "Amerika" is "intolerably repressive" and the "principal source of evil" in the world—an idea, according to Kramer, that "currently prevails at almost every level of cultural life," from our universities down to our "wretched pop music."[37]

★ ★ ★

Lest anyone regard such talk as the exclusive province of the conservative wing of the mainstream media, such treatment is actually more the rule than the exception. Matt Taibbi, who reports on politics for the onetime countercultural magazine *Rolling Stone,* sounds positively Coulterian when complaining of what he terms "the saddest collection of cowering, ineffectual ninnies ever assembled under one banner on God's green earth . . . politically irrelevant and permanently relegated to the sidelines, tucked into its cozy little cottage industry of polysyllabic, ivory tower criticism. When you get right down to it, the American left is basically just a noisy Upper West Side cocktail party for the college-graduate class."[38] One would expect, moreover, that the last institution to embrace this destructive stereotype would be the *New York Times,* which is universally perceived as ground zero of much-maligned sophisticated liberalism. And yet one finds on that paper's front page the disappointing news that Nancy Pelosi "lends herself to easy caricature by Republicans" because, you guessed it, "she is an unapologetic liberal."[39] The clear implication is that liberals really ought to apologize just for being liberals, a notion to which the *Times* editors are so committed that, to take one trivial but revealing example, during the Republican convention in New York City in 2004 its editors sent reporter John Tierney to Zabar's, the famed food store on Manhattan's Upper West Side, literally looking for liberal New Yorkers who might be "re-examining their consciences." Just why these liberal consciences required reexamination, Tierney did not even bother to say.[40]

* * *

While an extreme example, the *Times* depiction of Zabar's shoppers is unfortunately representative. Conservatives, as portrayed in the mainstream media, have "values," while liberals merely enjoy their elitist whims. In the right-wing *Washington Times,* owned by Sun Myung Moon's Unification Church, you'll find references to "conservative values" seven times as frequently as "liberal values"; in the *Washington Post* the ratio is four to one.[41] (In interviewing the far-right presidential candidate Sam Brownback, ABC's George Stephanopoulos, for instance, equated "pro-family" with Brownback's right-wing "social conservative . . . pro-life" positions as if the only families in America were the conservative kind.)[42] "In this day and age," the linguist Geoffrey Nunberg surmises, "it's assumed that liberalism is something most people would have qualms about owning up to. And when liberalism is mentioned in these mainstream newspapers, the context is almost always 'West Side liberalism' or 'Hollywood liberalism,' thereby suggesting a social clique rather than a philosophical school." After all, Nunberg notes, "Hollywood liberalism" isn't the same sort of thing as "Chicago economics." Rarely if ever do the media employ a phrase like "working-class liberals, Hispanic liberals, or black liberals," though they frequently do so when describing conservatives.[43]

"Liberalism" in contemporary parlance is considered by many in our political debate to be less a political philosophy than a fashion statement—and an offensive one at that. Indeed, when the late, much-admired editor Michael Kelly was charged with the stewardship of the top job at what had been for nearly half a century the flagship publication of American liberalism, the New Republic, he called liberalism a philosophy "of determined perversity," whose "animating impulse is to marginalize itself and then to enjoy its own company. And to make it as unattractive to as many as possible." If liberalism "were a person," Kelly explained, "it would pierce its tongue."[44] Kelly was eventually fired, but it was hardly the first, nor would it be the last, time that someone promoted in the media as a spokesperson for "liberalism" would embrace its least flattering stereotypes. Indeed, as any number of ex-TNR editors could explain, such a strategy was just about the most reliable route to widespread television appearances, high-paying speeches, and overall approval within the insider elite that Washington had to offer.

And yet, at the same time and in many of the same places, Americans continued to hold political views on issue after issue that corresponded almost exactly to those held by these same dreaded, dare-not-speak-their-name liberals. In fact, as liberals have moved toward the center, chastened by decades of internal division, perceived policy failures, and defeat at the polls, and the views of the public have edged leftward in many cases—perhaps in response to the excesses of right-wing Republican rule—we now have a situation in which not just majorities but massive supermajorities of the public tell pollsters that they hold views well to the left of what their political system produces: the very same positions ironically espoused by some of America's most famous and allegedly out-of-touch liberals.

* * *

Liberals have committed any number of serious errors in the past, and will likely continue to do so. Indeed, many, though certainly not most, of the accusations leveled against them over the years contain more than a few grains of truth. But even granting the reality of these missteps—to be discussed at length in later chapters—they pale in comparison to the dangers posed to America by the extremist right-wing political movement that currently controls the executive branch, the judicial branch, and, until recently, the legislative branch of our government, along with much of our mainstream media. Having been out of power for so long, liberals have had to, in fact, shake off some of their outdated ideological attachments and rethink what has worked in the past, what hasn't, and what might work in the future. Recent history has rendered contemporary American liberalism a far more pragmatic and politically sensitive creed than it was when it provided so inviting a target for conservatives and moderates during their campaign of character assassination in the late 1960s. Voters may have sensed this in 2006 as they repudiated six years of right-wing Republican rule and ushered a host of candidates into the House and Senate who, while eschewing the actual "liberal" label, made no apologies for their liberal views. Shortly before Election Day, ABC News' tip sheet *The Note*—which functioned for years among Washington insiders as the inner Beltway's equivalent of *Pravda*—was predicting that the White House was "on the precipice of making Iraq a 2006 political winner for the Republican Party," in part because "Democrats remain united in their disunity, defensiveness, and distraction." CNN senior political correspondent Candy Crowley instructed viewers to expect another Republican victory because, per usual, the Democrats have been "on the losing side of the values debate, the defense debate and, oh yes, the guns debate."[45] It was not until quite late in the race that the experts even realized that both the House of Representatives and the

Senate were in play, and this came about only after the extremely odd phenomenon of, as the pundit Paul Krugman described it, "Reluctant Democratic politicians [being] dragged by their base into taking highly popular positions."[46]

When the tsunami finally arrived, conservatives and their allies in the media tried to spin their defeat into some sort of victory. Rush Limbaugh insisted on the day after the election that "Republicans lost last night, but conservatism did not." George F. Will argued that voters "punished" Republicans "not for pursuing but for forgetting conservatism."[47] Many pundits even tried to paint the victors as somehow more conservative than those they defeated. This was nonsense. It was true that many voters had grown so disgusted with the incompetence, extremism, and corruption they saw in the Bush administration and the Republican congressional leadership that they might have voted for almost any plausible candidate. But the fact remains that every single Democrat who took a Republican or an open seat in 2006 was more liberal than his or her Republican opponent. Every single Democratic candidate favored increasing the minimum wage and embryonic stem-cell research, and opposed the privatization of social security. Not one argued for Bush's plan to eliminate the estate tax, and none supported either Bush's catastrophic war or the rest of his failed foreign policy. While virtually all Republicans, including most prominently both President George W. Bush and Vice President Dick Cheney, trotted out tried-and-true accusations of liberal "elitism," "softness," and even "pro-terrorism," their scare tactics failed to frighten voters. Republican advantages in incumbency, gerrymandering, money, and mobilization—even the advantage of having a wartime president—amounted to nothing.[48]

But why?

The answer, like virtually everything about American politics, is complicated. Obviously a great deal of credit must be accorded to the Republican Party itself, whose members demonstrated a degree of incompetence, corruption, and extremism previously unseen in American governance. But a key component of the Democrats' victory was the fact that despite almost everything you read, see, and hear about how conservative the country has grown in recent decades, Americans are in fact liberals. True, barely 20 percent of them are willing to accept the "liberal" label, but take a close look at virtually any wide-ranging, carefully conducted political opinion poll, and you'll be surprised at what you find. Pick any issue, foreign or domestic, social, economic, environmental, or even religious, and you'll find not just majorities but supermajorities of Americans in favor of the "liberal" position time after time after time.

If the label "liberal" remains relatively radioactive for many voters, this is hardly surprising, given the literally billions of dollars that conservatives have invested in its denigration. The November 2004 National Election Study (NES)—which tries to eliminate the "moderate" option—found 35 percent of those questioned calling themselves liberal compared to 55 percent conservative. A Pew poll at roughly the same time found 19 percent liberal, 39 percent conservative, with the balance preferring "moderate." In January 2006, a Democracy Corps poll found 19 percent calling themselves liberal versus 36 percent conservative.[49] These numbers were practically indistinguishable from the average for the past thirty years (20 percent liberal, 33 percent conservative, 47 percent moderate).[50] And yet when "moderates" were questioned by pollsters for Louis Harris and Associates in 2005, they turned out to share pretty much the same beliefs that self-described liberals did; they just couldn't bring themselves to embrace the hated label.[51] In fact, due primarily to the hijacking of the Republican Party by a coterie of extremist conservatives on issue after issue, a powerful supermajority of more than 60 percent of Americans questioned in these surveys almost always espouse the "liberal" alternatives. Indeed, most Americans' answers, believe it or not, frequently fall to the left of those espoused by many liberal Democratic politicians.

These numbers are quite impressive, given all the associations with which liberalism has been saddled of late. As the political psychologist Drew Western aptly observes, the word *liberal* for most Americans implies "elite, tax and spend, out of touch," and "Massachusetts."[52] And yet the Pew Research Center for the People and the Press in Washington, D.C., in conducting an extensive set of opinion polls over the past few decades, has demonstrated a decided trend toward increasingly "liberal" positions, by almost any definition. To offer just a few examples of this liberal-in-all-but-name attitude regarding economic and welfare policy, according to the 2006 survey, released in March 2007, roughly 70 percent of respondents believe that the government has a responsibility "to take care of people who can't take care of themselves"—up from 61 percent in 2002. The number saying that the government should guarantee "every citizen enough to eat and a place to sleep" has increased by a similar margin over the past five years (from 63 percent to 69 percent). Two-thirds of the public (66 percent)—including a majority of those who say they would prefer a smaller government (57 percent)—favor government-funded health insurance for all citizens. Most people also believe that the nation's corporations are too powerful and fail to strike a fair balance between profits and the public interest. In addition, nearly two-thirds (65 percent) say corporate profits are too high, about the same number who say that "labor unions are necessary to protect the working person" (68 percent). When it comes to the environment, a large majority (83 percent) supports stricter laws and regulations to protect the environment, while 69 percent agree that "we should put more emphasis on fuel conservation than on developing new oil supplies," and fully 60 percent of people questioned say they would "be willing to pay higher prices in order to protect the environment." Regarding so-called social issues, only 28 percent of respondents agree that school boards should have the right to fire teachers who are known to be homosexual, while 66 percent disagree. A 56 percent majority opposes making it more difficult for a woman to get an abortion, while 35 percent favor this position.[53] These findings reinforce previous polls like that in 2004 by NPR, the Kaiser Family Foundation, and Harvard University, which asked voters whether "the federal government should fund sex education programs that have 'abstaining from sexual activity' as their only purpose" or if "the money should be used to fund more comprehensive sex education programs that include information on how to obtain and use condoms and other contraceptives." The condom/contraceptive option won the day by a margin of 67 to 30 percent. Unsurprisingly, a similar number (65 percent) said they worried that refusing to provide teens with good information about contraception might lead to unsafe sex, while only 28 percent were more concerned that such information might encourage teens to have sex.[54]

Contrary to conventional wisdom, Americans even tend to side with liberals rather than conservatives in their attitudes toward religion. According to a 2006 study sponsored by the Faith and Progressive Policy Initiative of the Center for American Progress and conducted by the firm Financial Dynamism, 67 percent of voters believe that religious freedom is a "critical" part of their image of America, compared to less than three in ten who believe the Judeo-Christian faith specifically is critical to this image. Only 20 percent of American voters approve of leaders using the political system to turn religious beliefs into action. In terms of the role that religious and moral teachings should play in public debate about key issues, American voters do not focus on the issues of abortion, gay marriage, and the kind of topics that so exercise conservative Christian leaders, but would prefer to see their churches lead on issues such as alleviating "poverty and hunger" (75 percent), "homelessness" (61 percent), "government corruption" (58 percent), "terrorism" (56 percent), "the environment" (54 percent), and "health care" (52 percent). Americans specifically reject the conservative Christian desire to suppress science in the service of religious dogma. Eighty percent of those questioned agree that "faith and science can and should coexist. We can respect our belief in God and our commitment to the dignity of every human life by using our scientific knowledge to help those who are sick or vulnerable." The same overwhelming number endorses the view that "stem cell research can be a force for moral good rather than a moral failing."[55]

The Bush administration's mishandling of almost every aspect of its foreign policy, especially the war in Iraq, has led to equally impressive majorities rejecting the fundamental tenets of conservative foreign policy beliefs on behalf of their more liberal alternatives. Despite the historic advantage the president enjoys in defining foreign policy questions, particularly in times of war and high patriotism, coupled with the fact that this is a nation that has "lost" only one war in its 230-year history, added to a never-ending propaganda campaign led by the masterful Karl Rove and his minions, massive majorities of Americans sided with congressional Democrats in their 2007 showdown with Bush over ending the Iraq War without victory. In January 2007, for instance, Bush faced what Bloomberg News termed "record disapproval" of more than 60 percent for his policy of continuing the war as well as "the broader war on international terrorist networks." Just about the only support for Bush's neoconservative foreign policy could be found within the confines of the Republican base, which continues to constitute approximately 28 to 33 percent of Americans questioned.[56] While most Americans continue to understand that war—sometimes even the threat of preemptive war—can be necessary under certain circumstances, barely four in ten, according to the Pew poll, were willing to trust the conservatives in the Bush administration to make the right decision on whether to begin one.[57]

Each one of the positions espoused above—and many, many more that I lack the space to enumerate—falls firmly into that part of the political playing field of positions claimed by people routinely denigrated in one way or another as "liberals." Why, then, are less than a third of these people willing to own up to the label?

Part of the problem is historical. Like conservatism, which has rushed rightward in recent decades, liberalism has transformed itself as well, moving much closer to the center of political debate. Unfortunately, many in the media and, therefore, much of the public have been late in getting the news. The ideological transformation of both liberals and conservatives over the past thirty years is actually quantifiable. According to research undertaken by political scientists Keith Poole and Howard Rosenthal in the early 1970s, the voting records of those in the political middle of the House Republican delegation were approximately as conservative as Congressman Steven LaTourette of Ohio, whom the *Almanac of American Politics* termed as having "the most moderate voting record of Ohio's Republican members." Yet by 2003, the antitax group the Club for Growth contemptuously labeled LaTourette a "Republican in Name Only" for his insufficient fealty to conservative causes. In other words, what was once the party's center had become its far left. The average Republican congressman was, by this standard, 73 percent more conservative in 2003 than his counterpart thirty years earlier.[58] In the Senate, moreover, the move rightward proved even mor pronounced. Using the same statistical analysis cited above, the median Senate Republican voted twice as conservatively in 2003 as did his 1973 counterpart. The Republican center had, in fact, moved so far to the right that it was actually best represented by now defeated Senator Santorum, who famously compared gay Americans to practitioners of polygamy, incest, and bestiality.[59]

On the Democratic side, most Americans would be surprised to learn that the famously "liberal lion" Ted Kennedy urged his followers to reconsider their reflexive liberalism as early as 1985, when he warned: "We cannot and should not depend on higher tax revenues to roll in and redeem every costly program," and added, "The mere existence of a program is no excuse for its perpetuation, whether it is a welfare plan or a weapons system."[60] While the Poole/Rosenthal calculations found the average 2003 Democratic member of Congress to be 28 percent more liberal than his early-1970s counterpart, this was almost entirely due to the sudden political extinction of the party's conservative southern wing. Nonsouthern Democrats have actually traveled a bit to the right. The voting public's move slightly leftward during this period thereby creates the paradoxical situation in which both parties' positions are actually to the right of the country's real center of political gravity.[61] That liberals remain on the defensive regarding the accusation that their positions are out of step is more the product of effective conservative propaganda and credulous reporting than of any genuinely identifiable trends in public opinion, but it serves nevertheless to effectively prevent our political system from responding to the democratic demands of its citizens.

If this book serves only one purpose, it would be to help remove this logjam and thereby open the way for Americans to get the government they repeatedly say they want. The truth, it turns out, really can set us free.

PART

I

WHAT IS THIS THING
CALLED "LIBERAL"?

Liberalism: A Crooked Branch of Timber

Condemning

One reason liberals today find themselves vulnerable to vituperation from so many quarters simultaneously is the difficulty they face in explaining, even in the most rudimentary terms, their basic philosophical beliefs. While contemporary conservatives may actually ignore their own principles in practice, they can at least explain them. To be a modern-day American conservative bespeaks some combination of a philosophical commitment to limited government, laissez-faire economics, biblically based morality (often literally interpreted), and the use of unilateral military force. When conservative strategist Grover Norquist brags, "I don't want to abolish government. I simply want to reduce it to the size where I can drag it into the bathroom and drown it in the bathtub," he is hearkening back to a long and distinguished historical tradition, however overstated.[1] Conservatism is self-consciously ideological in a way liberalism is not. Milton Friedman argues that "freedom in economic arrangements is itself a component of freedom broadly understood, so economic freedom is an end in itself." This belief leads a conservative columnist like George F. Will to support policies like the privatization of social security irrespective of whether such a transformation would make the program more or less effective, but because of "reasons [that] rise from the philosophy of freedom."[2] Liberals are often understood to be "progovernment" or even "protaxation," but this reflects a fundamental confusion between ends and means. Liberals believe in "government" only insofar as it is necessary to achieve essential goals, including public welfare, investment, redistribution of income, defense, and so on. Conservatives, on the other hand, argue against government as a matter of principle: the less government involved, the better, period.

The fundamental values of contemporary American liberalism, however, resist easy summarization. As the literary critic Lionel Trilling observed back in 1951, "it is a large tendency rather than a concise body of doctrine."[3] Liberalism's bedrock belief in personal freedom, of thought, of expression, and of action, is derived from and defined by the philosophers of the eighteenth-century Enlightenment and its children, a group that includes John Locke, Baron de Montesquieu, Voltaire, David Hume, Jean-Jacques Rousseau, Immanuel Kant, Adam Smith, Thomas Jefferson, Thomas Paine, and James Madison.[4] A liberal society strives to maximize these freedoms for the largest number of citizens while at the same time protecting the rights and interests of the minority, whose ideas of personal freedom may conflict with those of the majority. This focus on the freedom and the personal dignity of the individual fundamentally distinguishes liberalism from the tenets of both the religious right and the Marxist left, which stress instead unquestioned obedience to a higher authority for the benefit of the collective.[5] Liberals find inherited and unquestioned belief systems—whether imposed by the Bible, the Koran, the Dialectic of History, or the Fatherland—to be anathema. — Cuss dislike

While the word *liberal* has come to imply many ideas and commitments over the past two centuries, only those that honor what the economist John Kenneth Galbraith termed "the emancipation of belief" are actually worthy of the name. No one caught the essential spirit of this commitment better than the German philosopher Immanuel Kant, who in 1784 explained, "Enlightenment is man's emergence from his self-imposed immaturity. Immaturity is the inability to use one's understanding without guidance from another. This immaturity is self-imposed when its cause lies not in lack of understanding, but in lack of resolve and courage to use it without guidance from another. Sapere Aude [Dare to know!] 'Have courage to use your own understanding!'—that is the motto of enlightenment."[6]

At the time he was writing, Kant believed, rather optimistically, that the "spirit of freedom is expanding even where it must struggle against the external obstacles of governments that misunderstand their own function." Indeed, this struggle remains with us today, as too many gov-

Awesome

ernments, including frequently our own, embrace an authoritarian philosophy of governance that denies citizens not only the power to question their leaders but also the ability to obtain the information they need to make informed decisions about choosing them. As the philosopher Thomas Nagel points out, whatever form of liberalism we may be discussing, it remains a fundamental precept that the power of the state over the individual be carefully limited:

> The sovereign power of the state over the individual is bounded by a requirement that individuals remain inviolable in certain respects, and that they must be treated equally. The state is a human creation, and it is subject to moral constraints that limit the subordination of the individual to the collective will and the collective interest. Those constraints have to be embodied in political institutions. They include not only the familiar freedoms of religion, expression, association, and privacy, but also equality of political status, equality before the law, and, in the welfare state version, equality of opportunity and fairness in the social and economic structure of the society.[7]

The term *liberal* originally entered the political lexicon in 1811 when a group of Spaniards proposed the adoption of a new constitution based on the French constitution of 1781. Its proponents called themselves the Enlightenment, and their platform included a strong dose of anticlericalism. From Spain, historian Ronald D. Rotunda explains, the term *liberal* traveled to Italy, France, and Britain, where it was naturally identified with the laissez-faire economic policies of William Gladstone in the nineteenth century.[8] British liberalism might aptly be termed "the revolt of reason," as its followers sought to wean the nation from its reliance on the twin powers of the church and the Crown. As liberal philosopher John Dewey would later note:

> The word [*liberalism*] came into use to denote a new spirit that grew and spread with the rise of democracy. It implied a new interest in the common man and a new sense that the common man, the representative of the great masses of human beings, had possibilities that had been kept

under, that had not been allowed to develop, because of institutional and political conditions. This new spirit was liberal in both senses of the word. It was marked by a generous attitude, by sympathy for the underdog, for those who were not given a chance. It was part of a widespread rise of humanitarian philanthropy. It was also liberal in that it aimed at enlarging the scope of free action on the part of those who for ages had had no part in public affairs and no lot in the benefits secured by this participation.[9]

Liberalism took a step toward our present understanding of the term with the formulation of a "New Liberalism" by L. T. Hobhouse in 1911.[10] New Liberals shared with classical liberals the notion that wealth was produced by individuals, but argued that these same individuals' prosperity relied on the health and security of the community.[11] Building on Hobhouse's insight, Dewey, America's most influential liberal thinker for more than half a century, advanced the cause considerably by arguing that "liberty" should be imagined not as an abstract principle merely to be admired but as "the effective power to do specific things"—things that could not be done by people enjoying only the theoretical ability to act on their freedoms. No longer could the slogan of political liberals be "Let the government keep its hands off industry and commerce," as the government became necessary to protect the individual's freedom from the growing power of just those forces. "There is no such thing as the liberty or effective power of an individual, group, or class," Dewey explained, "except in relation to the liberties, the effective powers, of other individuals, groups or classes."[12]

What this meant for liberalism was that the commitment to Enlightenment principles was insufficient if real-world forces—say, corporate trusts or monopolies—interfered with individuals' ability to realize them. The new view was initially adopted in the early 1900s by both Theodore Roosevelt's "Bull Moose" Republican Party and Woodrow Wilson's Democrats under the banner of "progressivism," where trust-busting and industry regulation became the agreed-upon responsibility of progressive governance. It was not until Franklin Roosevelt launched the New Deal in the early 1930s, however, that the actual term *liberal* come into widespread use in the United States. Faced with a crisis of capitalism on the one hand, and a global threat to liberal principles in the forms of socialism, communism, and fascism across Europe on the other, Roosevelt tossed aside old nostrums about economics and public policy and redefined the government's role in society. The new American liberalism would place it on the side of those individuals most in need of assistance against a wide array of forces whose combined power made a mockery of America's promise of freedom and liberty. As the party of "militant liberalism," FDR declared, Democrats would deploy the U.S. government to "protect its people against disasters once considered inevitable, to solve problems once considered unsolvable."[13] In contrast to what FDR called "the conservative party," which "honestly and conscientiously believes" that "in the long run, individual initiative and private philanthropy can take care of all situations," the "liberal party is a party which believes that, as new conditions and problems arise beyond the power of men and women to meet as individuals, it becomes the duty of the Government itself to find new remedies with which to meet them."[14] And so it did. Under Roosevelt's liberal leadership, the Democrats doubled their percentage of the popular vote in presidential elections. By 1934 they held more than 70 percent of the House and Senate.[15] They won five consecutive presidential elections—a feat no party had ever or has ever matched—and nine of the next ten congressional elections, as well.[16]

For the first time in its history the U.S. government accepted responsibility for providing a "safety net" for its citizens, embarking on what the social critic Irving Howe termed the "socialization of concern" by creating programs like social security and unemployment insurance, supporting workers' right to organize, and instituting a set of policies devoted to Keynesian stimulation of the economy.[17] And while, as Dewey noted back in 1936, liberalism's "philosophy has rarely been clear cut," it had come to represent an identifiable program: "that government should regularly intervene to help equalize conditions between the wealthy and the poor, between the overprivileged and the underprivileged."[18]

Just how successful these programs were in achieving their aims remains a matter of considerable debate. While economist J. Bradford

DeLong makes a valid point when he characterizes the entire New Deal as "badly handled, but a vast improvement,"[19] historian Lizabeth Cohen suggests that its impact "should be measured less by the lasting accomplishments of its reforms and more by the attitudinal changes it produced in a generation of working-class Americans who now looked to Washington to deliver the American dream."[20]

The introduction of pragmatism to liberalism was obviously necessary to make it meaningful in people's lives. But it also raises a question that liberals have never satisfactorily resolved, either philosophically or pragmatically: Just what are the limits of liberalism? What, in other words, is the proper mix of rights and responsibilities of the citizens of a liberal government, and how far should that government go in attempting to ensure that those rights and responsibilities are guaranteed to all?

Because liberalism arose as a matter of pure pragmatism with next to no theory in the first place and was led by a politician who prided himself on his willingness to try almost anything—Richard Hofstadter aptly termed the New Deal "a chaos of experimentation"—the subject of limits was never satisfactorily addressed.[21] Roosevelt's programs never cohered ideologically, in part because they were never intended to do so: almost anything considered both potentially effective and politically plausible could be considered. Arthur Schlesinger Jr. has argued, however, that liberalism's very lack of ideological coherence is one of its greatest strengths: "Liberalism in America has been a party of social progress rather than of intellectual doctrine, committed to ends rather than to methods. When a laissez-faire policy seemed best calculated to achieve the liberal objective of equality of opportunity for all—as it did in the time of Jefferson— liberals believed, in Henry David Thoreau's words, that that government is best which governs least. But, when the growing complexity of industrial conditions required increasing government intervention in order to assure more equal opportunities, the liberal tradition, faithful to the goal rather than to the dogma, altered its view of the state."[22]

Since Roosevelt, liberals have sought to expand the government's ability to improve the lives of ordinary citizens. During the 1960s they drew on the various liberation movements of the second half of the twentieth century—including but not limited to civil rights, feminism, gay rights, and Hispanic, Asian-American, and Native American movements—to address an almost endless array of social, cultural, and even sexual maladies. Predictably, the results have proven quite mixed. Liberals often paid a great deal more attention to their noble ends than to the means necessary to reach them, in part because their goals were themselves a great deal more controversial with their fellow citizens than they were able to understand or even envision. Yet even had those goals been as broadly popular as liberals apparently believed, it is far from clear that their aims were ever reasonably achievable in a democratic society.

Traditional politicians had always understood the delivery of services to include such amenities as a clean street or a patronage job, but how, even in the best of times, could anyone hope to "deliver" integration, equality, or "peace"? Even the more limited but still enormously ambitious aims of LBJ's Great Society proved beyond the abilities of the federal government—or perhaps any government. Writing in 1965, the critic Paul Goodman wisely noted that it was commendable when the government summoned its resources "to prevent or remedy social and physical evils, like urban poverty, exploitation of labor, traffic congestion, air pollution," but its traditional "safeguarding function is entirely different from government trying to make life excellent, to make society moral, civilized or magnificent."[23] Much unnecessary unhappiness might have been prevented if only liberals had paid greater heed to the liberal philosopher Isaiah Berlin's creed: To guarantee its citizens the full measure of "negative liberty" is the maximum goal a liberal society can hope to achieve, as it recognizes that "human goals are many," and no individual can choose what is best for all.[24]

* * *

In the decades following the New Deal, liberalism remained the fundamental bedrock of much of American political life, regardless of which party happened to be in power. "Should any political party attempt to abolish Social Security and eliminate labor laws and farm programs," President Eisenhower wrote his brother Edgar, "you would not hear of that party again in our political history."[25] The historian Alan Brinkley speaks of growing up in the 1950s and '60s with a strong sense of self-identification with the accomplishment of liberalism. In those days, the word required no complicated definitions, for it was, in many middle-class neighborhoods, in the very air and water that working people imbibed. "The achievements of liberalism were everywhere visible: the robust growth of the American economy, stabilized (at times at least) by the active use of Keynesian policies; the gradual expansion of the New Deal welfare and social insurance system, which had lifted millions of elderly people (and many others) out of poverty; and beginning in the early 1960s, the alliance between the federal government and the civil rights movement, an alliance that most white liberals believed gave liberalism a powerful moral claim to accompany its many practical achievements."[26]

Liberalism was understood by its proponents to be not merely triumphant in this era; rather, they considered it the only governing philosophy to be taken seriously. Arthur Schlesinger Jr. did not feel compelled even to address conservatives in his 1949 manifesto, *The Vital Center;* his ideological battleground existed exclusively in the territory between liberalism and Marxism.[27] Similarly, Lionel Trilling, in the enormously influential 1950 introduction to his collection of essays entitled *The Liberal Imagination,* complained that the United States simply lacked a viable conservative intellectual tradition. This troubled Trilling not because he particularly cared for conservatives, but because liberalism would likely grow weak and flaccid without a suitable philosophical partner with whom to spar on occasion. The absence of conservative ideas "does not mean," Trilling was at pains to explain, "there is no impulse to conservatism or to reaction." Rather, such impulses do not "express themselves in ideas but only in action or in irritable mental gestures which seek to resemble ideas."[28] Indeed, when in 1960 the sociologist Daniel Bell declared a decidedly premature "end of ideology" in America, he addressed himself exclusively to potential challenges to the prevailing liberal consensus, one that appeared to American intellectuals to be so universally accepted that it no longer qualified as an ideology but appeared instead to be another word for reality.[29] "These, without a doubt, are the years of the liberal," John Kenneth Galbraith wrote in 1964. "Almost everyone now so describes himself."[30]

Alas, the liberal hold on America's political imagination proved considerably more tenuous than these intellectuals imagined. As Bell himself pointed out in 1963, what he called the "New American Right" continued to articulate, quite forcefully, its agenda to dismantle the welfare state and "tame" the unions. This movement drew considerable power from mainstream business organizations, as the Western European and Japanese economic recoveries put pressure on American industry and led to a steady diminution in its manufacturing profits. The political impact of these developments was a revival of corporate militancy. Companies fired union activists without regard for the niceties of labor law and lobbied Congress to reverse New Deal–era regulations. They underwrote organizations like the U.S. Chamber of Commerce, whose publications attacked liberals for taking a "backroad to socialism," in the fast lane toward a "police state."[31] As early as 1947 the conservatives began to win striking political victories, including the Taft-Hartley Act, which severely constrained the rights of working people.

No American president would again succeed in sending liberal hearts soaring the way FDR had. As Schlesinger lamented at the time, "The existence of Franklin Roosevelt relieved American liberals for a dozen years of the responsibility of thinking for themselves." Only after his death did they "realize to what extent their confidence in the postwar period had rested on one man."[32] Harry Truman would, certainly, sponsor significant social and economic accomplishments—most famously, perhaps, the almost overnight integration of the U.S. armed forces. And in his spirited 1948 campaign, Truman would win a come-from-behind victory against New York governor (and heavy betting favorite) Thomas E. Dewey, despite challenges from the Progressive Party's Henry Wallace on his left and the Dixiecrat Strom Thurmond on his right.[33] But for most liberals, Truman's presidency felt like a painful hangover on the morning after decades of high living under FDR. When, in response to a strike by steelworkers, he threatened to draft the union men back to the factory, the *New Republic* denounced Truman for having dreamed up the "most vicious piece of anti-union legislation ever introduced by an American President."[34] The tone of the Truman administration also differed in kind from that of FDR's ideas-driven intellectual hothouse. Despite the hysterical rhetoric of the Chamber of Commerce and others, Truman ran a businessman's administration. Among senior appointees, forty-nine were bankers, financiers, and industrialists, including his secretaries of commerce, war, and defense and his undersecretary of state; *thirty-one* were generals or admirals; and seventeen were corporate lawyers.[35] As the journalist Howard K. Smith observed, "The effective locus of government seemed to shift from Washington to some place between Wall Street and West Point."[36]

Personality aside, much of this was inevitable. The spirit of liberal innovation that reshaped the economy and helped win the war was certainly flagging by the end of its second decade in power. In the late 1950s John Kenneth Galbraith complained,

American liberals have made scarcely a new proposal for reform in twenty years. It is not evident that they have had any important new ideas. Reputations for liberals or radicalism continue to depend almost exclusively on a desire to finish the unfinished social legislation of the New Deal. . . . On domestic matters, liberal organizations have not for years had anything that might be called a program. Rather they have had a file. Little is ever added. Platform-making consists, in effect, in emptying out the drawers.[37]

Following the Truman presidency the undisputed object of liberal affection was the two-time Democratic presidential nominee, Illinois governor Adlai Stevenson. In retrospect he was an odd choice. Stevenson was a snob, and in many ways not much of a liberal. He charmed intellectuals with his calls for a commitment to "cold-eyed humility" and a recognition that "our wisdom is imperfect and our capabilities . . . limited."[38] Though he might have been a classier fellow than General Eisenhower bookwise—an ironic egghead after liberals' own hearts—his politics were frequently indistinguishable from those of the plain-spoken military man.[39] (Following his election loss, a woman tried to soothe his feelings by telling him that he had "educated the country"; Stevenson replied, "Yes, but a lot of people flunked the exam.")[40]

It was Governor Stevenson's high opinion of his own intellect that was instrumental in defining in the public mind the "effete liberal" stereotype. Richard Nixon—who would soon make quite a career of exploiting exactly these tendencies among liberals—raged at "Adlai the Appeaser," said he had a Ph.D. from "Dean Acheson's College of Cowardly Communist Containment," and reminded voters that the country would be better off with a "khaki-clad" president than one "clothed in State Department pinks."[41] The right-wing *New York Daily News* referred to Stevenson as "Adelaide," reporting with almost comical homophobia that he "trilled" his speeches in a "fruity" voice, using "teacup words" that were reminiscent of a "genteel spinster who can never forget that she got an A in elocution at Miss Smith's finishing school."[42] Stevenson was, in fact, hardly less committed to the Cold War than Eisenhower, and though he opposed McCarthyism, he had no problem with dismissing teachers for being Communist Party members or with using the Smith Act to prosecute others. In this regard, he epitomized the weak-kneed response of so many liberals to what was among the most significant threats to civil liberties in the history of the republic, and later, the cause of much disillusionment on the part of young leftists with their tut-tutting liberal elders. While liberals were understandably eager to establish their Cold War bona fides, they were unable to strike a sensible balance between voicing their disapproval of communism and Communists while simultaneously defending constitutional guarantees that permitted Americans to make politically unpopular choices if they so desired. As a result, the right-wing Red Scare took place without the energetic opposition of those in the best position to blunt its effectiveness, and many, many innocent lives ended up in ruins thanks to what would later prove to be exaggerated—and in some cases imaginary—dangers.

In keeping with his profile in liberal cowardice, Stevenson also opposed both public housing and what he called "socialized medicine." He had little sympathy for much of the New Deal and spent far too much time making up his mind about the repeal of the Taft-Hartley Act. Regarding the great moral and political challenge of the day for American liberals, civil rights, he was notably AWOL.[43] In this respect, he was less brave, and less liberal, than the much-derided Truman. Irving Howe would later term "Adlaism" to be "Ikeism . . . with a touch of literacy and intelligence."[44]

By 1960, with Stevenson considered damaged goods by many who had supported him twice before, it fell to a new generation of liberals led by the dashing young senator from Massachusetts to breathe new life into the brand. Unlike Stevenson, but like his electorally more successful predecessors, John Fitzgerald Kennedy evinced an ambivalent relationship both to liberalism and to liberals themselves. Raised in splendor by one of America's wealthiest and most ambitious industrialists, Kennedy nonetheless managed to communicate that elusive "common touch" Americans demand in their politicians. And while his record on McCarthyism was truthfully worse than Stevenson's—his brother Bobby had actually worked for the liberal Antichrist, and Kennedy himself managed to miss the belated Senate vote for censure—by the time of his presidential campaign in 1960, the censure had temporarily taken the issue off the table for most voters. Owing to his widely promoted reputation for "vigor," the charming young man made good use of his father's fortune, revitalizing the stale clichés of liberalism that had gone on life support under Stevenson. Addressing a gathering of New York's Liberal Party, on whose presidential line he also ran, in September 1960, Kennedy explained:

> What do our opponents mean when they apply to us the label "Liberal"? If by "Liberal" they mean, as they want people to believe, someone who is soft in his policies abroad, who is against local government, and who is unconcerned with the taxpayer's dollar, then . . . we are not that kind of "Liberal." But if by a "Liberal" they mean someone who looks ahead and not behind, someone who welcomes new ideas without rigid reactions, someone who cares about the welfare of the people—their health, their housing, their schools, their jobs, their civil rights, and their civil liberties—someone who believes we can break through the stalemate and suspicions that grip us in our policies abroad, if that is what they mean by a "Liberal," then I'm proud to say I'm a "Liberal."[45]

Kennedy represented what the pollster and political scholar Stan Greenberg calls "Opportunity Democrats": liberals who interpreted their mandate to build on the legacies of the New and Fair Deals by finding ways, in the president's words, to allow all Americans to "share in the benefits of our abundance and natural resources."[46] More probusiness than their predecessors, Kennedy liberals prided themselves on their tough-mindedness with adversaries abroad. They were considerably less eager, however, to take on what the Swedish sociologist Gunnar Myrdal termed "the American Dilemma" of segregation and racial inequity. When, in his inaugural address, Kennedy promised to "pay any price, bear any burden," for freedom, he was implicitly excluding what he privately called "this Goddamned civil rights mess" from his definition. Indeed, despite rising tensions across the South, Kennedy did his best to ignore the issue, going so far as to delay before the 1962 midterm congressional elections an executive order that would bar discrimination in federal housing programs.[47] Politically, this was the prudent course to take. When, following the elections, he signed the order, pollster Lou Harris warned that 1962 had brought slippage in support not merely in the South, but also in "pivotal industrial states" and among blue-collar Catholics, including the Irish, who were more conservative, seeing few economic gains, and who were not sympathetic to black demands. Kennedy tried to proceed as cautiously as possible on civil rights, nervous not only about the fragility of the New Deal coalition on the race issue, but also with regard to the power of southern Democrats to bottle up his entire political agenda on the Hill should they come to view him as an ally of their adversaries.

Even so, events forced Kennedy's hand, as a young generation of black activists and church leaders made it more and more difficult for the president to stay out of the "mess" by forcing the issue and highlighting the contradiction between the nation's ideals and the practice of apartheid in the South. Cold War tensions also contributed to pressure the administration to live up to its soaring internationalist rhetoric. In 1963 Kennedy finally stepped up to the proverbial plate, calling the right to vote "the most precious and powerful right in the world," and promising that it would "not be denied to any citizen on grounds of his race or color."[48] He soon asked Congress for comprehensive civil rights legislation and preached in a televised address: "We are confronted primarily with a moral issue. It is as old as the Scriptures and is as clear as the American Constitution. The heart of the question is whether all Americans are to be afforded equal rights and equal opportunities . . . this Nation, for all its hopes and all its boasts, will not be fully free until all its citizens are free."[49] From that moment on the liberals' devil's bargain with southern segregation finally ended. Henceforth, no American politician could profess to call him- or herself a liberal without a bedrock commitment to the cause of complete political and social equality for all citizens, without regard to race, creed, or color.

In the national aftershock of Kennedy's assassination in November 1963, Lyndon Johnson appeared for a time to be the unlikely savior of American liberalism as he deployed his unique blend of ambition, obsession, and political genius to enact civil rights and welfare legislation the breadth and scope of which his predecessors had not even dared to dream. Following the 1964 election, armed with a landslide majority victory and the mantle of the slain hero, and carrying the legacy of liberalism on his back, Johnson took on the very issue his predecessors had so studiously avoided—retributive racial and economic justice—with tragic, if predictable, results. During the previous decade political scientist V. O. Key Jr. had observed in his classic work *Southern Politics in State and Nation* that the Republican Party in the South "scarcely deserves the name of party. . . . It wavers somewhat between an esoteric cult on the order of a lodge and a conspiracy for plunder in accord with the accepted customs of our politics."[50] And yet LBJ's commitments to voting rights and racial equality helped transform the Republicans almost overnight into the region's dominant political force. Johnson knew exactly what he was doing and famously prophesized, "We have to press for them [voting rights] as a matter of right, but we also have to recognize that by doing so we will destroy the Democratic Party."[51] Nobly, he did just that. "[The slaves] came in darkness and they came in chains," Johnson annouonced, his voice quivering as he signed the historic Voting Rights Act on August 5,

1965, striking down a series of legal barries constructed by white South-erners to prevent blacks from exercising their right to vote. "Today we strike away the last major shackle of those fierce and ancient bonds."[52]

Just six days later, massive riots broke out in Watts, Los Angeles, when a black driver was pulled over for drunkenness. They lasted for a full five days and were televised across the land, horrifying white middle-class America, including many of those whose hopes and ideals for peaceful integration of the races had been represented by Johnson's moving words earlier that week. The riots signaled to all that nothing about end-ing centuries of officially enforced discrimination was likely to be simple, easy, or without painful trauma for the nation. More than four decades later, we continue to live amid the ruins of the ensuing destruction.

Excluding the irredeemably racist—not a small number, unfortunately—the obvious political problem raised by forced integration for liberals was one of implementation: How could they avoid giving average Americans the impression that they were robbing (white) Peter to pay (black) Paul? Addressing the dilemma proved simple in theory, but all but impossible in practice.

Liberal programs designed to redress the results of centuries of dis-crimination against blacks immensely increased the insecurity of working-class whites, who were the primary constituency of the New and Fair Deals. These men and their families witnessed the unraveling of their livelihoods, their neighborhoods, their local school systems, and what appeared to be their entire way of life—not merely in the South but all across America. Had liberals had the foresight to focus on an overall strategy to uplift the poor and the middle class regardless of race, they might have had a fighting chance. Instead, they placed race at the center of their appeal and thus ensured the equivalent of a low-level race war between black Have-Nots and white Have-Littles. Regardless of who emerged on top, liberals were certain to lose in a fight between two of their most important political constituencies. Again, displaying what ap-peared to be moral bravery but was more accurately political naïveté, they chose to embrace fully the demands of the smaller, less powerful, but increasingly radicalized constituency of black America in its demands for a thoroughgoing reordering of American political and economic priorities. Instead of acknowledging and honoring the sacrifices they were demanding of working-class whites and offering compensation—or finding ways to ease the transition toward the color-blind society they envisioned—the same liberals branded their own political base as selfish and "racist." Because they did so largely from the security of their own safe, comfortable, and largely segregated enclaves in the Boston-Washington corridor, they added the politically potent ingredient of apparent hypocrisy to an already explosive cocktail.

Liberals lost their hold on the white working class almost everywhere in America. The year 1966 saw the reelections of John Tower in Texas and Strom Thurmond, running for the first time as a Republican, in South Carolina. Claude Kirk became the first Republican governor of Florida since Reconstruction, and in the year's biggest political story, former actor and GE spokesman Ronald Reagan took the governorship of California away from the liberal Pat Brown, promising a get-tough policy against students, minorities, and protestors of all kinds. Examining the middle-class politics of Macomb County, Michigan, more than twenty years later, the pollster Stanley Greenberg would discover:

> These white Democratic defectors express a profound distaste for blacks, a sentiment that pervades almost everything they think about government and politics. . . . Blacks constitute the explanation for their vulnerability and for almost everything that has gone wrong in their lives; not being black is what constitutes being middle class; not living with blacks is what makes a neighborhood a decent place to live. These sentiments have important implications for Democrats, as virtually all progressive symbols and themes have been redefined in racial and pejorative terms.[53]

Republicans could not be expected to pass up so pregnant a political opportunity. In the summer of 2005, Republican Party chair Ken Mehlman found himself compelled to apologize to black Americans for his party's efforts "to benefit politically from racial polarization."[54] But benefit they did. Liberals became identified among white working-class voters exclusively and disastrously as the champions of the black underclass. The same liberals who acted so callously toward the white working class at home found themselves stuck inside an unwinnable, dishonestly promoted, and apparently endless war in far-off Indochina—one in which they stood accused of treating the lives of American poor and working-class children as so much fodder for their (ultimately) discredited theories of dominoes and deterrence. The fact that the children of the elite enjoyed the option of sitting out the war with college deferments—meanwhile indulging in sexual and pharmaceutical experiments, and mocking both the war and the patriotic support it inspired in large, often outlandish political demonstrations—while working-class kids were perceived by middle America to accept their duty to defend the country and often die for it exacerbated the already deadly undercurrent of intra-Democratic class conflict. Blue-collar workers not only perceived their vulnerability to liberal caprice but came to view liberals as feckless and cowardly when they ultimately turned against the war as well. The unavoidable appearance of hypocrisy again incited rage, and the net result was the permanent destruction of the New Deal coalition.

The combined result of all of these events' occurring simultaneously was the igniting of an antiliberal explosion whose effects continue to shape our political universe more than forty years later. The most incendiary elements of this fateful admixture included:

• **Welfare payments**—particularly to minorities—that appeared to reward sloth and encourage irresponsible behavior, and to grow more and more generous.

• **Forced integration schemes** that had the effect of destroying neighborhood cohesion, reducing housing values, and turning primary schools into political battlegrounds.

• **Increasing inflation** that ate away at working people's income as it simultaneously led to higher taxation. Lyndon Johnson's refusal to ask the nation to forgo any form of "butter" to fund the "guns" of Vietnam created a kind of macroeconomic virus that wormed its way through the U.S. economy, resulting in the "diabolical double helix" of rising inflation and unemployment in the 1970s. High inflation rates produced nominally rising wages for workers but declining spending power in real terms, owing to "bracket creep" in the federal tax system. Middle-class Americans were working harder for less money, but found themselves being taxed at higher rates. Families with modest incomes also suddenly found themselves owning homes for which they could no longer afford the real estate taxes. Again, liberals largely ignored their plight and instead embraced these tax dollars as a source to fund social programs. Their unwillingness to deal with the problem inspired a middle-class tax revolt. In California a large majority of voters supported Proposition 13, which froze property taxes at 1976 levels and ultimately destroyed the quality of public education for schoolchildren, threatening a fundamental building block of the American dream. Republicans seized on the proposition's success and took the antitax campaign national, under the guise of a proposed 30 percent across-the-board federal income tax cut.

• **Permissive social morality,** including "government programs" that appeared to many to be offering not merely indulgence—which would be bad enough—but actual encouragement to lazy, ill-mannered, and sexually promiscuous individuals who gamed a corrupt system for personal gain when they were not out causing riots, looting stores, committing violent crimes, or all of the above. California governor Ronald Reagan and Alabama governor (and presidential candidate) George Wallace, together with President Nixon, added a new, pejorative meaning to the word *liberal*. Under the influence of their rhetoric, liberalism came to connote for key voters, as authors Thomas and Mary Edsall pointed out, "The favoring of blacks over whites and permissiveness toward drug abuse, illegitimacy, welfare fraud, street crime, homosexuality, anti-Americanism, as well as moral anarchy among the young."[55]

• **The use of the courts, rather than the electoral process,** to achieve liberal aims. Starting with the Warren Court's 1954 *Brown v. Board of Education of Topeka* decision declaring school segregation unconstitutional, liberals working with individual constituencies of victimized Americans attempted to achieve the most fundamental transformations of society imaginable by mere judicial decision. Desegregation decrees were quickly followed by barely less sweeping orders demanding institutionalized tolerance and often favorable treatment not only for blacks and women but also for gays, Hispanics, endangered species, and any other group with the ability to pursue a political agenda by class-action lawsuit.[56] In addition, the Supreme Court, already widely seen as a leading liberal institution, issued a series of decisions that reinforced the notion that liberals were going to conduct their assault on traditional morality whenever and wherever possible. In *Engel v. Vitale* (1962) and *Abington School District v. Schempp* (1963), the Court banned Bible readings and prayer in public schools. In *Griswold v. Connecticut* (1965), the justices overturned any state restrictions on contraception, and in *Mapp v. Ohio* (1961) and *Miranda v. Arizona* (1966), they handed down decisions that gave greater protection to criminal defendants. *Loving v. Virginia* (1967) outlawed state bans against interracial marriage.[57] This process culminated in 1973's *Roe v. Wade* decision, which had the effect of transforming not only abortion rights in America but also sexuality itself, and did so on the basis of an extremely convoluted and easily challenged legal reading. At the same time, Ralph Nader and his "Nader's Raiders" launched their crusade on behalf of the rights of American consumers, adding yet another liberal movement dedicated to forcing widespread social change through the use of judicial and administrative—rather than electoral-based—remedies. Such victories opened liberals up to the politically powerful—and not entirely unfair—charge by the likes of rightwing provocateur Dinesh D'Souza that these massive social changes had been imposed on Americans without regard for political process or the strongly felt preferences of significant majorities of Americans. The left has won virtually all of its victories in America not through the democratic process but by going around it, D'Souza complains: "How did abortion become legal? How did the left get its radical doctrine of secularism adopted? How has the left managed to overturn virtually all laws against pornography? How is gay marriage being pushed today? In every case, the left has relied on the courts to declare a 'right' and then enforce that right against the will of the American people and their elected representatives. In this sense, the biggest victories of the cultural left in the past few decades have all been achieved undemocratically."[58]

• **The shrinkage of the economic pie** and the fight over its remaining crumbs. The engine that drove the U.S. economy became overheated in the late 1960s and early 1970s in large measure owing to the Johnson administration's unwillingness either to consider a significant tax increase or to balance its foreign and domestic commitments with available resources. What the political scientist Theodore Lowi termed "interest group liberalism" pitted each group against the other in what—in an age of declining economic growth—appeared to be a zero-sum game that exacerbated intra-group animosities. And because it relied almost exclusively on administrative and judicial decision making, it also eluded any form of meaningful democratic control, thereby further isolating liberal constituencies from the larger public while simultaneously removing them from any concerted, cooperative, serious challenge to the more universal—and potentially politically galvanizing—aspects of social injustice.

• **Vietnam and the end of liberal anticommunism.** Yet another major fracture opened up between liberalism and much of its former middle-class constituency in the form of its retrenchment from its historic commitment to anticommunism. The catastrophe of Vietnam caused a quadruple fissure within liberalism: it diverted resources from the government that could have been used to sustain social progress; it isolated liberals from an increasingly angry (and ultimately nihilistic) antiwar movement made up of much of America's most articulate and eloquent college-educated young people who could have benefited from their guidance; it weakened the movement's association with the historic (and highly popular) cause of anticommunism; and finally, and most crucial, it robbed liberals of their self-confidence. Vietnam was the hurt that kept on hurting.

• **Vietnam and the collapse of the liberal / left alliance.** Vietnam alienated liberals not only from young people but from their political allies on the non-Communist and socialist left, who, understandably, held them responsible for helping to create a moral and political catastrophe. The relationship between liberals and "the left"—meaning socialists, Communists, anarchists, and, in the past, prairie populists—had always been a complicated one. Many of liberalism's most important ideas were lifted from these movements. Indeed, Milton Friedman has been heard to describe Norman Thomas's Socialist Party as having been "the most influential party in the history of this country," as "every one of its 1928 platform planks had later been enacted."[59] (Friedman was referring to the fact that the New Deal Democrats had borrowed rather liberally from Thomas, just as Woodrow Wilson had borrowed from Eugene Debs's Socialists, and Democrats under William Jennings Bryan had taken ideas from the Populist Party.) In the New Deal era and during World War II, a "popular front" mentality on all sides enabled liberals, socialists, and even Communists to work on many a common cause together. But during the 1950s liberals failed to find a workable compromise between their desire to protect civil liberties on the one hand and oppose Communist subversion on the other. Many fell prey to a Cold War hysteria that weakened their ability to defend the rights of those on the left with whom they disagreed to enjoy the rights of free expression that are so integral to liberal self-conception. At the same time, in the late 1960s and early '70s, many liberals who had overlearned these lessons failed to separate themselves from some of the counterproductive antics of the antiwar movement and the various minority and identity politics that also emerged. (Another benefit that had accrued to liberals from the radical lefts of the past was making them appear reasonable in the eyes of average, apolitical Americans, if only by comparison.) The net result was that liberals forfeited their own identities and became subsumed within an increasingly unpopular "left"—at least in the minds of voters who were expected to trust them with the reins of national leadership. Buoyed by the impression of uncontrollable chaos across the nation, particularly in leftist precincts in universities and urban ghettos, Republicans rode a right-wing backlash to victory in presidential election after election, employing a strategy like that enumerated in Richard Nixon's 1972 "Assault Book." This called on allies to portray Democratic nominee George McGovern as "the pet radical of Eastern Liberalism, the darling of the *New York Times,* the hero of the Berkeley Hill Jet Set; Mr. Radical Chic," with Nixon contrasted as "the Candidate of the Common Man, the Working Man."[60] Meanwhile, leftists tended to treat liberals with a mixture of pity and contempt. When the folksinger Phil Ochs sang "Love Me, I'm a Liberal," the song was intended to be a scorching indictment of liberal cowardice by a bitter adversary, not the good-natured ribbing one might expect from an affectionate ally.

• **A massive investment in opinion formation and management** by big business groups and wealthy right-wing individuals, including the creation of an interlocking web of well-funded think tanks, media companies, pressure groups, and pseudoscholarly centers designed to cover middle-class resentments with the patina of intellectual respectability. The inspiration for the network came from many sources, beginning with the widespread belief among wealthy Goldwater supporters in 1964 that they were unlikely to get a fair hearing from the nation until they could match liberals foundation for foundation, newspaper for newspaper, television network for television network. Beginning in August 1971, future Supreme Court associate justice Lewis Powell undertook a campaign to convince not only conservative billionaires but also ordinary businessmen that their way of life faced a threat not only from "the Communists, New Leftists and other revolutionaries who would destroy the entire system," but also from "perfectly respectable elements of society: from the college campus, the pulpit, the media, the intellectual and literary journals, the arts and sciences, and from politicians." Powell advised American conservatives that "strength lies in organization, in careful long-range planning and implementation, in consistency of action over an indefinite period of years, in the scale of financing available only through joint effort, and in the political power available only through united action and national organizations," and added, "Business must learn the lesson, long ago learned by labor and other self-interest groups. This is the lesson that political power is necessary; that such power must be assiduously cultivated; and that when necessary, it must be used aggressively and with determination—without embarrassment and without the reluctance which has been so characteristic of American business."[61] The fruits of subsequent efforts—supported by the combined contributions of billionaires like Richard Mellon Scaife, Joseph Coors, the Hunt brothers, the Olin, Bradley, and Koch family foundations, and later Sun Myung Moon and Rupert Murdoch—included the founding of a series of new and newly expanded conservative institutions, research grants, and prestigious-looking publications. Scaife's family foundations alone provided more than half a billion dollars over a period of four decades.[62] As a range of opportunities presented themselves, a new group of "neoconservative" intellectuals—former liberals who had switched sides in reaction to what they believed to be the excesses of liberalism and the antiwar movement—joined with familiar conservative voices like that of Robert Bartley, who would oversee the angry editorial pages of the *Wall Street Journal* for nearly thirty years, to begin the process of remaking the American public sphere into a space that privileged the views of conservative Christians, Fortune 500 CEOs, and unapologetic militarists and imperialists over those of their liberal opponents.

• **The politicization of knowledge.** Many in the media, and even in the funding world, tend to treat conservative counterestablishment research organizations like the Heritage Foundation and the American Enterprise Institute (AEI) as the corollary of allegedly "liberal" think tanks like the Brookings Institution and the Urban Institute, which have traditionally been associated with nonpartisan research. In the winter of 2007, for instance, the mainstream Pew Charitable Trust offered $2.2 million for a study on social mobility in America. The plan called for funding, as the *Wall Street Journal* explained, to "go to scholars at the American Enterprise Institute and Heritage Foundation, which have a conservative bent, and the Brookings Institution and Urban Institute, which are more liberal." In fact there is no analogy whatever to be made between what are largely political operations on the right, built on an extremely modest foundation of research, and honest policy-research organizations that employ both conservatives and liberals.

The AEI, which was founded in 1943, defines itself as an institution meant to defend "the principles and improve the institutions of American freedom and democratic capitalism—limited government, private enterprise, individual liberty and responsibility, vigilant and effective defense and foreign policies, political accountability, and open debate."[63] Its younger cousin, the Heritage Foundation, founded in 1973, boasts a mission statement that calls for its members "to formulate and promote conservative public policies based on the principles of free enterprise, limited government, individual freedom, traditional American values, and a strong national defense."[64] Its "scholars" are not scholars in the traditional sense, but more like political operatives. They are expected to spend at least as much time networking with reporters and government staffers as on research. Heritage expends a great deal of effort on tracking legislation and, frequently, shaping hearings as well as press coverage of those hearings. For these reasons, among many others, the right's "research" is not guided by academic standards of scholarship and evidence, and most of it would not stand up to such scrutiny. As Heritage president Edwin Feulner explained back in 1995, "We don't just stress credibility. We stress timeliness. We stress an efficient, effective delivery system." Burton Pines, a Heritage vice president, has added, "We're not here to be some kind of Ph.D. committee giving equal time. Our role is to provide conservative public-policy makers with arguments to bolster our side."[65]

While the foundation's burgeoning influence became visible to mainstream observers only with Ronald Reagan's 1980 election to the presidency, it had been building slowly for years. On October 3, 1983, at Heritage's black-tie tenth-anniversary banquet, Reagan himself declared, "Historians who seek the real meaning of events in the latter part of the twentieth century must look back on gatherings such as this."[66] Although Brookings, Carnegie, and even the Council on Foreign Relations are often called "liberal" by conservatives, this is clearly done for strategic reasons. Look at the Brookings mission statement: "The Brookings Institution is a private nonprofit organization devoted to independent research and innovative policy solutions. . . . Research at the Brookings Institution is conducted to inform the public debate, not advance a political agenda. Our scholars are drawn from the United States and abroad—with experience in government and academia—and hold diverse points of view."[67] The Urban Institute, similarly, explains that "to promote sound social policy and public debate on national priorities, the Urban Institute gathers and analyzes data, conducts policy research, evaluates programs and services, and educates Americans on critical issues and trends."[68]

Politics is a secondary concern in these institutes, if at all. The head of Brookings during the Clinton years was a Republican, as are many of its fellows. Much the same can be said of other so-called liberal think tanks. At the Council on Foreign Relations, not only is liberal bugaboo Henry Kissinger a mainstay, but its senior fellows include Max Boot, a hawkish neocon refugee from the hard-right *Wall Street Journal* editorial page, and Michael Gerson, the Christian evangelical former chief speechwriter for George W. Bush. Even the genuinely liberal think tanks, like the labor-supported Economic Policy Institute and the more recently formed Center for American Progress (where I have been a senior fellow since its founding in 2003), pay a great deal more attention to the precepts of honest academic scholarship than do their right-wing counterparts. Yet because the right has been able to pass off its ideological indoctrination as "policy research," it has succeeded in corrupting the foundation of data upon which policy and political debates must necessarily rest.

- **The retreat of liberal intellectuals from the public debate.** Just as conservatives were finding their voice in the public discourse, liberal intellectuals were forfeiting their own: withdrawing into university departments and embracing an impenetrable, specialized vernacular that effectively cut them off from any larger public than similarly trained specialists. During this period, as the sociologist Douglas S. Massey has written, "under the banner of postmodernism, deconstructionism, critical theory, or more popularly, 'political correctness,' what has become known as the 'academic cultural left' prosecuted their own private culture wars." During the course of this new campaign, liberalism was easily portrayed by its new enemies as an Orwellian parody of its former self, "suppressing free expression to ensure liberal orthodoxy and seeking to instill through indoctrination what it could not achieve politically at the polls."[69] But the truth of the matter was even worse. The militant foot soldiers of the "identity politics" began with what undoubtedly was a worthy notion: that individual experience is shaped by larger structures of power and oppression, and that these therefore need to be identified and challenged. Unfortunately, this practice devolved into a parody of itself as proponents seized upon curbing "offensive speech" on college campuses as the number-one priority of their political energies, just as the Reagan White House launched what can now be seen as a generation-long assault on the living standards and political power of America's poorest and most powerless citizens. Because so many leftists blinded themselves to the existence of, much less the consequences of, this relentless class war, Democrats and liberals were left without foot soldiers to fight back. Leftists also often tended to define one another as the "enemy," embarking on a destructive and debilitating campaign to prove that their own particular group's victimization trumped those of their closest competitors, thereby weakening their ability to achieve the necessary internal compromise and cooperation to resist the right's rise to power. The very idea of the "public good" became, in their texts, a means of oppression of the "other"—yet another subterfuge on behalf of ruling elites, whose interests liberals who fought for the rights of the poor and of working people were somehow suspected of serving.[70] These same leftists, meanwhile, were so concerned with perfecting the political speech patterns on campus—while devoting their scholarly research to the most arcane imaginable issues of social and intellectual discourse—that they effectively abandoned any participatory role in the larger political culture. As the late philosopher Richard Rorty noted, academic leftists somehow managed to convince themselves that "by chanting various Derridean or Foucauldian slogans they [were] fighting for human freedom," and yet their "political uselessness, relative illiteracy, and tiresomely self-congratulatory enthusiasm" resulted only in political impotence.[71] Hence, when right-wing "experts" took to the public airwaves to blame liberal programs for rising violence, inflation, taxes, racial animosities, and the like, they were often able to do so without opposition.

• **The globalization of capital and production.** World events proved no friend to liberalism, either. The globalization of production and mobility of capital chipped away at the power of both unions and the liberal state to defend and protect their workers' standard of living. Economist Dani Rodrik observed, "The fact that 'workers' can be more easily substituted for each other across national boundaries undermines what many conceive to be a postwar social bargain between workers and employers, under which the former would receive a steady increase in wages and benefits in return for labor peace." Firms could now threaten workers with dismissal should demands for higher wages or on-the-job protection prove too onerous.

• **Deindustrialization.** The hemorrhaging of manufacturing jobs in the American rust belt sent formerly liberal Democratic workers packing from places like Detroit, Cleveland, Buffalo, and Pittsburgh and ultimately moving into increasingly conservative Republican sun-belt states where economies were growing and private sector unions nonexistent, weakening liberals' ability to pursue their political, economic, or cultural agenda.

• **Out-of-control immigration.** Also undercutting American workers' bargaining power was an increasingly porous border, which, together with loosened immigration laws and enforcement, swelled the number of illegal immigrants in the United States, further depressing wages. Immigration in the period from 1989 to 2001 proved a full 76 percent higher than in the period from 1976 to 1988. The number of legal immigrants grew from 2.5 million during the 1950s to 9.1 million four decades later.[72] This put further pressure on workers' wages and offered fodder for a nativist reaction.

• **The collapse of private-sector unionism.** Buffeted by the events described above and unwilling to recognize the gravity of the situation, organized labor failed to react to the changes afoot in the U.S. economy and found both its numbers and its influence steadily diminished. The labor movement's hold on the American worker slipped steadily from 35 percent union membership in 1954 to barely a third of that half a century later.[73] The number of liberal foot soldiers declined accordingly.

★ ★ ★

How did liberals deal with what faced them when they finally awoke to the full extent of their nightmare? Following the almost apocalyptic annum of 1968–69, the Democratic Party tore itself to shreds in the aftermath of the assassinations of Martin Luther King Jr. and Robert Kennedy, the rioting, the disastrous Chicago convention, the apparently endless carnage in Vietnam, and the sense of impending doom that manifested itself in internecine warfare and a narrow presidential loss by Vice President

Hubert H. Humphrey, aided by the splitting off from the party of southern populist George Wallace. In the aftermath of the debacle of George McGovern's forty-nine-state blowout four years later, no full-throated liberal candidate managed to capture the Democratic nomination for the presidency again. Fred Harris, Mo Udall, Teddy Kennedy, and McGovern himself were among those who tried and failed. The term *liberal* itself became toxic, despite the fact that its adherents continued to form the base of the Democratic Party. Not surprisingly, none of the party's presidential nominees during this period—neither Jimmy Carter, elected in the wake of Watergate but in his quest for reelection trounced by Ronald Reagan following the double national humiliation of the Iranian hostage crisis and the Soviet invasion of Afghanistan; nor his vice president, Walter Mondale, the Democrats' hapless nominee in 1984; nor 1988's choice, the no less hapless Massachusetts governor Michael Dukakis—ever came close to mastering what remained of Roosevelt's coalition. None could effectively elude the *liberal* label or successfully shape it into something sufficiently strong to survive the attacks that it inspired. Under challenge from "neoliberal" Gary Hart, who assaulted what he called the "Eleanor Roosevelt wing" and insisted that "American liberalism was near bankruptcy," Mondale did warn his party that the time had come to "adjust liberal values of social justice and compassion to a new age of limited resources."[74] But he never explained what this meant, save that it involved the politically suicidal step of raising people's taxes. New York governor Mario Cuomo offered up a series of inspirational speeches from which liberals took great comfort, but proved unwilling to test his political appeal beyond the confines of his own state.

At the same time, Reagan set the tone for the continued assault on liberals with his farewell convention address when he charged, "The masquerade is over. It's time to . . . say the dreaded L-word; to say the policies of our opposition are liberal, liberal, liberal."[75] That year's Democratic nominee, Michael Dukakis, tried to sidestep the attack by declaring, "This election is not about ideology, it's about competence." Pointedly, in his convention speech, Dukakis paid homage to Harry Truman, John F. Kennedy (twice), and Lyndon Johnson, but Franklin Roosevelt was not mentioned even once. FDR was, in fact, the Republican lodestar in this election, not the Democratic one. As Reagan told his assembled admirers upon his departure in 1988, "I started out in the other party. But forty years ago, I cast my last vote as a Democrat. It was a party in which FDR promised the return of power to the states. . . . FDR had run on a platform of eliminating useless boards and commissions and returning autonomy to local governments and to the states. That party changed—and it will never be the same. They left me; I didn't leave them."[76]

Meanwhile, the Republican candidate, Vice President George Bush, sneered, "Liberal, liberal, liberal," at his opponent as if the term conjured up images of serial killing and sexual perversion. "My opponent's views on defense are the standard litany of the liberal left," Bush explained to a San Diego audience. "The way he feels, I don't know if he could be comfortable in a great Navy town like this. I wouldn't be surprised if he thinks a naval exercise is something you find in the Jane Fonda *Workout Book*."[77] Down in North Carolina, Bush was far harsher: "I don't understand the type of thinking that lets first-degree murderers who haven't even served enough time to be eligible for parole so they can rape and plunder again, and then isn't willing to let the teachers lead the kids in the Pledge of Allegiance."[78] In the campaign's final moments Dukakis did offer up a tepid defense, explaining, "Yes, I'm a liberal in the tradition of Franklin Roosevelt and Harry Truman and John Kennedy." Yet what his left hand had given, his right immediately took back, and Dukakis promised to terminate "the most liberal borrowing and spending spree in American history."[79] (The candidate was apparently unaware that he had accepted the enemy's definition of the term as he embraced it.)

Having fought his way back to the Arkansas governor's office after having been turned out of it once before, Bill Clinton understood the degree to which liberals had been demonized in much of the country, and he became the first Democratic presidential candidate to confront the problem head-on. He bested his opponents in 1992 by casting himself on the popular side of the antiliberal arguments as an opponent of busing, bureaucracy, and big government, and the scourge of specialized liberal interests and secular immorality.[80] Clinton called for a "New Covenant" that would "honor middle-class values, restore the public trust, create a new sense of community, and make America work again"[81] He backed up his words with proposals for a middle-class tax cut, a national service, and a series of programs designed to promote public/private sector cooperation, many of which were borrowed from the Democratic Leadership Council, a group of probusiness, self-consciously "centrist" Democrats founded explicitly to combat the liberal dominance of the party. Clinton also embraced a number of conservative positions on social issues, including support for the death penalty, a stand he emphasized by interrupting his campaign to sign a death warrant in Arkansas for a barely competent individual. He also fought the party's soft-on-crime image by proposing the use of military-style boot camps for first-time offenders and challenged its too-dovish-to-be-trusted reputation by supporting the use of military force in the Balkans and in the Persian Gulf. The only time he actually spoke "the L-word" during the campaign was to deny its relevance, describing himself as "neither conservative nor liberal."[82]

Clinton's relationship with both liberals and liberalism during his two terms in office resists easy summarization. Never comfortable with the term himself, he avoided it as he sought simultaneously to redefine it. Two years before his presidential campaign, he had explained to a convention of the centrist Democratic Leadership Council, "Too many of the people who used to vote for us, the very burdened middle-class we are talking about, have not trusted in national elections to defend our national interests abroad or put their values into social policy at home, or to take their tax money and spend it with discipline." Clinton would eventually embrace what John F. Harris would term "a mild but innovative brand of liberalism that favored economic growth over redistribution, insisted that government pay its way rather than rely on budget deficits and embraced free trade rather than taking refuge in protectionism."[83]

Many liberals intuited, rightly or wrongly, that Clinton secretly sided with them in his heart of hearts, but wished he had been willing to risk more political capital on their behalf. Perhaps Clinton's most significant achievement was winning the presidency as a Democrat twice without allowing the liberal label to be hung as the equivalent of a political noose around his neck. Clinton employed liberals, he listened to liberals, and he often sympathized with liberals, but he was not himself a liberal—except in the expansive definitions of his conservative opponents. Just as FDR was a "juggler," who never let his right hand know what his left was doing, Clinton was a "triangulator," adopting ideas from all sides of the ideological spectrum and adapting them to his own purposes. While he supported the expansion of women's rights, family leave policies, and environmental protection, as authors John Micklethwait and Adrian Wooldridge note, he was also a "fiscal conservative who balanced the books, reined in spending, promoted free trade, oversaw a Wall Street boom, signed a welfare overhaul and supported tough crime policies that many old-style liberals once regarded as barbaric."[84] Following the debacle of the 1994 midterm elections when his party was humiliated by Newt Gingrich and his "Contract with America," Clinton embraced a series of policies designed to hopscotch around the political spectrum, from budget cuts in entitlement programs to support for school uniforms and tough sentencing laws that were designed to appeal more to conservatives than to liberals or moderates. In an odd but somehow exemplary sop to these same voters, Clinton even criticized his own tax hike as being too tough on the rich.

But it was not enough; whatever he did would not have been enough. The American right wing wished to repeal the 1960s, which it blamed, literally, for the collapse of Western civilization. As Gingrich explained soon after becoming Speaker of the House, from 1607 to 1965, "there was one continuous civilization built around a set of commonly accepted legal and cultural principles. Here's how we did it until the Great Society messed everything up: don't work, don't eat; your salvation is spiritual; the government by definition can't save you; governments are into maintenance and all good reforms are into transformation. From 1965 to 1994, we did strange and weird things as a country. Now we're done with that and we have to recover. The counterculture is a momentary aberration in American history that will be looked back upon as a quaint period of Bohemianism brought to the national elite." This counter-cultural elite, he continued, "taught self-indulgent, aristocratic values without realizing that if an entire society engaged in the indulgences of an elite few, you could tear the society to shreds."[85]

Nowhere was the rejection of the liberal elite clearer than in the right's reaction to the joint presidency of Bill and Hillary Clinton. Right-wing Supreme Court nominee Robert Bork compared the decade of their rule to a "mini–French Revolution." Culturally, the Clintons represented much about the 1960s that social conservatives found threatening, and indeed, Bork saw in the couple "the very personifications of the Sixties generation arrived at early middle age with its ideological baggage intact."[86] In fact, he was not entirely wrong. Bill Clinton and Hillary Rodham did meet while working on the McGovern campaign. Once married, Hillary Clinton did work outside the home and use her maiden name for a while, and clearly behaved as a full partner in her husband's presidency. Clinton socialized easily with gays and African Americans, and enjoyed hanging with Hollywood starlets and aging rock musicians. As Thomas Edsall notes, "Issues rooted in the questions of women's rights and their new roles, sexual freedom, personal responsibility, and the social control of male behavior, dominated not only the impeachment process, but also the entire Clinton presidency."[87] To many Americans, Hillary Clinton, in particular, inspired a series of emotional reactions that no amount of reassurance could temper. These included, according to a useful cataloging by the *Economist*'s "Lexington," "fears of successful professional women who look down their snooty noses at rednecks and stay-at-home mothers. Hatred of bossy liberals who want to impose a National Health Service and other bureaucratic monstrosities. Disdain for holier-than-thou lefties who ride their husbands' coat-tails to power and wealth."[88] Note that none of these objections addressed the substance of the Clintons' politics—they were, in fact, extremely cautious politically, well to the right of most public opinion polls on most issues—but focused instead almost exclusively on sex, culture, and personality. Clinton may have "dared to know," but only occasionally did he "dare to say," so ferocious and relentless was the right-wing attack on the first couple once they took up residence in the White House. Even so, it was difficult to imagine that Bill Clinton could be said to represent the same 1960s culture that produced an Abbie Hoffman, a Timothy Leary, or even a Charles Manson—as so many Republicans seemed to believe. Danny Goldberg, a music business executive and liberal activist, noted with an air of disappointment:

> [Clinton] was not at Woodstock, not at any American antiwar rallies. His musical hero is Elvis Presley, not Dylan or Hendrix. He plays the saxophone, not the guitar. His erotic posture resembles that of the macho fifties "rat pack" that entranced his hero John Kennedy, not the sexual liberation of the sixties. Clinton is a brilliant type. A careerist, driven to escape the poverty of his upbringing and always focused on conventional achievement, in many ways more influenced by the culture of the fifties than the sixties. While conservatives thought Clinton was being disingenuous when he said he had smoked marijuana once but "did not inhale," I along with many former hippies feared that Clinton was telling the truth.

Most Americans appeared to concur, and as a result, when 1996 Republican presidential nominee Robert J. Dole took up the tradition and bellowed "Liberal, liberal, liberal Bill Clinton," it was treated more like the ravings of a slightly disturbed old man than as a valid critique that demanded a political response. Dole went soundly down to defeat.[89]

While Clinton revived Democratic hopes for winning national elections, he did not do much for liberalism. Most of the traditional progressive organizations had fallen into such profound disarray, weakened by internal divisions and depleted membership, that they could rarely extract any price from Clinton in exchange for their support. These organizations, from labor unions to civil rights, environmental, feminist, and religious groups, all stood by Clinton when conservatives exploited his sexual affairs to try to drive him from office. Aside from an emotional bonding over common enemies, however, little warmth or mutual affection existed between them.

This troubled relationship would continue with the Democratic candidates who followed in Clinton's wake, though neither his vice president, Al Gore, nor Massachusetts senator John F. Kerry would prove anywhere near as skillful in negotiating its various shoals. Gore's inability to appeal to his party's left wing left him vulnerable to a kamikaze third-party challenge from Ralph Nader that ended up providing Bush with enough votes to throw the election to a Republican-dominated Supreme Court. (To be fair, much of the progress Democrats had made in attracting support from social conservatives was undone by the Lewinsky affair, together with Clinton's no less catastrophic unwillingness to come clean about it, which considerably complicated Gore's task.)

Kerry, meanwhile, did succeed in uniting the party, largely because Bush had revealed himself to be an extremist ideologue—and an incompetent one at that—who did not offer either liberals or moderates the luxury of minor distinctions. Yet Kerry also specifically avoided embracing symbolic liberal positions, even those that enjoyed supermajority support. Like Gore and Clinton before him, most, if not all, of the positions he took would have been considered typical of the conservative platform in American politics a generation earlier. And like Gore before him, Kerry suffered in the polls, despite his moderate demeanor and generally popular positions on the issues, because he found himself repeatedly on the defensive on cultural issues. In particular, he seemed to lack the devotion to religious symbols demanded by Christian evangelicals, who now made up nearly a quarter of the electorate and whose views had come to dominate the Republican Party. Though both Gore and Kerry were churchgoing men with sterling culturally conservative credentials, their party was dominated by secular Americans who demanded that their nominee repudiate the core wish list of conservative Christians. During the primary process Gore had felt compelled to affirm his support for legal abortion, support strong laws for registering guns, and favor civil unions for gays. But what was taken for normality in the Democratic loyalist world was incendiary in large parts of America outside of it, particularly against the backdrop of the cultural and Clinton wars.

John Forbes Kerry, meanwhile, would prove an even easier target, culturally, for his enemies. He was not merely a scion of great wealth who married into one of the largest private fortunes in the world, he had embraced the symbols of this wealth, and Republicans were able to define him with it. He not only had yachts and massive houses all over the country (including wealthy retreats like Sun Valley and Nantucket) but favored sports like windsurfing and snowboarding and sported an outspoken foreign wife with a strange accent. Like Gore, Kerry was uncomfortable exploiting his religious convictions for political gain, though by now this had become a near-obligatory ritual for all American politicians. Even worse, he hailed from the most liberal state in America, one in which a female judge—the wife of the liberal ex–*New York Times* columnist Anthony Lewis—had just decided to legalize gay marriage. Conservatives, having honed their techniques over a period of decades, exploited most of these weaknesses with an almost comically inane, but wickedly effective, campaign of mockery and denigration. Bush's secretary of commerce told reporters he thought Kerry "looks French." House majority leader Tom DeLay began his speeches with the quip "Good afternoon, or, as John Kerry might say: 'Bonjour!'" Here "French" was used to connote both elitism and anti-Americanism, according to the semiotic signaling of conservative talk radio and cable TV discourse. The NRA, author Tom Frank later noted, came up with an image that perfectly encapsulated the entire ridiculous enterprise: an elaborately clipped French poodle in a pink bow and a Kerry-for-president sweater over the slogan "That dog don't hunt."[90] By 2004 it would have been impossible to imagine a more appropriate symbol for American liberalism—and with it the funny-were-it-not-so-serious decline in the standards of American political debate in which liberals were forced to make their case. The reason for the effectiveness of this transparently absurd line of attack lay as much in the gullibility of the voting public as in the vulnerability of Kerry and the liberals who supported him. Nobody took a poll on it at the time, but it was probably not much more difficult to find an average American voter who could discourse about French poststructuralist theorists like Jacques Derrida or Jean Baudrillard than to locate one who could knowledgeably explain what John Kerry and his fellow "Massachusetts liberals" actually believed.

Hunting dogs or no, it was a real problem.

What Do Liberals Believe, Anyway?

At the risk of repeating myself, this needs to be stressed again, as it underlies almost every argument in this book: liberalism is notoriously difficult to define (and this is one of many reasons it is so easy to caricature). Growing out of the Enlightenment and the rejection of the divine right of both kings and churchly powers to rule over the lives and thoughts of individuals, it implies both a set of rights like those enumerated in the Constitution and Bill of Rights and a set of social and political movements spawned with the goal of humanizing industrial capitalism and relations between nations. The great Russian liberal philosopher Alexander Herzen made this point beautifully when, living in exile in London among fellow revolutionaries spouting socialism, anarchism, communism, and nihilism, among other isms, he marveled at his hosts: "England . . . They invented personal liberty, and they know it, and they did it without having any theories about it."[1]

Without much in the way of theory, as Herzen notes, liberals share a fundamental commitment to the values of the Enlightenment: in the force of reason and the ability of men and women to join together to create a society for the common good. This belief distinguished them from the theocrats of their day, as it does for liberals in our own. When George W. Bush explains that he believes that God speaks to or through him and his presidency—a fact that has often been reported—he is explicitly placing himself outside this tradition. Even so, classical liberalism remains a rather large, unwieldy tent and does not offer much to go on from a political standpoint. "Daring to know" gets one only so far, as people tend to "know" different things, based on their own prejudices, preconceptions, and life experiences.

As it has developed during roughly the past 250 years, contemporary liberalism may be understood in its present incarnation to hover between two philosophical poles loosely defined as "rights-based" liberalism, which derives from the writings of twentieth-century political philosopher John Rawls, and "communitarian" liberalism, which arose in large measure as a response to Rawls's writings but also owes a great deal to the "republican" beliefs that animated the visions of many of America's founders. Like Immanuel Kant before him, Rawls argued that the moral judgments of ordinary people are the proper departure point for political morality. All of us possess an "inviolability founded on justice that even the welfare of society as a whole cannot override." For instance, even if racism or sexism could be shown to maximize social utility, he says, each would still violate our basic sense of fairness. Within these confines, however, Rawls sought to define a political space he called "justice as fairness." He focused on what he termed "procedural justice," whereby a society could design political procedures that embody the moral ideal of justice. The fulcrum of Rawls's approach is his famous metaphor of a "veil of ignorance," in which we seek to create a society from an original state in which "no one knows his place in society, his class position or social status, nor does anyone know his fortune in the distribution of natural assets and abilities, his intelligence, strength and the like." This scenario also assumes "that the parties do not know their conceptions of the good or their special psychological propensities."[2] In such a thought experiment, as Rawls explained it in the famous last sentence of his masterwork, A Theory of Justice, "Purity of heart, if one could attain it, would be to see clearly and to act with grace and self-command from this point of view."[3]

Rawls's "veil of ignorance" has served as the foundation of most philosophical arguments over the meaning of liberalism since its introduction in 1971. And while it provides a useful starting point for the construction of a genuinely liberal society, it misses a great deal as well. Rawls focuses almost entirely on material wealth, for instance, at the expense of other forms of social good. He ignores the power of groups to shape one's personal identity—an inconvenient fact, to be sure, but one that is necessary to understand politics at almost any level. Rather amaz-ingly for a liberal, Rawls also does not address the power of institutions such as corporations—perhaps the central economic reality of our time—to shape the public sphere for their own advantage. Rawls's con-ception may appear to be utopian, given that we currently live in a soci-ety in which identity politics tends to divide groups against one another, and where social and economic inequalities are presently exploding. Judged by the standards of the history of the progressive political imagi-nation, however, it's a pretty tame affair. As John Schaar observes, "The world [Rawls] presented looks distressingly like the one we have, but with a little more equalization of income and welfare."[4]

For the purposes of defining liberalism today, the most common ob-jection to the Rawlsian paradigm comes from the communitarians, who borrow considerably from the same republican precepts of America's founders that come into conflict with the more liberal ideas popular at the time of America's origins more than two hundred years ago. To what degree, asks the political philosopher Michael Sandel, are our liberal virtues fashioned in relative isolation, and to what extent can they be found embedded in relations with others?[5] Are we, ultimately, atomistic, individual beings or members of various interlocking communities? "Rawlsian liberalism defines certain actions as beyond the bounds of a decent society," Sandel complains, "but wherein lies its commitment to the good, the noble of purpose, the meaning, as it were, of life?"[6]

For guidance in these intractable liberal positions, the historian James T. Kloppenberg suggests we turn to one of civilization's oldest moral traditions, and one whose roots are shared by most Americans: Christianity. Conceptually, Kloppenberg notes, the central virtues of liberalism descend directly from the cardinal virtues of early Christian-ity: "prudence, temperance, fortitude, and justice." He adds that "the liberal virtues of tolerance, respect, generosity, and benevolence like-wise extend St. Paul's admonition to the Colossians that they should practice forbearance, patience, kindness, and charity."[7]

This view is reinforced by the arguments of Jürgen Habermas, post-war Europe's most significant liberal philosopher and perhaps the last great voice of the once preeminent (and neo-Marxist) Frankfurt School. "Christianity, and nothing else, is the ultimate foundation of liberty, conscience, human rights, and democracy, the benchmarks of Western civilization," Habermas told then cardinal Joseph Ratzinger, now Pope Benedict, during a January 2004 conversation. "To this day, we have no other options [than Christianity]. We continue to nourish ourselves, from this source. Everything else is postmodern chatter."[8] No one understood this better than Franklin Delano Roosevelt. Asked by a reporter about his political philosophy, FDR replied, "Philosophy? I am a Christian and a Democrat—that's all."[9]

To add greatly to the irony of tracing the philosophical roots of modern liberalism to the earliest teachings of a religion whose fundamentalist followers find so much to revile in it, let us consider that perhaps the clearest evocation of what it means, philosophically, to be a liberal across both space and time can be found in the work of another political pioneer whose writings are conveniently ignored by the right-wingers who so frequently invoke his name: Adam Smith. In *The Wealth of Nations*—perhaps the founding text of capitalist philosophy—the proud liberal wrote: "No society can surely be flourishing and happy, of which the far greater part of the members are poor and miserable. It is but equity, besides, that they who feed, cloath and lodge the whole body of the people, should have such a share of the produce of their own labour as to be themselves tolerably well fed, cloathed and lodged."[10]

Still, liberalism is not a synonym for humanitarianism. As Paul Starr notes, liberals demand some form of reciprocity from their beneficiaries in exchange for their generosity. "By rooting ordinary aid to the poor in a norm of reciprocity, a liberal state may help to preserve the dignity of its beneficiaries and their sense that other people do not regard the assistance they receive as shameful because they are getting something for nothing."[11] The goal of liberalism is not societal equality itself, which is not merely impossible to achieve but quite likely impossible to define. Rather it is equality of opportunity, where every citizen is entitled to the same chance to fulfill his or her potential regardless of the circumstances of birth, financial status, race, sexual orientation, gender, whatever.

Everyone gets the same chance, and we're all in the business of providing that chance, together.

Liberalism has never entirely successfully escaped what Irving Howe called "the paradisial vision that is deeply lodged in the American imagination." Thus, Howe notes, we must add to its legacy "a strand of deep if implicit hostility toward politics per se—a powerful kind of moral absolutism, celebrating conscience above community, which forms both its glory and its curse." In this implicit rejection of politics, liberalism often appears, in the trenchant criticism of Lionel Trilling, to congeal into the simplistic notion "that the life of man can be nicely settled by correct social organization, or short of that, by the election of high moral attitudes."[12] Herein lies one of liberalism's most glaring weaknesses, and one that consistently mitigates its political effectiveness. Because many liberals believe themselves to be "above politics," they are unwilling or unable to commit themselves to the kinds of political compromise and cooperation that make political wheels spin. This was the flaw in many of the most idealistic programs of the Great Society era as well as an important factor in inspiring the backlash that followed. Today, we see it most clearly in Ralph Nader's kamikaze presidential campaigns, which continue despite having helped lay the groundwork for the ascension to the presidency of the single most reactionary individual ever to hold the office, but it is visible in so many liberal enterprises that one might fairly conclude that it is endemic to the philosophy itself.

In summary, we might term political liberalism to be "deliverable justice as fairness." Yet as any philosophically serious liberal well knows, we live in a universe of profound limits to our ability to "do good" or even to identify it. Daring to know, after all, is not the same thing as knowing; what is morally desirable may not be pragmatically achievable. Your author's understanding of contemporary American liberalism embraces pragmatism without shame or apology. What is not deliverable by government, we leave to parents and clergy and the like, though we affirm the values that support liberal beliefs: values that derive, it turns out, from the social gospel.

In the world at large, for instance, a genuinely liberal U.S. foreign policy might imply a degree of knowledge, understanding, patience, and perseverance that lies beyond the horizon of our collective capacity. As the great liberal theologian and philosopher Reinhold Niebuhr wrote back in 1952, Americans may fancy themselves to be "tutors of mankind in its pilgrimage to perfection," but we are more likely to "bring calamity upon ourselves and the world by forgetting that even the most powerful nations . . . remain themselves creatures as well as creators of the historical process."[13] Indeed, the historical process and its various legacies, as we have seen, offer no end of interference with our wishes to improve the lot of the unfortunate among us, to say nothing of the fate of mankind. In that regard, conservatives—whose philosophical precepts invite no such efforts—have a much easier time of things when attempting to marry elegant theory with uncooperative reality. With liberalism, idealism provides the foundational ingredients, but realism the necessary leavening; it is in locating the proper balance between the two that lies, as Shakespeare might say, "the rub."

3

What Does Liberalism Look Like?

As the previous chapter was pitched at a rather lofty level, it now behooves us to ask what liberals want, not in theory, but in actual practice, brought down to the level of the reality of everyday life. A simple way of explaining the overall goals of contemporary American liberalism would be to point to the success of social policies in places like western Europe, and particularly in northern Europe. (I am leaving Canada largely out of this discussion, though a similar case could be made for it, because Canadians, unlike Americans and Europeans, do not face any credible military threats, and so see no need to devote a significant portion of their GDP to defense.)

Conservatives so consistently denigrate the amazing achievements of twenty-first-century Europeans that one can't help but wonder what has them so worried. "If you want a lower standard of living," conservative policy experts Grace-Marie Turner and Robert Moffit argued in a December 2006 op-ed, "the Europeans have the right prescription." Their argument echoes views, as the *New Republic*'s Jonathan Cohn notes, that are popular across the conservative spectrum, from *Newsweek*'s Robert Samuelson ("Europe is history's has-been") to the *National Review*'s Jonah Goldberg ("Europe has an asthmatic economy") to the *New York Times* pundit David Brooks ("The European model is flat-out unsustainable").[1] Conservatives have been making exactly these arguments for roughly five decades now, yet these same European nations have by almost every measurement—individual rights and community, capitalist enterprise and social solidarity, and even personal mobility—proven superior to the United States.[2] Despite some significant philosophical distinctions, what in practice Americans call "liberalism" is known in Europe as "social democracy." By any name, however, and allowing for differences in national preferences, character, history, racial and ethnic makeup, and so on, the progress that Europeans have made toward the goal of "justice as fairness" ought to be enough to make most Americans—and not just liberals—ashamed and envious.

The workers of France, Belgium, Ireland, the Netherlands, and Norway all produce the same goods and services as the United States or more, and thereby enjoy higher productivity per hour worked than do U.S. workers.[3] The reasons for this are myriad, but almost all of them contradict conservative conventional wisdom. According to conservative ideology, high tax rates are supposed to kill personal initiative and depress growth, but they are much higher and more progressive across Europe than in the United States. Welfare payments—again, allegedly the means by which the personal initiative of poor people is destroyed—are based in Europe on universal entitlements, with little, if any, means-testing.[4] Finally, union membership, also the bane of conservative propagandists in the United States, ranges from 70 percent of the workforce in Norway to over 95 percent of the workforce in Finland, more than six times its level in the United States.[5]

While these societies are hardly utopias—much of Europe remains riven by apparently insoluble Islamic immigration crises and relatively high unemployment—the benefits provided by many if not most of these societies would, for most Americans, prove a wonder to behold. Despite the fact that Americans work nearly four hundred more hours a year than those famously industrious Germans, and more than workers in virtually every western European nation by a considerable margin, these same states somehow sponsor far more generous programs of training and job mobility, and pay generous unemployment benefits. Families receive periods of paid maternity and paternity leave. Europeans also enjoy high-quality public health and education provisions, and all manner of public services, from parks to efficient and inexpensive public transport systems, that are not available anywhere in the United States.[6] To give just one example, Denmark spends nearly one-third of its gross domestic product on government-run benefits and taxes its citizens at an equivalently high rate. Its top bracket is 63 percent, nearly double the highest rate in the United States. With these revenues, the state spends more than 5 percent of its GDP on the unemployed and more than 2 percent alone on "flexicurity" labor market programs to help retrain displaced workers. This compares with a feeble 0.16 percent in the United States, which is by far the lowest in the Organisation for Economic Co-operation and Development (OECD).[7] Partly as a result, in mid-2006 Denmark's unemployment rate was just 3.6 percent, well below the 4.7 percent in the United States. According to the Economist Intelligence Unit, Denmark's "Quality of Life" index proved superior to that of America as well, with advantages like universal health care and day care, and a poverty rate of just 4.3 percent, compared with 17.1 percent in the United States. (America has the second-worst record among OECD nations.) Meanwhile, Denmark is, at this writing, enjoying a small budget surplus, equal to approximately 0.65 percent of its GDP. The United States, meanwhile, is saddled with ever-exploding deficits, currently reaching 4.5 percent of GDP, and rising.[8]

Denmark is hardly exceptional. In Finland, for instance, citizens are entitled to state-funded educational, medical, and welfare services, literally from the cradle to the grave. Finns pay nothing, ever, for education, including both infant and child care as well as medical and law school—to say nothing of their monthly stipend for expenses. And they produce perhaps the best educational test results in the world. (This is true even though they don't go in for standardized tests.) According to 2003 OECD surveys, Finland ranks no. 1 in student reading ability, no. 1 in student science ability, no. 2 in student problem-solving ability, and no. 2 in student mathematics ability. The United States, by contrast, ranks no. 12, no. 19, no. 26, and no. 24, respectively.[9]

When comparing social policies in the United States and the advanced nations of Europe, such disparities are the rule, rather than the exception. According to the most recent census figures, nearly sixteen million Americans are living in "deep or severe poverty"—a category that includes individuals making less than $5,080 a year, and families of four bringing in less than $9,903 a year. Of these, barely 10 percent receive welfare in the form of Temporary Assistance for Needy Families and just slightly more than a third receive food stamps.[10] Apart from cases of "severe poverty," one in six American households earned less than 35 percent of the median income in 2000. (In Britain, among the least equitable of European nations, that proportion is fewer than one in twenty.)[11] America's relatively niggardly welfare system, even in its most generous incarnation, raised poor incomes only moderately, and reduced the proportion of adults in poverty from 26.7 to 19.1 percent.[12] In Germany, France, and Italy, meanwhile, the proportion of adults in poverty hovers at around just 7 percent. As for the elderly—where America's social security program presents the country at its most beneficent—the nation manages to reduce poverty levels from nearly 60 percent before transfer payments to just below 20 percent. Yet the Europeans improve on this performance by significant margins as well. Germany, France, and Italy leave only 7.6, 7.5, and 6.5 percent of their elderly populations living in poverty, respectively. And what is perhaps worse, while roughly a quarter of all American children are condemned to grow up in poverty, the analogous proportions for the countries cited above are just 8.6, 7.4, and 10.5 percent.[13] The lack of progress in this area in the United States is one reason American conservatives insist on making these programs so stingy. The truth is that, when it comes to social mobility, these European nations prove far more successful in providing what might be called "the Nordic Dream"— or even "the British Dream"—than the romantic notion of "the American Dream" that schoolchildren are taught to cherish. This is true at nearly every level of society. According to two separate studies based on a set of data collected over a period of five decades the Nordic countries enjoy considerably greater degrees of social mobility than do Americans. In the United States, a son's earnings are more than twice as likely to be closely related to those of his father than in most Nordic nations, and even Britain does a much better job at offering second-generation earners a higher probability of economic improvement than does the United States. This is true across the board, but is most dramatic for those stuck at society's bottom rungs.

Europe's more generous welfare system has actually proven more successful than America's in reducing the size of these payments by moving people off welfare—which is, after all, supposed to be the goal of such programs. In the Nordic nations, for instance, three-quarters of those on welfare had moved up and out of the system by the time they reached their forties, but barely more than half of their American counterparts had. As the editors of the *Economist* put it, "In other words, Nordic countries have almost completely snapped the link between the earnings of parents and children at and near the bottom. That is not at all true of America." In Britain, too, fully 70 percent of those enmeshed in the welfare system had moved out within a single generation—again, a higher percentage than in America. The magazine points to the generous tax and welfare provisions for families as "the obvious explanation for greater mobility in the Nordic countries . . . especially when compared with America's."[14]

Now look at some other significant differences:

No-Vacation Nation. The United States is the only wealthy industrialized nation not to legislate any paid time off and holidays for its workforce. Austria and Britain both offer four weeks, Denmark gives thirty work days, and even Japan mandates ten days. The United States guarantees nothing, with low-wage and part-time workers, not surprisingly, suffering the most. Only 69 and 36 percent of them, respectively, enjoy any vacation time at all.[15]

Children and Health. With America's wasteful and expensive system of public health, and family-unfriendly employment laws, its children face a whole host of impediments to their development potential that are all but unknown across much of Europe. The United States and South Africa are the only two developed countries in the world that do not provide health care for all of their citizens.[16] Nationally, 29 percent of children had no health insurance at some point in the last twelve months, and many get neither checkups nor vaccinations. The United States ranks eighty-fourth in the world for measles immunizations and eighty-ninth for polio.[17] These figures are particularly shocking given that Americans spend almost two and half times the industrialized world's median on health care, nearly a third of which is wasted on bureaucracy and administration.[18] As the New Yorker's Malcolm Gladwell notes:

> Americans have fewer doctors per capita than most Western countries. We go to the doctor less than people in other Western countries. We get admitted to the hospital less frequently than people in other Western countries. We are less satisfied with our health care than our counterparts in other countries. American life expectancy is lower than the Western average. Childhood-immunization rates in the United States are lower than average. Infant-mortality rates are in the nineteenth percentile of industrialized nations. Doctors here perform more high-end medical procedures, such as coronary angioplasties, than in other countries, but most of the wealthier Western countries have more CT scanners than the United States does, and Switzerland, Japan, Austria, and Finland all have more MRI machines per capita. Nor is our system more efficient. The United States spends more than a thousand dollars per capita per year—or close to four hundred billion dollars—on health-care-related paperwork and administration, whereas Canada, for example, spends only about three hundred dollars per capita. And, of course, every other country in the industrialized world insures all its citizens; despite those extra hundreds of billions of dollars we spend each year, we leave forty-five million people without any insurance.[19]

And remember the Finns? Not surprisingly, perhaps, they devote less than half of what we do to medical care, as a percentage of GDP, and yet their infant mortality rate is half that of the United States—and one-sixth that of African-American babies—while their life expectancy rate is greater.[20] (The United States ranked forty-second, behind not only Japan and most of Europe but also Jordan, Guam, and the Cayman Islands, according to the most recent census figures.)[21]

Perhaps all that education has made them smart enough to invest in preventative care and universal coverage.[22] Conservatives, members of the American medical industrial complex, and other defenders of the U.S. status quo frequently berate the European health care alternative because, they say, the care that patients receive there is both less responsive and less advanced than that available to Americans, however much more we may have to pay for ours. These claims tend to evaporate under even minimal scrutiny. Jonathan Cohn reports, for instance, that American patients wait longer, on average, for routine treatments than those in France and Germany. Moreover, hospitals in those two nations also provide new mothers more than four days to recover, while insurance companies insist that doctors send American mothers home after only two. Swedes enjoy better success rates treating cervical and ovarian cancers. The French best the American system when it comes to stomach cancer, Hodgkin's disease, and non-Hodgkin's lymphoma. The French also benefit from more cancer radiation equipment than Americans. And despite so many American boasts on exactly this topic, Germans get the most hip replacements. In the area where one hears the loudest cheers for the American system—making new cancer treatments available to patients as quickly (however expensively) as possible, the United States is merely tied with Austria, France, and Switzerland. Of course, the U.S. system does not do everything poorly. Cohn points to the world's highest cure rate for "some cancers—including breast and prostate cancer," but it's hard to connect these to our system of health care delivery. And finally, he rightfully asks, if the less expensive, more efficient, and more universal European system "means worse health care overall, then why do so many studies show the U.S. scoring so poorly on international comparisons, including those examining 'mortality amenable to health care'— a statistic devised specifically to test the quality of different health care systems across the globe?"[23]

Just how did the Europeans get so smart? The education figures tell a similar story. Although the United States devotes roughly the same proportion of national income to education as the European Union nations, on average, European nations all rank higher in math and science. They also enjoy, on average, an additional year of education and have a higher proportion of young people in higher education.[24]

Toward a Humane Society. Socially, the values of Europe strike most liberals as far more humane than our own. As amazing as it may sound to many Americans, candidate countries for EU membership must first abolish capital punishment as a condition for entry; in fact, it is the very first condition listed.[25] Gay marriage is the law in Belgium, the Netherlands, and even Catholic Spain, while gay civil unions are officially recognized by Norway, Sweden, Iceland, France, and Germany. Although Americans prove to be evenly divided when asked by pollsters whether "homosexuality is a way of life that should be accepted by society," European acceptance levels range from 72 percent in Italy to 83 percent in Germany.[26] While the names of many, mostly conservative, European parties do contain the word *Christian* (as in "Christian Democrat"), they are far less eager to inject their own parochial understanding of biblical injunctions into politics. This is particularly true in England, the most Americanized of "European" nations. During the 2005 election there, Conservative candidate Michael Howard raised none of what Americans consider "social" issues like abortion or gay marriage, which proved so important an element in Bush's 2004 campaign. When he appeared at the pulpit at the Tabernacle Christian Centre near the outskirts of London, he mentioned neither God nor religion during a twenty-minute speech. In an almost perfect contrast to George W. Bush, Howard called for a massive increase in British foreign aid,[27] which speaks to yet another of Europe's great advantages over the U.S. political system: the relatively responsible positions its conservative parties take toward issues of social solidarity and genuinely "compassionate conservatism." In Norway, for instance, even the conservative investment community that manages the country's enormous $300-billion-plus government pension fund refuses to invest in companies with whose social practices it disagrees.

Additionally, Francis Fukuyama, the noted political theorist whose "End of History" thesis so captured the imaginations of American conservatives eager to pronounce their own society as the final development point of world political history, finds that the European Union's "attempt to transcend sovereignty and traditional power politics by establishing a transnational rule of law is much more in line with a 'posthistorical' world than the Americans' continuing belief in God, national sovereignty, and their military."[28] Certainly the EU has disappointed many of its expectations, but members' willingness to compromise their sovereignty for the improvement of all on matters sometimes central to national identity is an example from which many American liberals also find inspiration.

Sex, Guns, and Death. Because Christian conservatives and the gun lobby do not enjoy the power to shape public policy in Europe and Canada, their children are also safer than are ours. Canadian and European teenagers do not have to contend with restrictive laws that deny them access to truthful sex education and contraception, or with federally funded programs that deliberately misinform them about the dangers associated with sex to try to scare them into abstinence.[29] Canadian and European young people are about as active sexually as Americans, but teenage American girls are five times as likely to have a baby as French girls, seven times as likely to have an abortion, and seventy times as likely to have gonorrhea as girls in the Netherlands. In addition, the incidence of HIV/AIDS among American teenagers is five times that of the same age group in Germany.

As for violent deaths, the United States must contend with the power of the conservative National Rifle Association, which not only lobbies to prevent background checks to keep guns out of the hands of criminals and terrorists, but also insists that when such checks are conducted, the evidence amassed must be destroyed within twenty-four hours. The result: American children are sixteen times more likely than children in other industrialized nations to be murdered with a gun, eleven times more likely to commit suicide with a gun, and nine times more likely to die from firearms accidents. These figures are hardly surprising when one considers the fact that the rate of firearms homicide in the United States is nineteen times higher than that of thirty-five other high-income countries combined.[30]

One could fill an entire book with examples and statistics that demonstrate the multiple means by which various European governments better serve their citizens than does our own. Apologists for American failures in these areas point to characterological, ideological, and historical reasons why Americans shy away from more effective delivery and distribution systems for the services they need to live healthy, prosperous lives. Liberalism, as the political scientist Paul Starr correctly argues, derives from different roots than European social democracy, and the accomplishments of a system based on the latter are not immediately transferable to the former.[31] But in most of these cases, what prevents the realization of the kind of government and society Americans say they desire is less a matter of choice than of imposition. Powerful lobbies buy themselves the right to rip off Americans with perfectly legal payments to politicians and then pretend that somehow this legalized larceny represents the true desire of a public that is perennially kept in the dark. Policies with strong majority support such as universal health care and paid maternity leave are written off as liberal or even socialistic, as if that ends the argument then and there. What this book aims to do in the pages that follow is to tear down those barriers to coherent argument and pragmatic practice. Remove the bugaboo from the word *liberal*, I argue, and the policies of a sensible populace naturally follow. Unfortunately, doing so is a great deal more difficult that it looks, and in the following chapter, I attempt to explain why.

— 4 —

So What's the Problem?

Most of what you've read so far raises an obvious question: If most Americans agree with liberal priorities on so many issues, and if the liberal/social democratic model of governance delivers a far superior program of goods and services so much more effectively for so many people, why, then, is liberalism presently in such dire straits politically? Why are so few Americans—a strong majority of whom endorse most of its specific goals—eager to identify themselves with its traditions? Why are liberals doing so badly in both the political arena and with the media punditocracy?

Of course, this conundrum would be less daunting if we could point to a single, simple explanation, such as "Liberals are too damn elitist," or "Liberals hate God," or another of the nostrums frequently repeated on any given Rush Limbaugh—or even mainstream media—program. It would also be considerably easier if one could pick a single or even a handful of obvious villains, as in, say, "conservatives" or "corporations" or "the media," or even liberals themselves. Alas, the afflictions that presently beset American liberals and liberalism are myriad, mutually reinforcing, and devilishly difficult to untangle. To do justice to each one would require another book or three. Other obstacles are unavoidable, given the historical circumstances. Yet a third set is due to the design and successes of a well-financed, well-organized, and well-disciplined conservative movement in the United States, coupled with a quiescent mainstream media that fails to challenge its steady stream of false information and frequent slander of its opponents.

What follows is a depressingly lengthy—but incomplete, nevertheless—list of problems liberals must somehow overcome if they are to return to the honorable position they once held in American politics. They are not

presented in any particular order or category, as each is in some way related to many others, and few, if any, can be said to derive from a single
cause.

The Word *Liberal* Itself. As discussed above, the conservative
movement—frequently aided by the putatively liberal members of the
mainstream media—has invested many billions of dollars in sullying the
good name of liberals and making a mockery of their true beliefs. This
effort involves well-funded foundations, think tanks, newspapers, cable
stations, talk-radio programs, Internet sites, gossip columnists, PBS programs, publishing houses, and network broadcast programs—to say
nothing of the resources of the Republican National Committee—all of
whom have made a concerted effort to vilify and dishonor the term
liberal, associating it with all manner of weakness, treachery, and immorality. Whether the "world outside" actually matches what the public
philosopher Walter Lippmann called "the pictures in our heads" is in
many cases irrelevant. If Americans associate negative qualities with the
word *liberal,* they will be unlikely to pay attention long enough to listen
to arguments to the contrary.

Racial and Ethnic Conflict. Lyndon Johnson correctly predicted that
his championing of the 1964 Civil Rights Act would destroy the Democratic Party in the South. In many areas of the nation, white middle- and
working-class voters simply refuse to vote for a party they associate
with black and brown people. The loss of the once "Solid South" has
translated into an electoral map that has put the Democrats at an apparently permanent disadvantage in electoral politics and has rent apart
the New Deal coalition that succeeded so frequently in electing presidents between 1932 and 1968 and dominating Congress through 1980.
Moreover, as the South and parts of the West have fallen to Republicans,
moderates and liberals have been replaced by extreme right-wingers
who have purposely sought to highlight the explosive issues that continue to tear liberalism apart. It's an endless cycle, and one that liberals
are presently at a loss to address.

Within the remaining constituencies, the legacy of the collapse of the civil rights movement is the intense hostility of many of the groups forced to compete for what remains of its spoils. In the post–civil rights era, for instance, the black and Jewish leaderships have constantly been in conflict over affirmative action and quota preferences; blacks and gays have fought over whether civil rights protections should be extended to Americans on the basis of sexual orientation; Asian Americans and blacks have experienced conflict over various urban issues; working-class whites have battled with blacks about job preferences and antidiscrimination legislation in housing laws and school busing; and immigrant groups have clashed with labor unions over job and border issues.

Class Conflict. Liberals are unavoidably divided by class. On the one hand, the coalition's bedrock economic constituency is made up of wage workers, small-business owners, and the poor. On the other, its no-less-bedrock cultural constituency consists of professionals, artists, academics, and public-sector service workers. According to the Pew Research Center, the culturally liberal group makes up about 40 percent of all Democratic voters, but only 19 percent of all registered voters. These voters are predominantly white, and a majority are female. They are, as a group, better educated than the rest of the country, less religious, more urban, less married, and wealthier. They strongly support abortion rights and gay marriage, do not worry much about pornography, and rarely own guns.[1] Needless to say, these values frequently find themselves in conflict with those professed by the white working-class voters—especially white male voters—particularly in nonurban areas. To give just one example, according to a Pew survey released in 2007, two-thirds of working-class Democrats have a favorable view of Wal-Mart, while a majority of professional-class Democrats consider it to be something akin to evil incarnate.[2] These divisions, too, are endlessly exacerbated by conservatives in the media and elsewhere, who seek to paint cultural liberals as "effete," "elitist," "arrogant," and prone to meddling in the lives of those for whose values they feel contempt. This constant refrain on almost all cable news shows and talk-radio programs frequently makes its way into the mainstream media discourse—often, alas, purveyed by alleged liberals.

Abortion Politics and Gender Conflict. Even though liberals are more likely to be female than male—possibly the result of what linguist George Lakoff terms a cooperative "nurturing" framing of the issues rather than a more competitive narcissistic one—the politics of abortion has nevertheless proven extremely costly in recent decades. Abortion has become the litmus test in recent years for Democratic candidates and liberal voters, but the position they have staked out is one that does not enjoy majority support. (Recall that his vetoing of the so-called partial-birth abortion ban was one of very few occasions when President Clinton knowingly chose to defy majority public opinion on a major political issue during the course of his eight years in office.) Abortion has the triple disadvantage of saddling liberal politicians with an unpopular position relating to restrictions on abortion in many parts of the country where the issue remains salient and powerful; of creating barriers for those politicians whose liberal credentials are strong on all other issues but who, for reasons of religion or philosophy, cannot endorse abortion; and of strengthening the perception among common people that liberals are antireligious, antidemocratic, and indifferent to their values.[3] All this serves no one.

Secular / Religious Conflict. Author Gregory Rodriguez points out that before 1972, "both major parties were essentially indistinguishable in their approach to religion. The activist cores of both were dominated by members of mainstream religious groups: the GOP by mainline Protestants and the Democratic Party by Catholics and Jews." But with the takeover of the party by the forces of the "New Politics," he identifies

a profound shift from what had been the cultural consensus in American politics. Whereas only 5% of Americans could be considered secular in 1972, fully 24% of first-time Democratic delegates that year were self-identified agnostics, atheists or people who rarely, if ever, set foot in a house of worship. This new activist base encouraged a growing number of Democratic politicians to tone down their appeal to religious voters and to seek a higher wall separating church and state. With little regard for the traditionalist sensitivities of religious people within or outside of the party, the Democrats also embraced progressive stances on feminism and homosexuality that the public had never openly debated.[4]

Because liberals are perceived to be the most secular segment of the population, and because so many Americans believe it important to vote for people who represent their own personal belief systems—or at least claim to—this secularism is a significant political disadvantage in an increasingly religious society. Twenty-three percent of voters surveyed on Election Day 2002 in the national exit polls described themselves as "born-again or evangelical" Christians who cast their vote on the basis of "moral issues." These voters chose George W. Bush by a margin of 78–21, and skew the system against liberals by virtue of sheer numbers.

Foreign Policy Conflict. Liberals have never settled the fundamental discrepancy between their pre-Vietnam (largely) hawkish selves, and their post-Vietnam (largely) dovish ones. Frequently, the two sides end up opposing each other with greater enthusiasm than they do their putative opponents. They are likewise rarely if ever able to agree on the most fundamental aspects of foreign and military policy, and thereby tend to try to paper over these differences by what amounts to the adoption of either an equivocal position or one of obfuscation, when what the public demands is the appearance of strength and clarity in exactly this context.

The Politics of Victimization. Beginning in the early 1970s, liberals began to see themselves as a coalition of victims seeking redress rather than a majority movement that represented the interests of most Americans. Women, religious minorities, ethnic minorities (including blacks, Hispanics, Native Americans, and Asian Americans), gays and lesbians, the handicapped, and the socially and economically disadvantaged all sought to demand redress from the system for historic wrongs. In some cases, they insisted on retributive action; in others, they merely wanted to enjoy the fruits of American society as equal citizens. This situation not only gave rise to massive degrees of resentment among a majority who felt themselves forced to make sacrifices they could ill afford on behalf of those whose values they may not have supported, it also provided easy political targets and extremely valuable organizational issues for right-wing campaigns. This occurred for nearly twenty years around issues of race, crime, welfare, abortion, and affirmative action as well.

The Problem of "Checklist Liberalism." Just days before he lost the 2006 Democratic senatorial primary in Connecticut, Joe Lieberman gave voice to the prevailing view of professional politicians' calculations: "Did I keep in touch with Democrats? You bet I did. . . . I have the support of most of the key inner constituencies, advocacy groups within the Democratic Party: the AFL-CIO, the League of Conservation Voters, Defenders of Wildlife, Human Rights Campaign, NARAL, Planned Parenthood PAC. They wouldn't support me if I lost touch with them."[5] The fact that Lieberman had, in fact, lost touch with Americans on the most important issues of all—the war in Iraq, and the need to oppose the Bush administration's power grab across the board—apparently did not enter into his calculation. Lieberman was particularly tone-deaf on these most central of issues, and proved the architect of his own humiliation in this regard, but the notion that the groups he cited could prove a winning coalition nationally when it could not win even a single blue-state Democratic primary points to the obvious limitations of this approach as a political strategy.

Short-Termism. As E. J. Dionne notes, while conservative organizers tend to pay close attention to long-term goals and institution-building from the bottom up, liberals often focus on favorite causes and favorite candidates, notably in presidential years, to the exclusion of longer-term strategizing. For instance, the wealthy donors who bankrolled grassroots organizing in the 2004 presidential campaign withdrew immediately afterward. They created the multimillion-dollar effort America Coming Together (ACT), and then, as Democratic congressional leader Rahm Emanuel bemoaned, "They walked off the field." In contrast, observes Amy Chapman, executive director of Grassroots Democrats, which raises money for state party organizations, among conservatives "everyone plays a role in supporting the party and building a party structure."[6]

The Issue of "Implementation." Liberals have a great many good ideas. But ideas remain just that until they are implemented, and here, liberals have been overly impatient and frequently unconcerned with the (necessarily) unpredictable results of their policies. The popular reactions to the busing of schoolchildren or the implementation of race-based affirmative action programs are but two of many example where good intentions were not only insufficient but may have proved counterproductive. Too often liberals depend on the weight of sensible argument to carry the day, and dismiss those who oppose them as simply failing to "see the light." Former communications chief Michael Waldman recalls President Clinton's frequent frustration with those he termed "these reformers," who "think that if you wave the wand you'll get reform."[7]

"Sucker" Centrism. Pushed by the mainstream media to "rise above politics" and appeal to a conservatively defined political "center," liberals are forever proving that they would rather enjoy the illusion of bipartisan cooperation than actually win their political battles. Business lobbies, for example, have learned to support the conservative agenda even when it is irrelevant to their own interests, for they realize that with conservatives in power, they will be fighting over spoils with winners, rather than over recriminations with losers. The differences between each side's commitment to victory at all costs became evident to all when, during the election conflict in Florida in 2000, conservatives spent millions to secretly orchestrate what their right-wing pundit Paul Gigot approvingly termed a "bourgeois riot" designed to shut down a potentially unfavorable vote count, while Democrats actually instructed their supporters to leave the state lest they be accused in the national media of showing bad manners. But they are also evident in small ways across nearly every aspect of the nation's political business. For instance, in the summer of 2006, the National Federation of Independent Business, the small-business lobby, argued on behalf of what economist and columnist Paul Krugman termed "the bizarre, hybrid wage-and-tax legislation" before the Senate, which would have raised the minimum wage while sharply cutting taxes on very large estates. Neither part of the provision would have benefited small businesses: minimum-wage increases would have raised their costs, and the repeal of the estate tax would have vastly increased the size of the federal deficit while benefiting a total of only 135 small businesses a year, according to Congressional Budget Office calculations, but they were willing to take one for their team. Now compare that with liberal interest groups like the Sierra Club, the environmental organization, and NARAL, the abortion-rights group, both of which endorsed Senator Lincoln Chafee, Republican of Rhode Island, for reelection. The Sierra Club's executive director explained, "We choose people, not parties." But Krugman notes, "While this principle might once have made sense, it's just naïve today. Given both the radicalism of the majority party's leadership and the ruthlessness with which it exercises its control of the Senate, Mr. Chafee's personal environmentalism is nearly irrelevant when it comes to actual policy outcomes; the only thing that really matters for the issues the Sierra Club cares about is the 'R' after his name."[8] (Chafee lost, in any case.) If the Republicans had maintained control of the Senate, Senator James Inhofe, who complains that global warming is "the greatest hoax ever perpetrated on the American people," would continue as chair of the Senate Environment and Public Works Committee, while the majority leader would have undoubtedly been someone who shared Bill Frist's view that abortion equals murder. Too many liberals are simply too high-minded to worry about actually winning.

Indiscipline and Political Disorganization. "That liberals are divided in outlook and endeavor while reactionaries are held together by community of interests and the ties of custom is well-nigh a commonplace," wrote John Dewey in 1935.[9] Speaking from the perspective of contemporary history, Dewey was living in a liberal organizational paradise. At the height of the post–New Deal party system of the 1950s and 1960s, the Democratic Party was supported by a powerful and interlinked network of nationally, locally, ethnically, and occupationally grounded organizations, integrated with an equally rooted Democratic Party structure, and represented middle-income Americans on pocketbook matters. All of these have weakened considerably, for a variety of reasons, including the time demands on two-income families, the siren song of television, and changes in the global economy. Today, lower-income Americans— the ones represented by Democrats—are barely a third as likely as the affluent to belong to an organization that takes a stand on public issues.[10] The most significant loss among this sector has been the decimation of America's union movement. Once representing the wage earners of approximately a third of America's families, today, in the private sector, they represent not even a tenth.[11] As political scientists Jacob Hacker and Paul Pierson observe, "Amid the ongoing debate over whether unions are good for the economy, we often forget that they have always been crucial political actors, helping workers identify common issues, informing them about political and policy considerations, and shaping political debates. No organization representing working families today has anything remotely like the same reach, influence, or cohesion as American unions did during their halcyon years."[12] A 2005 study commissioned by the liberal donor group Democracy Alliance pointed to many of the areas in which liberals put themselves at an organizational disadvantage when compared to their highly motivated and well-disciplined conservative counterparts:

> Conservatives systematically invest in non-electoral, social, religious and cultural networks to wage a "permanent campaign" that continuously dialogues with people around conservative values outside of election season and then inspires them to make conservative electoral choices. Progressive capacity concentrates efforts on the eve of election, while

conservatives work to create conservative culture and work to produce conservative voters year-round.[13]

As Thomas Edsall sagely observes,

Perhaps most important is the difference in the linkage between the party and the network of allied interest groups on each side of the aisle. Conservatives and the Republican Party were unified by the shared goal of ending their minority status and taking the reins of power. For Grover Norquist, president of the Americans for Tax Reform, Feulner of the Heritage Foundation, Weyrich of the Free Congress Foundation, the former Moral Majority president Jerry Falwell, Pat Robertson of the Christian Broadcast Network, Dirk Van Dongen, president of the National Association of Wholesale Distributors, John Engler, president of the National Association of Manufacturers, and a host of others in charge of organizations on the right side of the spectrum, the Republican Party is their political arm, an integral part of their public lives, and crucial to their ability to press policy and legislative agendas. . . . In contrast, the mainstay organizations of the left were created when liberals and Democrats were in power. Their function was to influence sympathetic decision makers who controlled both branches of Congress for many decades, not to wrest power from adversaries. Virtually every leader of the liberal network is a Democrat. But Ralph Neas of People for the American Way, Nan Aron of the Alliance for Justice, and Wade Henderson of the Leadership Conference on Civil Rights all see themselves and the goals of their respective organizations as separate and distinct from the Democratic Party. On the left, this separation applies almost across the board to include the NAACP, the ACLU, Common Cause, the American Association of University Women, the Children's Defense Fund, NARAL Pro-Choice America, the Human Rights Fund, the National Organization of Women, and so on.[14]

This "urge to purge" on the part of many progressives was on display at what is probably the largest annual gathering of progressive activists, the national "Take Back America" conference, sponsored by the Campaign for America's Future. As Todd Gitlin reported, Kim Gandy, the president of the National Organization for Women, took the stage at its 2005 annual gathering to denounce John Kerry, the Democratic Party's 2004 nominee; Jim Wallis, the left-wing evangelical leader; and Bono, the U2 superstar and global humanitarian who has proven willing to work with the Bush administration to try to reduce disease and starvation in Africa. "If this is what it means to be a big tent," she insisted, "then I say let's keep the skunk out of the tent." She was followed to the podium by Jesse Jackson, who likened progressives to "the third rail of American politics." The first two rails, Jackson explained, were the two parties. The third was "a strong independent force." As Gitlin rightly noted, Jackson's metaphor may have been unwittingly revealing. "Third rails may carry the power, but they are also lethal." Sadly, he reports, both Gandy and Jackson drew standing ovations.[15] Elections are not won by subtraction, and coalitions are not built on the basis of purity tests. But this is a fact of political life that all too many influential voices on the left refuse even to recognize.

Base Weakness. "There are twice as many angry conservatives in this country as there are angry liberals," notes Democratic direct-mail specialist Hal Malchow. "Liberals by their very nature don't get as angry as conservatives do."[16] Because roughly 30 percent more Americans describe themselves as conservatives than liberals—and because these conservatives are, on average, more motivated and better served by a well-funded, well-disciplined political structure augmented by a massive talk-radio and cable-television communications empire—a right-wing politician can win elections while taking positions that are vastly at odds with those held by a significant majority of his constituents, just so long as those who support him remain more committed to his victory than do the larger number of people (and funders) who would prefer his defeat. The conservative movement is supported by right-wing religious organizations like the Family Research Council, the Traditional Values Coalition, Focus on the Family, and the Southern Baptist Convention; wealthy foundations like Scaife, Bradley, Olin, Koch, Smith Richardson,

Carthage, and Earhart; a vast array of think tanks, including the American Enterprise Institute, the Cato Institute, the Free Congress Foundation, the Heritage Foundation, and the Manhattan Institute; numerous business organizations, including the Business Roundtable, the U.S. Chamber of Commerce, the National Association of Manufacturers, and the National Federation of Independent Business; and the entire News Corp empire, including Fox News, as well as almost all of talk radio, most of cable television, and much of the print punditocracy, including most particularly the martial editorial pages of the *Wall Street Journal*.

The liberal equivalents of this potent apparatus are either anemic, forty years behind in organizing techniques and investment, or nonexistent. Take the example of mega-churches. Just before the 2004 election, former Christian Coalition chief Ralph Reed explained, rather cogently, that Bush would win the election because Christian conservatives would all go to church on Sunday, would be reminded to vote, and would be driven to and from polling places, if necessary. Liberals, in contrast, went nowhere on Sundays, and indeed did not congregate anywhere, anytime at all. Conservative mega-churches, moreover, also provide a central focus for the lives of many of their members to a degree that has no corollary in liberal life. As Thomas Edsall points out, these institutions have become seven-day-a-week service providers, using a business model and "corporate-style growth strategies . . . giving them a tremendous advantage in the battle for religious market share." They make available day care, singles groups, political debates, game nights, bridge clubs, affinity gatherings for everyone from motorcycle enthusiasts to weight watchers, book clubs, softball teams, AA sessions, church cafés, gathering places for teenagers, free financial advice, low-cost bulk food, music studios, divorce counseling, help for parents of autistic children, meals for the elderly, a "car ministry" that repairs donated vehicles, and even a "fidelity group" for men with "sexual addictions." Some mega-church complexes include banks, pharmacies, and schools; others offer test preparation assistance and help in filling out tax forms and in buying houses.[17] Given the centrality of their proselytizing mission, they also continually expand their numbers.

The conservative base is naturally much wealthier than the liberal base. Republicans are the party of CEOs, of the managerial elite, of successful entrepreneurs, and of successful small-business people.[18] It is, as Edsall notes, the party of well-to-do white-collar workers, stable families, and those belonging to rising rather than to waning religious movements. Twice as many voters in the bottom third of income brackets were not registered to vote when compared with the rest of the electorate, according to the 2004 National Election Study (NES).[19] Liberals, moreover, must rely for their funding upon people who are not serving their own interests economically, which is, at best, a tricky tactic to pull off. John Olin, namesake of the right-wing Olin Foundation, reportedly said he saw his role as "using my fortune to protect the system that made it possible." Liberal funders, meanwhile, must address the very inequities in the system that have helped make them wealthy enough to be funders in the first place.

This difficult task is made more so by the fact that conservatives, and many in the media, appear to believe that rich people have no business caring about poor people in the first place. During the opening months of John Edwards's 2008 presidential campaign, for instance, the *Washington Post* devoted far more attention to his personal finances than to his plans for universal health care. Bill Hamilton, an editor at the paper, defended its stop-the-presses front-page treatment of the routine sale of Edwards's house by explaining to the *Post*'s ombudsman that the article was justified because it involved a "presidential candidate [who] just happens to be a millionaire who is basing his campaign on a populist appeal to the common man."[20] The *New York Times* proved similarly obsessed. For instance, in an alleged news story entitled "Edwards Talks Tough on Hedge Funds," Leslie Wayne observed, "Mr. Edwards has made poverty his signature issue, a topic that stands in sharp contrast to his own $30 million net worth."[21] Of course, owing to U.S. campaign finance laws, it is awfully difficult to run for the presidency without also being a multimillionaire. And if you're an actual poor person, it's impossible. (All of the people who ran for president in 2008 were millionaires.) Yet MSNBC host Tucker Carlson, as Jamison Foser noted, termed

Edwards's work for a perfectly legal and legitimate hedge fund to be "corrupt, or at least questionable" and demanded, "What the hell is a man of the people doing working for a hedge fund?" But there's no problem with a government for the rich by the rich. Mitt Romney, for instance, claimed a net worth of $350 million, and ex–New York mayor Rudy Giuliani pocketed more than $16 million in 2006 alone, but as Fox News's Neil Cavuto put it, "The GOP guys are not pretending to be, you know, great poor advocates, right?"[22] Since actual poor people are de facto disqualified from running for president, then, we might as well forget all about them.

Republican strategists recognize their advantages and plan their campaigns accordingly. Using the resources of government—up to and including creating massive levels of debt in order to pay off political contributors with public funds—they divert these funds to their troops to ensure their continued health and wealth.[23] Under the Bush administration, right-wing organizations have found themselves to be the beneficiaries of extremely generous government largesse. A single grant-making program, federal aid to abstinence education, for instance, has granted more than $50 million to such organizations as Carenet Pregnancy Services of DuPage, Illinois, an evangelistic organization that exists to help women who experience unplanned or unwanted pregnancies "choose life for their unborn babies"; Door of Hope Pregnancy Care Center in Madisonville, Kentucky, an organization "committed to the belief in the sanctity of human life, primarily as it relates to the protection of the unborn"; and Bethany Crisis Pregnancy Services in Colorado Springs, Colorado, which warns women considering abortion, "Your pregnancy ends with death. You may feel guilt and shame about your choice. You will remember taking a life."[24]

In recent years the liberal base has begun to develop itself via the organizational talents and commitments of the "netroots" on the Internet, along with the creative talents of nascent pressure groups like MoveOn. Such developments are undoubtedly cause for cautious optimism among liberals, but as of now, they do not compare to their right-wing counterparts.

The Outsourcing of Liberal Activism. One of the consequences of the organizational weakness of the liberal base is the lack of committed activists willing to knock on doors, man phone banks, and drive voters to the polls on Election Day. The diminution of the union movement has also decreased the number of available foot soldiers for the unglamorous, unpaid parts of political work that can make all the difference in a close election. The professionals' solution has been to outsource that work to intermediary organizations whose professionally trained canvassers are paid to take a cause or case for a particular candidate to individual voters. Conservatives, by contrast, tend to work through their mega-churches and organizations like Focus on the Family, whose members' local roots make their pitches—and their strategic judgments about the people they seek to reach—far more effective, since voters are speaking to their friends and neighbors, rather than paid strangers.[25]

The Globalization of Production. The average hourly wage of a U.S. worker, according to the 2006 Economic Report of the President, fell, in constant 1982 dollars, from $8.21 in 1967 to $8.17 in 2005. Many factors helped contribute to this decline, but certainly a major one was the fact that in China in 2005, the legal minimum wage was just 41 cents an hour (which was higher than in some other nations), and many companies were allowed to skirt even that.[26] The position of the business community, supported by the Bush administration, was stated by Hewlett Packard CEO Carly Fiorina, who declared, "There is no job that is America's God-given right anymore."[27] The fact that global corporations can and do outsource their labor to nations where labor is cheapest and environmental regulation most lax severely restricts the ability of liberals to use their traditional fiscal and economic tools to generate economic growth and good jobs for American voters. It also significantly reduces the power of its primary constituency, organized labor. In 1969 well-paying, unionized manufacturing jobs accounted for 26.3 percent of all employment; by 2005, they amounted to only 10.9 percent of national employment.[28]

A Corrupt Campaign Finance System. It is no secret that the party that lavishes its legislative and executive power on advancing the interests of big business and wealthy Americans is going to have an easier time finding resources to continue to do so than one whose fealty lies with working people and ordinary Americans. On a corporate level, according to the Center for Responsive Politics, a decade ago political donations from nineteen key industry sectors were split roughly evenly between the parties. Today the GOP holds a two-to-one advantage in corporate donations.[29] As for individual donors, those who give money to campaigns are typically much wealthier than most Americans. In 2000 just one out of eight U.S. households enjoyed annual incomes of more than $100,000. However, this same 12 percent of Americans comprised fully 95 percent of those who gave over a thousand dollars to a political campaign that year.[30] According to research by Harvard political scientist Andrea Campbell, the parties each directly contacted about a quarter (the Democratic Party) to a third (the Republican Party) of the wealthiest Americans in 2000, compared to a bit less than 15 percent in the 1950s. Wealthy Republican-oriented voters are generally much easier—and less expensive—to reach than poorer ones, because wealthy people pay more attention to the media than do poor ones. In a 2003 poll of people's political knowledge, a majority of the richest 5 percent of Americans answered the survey questions correctly, compared to just 20 percent of the poorest.[31]

Complex Issues, Simplistic Debate. Liberals suffer from a relative difficulty in viewing politics in a complex fashion, at least when compared to conservatives. Bill O'Reilly postulates the conservative dominance of the talk-show format to be the result of these differences: "Conservative people tend to see the world in black and white terms, good and evil. Liberals see grays. In any talk format, you have to pound home a strong point of view. If you're not providing controversy and excitement, people won't listen, or watch."[32] O'Reilly's offhand observation is actually consistent with the results of the most comprehensive review of personality and political orientation to date: a 2003 meta-analysis of eighty-eight prior studies involving 22,000 participants. The researchers—John I. Jost of NYU, Arie Kruglanski of the University of Maryland, and Jack Glaser and Frank Sulloway of Berkeley—found that conservatives are more eager than liberals to reach quick decisions and to stick to them, regardless of counterevidence. Conservative personality types demonstrate an extremely limited tolerance for ambiguity—or what George W. Bush would call "nuance"—while liberals, according to Jost, are more likely to exhibit intellectual curiosity and are "more likely to see gray areas and reconcile seemingly conflicting information."[33] Yet another study, this one published in the journal *Nature Neuroscience* in the autumn of 2007 by scientists at New York University and UCLA, found that "liberals had more brain activity and made fewer mistakes than conservatives" when seeking to recognize the difference between a W and an M in repeated experiments. This indicated, according to Frank J. Sulloway, a researcher at UC-Berkeley's Institute of Personality and Social Research, that "liberals were 4.9 times as likely as conservatives to show activity in the brain circuits that deal with conflicts, and 2.2 times as likely to score in the top half of the distribution for accuracy." Based on these results, liberals were deemed by the study's authors to be more likely to accept new social, scientific, or religious ideas, even should they conflict with previous beliefs.[34] These traits are also consistent with the argument of author Jeffrey Scheuer, who notes that the liberal discourse demands complexity "not just of government but, inferentially, of society and of causality itself." Even when liberal voices for change are "simplistic or sloganeering, demanding peace, jobs, equality, or a greener planet, the underlying values are more inclusive and far-reaching."

Television quite obviously has no use for this kind of subtlety. It atomizes, compartmentalizes, manipulates, disjoins, disintegrates, wrenches from context, ignores, and changes the subject whenever it feels like it. It does not sit still for complex arguments. "Television," Scheuer notes, "systematically 'keeps it simple, stupid.'"[35] The problem is compounded by the fact that, as Tim Rutten of the *Los Angeles Times* admits, "Today, there are an increasing number of stories of great consequence—like Enron—whose complexity too often simply outstrips the competency of many of the reporters assigned to cover them." Rutten continues: "By and large, the people now running major news operations don't want to take the time or pay the money that it would take to field suitable reporters. Much more interesting to editors and producers are the personal, gossipy stories that focus on personalities. In business reporting, for instance, the collapse of Enron—the most massive business failure in business history, perhaps—was preceded not merely by ignorance but by celebration of the criminals who were taking the company down." Not long after Enron's collapse, the Conference Board published a pseudonymous piece by a "longtime publishing insider" who diagnosed the problem as follows: "Most of the mainstream business media has been too busy morphing CEOs into celebrities and giving us guided tours of their royal lifestyles. There's been no time to do reality checks on their balance sheets and business practices. Instead, 'the press gave us personal information about Ken Lay's brilliance, his wife's wonderful taste in furniture, and the glamorous lives of other business executives,' says Ron Berenbeim, the Conference Board's expert on business ethics. 'They didn't think we were interested in those boring footnotes in the balance sheet and earnings reports.'"[36]

That analysis can be applied to almost any major issue in American politics. Jacob Hacker and Paul Pierson, together with a team of researchers, examined the manner in which *USA Today,* America's largest-circulation daily newspaper, covered the 2001 Bush tax cuts. These were the administration's single most important pre-9/11 political priority, and perhaps the single most consequential piece of domestic legislation in twenty years. In *USA Today*'s seventy-eight stories about the tax cuts, only six dealt with the actual content of the tax bill, and only one with its likely results. All the rest were pure politics and personality: reporting of the type that one might get if *People* magazine focused its reporting on Washington rather than on Hollywood. The *New York Times* was marginally better, with 126 stories, almost a third on the front page. Again, nearly 60 percent focused on the politics and only seven stories total on the massive redistribution of resources from poor and middle-class Americans to wealthy ones. But far more Americans get their news from television and right-wing talk radio than from either the *Times* or *USA Today*, and in those media almost all of the issues were ignored in "debate," with the main topic of conversation being simply "tax cuts," as if Bill Gates and the person who scrubs the toilets at Microsoft's Redmond, Washington, offices would benefit equally from them. It is nearly impossible to imagine an effective political counter to the simple conservative nostrums that cannot be mocked, parodied, and effectively parried by virtue of the liberals' inability to find a medium willing to do the complexity of their worldview justice.

Now add to all of the above the fact that the liberal case itself is not merely more complicated for the majority of people to understand in a sound-bite society, but it is also, properly understood, more demanding. As Barack Obama explains so eloquently, "It's easy to articulate a belligerent foreign policy based solely on unilateral military action, a policy that sounds tough and acts dumb; it's harder to craft a foreign policy that's tough and smart. It's easy to dismantle government safety nets; it's harder to transform those safety nets so that they work for people and can be paid for. It's easy to embrace a theological absolutism; it's harder to find the right balance between the legitimate role of faith in our lives and the demands of our civic religion. But that's our job."[37]

Moral Hypocrisy? No Problem. George Will defines "conservatism" as "realism about human nature."[38] If so, it's often other people's natures, not conservatives' own. Because liberals tend to believe that they have to live up to the ideals and principles they preach, they severely limit their appeal to people who know, deep inside, that they cannot eschew certain kinds of personal behavior that would be inconsistent with the politics to which they dedicate themselves in public. It's not that liberals are never hypocritical. They are, of course. You could fill an entire 757 airliner and then some with hybrid-driving Hollywood environmentalists and liberal politicians—that is, if they weren't hopping around the globe in their gas-guzzling private planes. But liberals pay a price for this hypocrisy, and the honest ones admit to a sense of shame about the disjunction between their words and their actions. The dishonest ones are held to account by the honest ones, and it costs them in terms of both credibility and popularity. The media has an endless fascination with the topic; for example, Hollywood environmentalist Laurie David's private plane use—first reported by yours truly in the *Atlantic Monthly*—is as well known to much of the public as her advocacy for the environment.[39] Conservatives, however, appear to have reached an understanding among their followers that if a politician or a pundit professes to be in favor of virtue, it matters little that he practices vice. Conservative voters want their representatives to speak out against fornication, gambling, and drug abuse, but they are happy to embrace leaders like Newt Gingrich, Bob Livingston, Bob Barr, Henry Hyde, Dan Burton, and even Bob Dole, all of whom railed against Bill Clinton's love life but were adulterers themselves.[40] Hypocrisy is a significant political problem for a liberal because it implies both insincerity and inauthenticity. For a conservative, however, it turns out to be far more important to talk the talk than to walk the walk.

No historical figure in America is more revered today by conservatives than Ronald Reagan, a man who was divorced, estranged from some of his children, and completely unfamiliar with his grandchildren; rarely if ever set foot in church; invited gays to spend the night together in the White House; supported the rights of gays to teach in public schools; and, as governor of California, signed what was then perhaps America's most permissive law on abortion.

Sexual harassment is also not a bad career move on the right, or so we can glean from the careers of conservative talk-show hosts John McLaughlin and Bill O'Reilly, both of whom paid massive cash settlements to former employees regarding some extremely embarrassing and explicit sexual harassment charges. ("Guys, if you exploit a girl, it will come back to get you," wrote the man who detailed his unreciprocated loofah-filled sexual fantasies to his producer, Andrea Mackris, on the phone in a comically ill-timed children's book. "That's called 'karma.'")[41] And in the case of Representative Mark Foley's famous homosexual e-mails with young congressional pages, much of the Republican leadership was well aware of his exploits but chose to protect, rather than punish, his predatory behavior. The Ethics Committee, which investigated the matter, explained, "Some may have been concerned that raising the issue too aggressively might have risked exposing Rep. Foley's homosexuality."[42] When the time came to choose new leaders to head up the 2007 Republican minority, however, few members of the leadership suffered any penalty, as much the same slate of leaders was chosen again. Meanwhile, one hopes the Hypocrisy Hall of Fame, once it's created, reserves a place for Foley's now-famous reaction to the revelation of Bill Clinton's relationship with Monica Lewinsky. "It's vile," he said at the time. "It's more sad than anything else, to see someone with such potential throw it all down the drain because of a sexual addiction."[43]

Whether Foley, who merely flirted with underage congressional pages but did not have sex with them until they were of age, or any of the public servants named above deserves to be challenged by Republican senator Larry E. Craig of Idaho, a co-chair of Mitt Romney's presidential campaign, who was repeatedly arrested for allegedly soliciting homosexual sex in men's bathrooms and who pleaded guilty to misdemeanor disorderly conduct after apparently having attempted to solicit a police officer and yet continues to deny that he is gay, I will leave to the reader. Back in 1998, Craig complained of a proposed censure resolution for Bill Clinton, "It's a slap on the wrist. It's a 'Bad boy, Bill Clinton. You're a naughty boy.' The American people already know that Bill Clinton is a bad boy, a naughty boy. I'm going to speak out for the citizens of my state, who in the majority think that Bill Clinton is probably even a nasty, bad, naughty boy." (To be fair, Craig's insistent claim of innocence is at least as compelling as that of the Florida Republican representative and titular head of the McCain campaign there, Bob Allen, who told cops that he had offered to perform oral sex in a public bathroom because, as the only Caucasian in the restroom, he felt he was "in danger of being robbed.")[44]

Undoubtedly, Messrs. Foley and Craig must have feared exposure as homosexuals to their fellow Republicans, including the Louisiana senator, and former southern regional chair of Rudy Giuliani's presidential campaign, David Vitter, who said of the party's crusade to ban gay marriage, "I don't believe there's any issue that's more important than this one." (Vitter said this in June 2006, while parts of the city of New Orleans were figuratively, if no longer literally, underwater.)[45] The married congressman and father of four, who during the Clinton impeachment crisis had declared the president to be "morally unfit for office, and guilty of helping to further drain any sense of values left to our political culture," was discovered, alas, in the summer of 2007 to be an enthusiastic client of the so-called DC Madam, as well as of a few of the working women of New Orleans.[46]

Then again, all of the above might have faced stiff competition in the battle against Clinton's "sexual addiction" from their then-fearless leader, Newt Gingrich, who managed to lecture the rest of us about personal morality after he

- left his first wife, who had put him through college, by announcing their separation in the hospital room where she was recovering from cancer surgery, and telling a friend, "She's not young enough or pretty enough to be the wife of the president. And besides, she has cancer";
- left his family to depend on church alms owing to his refusal to pay child support;
- married a much younger woman six months later;
- called his second wife at her mother's home on her mother's birthday following her diagnosis with multiple sclerosis and announced another divorce;
- married a former congressional aide, twenty-three years his junior, with whom he has since admitted he was also having an affair.[47]

And while he may not be proud, it remains odd that none of the above managed to give Gingrich pause as he and his colleagues—including fellow adulterers House majority leader Bob Livingston (R-LA) (who was to succeed Gingrich) and Judiciary Committee chair Henry Hyde (R-IL)—led the charge to impeach the president for lying about sex.

The right-wing's hypocrisy does not stop at the pants zipper. Self-appointed virtuecrat William Bennett made millions railing against the immoral behavior of the rest of us on talk radio and both cable and network TV while secretly gambling away more than $8 million of his ill-gotten gains at the blackjack tables in Vegas. (How many underprivileged students could have gone to the parochial schools about which Bennett speaks so rapturously on that money?) And Rush Limbaugh, who tastelessly mocked the late Jerry Garcia as "just a dead doper" and once lectured on his syndicated TV show, "If people are violating the law by doing drugs they ought to be accused and they ought to be convicted and they ought to be sent up," turns out to be an illegal doper himself.[48]

* * *

If one assumes that sin is roughly equally distributed among Republican and Democratic voters (within any given state), then clearly the red staters are outpacing their blue counterparts in almost every activity alleged to provide a path to eternal damnation. According to a dossier collected by the *American Prospect:*

- In red states in 2001, there were 572,000 divorces. Blue states recorded 340,000.
- In the same year, eleven red states had higher rates of divorce than any blue state.
- In each of the red states of Louisiana, Mississippi, and New Mexico, 46.3 percent of all births were to unwed mothers. In blue states, on average, that percentage was 31.7.
- Delaware has the highest rate of births to teenage mothers among all blue states, yet seventeen red states have a higher rate. Of those red states, fifteen have at least twice the rate of that of Massachusetts. There were more than 100 teen pregnancies per 1,000 women aged fifteen to nineteen in five red states in 2002. None of the blue states had rates that high.
- The rate of teen births declined in forty-six states from 1988 to 2000. It climbed in three red states and saw no change in another.
- The per capita rate of violent crime in red states is 421 per 100,000. In blue states, it's 372 per 100,000.

- The per capita rate of murder and nonnegligent manslaughter in Louisiana is 13 per 100,000. In Maine, it's 1.2 per 100,000.
- As of 2000, thirty-seven states had statewide policies or procedures to address domestic violence; all thirteen that didn't were red states.
- The five states with the highest rates of alcohol dependence or abuse are red states.
- The five states with the highest rates of alcohol dependence or abuse among twelve- to seventeen-year-olds are also red states.
- The per capita rate of methamphetamine-lab seizures in California is 2 per 100,000. In Arkansas, it's 20 per 100,000.
- The number of meth-lab seizures in red states increased by 38 percent from 1999 to 2003; in the same time frame, it decreased by 38 percent in blue states.
- Residents of the all-red mountain states are the most likely to have had three or more sexual partners in the previous year, while residents of all-blue New England are the least likely to have had more than one partner in that time span.
- Residents of the mid-Atlantic region of New York, Pennsylvania, and New Jersey were the most likely to be sexually abstinent, while residents of the all-red western south-central region (Texas, Oklahoma, Arkansas, Louisiana) were the least likely.
- Five red states reported more than 400 cases of chlamydia per 100,000 residents in 2002; no blue state had a rate that high.
- The per capita rate of gonorrhea in red states was 140 per 100,000; in blue states, it was 99 per 100,000.[49]

This tolerance for hypocrisy on the part of red-state voters is no less apparent when it comes to tax and spending policies. Yes, we hear much from conservative politicians about the need to reduce government handouts. But according to a study by the conservative Tax Foundation employing the U.S. Census Bureau data, during the fiscal year 2004, New Mexico, Alaska, West Virginia, Mississippi, and North Dakota all enjoyed considerably more revenue from their taxpayer-funded government than they paid. Conversely, the citizens of New Jersey, Connecticut,

New Hampshire, Minnesota, and Illinois all paid much more in taxes than they took back. The taker states all went for Bush; the giver states all went for Kerry.[50]

A Biased Election System. One of the more distressing aspects of the liberals' contemporary predicament is that aside from the money issues, the American electoral system is weighted in favor of conservatives. Liberal voters tend to concentrate in a few, largely urban, areas, and hence can easily be gerrymandered into a smaller number of congressional seats. Even though Al Gore beat George W. Bush by more than a half million votes in the 2000 popular vote, Bush still won forty-seven more of the 2002 congressional districts than Gore. During that election, Democrats won their seats with an average of 69 percent of the popular vote, while the Republicans averaged just 65 percent in their contests. Republicans, moreover, won forty-seven races with less than 60 percent of the vote, while Democrats won only twenty-eight such victories.[51] The net result is that Republicans wasted far fewer votes in places where their supporters were bunched into a single district.

Consider the following comparison: Democrats received 54.8 percent of the popular vote cast in 2006, which is a far more powerful mandate than the Republicans received in 1994, when they garnered only 51.6 percent of the vote. But while the Republicans won 230 seats that year, the Democrats' significantly higher percentage of the vote earned them only 1 additional seat, for a total of 231.[52] (Casual observers might have been confused by the contrasting media coverage of the two shifts. For instance, as Paul Krugman pointed out, following the 1994 GOP victory, in which Republicans enjoyed a 7-point advantage over Democrats in the popular vote, *Time* featured a charging elephant on its cover. But following the larger, 8.5 percent Democratic landslide in 2006, the magazine's cover pictured two concentric circles together with the announcement, "The center is the new place to be.")[53]

In the Senate the imbalance is even more pronounced. Democratic candidates for the Senate in 2000 carried the combined popular vote by a margin far greater than that by which Al Gore topped George W. Bush's vote. But of course they failed to carry a majority of seats. Assuming senators represent half their states' residents, the forty-nine Democrats in the new Senate represent approximately 40 million more Americans than the forty-nine Republicans.[54] The net result is considerably less representation for liberals than for conservatives. In most red states, Republicans enjoy a modest advantage over Democrats, but it is generally enough to win. In blue America, however, Democrats waste what is an overall fifteen-point advantage.[55] Owing to these disparities, a voter in Alaska or Wyoming enjoys a vote that is seventy times more influential than my own is in New York. And given the fact that the Constitution stipulates that "no State, without its Consent, shall be deprived of its equal Suffrage in the Senate," coupled with the rule that requires a two-thirds majority of both houses plus three-quarters of all state legislatures for passage of any new constitutional amendment, a snowball's chance of surviving an eternity of hellfire and damnation looks like a better bet.

Part of the liberals' problem here is of their own making. Democrats simply do not distribute themselves well in a nation in which small states carry outsized political power. Added to this pattern is the hell of good intentions that derives from past support for voting-rights laws designed to create districts in which racial and ethnic minorities enjoy a majority. Given that many of these representatives have managed to create districts in which they regularly enjoy victories that garner them more than 80 percent of votes cast, the ironic result of their creation is to ghettoize their voters politically and actually weaken their national representation. While liberals have traditionally supported these laws as a necessity to ensure voting rights for minorities in the South, in many places, they have outlived their usefulness and become an undue burden on the very people they once benefited. "As populations of solidly Democratic African Americans are squeezed into fewer and fewer districts," notes political scientist David Epstein, "the surrounding 'bleached' districts have higher chances of electing Republicans." His research demonstrates that with the rise of the Republican Party's fortunes in the South, the new electoral math dictates that for every extra majority-minority district created, two extra Republicans get elected from surrounding districts.[56] No wonder the Republicans voted so strongly to support the renewal of the Voting Rights Act in 2006, even though as a party they have no elected national minority representatives.

The Conservative Punditocracy. It's a cliché that the media is biased in favor of liberals, but a profoundly outdated one. The accusation, while true thirty years ago, perhaps, has been overtaken by the growth of a massive conservative media establishment that, to a considerable degree, has not only displaced the old media but simultaneously transformed it (a process I described in *What Liberal Media?*).[57] Whether one agrees about the overall orientation of the mainstream media, the argument as it pertains to the opinion media—the "punditocracy," as I have named it—is pretty much rock-solid. In surveying the political spectrum of professional punditocracy, it's hard to see where the liberal side gets a fair shake in any of it.

One reason conservatives have been so successful in recent years is their tactic of setting up debates in which there is a "conservative" on one side and someone who is not quite as conservative, but still no liberal, on the other. This dynamic has significant political consequences. Since the right has grown so successful in demanding representation, television and radio bookers (even on allegedly liberal outlets like PBS and NPR) are happy to pit right-wingers against moderates, moderate conservatives, and down-the-middle reporters, giving the "liberal" point of view no airing whatever. This phenomenon is promoted by right-wingers who like to pretend that CNN, with its longtime stable of commentators (including Robert Novak, William Bennett, Glenn Beck, Lou Dobbs, and Jonah Goldberg), and MSNBC, with shows hosted by former Republican congressman Joe Scarborough and right-winger Tucker Carlson—and, for a while, Michael Savage—are by definition "liberal" because they are not Fox.

For this, among other reasons, liberals are all but invisible on the Sunday-morning public affairs shows, perhaps the most influential of media platforms. In 2006 Media Matters conducted a content analysis of ABC's *This Week with George Stephanopoulos,* CBS's *Face the Nation,* and

NBC's *Meet the Press,* classifying each one of their nearly seven thousand guests from Bill Clinton's second term, George W. Bush's first term, and 2005 as Democrat, Republican, conservative, progressive, or neutral. Despite its having been produced by a liberal think tank, the study's grading of the guests proved to be extremely generous to the right-wing side, and therefore precludes any credible claims that it's a product of liberal bias. For instance, liberal-hater Joe Klein, who calls Democrats "a party with absolutely no redeeming social value . . . a really boring and flat party," and claims they "make fools of themselves even when they speak the truth," was coded "progressive."[58] Cokie Roberts and David Broder, both of whom had all but declared open war on Democrats and liberals during the previous decade, as well as former GE chairman Jack Welch, were classified as "neutral." Its key finding: "The balance between Democrats/progressives and Republicans/conservatives was roughly equal during Clinton's second term, with a slight edge toward Republicans/conservatives: 52 percent of the ideologically identifiable guests were from the right, and 48 percent were from the left. But in Bush's first term, Republicans/conservatives held a dramatic advantage, outnumbering Democrats/progressives by 58 percent to 42 percent. In 2005 the figures were an identical 58 percent to 42 percent."

In addition, it found "more panels tilted right (a greater number of Republicans/conservatives than Democrats/progressives) than tilted left" for every single year of the study. In some years the gap was as high as four to one. Moreover, congressional opponents of the Iraq War were all but banished from the Sunday shows, particularly in the period just before it was launched.

When spokespeople for the shows were contacted to explain the disparity, they claimed that they go where the action is, and today the action is Republican/conservative. (Though it should be noted that *Face the Nation* was considerably fairer to liberals than *Meet the Press* or *This Week*.) But of course, were that true, then the Clinton years would have been just as tilted in favor of Democrats/progressives as the Bush years have been toward Republicans/conservatives. When the study was updated to take account for 2006, little if anything had changed, despite an election in which Democrats defeated Republicans with what amounted to a sweep of every single open seat. Yet even after twelve years in the liberal wilderness, in the week following this dramatic repudiation of George W. Bush's war policies in Iraq, whom did *Meet the Press* rush out to book for its first postelection program? Republican war supporter John McCain, who was not even up for reelection but leads the league in Sunday-show appearances, and independent war supporter Joe Lieberman, who had been repudiated by his own party as a result of his prowar position. Together with Secretary of State Condoleezza Rice, McCain had twice as many solo interviews on these programs as any Democrat. Right-wing journalists and pundits also enjoyed a two-to-one booking advantage over their liberal counterparts in these programs' regular discussions and roundtables.[59]

These shows feel empowered to engage in an agenda-setting discussion with a panel of mostly right-wing politicians, followed by a journalists' panel in which conservatives are paired almost exclusively with down-the-middle reporters, rather than writers or thinkers who might credibly represent the liberal side. Every week George Stephanopoulos seeks the wisdom of the deeply right-wing George Will and the "neutral" (though personally conservative) Fareed Zakaria. (Sam Donaldson, a liberal, had previously been an exception to this rule, though few liberals would have picked him to represent their side.) The guest list for the far more influential *Meet the Press* tells a similar story. Why, asks the original study's author, Paul Waldman, "would the producers of the shows believe that a William Safire (56 appearances since 1997) or Bob Novak (37 appearances) is somehow 'balanced' by a Gwen Ifill (27) or Dan Balz (22)?"

Indeed, as far as critical commentary goes, with the occasional exception of E. J. Dionne, not a single unapologetic liberal is invited on any of these shows, save perhaps for an annual appearance as a kind of anthropological curiosity. Tune in to every show every week for a year, and you are unlikely to see Frank Rich, Paul Krugman, Hendrik Hertzberg, Harold Meyerson, or anyone associated with the *Nation*, the *American Prospect*, the *Washington Monthly*, the *New York Review of Books*, *Salon*, *In*

These Times, Mother Jones, or even the liberal remnant of the *New Republic.* Keeping with these tendencies, when Katie Couric introduced her "free speech" segment during her debut performance in the anchor chair for the *CBS Evening News,* she waited nine full nights before speaking with a liberal, though she managed to find room for Rush Limbaugh during the first week. PBS's primary pundit program, Jim Lehrer's *Newshour,* had long pitted Paul Gigot, a hard-right conservative and now editor of the extremist editorial pages of the *Wall Street Journal,* against Mark Shields, a former political consultant who says he does not subscribe to any ideology at all. Gigot has since been replaced by David Brooks, a former editor of the *Weekly Standard* and protégé of William Kristol, who also takes a far more aggressive ideological position on issues than his putative liberal partner. In a study of the program's guest list over a six-month period spanning October 2005 through March 2006, the media monitoring group FAIR found Republican sources outnumbered Democrats two to one. Even allowing for the fact that in a Republican administration, "newsmakers" are going to skew to the party in power unless a significant effort is made to achieve balance, the PBS program compares unfavorably with that of NPR, whose skew toward Republicans stood at just over three to two.[60]

On cable television, the situation is far worse for liberals. Until MSNBC gave Keith Olbermann his own show, not a single liberal was to be heard. Fox had O'Reilly, Gibson, Hume, and Neil Cavuto, with Sean Hannity knocking about his handpicked "liberal" punching bag, Alan Colmes, every night, and Oliver North, John Kasich, Cal Thomas, and Fred Barnes on weekends. MSNBC had Joe Scarborough and Tucker Carlson. (The centrists Larry King [on CNN] and Chris Matthews [on MSNBC] also hosted shows, though Matthews, at least, is the kind of centrist whose cup runneth over at the sight of George Bush standing beneath a MISSION ACCOMPLISHED sign.)

By now no one apart from perhaps its PR staff doubts that Fox News broadcasts are deeply slanted to reflect whatever propaganda offensive upon which the Bush White House has recently embarked. (Even the tireless PR group doesn't always manage to get its "fair and balanced" memos all the way to the top. At the 2007 World Economic Forum in Davos, for instance, when Rupert Murdoch was asked whether his News Corporation had successfully managed to shape the agenda on the war in Iraq, he answered, "No, I don't think so. We tried.")[61] For instance, when during the 2006 election the president brazenly asserted that if the voters rejected Republicans in the 2006 election, "the terrorists win, and America loses," the network's vice president for news sent out a staff memo instructing his minions to "be on the lookout for any statements by the Iraqi insurgents who must be thrilled at the prospect of a Dem-controlled Congress."[62] In fact, the International Institute for Strategic Studies estimated in 2004 that Bush's invasion of Iraq had aided al-Qaeda to recruit as many as eighteen thousand terrorists eager to attack the United States and its interests across the world.[63]

When the Democratic presidential candidates, led by John Edwards, pulled out of the March 2007 debate that was to be cosponsored by the Nevada branch of the party and Fox News, the Wall Street Journal editorial page rendered the story thus: "The left blogosphere thinks the most popular cable-news network leans too far right, and so Democrats should not legitimate it by appearing." That is true as far as it goes, but it does not go nearly far enough, as it fails to examine Fox's reaction to the Democrats' decision. On The Beltway Boys, Morton Kondracke likened Nevada Democrats to Communist propagandists. Bill O'Reilly found similarities between "radical" Nevada voters and Nazis. The channel's vice president, David Rhodes, accused Nevada Democrats of being "controlled by radical fringe out-of-state interest groups." As Media Matters' Eric Boehlert pointed out, "Of course, a real news organization wouldn't issue a nasty statement like that, nor would it give the statement exclusively to Matt Drudge, which Fox News did."[64]

As the scrupulously fair-minded reporter Ronald Brownstein notes, "Through its language, its news decisions and its hosts—[Fox] generally functions more like a cog in the Republican message machine than as a conventional news organization that attempts to abide, however imperfectly, by the traditional standards of (yes) fairness and balance."[65]

Fox, like the American Enterprise Institute, the Heritage Foundation, and the *Washington Times,* is a conservative counterestablishment institution designed to ape the functions of establishment organs, doing double duty by firing up the troops with custom-crafted ideological spin, "analysis," and phony scholarship while confusing the rest of the world with nonsense disguised as news. A 2004 Center for Media and Public Affairs study found that at the height of the presidential campaign, just 13 percent of Fox News panelists' comments on Democratic candidate John Kerry were positive, compared with 50 percent for Bush. As Fox London bureau chief Scott Norvell has put it, "Even we at Fox News manage to get some lefties on the air occasionally and often let them finish their sentences before we club them to death and feed the scraps to Karl Rove and Bill O'Reilly."[66]

Much of the mainstream media has played along with the Fox charade. The *Wall Street Journal* went so far as to publish a correction when a reporter termed the network to be "sympathetic to the Bush cause and popular with Republicans." (And this was long before Murdoch's successful takeover bid.) With the exception of a few combative on-air counterattacks—most notably by Bill Clinton and Barney Frank—so, too, have liberals and Democrats, some of whom have offered themselves as willing accomplices. The network has made a specialty of promoting what might be termed "Even the *New Republic* Liberals"—that is, liberals who specialize in bashing other liberals and liberalism. As Alex Koppelman demonstrated on Salon.com, Fox frequently features the likes of Susan Estrich complaining that Al Gore has gone "off the deep end" when he lays bare the administration's deception in the "war on terror." Pat Caddell whines that only "the real fringe of this party" wants to unseat Joe Lieberman.[67] And, of course, barely a night passes that nasty Alan Colmes does not punch poor Sean Hannity in the knuckles with his face.

Fox viewers, according to a study by the University of Maryland's Program on International Policy Attitudes, are decidedly misinformed about the world relative to viewers of CBS News or listeners of NPR. A recent survey by the Pew Research Center found viewers of *The Daily*

Show and *The Colbert Report* likely to be better informed than the average Fox News consumer. But the impact of Fox's brand of fake news is not limited to its own viewers. When in April 2007 anchor Katie Couric misreported on *CBS Evening News* that Barack Obama "grew up praying in a mosque," she was citing a discredited Fox report that had appeared three months earlier.[68]

It's not merely what is reported as "news" on Fox that is slanted beyond any sensible measure to vilify liberals and Democrats. Consider the messages the network sends its readers in its on-screen crawl during its coverage of political issues. Among the highlights:

"Attacking Capitalism: Have Dems Declared War on America?" (2/18/06)

"Dems Helping the Enemy?" (5/22/06)

"A Lamont Win, Bad News for Democracy in Mideast?"(8/8/06)

"Have the Democrats Forgotten the Lessons of 9/11?"(8/8/06)

"Is the Democratic Party Soft on Terror?" (8/8/06)

"Are Congressional Democrats Killing Spirit of Bipartisanship?" (1/3/07)

"The #1 President on Mideast Matters: George W. Bush?" (8/14/06)

"Is the Liberal Media Helping to Fuel Terror?" (8/16/06) [69]

It's nonsense like the above that, in all likelihood, led that noted media analyst Bart Simpson to muse to his psychiatrist, "And then I had this dream that my whole family were just cartoon characters and our success had led to some crazy propaganda network called Fox News."

Even outside of Fox, one can discern a similar drift toward Rovian disinformation in reporters whom few would associate with conservatism. These examples have grown so common, in fact, that they elicit little controversy or complaint, even when they perfectly reflect Republican campaign charges rather than any remotely defensible "objective" questioning or reliable information. How many viewers discerned anything unusual when MSNBC chief congressional correspondent Norah O'Donnell demanded of Democratic congresswoman Loretta Sanchez that she go "on the record" with a "promise" that Democrats would "not issue tens or hundreds of subpoenas to the White House when it comes to Katrina, Iraq, and a number of issues" that would "make the president's final two years in office a living hell"? Earlier in the segment, which also included a discussion with Representative Trent Franks (R-AZ), O'Donnell suggested that reviewing Democratic voting records on wiretapping and detainee abuse "helps [the White House] make a compelling argument" that "Democrats are weak when it comes [to] defense." As Media Matters for America noted, on the August 31, 2006, edition of *Hardball*, O'Donnell asked Democratic strategist Bob Shrum if "part of the problem that the Democrats have is they don't have a message to respond to the president" on the Iraq War. The following day, O'Donnell asked MSNBC political analyst Ron Reagan if withdrawing from Iraq would "essentially hand a victory to the terrorists."[70] While one might be tempted to consider these examples particularly egregious in the hothouse culture of talk TV, they are, in fact, fairly typical. To my knowledge, nobody has ever pointed to Norah O'Donnell as an example of an especially conservative correspondent; rather, she is thought to have no ideology at all. In the context of contemporary cable TV, however, an alleged lack of ideology is difficult to distinguish from a set of Karl Rove–dictated talking points. The truth is, as Fox is winning the ratings war on cable, the other stations—even the broadcast stations— are rushing to emulate its success by adopting its biases. As ex–ABC News political director Mark Halperin so helpfully explained during a friendly visit to Bill O'Reilly's program, he and his colleagues have found Fox to be a model broadcast. "If you want to thrive like Fox News Channel—[if] you want to have a future—you better make sure conservatives find your product appealing."[71]

In truth, while one is loath to give credence to what some would happily term "conspiracy theories," the evidence demonstrates that even at MSNBC—which conservatives like to yoke together with CNN as a "liberal" alternative to Fox—liberals have been put on notice that they may go only so far. Back in 2003, when the longtime liberal and former daytime talk-show host Phil Donahue was given a show on the network, he enjoyed what were then the network's highest ratings in prime time, and they were rising. Still, the show was canceled, not because of its ratings but, according to an internal NBC News memo that was widely reprinted, because its executives felt that Donahue presented a "difficult public face for NBC in a time of war. . . . He seems to delight in presenting guests who are anti-war, anti-Bush and skeptical of the administration's motives." Its authors feared that the host would become "a home for the liberal antiwar agenda at the same time that our competitors are waving the flag at every opportunity." At the same time MSNBC announced it was hiring former Republican congressional leader Dick Armey, former Minnesota governor Jesse Ventura, and the right-wing shock jock Michael Savage, who soon had to be fired for telling a gay caller that he was a "sodomite" who should "get AIDS and die." Even before his show was taken off the air, Donahue later revealed, he had been instructed by the network brass that he must feature at least two conservative guests every time he booked a liberal. After former sportscaster Keith Olbermann joined the network, he soon found himself in trouble, he later said, for putting liberals on the program "on consecutive nights." On the shows hosted by conservatives and by the mercurial Matthews, however, the network brass apparently evinces no discomfort whatever about conversations that are dominated by the right.[72]

Should anyone get the notion that CNN is somehow a viable liberal alternative to all of the above, well, think again. There the problem is not only the plethora of conservative commentators, but also the network's willingness to deliberately downgrade its own professed journalistic standards in pursuit of Fox's audience. Perhaps the most egregious example yet of the effects of this pursuit occurred in May 2007, when CNN Headline News devoted a full hour of programming to the crackpot views of its own right-wing radio talker and self-described "rodeo clown," Glenn Beck, for a program entitled "Exposed: Climate of Fear." Shortly before the broadcast, the host had publicly compared Al Gore to Adolf Hitler and warned falsely that global warming activists wanted the United Nations to run the world and to implement a "global carbon tax." (The network followed up with another Beck special, "Exposed: The Extremist Agenda," which sounded the alarm about the dangers emanating from

American Muslims.) Although Beck's special actually landed the network in last place during its broadcast, it nevertheless added credence to the view that journalism—even on CNN—cannot treat complex issues even remotely responsibly. "Climate of Fear" appeared long after the Intergovernmental Panel on Climate Change decreed the fact of global warming to be "unequivocal," yet somehow the network believed it legitimate to lend credibility to the same discredited, industry-financed conservative fantasists to whom virtually no reputable scientist any longer gave credence.[73] The show was broadcast during the same period when the network entirely ignored the Bush administration's refusal to implement a Supreme Court ruling that it adhere to the global warming–related provisions of the Clean Air Act.[74] ABC News likewise found Beck's views so enlightening that they were willing to share him as a commentator. What possible other explanation could there be, given the man's meager ratings, his (admitted) journalistic inadequacies, and his frequently offensive racist rants against Arabs and others, than a desperate desire to attract a portion of Fox's right-wing audience?

Beck's campaign has an analogue on CNN in Lou Dobbs's crusade against immigration. Dobbs, who previously admitted to contributing to the Republican National Committee, changed his stripes a bit during George W. Bush's presidency and undertook a crusade on behalf of the pocketbooks of middle-class Americans. So far, so good, a liberal might conclude, but Dobbs defined as part of this crusade a particularly virulent variant of the old American nativist distrust of immigration. For instance, he frequently informed his viewers that one-third of the inmates in the federal prison system were illegal immigrants. According to the Justice Department, however, only 6 percent of prisoners in this country are noncitizens (compared with 7 percent of the population). One of his correspondents claimed that, owing to Mexican immigration, the United States had experienced seven thousand cases of leprosy over the previous three years—a figure that was close to twenty times the actual number of cases. In support of this phony number, he called upon a guest with no particular expertise in the topic, whose past speeches included the claim that Mexican immigrants had a habit of molesting children. Remember, CNN, like MSNBC, is somehow considered to be a "liberal" alternative to Fox, and is frequently denounced by conservatives and characterized by reporters as such.[75]

* * *

Meanwhile, even with all of the above, cable TV is practically a liberal Fantasy Island compared to talk radio, which is so benighted from a liberal standpoint that Bill O'Reilly actually falls on the left side of its spectrum. A 2007 study released by the Center for American Progress and Free Press found it "conservative, and 9 percent is progressive." And that disparity isn't limited to small-town radio in areas that lean conservative: in the top ten radio markets, "76 percent of the programming . . . is conservative and 24 percent is progressive."[76]

The natural conservative tendencies of these shows' corporate paymasters are, moreover, reinforced by the conservative tendencies of many of its advertisers. In 2006 an internal ABC memo was leaked revealing the existence of an advertiser "blacklist" against the liberal radio network Air America. Some ninety major corporations demanded that their ads be pulled from radio stations that ran Air America programming on the ABC Radio affiliate network, and ABC complied.[77] The episode recalled a comment in the trade publication *Advertising Age* when Al Gore was proposing to launch what looked like it might be a progressive TV network (later known as Current). A Fox News executive explained, "The problem with being associated as liberal is that they wouldn't be going in a direction that advertisers are really interested in. . . . If you go out and say that you are a liberal network, you are cutting your potential audience, and certainly your potential advertising pool, right off the bat."[78]

* * *

The situation in print is not as dire as in the electronic media, but still stacked against the liberal viewpoint. Numerous newspapers, like Rupert Murdoch's *New York Post* and the Unification Church's *Washington Times*, function less as news-gathering institutions than as right-wing Republican propaganda outlets. For instance, in early 2007, in a remarkable journalistic circle jerk of self-referentialism, the *Washington Times'* Greg Pierce reported on the Republican National Committee's "key findings" about leading 2008 Democratic presidential candidates by printing the title of each of the RNC's accusations verbatim, adding only that the alleged "findings" were not "a pretty sight." He neglected to mention, however, that the so-called findings in turn cited *Washington Times* articles, columns, and editorials a total of fourteen times. Among the "findings": Senator Barack Obama of Illinois, "an inexperienced, insulated, arrogant, unabashed liberal"; New Mexico governor Bill Richardson, a "self-promoting Washington insider with a controversial record."[79] As Media Matters' Jamison Foser pointed out at the time, *The Politico's* Mike Allen—formerly a top correspondent for *Time* and the *Washington Post*—touted this piece for its "just-the-facts" and "sophisticated" nature in a seven-hundred-plus-word article that somehow managed to avoid including a single fact from the purportedly "fact-based" documents.

Unhappily, much of this dynamic is replicated across the nation's editorial pages. The *Wall Street Journal's* editorial page is far more conservative than any national newspaper's page is liberal, including particularly that of the *New York Times,* to which it is frequently compared. What's more, it is also considerably less enamored with the traditional commitment of journalists to standards of accuracy and evidence. Long after the so-called Swift Boat Vets and POWs for Truth spread demonstrable falsehoods about John Kerry's war record, for instance, the *Journal* editors endorsed these lies as "no doubt contentious, but . . . of a piece with the contemporary bipartisan standards of adversarial politics."[80] Such views are all too typical of a page that has historically placed its own ideological obsessions above inconvenient truths—including truths that happen to appear in the excellent news pages of the pre–Rupert Murdoch *Wall Street Journal*.

During the Bush era readers of the *Washington Post* have noticed a decided march of that paper's editorial pages into conservative territory, particularly in its support of Mr. Bush's war. As Democratic representative David Obey (D-WI) noted on the floor of the House during a spring 2007 war debate, "Let me submit to you the problem we have today is not that we didn't listen enough to people like the *Washington Post*. It's that we listened too much. They endorsed going to war in the first place. They helped drive the drumbeat that drove almost two-thirds of the people in this chamber to vote for that misguided, ill-advised war."[81]

Then there are the op-ed pages. In 1999, before newspapers scrambled to offer jobs to even more right-wingers to keep up with the new Bush era, *Editor & Publisher* undertook a survey of the syndicates. It discovered that of the top ten columnists carried in papers with a combined circulation of over ten million, six were conservatives, three were liberals, and one was a centrist. The top two columnists, James Dobson of the right-wing group Focus on the Family, and Cal Thomas, a former official of the Moral Majority, present Christian right views in more than five hundred newspapers each. Right-wingers (and Christians) Robert Novak and George Will ranked next in popularity.[82]

Eight years later, my colleagues at Media Matters for America undertook an updated version of the *Editor & Publisher* study and found that if anything, the situation had, from the perspective of ideological balance, worsened considerably. Typical of Media Matters' methodology, the study employed extremely generous definitions of *progressive* in order to allay potential accusations of bias. Its key findings included these:

- Sixty percent of the nation's daily newspapers print more conservative syndicated columnists every week than progressive syndicated columnists. Only 20 percent run more progressives than conservatives, while the remaining 20 percent are evenly balanced.
- In a given week, nationally syndicated progressive columnists are published in newspapers with a combined total circulation of 125 million. Conservative columnists, on the other hand, are published in newspapers with a combined total circulation of more than 152 million.
- The top ten columnists as ranked by the number of papers in which they are carried include five conservatives, two centrists, and only three progressives.

- The top ten columnists as ranked by the total circulation of the papers in which they are carried also include five conservatives, two centrists, and only three progressives.
- In thirty-eight states, the conservative voice is greater than the progressive voice—in other words, conservative columns reach more readers in total than progressive columns. In only twelve states is the progressive voice greater than the conservative voice.
- In three out of the four broad regions of the country—the West, the South, and the Midwest—conservative syndicated columnists reach more readers than progressive syndicated columnists. Only in the Northeast do progressives reach more readers, and only by a margin of 2 percent.
- In eight of the nine divisions into which the U.S. Census Bureau divides the country, conservative syndicated columnists reach more readers than progressive syndicated columnists in any given week. Only in the Middle Atlantic division do progressive columnists reach more readers each week.

The study's author, Paul Waldman, notes that these numbers imply far more "reach" among readers than news of declining print circulation might imply. The Newspaper Association of America estimates that each copy of a weekday paper is read by an average of 2.1 adults, while each Sunday paper is read by an average of 2.5 adults, creating a total readership of over 116 million people daily and another 134 million on Sunday. What's more, Waldman notes, a 2006 Pew Research Center study found that 66 percent of those who say they follow political news closely regularly read newspapers, a much higher figure than for any other medium. These are the people public opinion specialists term *influentials*, those whose views tend to affect those of their friends, families, and wider communities.[83] And with regard to appearances by guest columnists, upon his retirement as president of the conservative think tank the American Enterprise Institute in October 2007, Christopher DeMuth bragged that "AEI essays appear more frequently than those from other think tanks of all persuasions, not only in the opinion pages of the *Wall*

Street Journal but also those of the New York Times and Washington Post.[84] Therefore with few exceptions these "influentials" are receiving more conservative-oriented arguments than liberal ones.

In the newsweeklies, the situation is more complex. U.S. News & World Report, which has a considerably smaller circulation than Newsweek or Time, employs columnists who tend toward the center or center-right. It employs no actual liberals, but its most prominent pundits—former White House aide David Gergen, reporter and television personality Gloria Borger, and owner Mortimer Zuckerman—have their feet planted in the political center, wherever that happens to be at the time. (The magazine's other major voice, Michael Barone, is clearly right of center.) At Newsweek, which lags behind Time in both circulation and prestige—but only by a bit—the mixture of liberals and conservatives is actually slightly balanced toward the liberal side. Jonathan Alter, Anna Quindlen, and Eleanor Clift play the left side of the field, while George F. Will and Robert Samuelson play the right. (President Bush's former top speech-writer, the conservative evangelical Christian Michael Gerson, was re-warded upon leaving the White House with the same enviable dual Newsweek–Washington Post job enjoyed by both Will and Samuelson, but none of Newsweek's liberals.)

At Time, however, the oldest, most venerable, most influential, and highest-circulation magazine, the stable of columnists is dominated not merely by conservatives but also by writers whose animating inspiration appears to be the need to slander liberals at every opportunity in lan-guage that is hardly distinguishable from that heard from Rush Limbaugh or the celebrated Time cover girl Ann Coulter. It's as if the magazine made a conscious decision to emulate the Wall Street Journal, with gener-ally accurate and respected news pages paired with angry and often vi-ciously antiliberal opinion pages.

Time's chosen columnists are not only abusive to liberals and Demo-crats; they are obsessive in their abusiveness. Neoconservative Charles Krauthammer, who enjoyed a column at the magazine for nearly twenty-five years, described Democrats as "rank hypocrites" with "nothing to of-fer on Social Security . . . nothing to offer on the war in Iraq . . . nothing to offer on the idea of how to manage ourselves in the UN . . . obstructionist." Moreover, "they have trashed two centuries of tradition." Democrats were "gleeful, and shamelessly hypocritical . . . dishonest, disreputable and disgraceful. . . . The Democrats have no ideas on these issues, and what they are is obstructionist." When Vice President Gore criticized the Bush administration for its pattern of deception, which has been demonstrated, Krauthammer, a psychiatrist, joked that he had "gone off his lithium," and added, "The biggest cheers for Gore must have been coming from caves in Afghanistan and diehards in Fallujah."[85] When Gore sought to warn the nation and the world of the dangers of global warming, Krauthammer returned with an attack in *Time* against his alleged "Limousine Liberal Hypocrisy."[86]

Krauthammer was joined in his vendetta by longtime *Time* columnist Joe Klein, who noted, after Gore made his prophetic speech, that the vice president "looked like a madman." Again, Klein calls himself a "radical moderate," but his modus operandi toward liberals is slander and abuse. The phrase "Democratic ideas," he guffaws, "is an oxymoron."[87] Writing about the marriage troubles of three Republican presidential candidates in March 2007—who together have had nine marriages among them—he explained that they are "moderate candidates who live like liberals." At a foreign policy breakfast Klein shouted out from the back of the room, apropos of nothing in particular, "Democrats will not succeed in upcoming elections if their message is that they hate America—which is what has been the message of the liberal wing of the party for the past twenty years." Clarifying his remarks on a blog post, he explained that the "left wing of the Democratic Party"—not "liberals"—has a "hate America tendency."[88] But of course the discussion was of potential presidential candidates. Apparently Klein meant to define Hillary Clinton, Barack Obama, John Edwards, and Bill Richardson—to say nothing of John Kerry and Al Gore—as "left-wing" America-haters.

Klein leveled these irresponsible and unsupported attacks while considered the single most "liberal" columnist at the magazine, for in addition to Krauthammer, his only colleague in the political stable during the late Clinton years and the first six years of the Bush administrations was Andrew Sullivan. Before he experienced an anti-Bush conversion, Sullivan reminded many readers of Joe McCarthy in the uncontrollable and unsupported vitriol he directed toward liberals. He notoriously suggested that Gore voters could not be trusted to be loyal Americans after 9/11, and shortly thereafter insisted, "It didn't change the far left, who saw it as another reason to hate America." When the Iraq War began, he argued, again without evidence, that "many liberals found themselves, I think, for partisan reasons sort of almost wanting this to fail." In Sullivan's view, Harvard is a "Stalinist, PC, left-wing university," and upon the death of the great liberal economist and public intellectual who made the university his home, John Kenneth Galbraith, he wrote, "the only response to a person like that is sadness mixed with contempt."[89]

When Sullivan left *Time* in early 2007 for the *Atlantic Monthly,* shortly after he became the kind of anti-Bush liberal whose loyalty he so frequently impugned, the magazine's new managing editor added to its stable the much admired neoliberal Mike Kinsley, founding editor of *Slate;* the magazine's former editor, centrist Walter Isaacson of the Aspen Institute; and William Kristol of the *Weekly Standard.* The first two appointments were probably welcomed by most observers. Kinsley, perhaps the most talented columnist in America, is a self-defined "neoliberal" who delights in tweaking other liberals and adopting conservative positions on the basis of liberal arguments. Isaacson, meanwhile, is one of the country's most admired biographers. It was the third appointment that raised the most eyebrows, given that Kristol was not only a die-hard right-wing supporter of the Bush administration who took every available opportunity to attack both the patriotism and courage of liberals, but also perhaps the pundit whose previous analysis had been most profoundly discredited by reality. For instance, when the Starr report was issued during the Monica Lewinsky scandal, causing almost universal revulsion among Americans, Kristol wrote a cover editorial for his magazine that headlined the report as "Starr's Home Run," portraying its author as Mark McGwire and calling for Clinton's immediate impeachment. And at the outset of the Iraq War, Kristol dismissed predictors of Shiite-Sunni strife as purveyors of "pop sociology," insisting, "Iraq's always been very secular."[90]

Kristol termed those Americans with the foresight, common sense, and courage to oppose Bush's calamitous invasion of Iraq to be exclusively "liberals . . . who can always be counted on to favor tyranny over anything that strengthens American power however marginally." At the time, the calumny would have applied to the likes of General Anthony Zinni, Lieutenant General William Odom, Major General John Batiste, George H. W. Bush's national security adviser and coauthor General Brent Scowcroft, former national security adviser Zbigniew Brzezinski, former vice president Al Gore, dozens of U.S. senators, hundreds of U.S. representatives, and millions upon millions of Americans.

When it comes to liberals and Democrats, Kristol, a former right-wing Republican operative, is as prone as his conservative colleagues to insinuating disloyalty whenever a right-wing talking point is questioned. Connecticut Democrats were "drive[n] crazy" by Joe Lieberman, he explained, because "he's unashamedly pro-American." Following the U.S. massacre of innocent civilians at Haditha, he announced, again, without evidence, "The anti-American left can barely be bothered to conceal its glee."[91] (Kristol, like Krauthammer, was let go at the end of 2007, but immediately hired as a weekly columnist for the *New York Times* Op-Ed page.)

A stronger argument for the unchallenged antiliberal bias of the punditocracy would be hard even to imagine, but *Time* still managed to provide one when, in late April 2007, it announced the hiring of ABC News political director Mark Halperin, who was already on record arguing that mainstream reporters were "overwhelmingly liberal" and that they "hate the military."[92] Then, as if to add insult to injury, *Time* hired Ana Marie Cox to run its Web site. Though she was a putative liberal, her reputation rested almost exclusively on her experience as the editor of a D.C. gossip Web site, Media's "Wonkette," where her posts included reports on the "ass-fucking" antics of a young Republican congressional aide; she later translated her fame into a six-figure book contract. If *Time*'s editors had been trying to prove its columnists' contentions about the inherent perversity—sexual and otherwise—of media liberals, it could hardly have picked a more appropriate hire.[93]

The operation and net result of the system described above were accurately described by Al Gore: "Something will start at the Republican National Committee . . . and it will explode the next day on the right-wing talk-show network and on Fox News. . . . And then they'll create a little echo chamber, and pretty soon they'll start baiting the mainstream media for allegedly ignoring the story they've pushed into the zeitgeist. And then pretty soon the mainstream media goes out and disingenuously takes a so-called objective sampling, and lo and behold, these RNC talking points are woven into the fabric of the zeitgeist."[94]

The right-wing advantage has grown so enormous in opinion-oriented public discourse that it has become all but impossible to ignore, even by those who benefit most from it. In the past, it was the rare conservative who was willing to admit the depth of the stranglehold. While researching my 2003 book *What Liberal Media?* I discovered the following admissions. Rich Bond, former chair of the Republican Party: "There is some strategy to it [bashing the 'liberal' media]. . . . If you watch any great coach, what they try to do is 'work the refs.' Maybe the ref will cut you a little slack on the next one."[95] James Baker, who ran George H. W. Bush's second presidential campaign, among many other Republican and Bush family projects: "There were days and times and events we might have had some complaints [but] on balance I don't think we had anything to complain about."[96] Pat Buchanan, among the most conservative pundits and presidential candidates in the history of the republic, finding that he could not identify any allegedly liberal bias against him during his presidential candidacies: "I've gotten balanced coverage, and broad coverage—all we could have asked. For heaven sakes, we kid about the 'liberal media,' but every Republican on earth does that."[97] And even William Kristol, without a doubt the most influential Republican/neoconservative publicist in America today, has come clean on this issue. "I admit it," he told a reporter. "The liberal media were never that powerful, and the whole thing was often used as an excuse by conservatives for conservative failures."[98]

Back then, one had to be an unusually honest, or perhaps perspicacious, conservative to acknowledge that whatever advantage liberals may once have had when issues were debated had evaporated long ago. The evidence is so strong that even the compulsively dishonest Ann

Coulter admits, "We have the media now." Bill O'Reilly, who has proven himself capable of believing almost anything, including, according to one report he did in June 2007, the existence of a "national underground network" of pink-pistol-packing lesbians roaming "all across the country," raping girls, attacking guys, and forcing ten-year-olds to become gay,[99] warns, "Don't believe the right-wing ideologues when they tell you the left still controls the media agenda. It does not any longer. It's a fact."[100] The conservative analyst Bruce Bartlett admits in National Review Online that "the idea the media now tilt toward liberals is absurd."[101] The *Weekly Standard*'s Matt Labash, meanwhile, avers just how much fun it was to play the game while it lasted. "We've created this cottage industry in which it pays to be unobjective. It pays to be subjective as much as possible. It's a great way to have your cake and eat it, too. Criticize other people for not being objective. Be as subjective as you want. It's a great little racket. I'm glad we found it."

Amazingly, after all of the above, the con still works. Mark Halperin argued in late 2006 that the mainstream media still needed to "prove to conservatives that we understand their grievances" and that "if I were a conservative, I understand why I would feel suspicious that I was not going to get a fair break at the end of an election. We've got to make sure we do better, so conservatives don't have to be concerned about that. It's just—it's not fair." Is it any wonder that this same network felt compelled to use Rush Limbaugh as a commentator on liberals? It turns out, according to Mr. Limbaugh, that liberals are "prejudiced."[102]

The Ruthlessness/Corruption Gap. Liberals suffer politically from their dedication to good government; liberalism as an animating political philosophy makes no sense in any other context. When liberals take office, they devote themselves to what they understand to be the public interest: doing the greatest good for the greatest number. They also like to play by established rules, for much of what liberals understand to be fundamental to their political philosophy involves procedure, fairness, good governance, and so on. While they are not, as a rule, above passing laws designed to maximize their political advantage, it would nevertheless be unusual for a liberal politician to pass laws clearly detrimental to the public interest purely for partisan purposes. No liberal would ever, as conservatives do routinely, issue an invitation to private-interest lobbyists to come in and write their legislation and then brag about it to the media afterward.

When it comes to public office, conservatives have few such scruples. Their philosophical contempt for government and public service frequently spills over into a form of contempt for the very jobs they have pledged themselves to undertake. As the political scientist Alan Wolfe explains, "Conservatives cannot govern well for the same reason that vegetarians cannot prepare a world-class boeuf bourguignon: If you believe that what you are called upon to do is wrong, you are not likely to do it very well."[103] The levers of government therefore can become little more than the means through which they reward their supporters, punish their enemies, and prepare for the next battle, and the public interest be damned.

When, for instance, following the midterm elections in 2002, George W. Bush offered up an extremely rare expression of concern about the deficits caused by his tax cuts for the wealthy, inquiring— according to former treasury secretary Paul O'Neill—about yet another massive tax cut, "Didn't we do the investment package already?" he was shot down by his adviser Karl Rove. This came shortly after Vice President Cheney explained to O'Neill, "Reagan proved that deficits don't matter. We won the elections. This is our due." This account was of a piece with an anecdote told that same year by John DiIulio, the conservative University of Pennsylvania political scientist who ran the White House Office of Faith-Based and Community Initiatives. "There is no precedent in any modern White House for what is going on in this one," DiIulio told journalist Ron Suskind. The Bush operation contained "a complete lack of a policy apparatus. . . . What you have is everything— and I mean everything—being run by the political arm."[104]

Veteran Congress-watcher Norman Ornstein, who works at the right-wing American Enterprise Institute, terms the Republican modus operandi "the middle-finger approach to governing."[105] In support of their collective middle finger, the Republicans in Congress created what they called the "K Street Project," designed to institutionalize their power regardless of popular will. By forcing corporations to hire only Republican lobbyists and then demanding that these same lobbyists subordinate individual projects to the larger demands of the right-wing Republican agenda—in exchange for their turn at the feeding trough—they have successfully assembled the political equivalent of an infantry division made up of 1,200 committed foot soldiers. Any attempt to distinguish between the Republican Party and the big-business lobbies has become an exercise of Talmudic complexity. In fact, they are mostly interchangeable, often existing inside the same body. Take the example of former RNC chair Haley Barbour. A founder of one of the most influential lobbying firms in Washington, Barbour earned millions from companies with interests that are frequently at odds with those of most consumers, including tobacco (Brown & Williamson Tobacco, $120,000 yearly; Lorillard Tobacco, $440,000); drug companies (Bristol-Myers Squibb, $200,000; GlaxoSmithKline, $120,000); the long-term health care and maintenance organization industry (Kindred Healthcare, $320,000; Med-Cath Corporation, $320,000; UnitedHealth Group, $320,000; Alliance for Quality Nursing Home Care, $520,000); and major electric utilities (Electric Reliability Coordinating Council, $440,000; Southern Company, $200,000). Even so, he managed to win the Mississippi governorship with 53 percent of the vote.[106] Longtime *Washington Post* political reporter Thomas Edsall notes that "the fear of being labeled 'liberal' . . . has led to some reluctance to send reporters out to cover the extraordinarily lucrative relationship between Republicans and business."[107] However, details occasionally leak out. In 2006, for instance, Housing Secretary Alphonso Jackson, a friend and former Dallas neighbor of George W. Bush's, told a group of real estate officials that he once canceled a government contract because the contractor had said unkind things about the president. The inspector general for the Department of Housing and Urban Development conducted an investigation and discovered that the secretary had ordered his staff to avoid contractors who associated with Democrats and reward only Republican contributors and friends. This is contrary to the law, but not, apparently, contrary to the daily practice of how conservatives govern.[108]

In fact, inside the Bush White House, governance was altogether beside the point. Karl Rove actually institutionalized the purposeful misuse of taxpayer funds for political purposes. Officials in the U.S. Treasury and Commerce departments have admitted that they were subject to regular briefings by White House officials—Rove's Asset Deployment Team—tied to each two-year election cycle, designed to coordinate the announcement of high-profile cabinet secretary visits bearing goodies from the federal treasury focused almost exclusively on battleground states and vulnerable Republican districts.[109]

While the past decade presents a veritable cornucopia of examples of conservatives' forgoing their commitment to small government in order to reward their political friends and allies, the 2003 Medicare overhaul will stand forever as a monument to the exploitation of taxpayer-funded largesse. The story goes as follows: beginning with his January 2003 State of the Union address, President Bush pledged to keep the total cost of his proposed Medicare drug benefit to $400 billion over ten years. But Richard Foster, chief actuary at the Office of the Actuary, Centers for Medicare and Medicaid Services, did his own estimate and put the cost at approximately $540 billion. This figure remained a secret while the bill was being debated, however, because Foster had been warned that he would be fired should the truth leak out. His boss, Medicare chief Thomas Scully, was at the time in the process of nego-tiating himself a new lobbying job with one of the bill's beneficia-ries.[110] Shortly after Bush signed the program into law in December 2003, the White House revised its projection to $534 billion, but refused to offer any details of its calculations. That figure turned out to be wildly inaccurate as well. In February 2005 the White House released budget figures putting the cost of the ten-year tab for the Medicare prescription drug benefit at more than $1.2 trillion in the coming decade.[111] But even *these* numbers underestimated the colossal cost of this legislation. When in the 2004 Medicare trustees report the actuaries presented the cost, in present values, of the program, it came to $21.9 trillion, of which $16.6 trillion remained unfunded. How much is $16.6 trillion? Well, as conser-vative budget analyst Bruce Bartlett—who was himself fired from his right-wing think tank—points out, if the Medicare drug benefit were repealed, then "Social Security could be funded forever without having to raise taxes or cut benefits, and the federal government would still be able to cut $7.1 trillion off its long-term indebtedness."[112] What is alarming, Bartlett notes, is that, if the history of the program is any guide, these estimates are also much too low, and will eventually eat up what is the equivalent of every single tax dollar the government now receives.

While the costs of the package may be staggering beyond imagination, its benefits proved strikingly modest. The bill did nothing to reduce the spiraling cost of prescription drug prices. It specifically rejected—and actually outlawed—the technique that Medicaid and the VA employ to restrain drug prices, which is to use the bargaining power of their respective numbers to force companies to hold down costs. This had the effect, according to research by the National Academy of Sciences, of reducing the cost of drugs by 15 percent.[113] But at the behest of the pharmaceutical lobby, which contributed over $20 million to the Republicans in 2002 alone, the bill expressly forbade the government from taking advantage of this cost-saving mechanism. At the behest of the insurance industry— which spent $100 million on federal lobbying in 2003—Congress required that recipients contract for private insurance, even in places where it's not available. As Alan Wolfe pointed out, "To make sure government agencies didn't administer the benefit, they lured in insurance companies with massive subsidies and imposed almost no rules on what benefits they could and could not offer. The lack of rules led to a frustrating chaos of choices. And the extra costs had to be made up by carving out a so-called 'doughnut hole' in which the elderly, after having their drug purchases subsidized up to a certain point, would suddenly find themselves without federal assistance at all, only to have their drugs subsidized once again at a later point. Caught between the market and the state, Republicans picked the worst features of each."[114] When the more-than-one-trillion-dollar figure was finally revealed, Bush spokesperson Scott McClellan did what Bush administration figures almost always do when their statements conflict with reality: "Our cost estimates for the drug benefit are the same as they've been in the past," he lied.[115]

During the vote in the House of Representatives on the bill, objections came not merely from disgruntled Democrats but also from a handful of off-the-reservation Republicans, shocked by its expense. The bill would have failed to pass under the normal rules of voting, but the House Republican leadership (including Billy Tauzin, who, like the head of Medicare, was readying himself for a lucrative new career as head of the PhRMA lobby) chose to hold the longest recorded vote in modern House history in order to twist the necessary arms to win passage. While House votes generally take fifteen minutes, this one took fully three hours. (When then Democratic majority leader Jim Wright left voting open for an extra ten minutes in 1987, his counterpart, a representative from Wyoming by the name of Dick Cheney, termed the action to be "the most arrogant, heavy-handed abuse of power in the ten years I've been here.")[116]

Even so, the bill almost failed. House majority leader and Republican boss Tom DeLay apparently told Congressman Nick Smith, Republican of Michigan, whose son was running for his office, that a switch of his vote from "nay" to "yea" would be worth $100,000 to his son's campaign from "business interests," according to Smith's original recollection. This would be a felony if true. But after Smith refused the offer, he recanted his story, as so many witnesses had done before him.[117]

Ultimately this bill was more fiction than fact. Its combination of mountainous costs and minuscule benefits was due to the fact that it was really just a massive bait-and-switch game designed not only to fatten the coffers of the drug and insurance industries but, more significantly, to reward corporate contributors with massive taxpayer subsidies in the form of government reimbursements for corporate employee obligations to the tune of $660 per retiree per year. The numbers, once again, were barely believable. As the Wall Street Journal reported, the good news for the party's funders included $4 billion for GM, $1.3 billion for Verizon, and $572 million for BellSouth. BusinessWeek estimated a gross subsidy of $8 billion a year: $6.5 billion for the subsidy itself and $1.5 billion because Congress had made it tax free so that under accounting rules, it could be added to the corporate bottom line immediately.[118] If one includes the Bush energy bill, then at least sixty-one of

Bush's major fund-raisers directly benefited in their business enterprises from the passage of this legislation; investments of thousands of dollars yielded payoffs, in some cases, in the tens of millions.[119] What the conservatives were doing was exactly the same thing that Boris Yeltsin and his cohorts had done before his successful reelection: selling off the resources and obligations of the federal government for their own personal and political gain. And they did so without shame, scandal, or even much scrutiny. It's hard to imagine that anyone, save the immediate beneficiaries of this corrupt bargain, together with their ideological and political cronies, would actually endorse such behavior. And yet somehow liberals still retain a reputation for fiscal irresponsibility based on actions taken more than forty years ago.

The Purposeful Exploitation of Racial Fear and Loathing. "One of the greatest problems of democratic civilization," the renowned liberal theologian Reinhold Niebuhr wrote in 1944, "is how to integrate the life of its various subordinate ethnic, religious, and economic groups in the community in such a way that the richness and harmony of the whole community will be enhanced and not destroyed by them." Niebuhr dismissed those who at the time trusted in what he termed the hoped-for "frictionless harmony of ethnic groups" and "their eventual assimilation in one racial unity." Instead, he called on "democratic society" to use "every stratagem of education and every resource of religion" to fight the influence of racial bigotry—a bigotry that would not wither away simply as a result of material prosperity.[120] No easy task, to be sure, and liberals have failed at least as often as they have succeeded in attempting to address the issue. Still, they have tried. Almost all of us suffer from racist fears and impulses on occasion, liberals as well as conservatives. The primary political difference between liberals and conservatives, however, is that the former seek to transcend these fears for the purposes of building transracial coalitions, while too many conservatives prefer to exploit them. It is no accident, after all, that the Republican Party contains not a single black man or woman in the House of Representatives, in the Senate, or in a governor's chair. While no one ever says so aloud, blacks are demonized by conservatives so that they might more effectively exploit the fears of white Americans. We have seen examples of this tactic over and over, from the Jesse Helms ads with white men losing jobs to blacks, to George H. W. Bush's notorious invocation of Willie Horton. More recently, in 2006, when Tennessee senator Bob Corker was falling behind in a race with black representative Harold Ford, the Republican National Committee ran an ad that began with a scantily clad white woman declaring excitedly, "I met Harold at the Playboy party!" She returned at the end of the ad with a seductive wink, saying, "Harold, call me." As Drew Western notes, "The obvious goal was to activate a network about black men having sex with white women, something about which many white men, including those who are not consciously prejudiced, still feel queasy." Westen further observes:

> The "call me" line came just after the ad had ostensibly ended with the following words on the screen: "Harold Ford. He's Just Not Right." When I first saw the ad, I thought the syntax was peculiar. What did they mean by "He's just not right"? That's a term often used to describe someone with a psychiatric problem, and no one was suggesting that Ford was deranged.
>
> Then I realized what was wrong. If you were going to use that syntax, you'd say "He's just not right for Tennessee." What the viewer of the ad is not aware of (unless he or she is Tweetie Bird, or has trouble pronouncing r's), is that another network is being activated unconsciously. This second network was primed not only by the racial associations to the ad itself but by the broader campaign emphasizing that Ford isn't "one of us": "He's just not white." Then came a Corker radio ad, whose cover story was again to compare and contrast Corker and Ford on the extent to which they're really Tennesseans. Music plays continuously in the background, but every time the narrator turns to talk about Ford, the listener is exposed to the barely audible sound of an African tom-tom.[121]

Republicans professed to disassociate themselves from the television ad, but it received so much free airtime as a result of the media controversy that it more than did its duty with the voters. John McCain was so impressed, he hired the ad makers for his presidential campaign.

A commercial like this is part and parcel of conservatism's fundamental appeal in contemporary politics. America's most popular conservative talk-show host, Rush Limbaugh, once told an African-American caller to "take that bone out of your nose." "The NAACP should have riot rehearsals," he announced on another occasion. "They should get a liquor store and practice robberies." When Senator Carol Moseley-Braun's name was mentioned on his program, Limbaugh played the theme song "Movin' On Up" from the 1970s black sitcom *The Jeffersons*. "Have you ever noticed how all newspaper composite pictures of wanted criminals resemble Jesse Jackson?" he asked listeners.[122] He was forced to "resign" in disgrace from his job at ESPN after making what the network described as "insensitive and inappropriate" comments about an African-American NFL quarterback. He has even made tasteless sexual jokes about Barack Obama. The more serious point here is that so long as people's racial animosities are stoked and their fears encouraged, these feelings are likely to overwhelm their hopes.

The Weakening of Organized Labor. Back in the 1950s and 1960s a powerful network of labor organizations, integrated with a locally based Democratic Party structure, represented middle-income Americans in political, economic, and cultural matters. They helped workers identify common issues, informed them about political and policy considerations, helped shape their long-term philosophies, and turned them out for rallies and votes, much like what the mega-churches do today for conservatives. This movement also once provided Democrats with much of their political support, through funding, registration drives, solidarity campaigns, political campaigns, and all-important generation-to-generation political acculturation, assuring a sustainable future for all concerned. All that is but a memory today. Union membership in the United States has fallen from 35 percent in the 1950s to 11 percent today, and barely 8 percent in the private sector.[123] Even today, it is union membership that—statistically speaking—distinguishes a working-class liberal from a working-class conservative. In the 2004 election George W. Bush bested John Kerry among white men by a 62–37 percent margin, but Kerry carried white men in unions by a 59–38 percent margin. Bush likewise prevailed among white women by 55–44 percent, but Kerry carried unionized women workers by 67–32 percent.[124] Had union membership remained at its 1950 or 1960 levels, the presidency would have been Kerry's. Had the union movement provided anything like the wealth of services that it once provided for its membership, the entire character of our politics would be profoundly different. In fact, the opposite has taken place: as labor has declined, the number of conservative groups representing big business has exploded. A report issued by the American Political Science Association in 2004 noted that less-advantaged Americans "are so absent from discussions in Washington that government officials are likely to hear about their concerns, if at all, from more privileged advocates who speak for the disadvantaged. Politicians hear most regularly about the concerns of business and the most affluent."[125]

The Liberal Crisis of Confidence. All of the above factors have led liberals to a place where many if not most of them are no longer entirely certain of what they believe or how strongly they believe it. Part of this problem is endemic to the ideology itself. As discussed earlier, American liberalism lacks a clear core of easily described philosophical foundations. But the liberal tradition is also one that—in decided contrast to that of conservatism—has historically been characterized by self-doubt. As Alan Brinkley observes, liberal critics of liberalism "are not simply the countless disheartened liberals who are frustrated most of all by liberalism's political failures and who blame them on the craven timidity of Democratic politicians. Liberal philosophers and intellectuals have also offered damning critiques of all the basic premises of liberal thought."[126]

Certainly no less debilitating are the combined effects of the past thirty years of political history, and liberals' inability to make much headway against all of the various rifts, conundrums, and confusions described above. As James Bryce observed during his travels throughout America at the close of the nineteenth century, following a failed election, "The average man will repeat his arguments with less faith, less zeal, more of a secret fear that he may be wrong, than he did while the majority was still doubtful; and after every reassertion by the majority of its judgment, his knees grow feebler until at last they refuse to carry him into the combat."[127] Liberals today have simply lost too many elections, and it shows. According to a July 2006 poll by Democracy Corps, 68 percent of Americans believe that the Republican Party knows what it stands for, while only 45 percent say the same thing about the Democrats.[128] The Republicans did mismanage the government so egregiously between 2000 and 2006 that they discredited themselves sufficiently to enable a Democratic landslide. But as *National Review*'s Rich Lowry put it so eloquently, "Liberals cannot count on conservatives being associated with corruption, incompetence or an unpopular war forever."[129]

PART

II

AND WHY DO THEY
HATE AMERICA?

The thesis of this book, you may have noticed, is that our current political debate is characterized by myriad misperceptions about liberals—misperceptions that prevent the realization of the genuinely kinder and gentler America that most of us desire. In some cases conservatives have invested millions—even billions—in perpetrating these misperceptions as a deliberate political strategy designed to marginalize their opponents and clear the field for their politically unpopular programs. In other cases liberals have themselves failed to articulate the alternatives they offer in a manner that would enable Americans to recognize their own views—and interests—in liberal proposals. The media-aided campaign of demonization against anything and everything liberal has proven so influential that Americans rarely get to see or hear an actual liberal response to a particular problem.

In the pages that follow, I've tried to assemble what I consider to be the most significant accusations—both politically and pragmatically—against liberals. These have not only achieved the status of conventional wisdom, but are slanders that have become so successful that they no longer even need to be repeated by conservatives but are merely assumed. My aim is to demonstrate that not only are most of these charges untrue, misguided, and/or outdated, but in many cases—when one bypasses the typical propaganda channels and goes to the trouble to research and scrutinize the available evidence—they end up applying far more accurately to those leveling the accusation than to the alleged perpetrators. My hypothesis is simply this: correct the lies, half-truths, and outdated assumptions about liberals and liberalism that have taken root in the minds of most voters; improve their understanding of the actual impact of the past eight years of conservative rule and the past forty years of conservative agitation; and we get our country back. It sounds simple, I know, but it's not so easily done.

5

Why Do Liberals Hate Patriotism?

It is a given in American political discourse that conservatives are more patriotic than liberals. The "antipatriotic liberal" meme is a staple not only of conservative attacks on liberals in the media and in politics but of everyday political conversation. Newt Gingrich's famous description of Democrats as "the enemy of normal Americans" is one of many iterations of this well-worn theme. As Thomas Frank observed, "When the chairman of the Republican National Committee in 1992 announced to a national TV audience, 'We are American' and 'those other people are not,' he was merely giving new and more blunt expression to a decades-old formula."[1]

In an extensive Pew Research Survey published in March 2007, 61 percent of Republicans called themselves "very patriotic," while only 45 percent of Democrats did. (Significantly, however, the Republican number has been dropping and the Democratic percentage rising; an earlier Pew poll also found that African Americans, considered perhaps the most reliable of liberal voting blocks, were also among the most patriotic, as "eighty percent of black Americans . . . strongly identify themselves as patriotic.")[2] But patriotism is one virtue for which talk is particularly cheap. So let's look into the issue a little more deeply.

First, note that conservatives deem only certain American groups and institutions to be legitimately "patriotic." That list would include the military, conservative Christian churches, NASCAR, the Grand Ol' Opry, and holiday parades (both patriotic and Christian), but would exclude unions, jazz festivals, mainstream Christian churches and non-Christian houses of worship, pickup basketball games, nearly all moviemaking, and protest marches. Red states are considered to be by mere definition more patriotic than blue states. Recall that following

9/11, Andrew Sullivan, the (then) conservative blogger, warned Americans—à la Joe McCarthy—to be alert about traitors in their midst, whom he helpfully identified not as among people living in "the middle part of the country—the great red zone that voted for Bush" but as among Gore voters—the majority, by the way, and particularly in the city where the Twin Towers attack had taken place. Nevertheless, Sullivan professed to spy a "decadent left in its enclaves on the coasts [that] is not dead—and may well mount a fifth column."[3]

Let's stipulate that the above description of *patriotism* is the product of both ideological manipulation and McCarthyite insinuation, and can be rejected out of hand. (It's hard to square, anyway, with the fact that both Nashville, Tennessee, and Austin, Texas, the twin homes of country music, went Democratic by significant margins in 2004.)[4] But even if we were to accept this skewed institutional association of patriotism with, say, the military, the argument fails to stand up to scrutiny. David Broder, the "dean" of Washington conventional wisdom, attacked a 2007 speech by General Wesley Clark before a Democratic gathering in Washington because the general "repeatedly invoked the West Point motto of 'Duty, Honor, Country,' forgetting that few in this particular audience have much experience with, or sympathy for, the military."[5] Here Broder gives more polite voice to the same prejudices expressed by Rush Limbaugh et al., who insist that, by definition, a liberal "hates the military, hates America, hates Bush, hates the world except for France and Germany."[6]

The devotion of conservatives to America's military seems to consist, primarily, of two aspects: expressing one's love rhetorically while specifically avoiding service oneself, and refusing to offer appropriate funding or support either for soldiers fighting abroad or wounded veterans returning home. As with patriotism, Republicans do like to trumpet their devotion to the military with greater enthusiasm than Democrats,[7] but this is one case in which it's far more instructive to consider what people do, rather than what they say. Because the issue of the military is so fundamental to an understanding of the concept of patriotism, it is worth examining in detail the respective positions of conservatives and liberals toward the men and women who put themselves in harm's way to keep us safe.

CONSERVATIVES AND THE MILITARY I

The "Chickenhawk" Issue. At a gathering of New York's Conservative Party before the 2004 elections, Karl Rove, the architect behind President Bush's election victories, explained to the admiring throng, "Liberals saw the savagery of the 9/11 attacks and wanted to prepare indictments and offer therapy and understanding for our attackers." Conservatives, he said, "saw the savagery of 9/11 and the attacks and prepared for war."[8] This was nonsense; nearly 90 percent of liberals supported the U.S. military response against al-Qaeda in Afghanistan. (Liberals, unlike Rove and his patrons in the Bush White House, tend to believe that when one is attacked, it is appropriate to respond against those responsible, rather than against another group of people in another part of the world who had nothing whatsoever to do with the attack.) Still, Rove's casual slur points to another problem with conservatives. While he talks tough, Karl Rove—like, Bush, Cheney, et al.—has had no experience with the military save that of perhaps waving to soldiers on parade from a nearby sidewalk. Military service is something that powerful conservatives profoundly admire . . . but only in other people. Since the creation of an all-volunteer professional army in June 1973, military service has been the purview of a tiny minority in this country, but even when it was considered by law to be a matter of duty rather than one of choice, many conservatives—including many of those most eager to deploy the military for purely political purposes—managed to avoid wartime service. Moreover, in virtually all cases, these conservatives supported the war then being fought in Vietnam; they merely believed that others should be the ones to fight it. One can debate the ethical responsibility of a young person who refuses to fight in a war he or she does not support; having never been faced with this choice personally, I am reluctant to moralize about it. But how is it possible to defend those, like young Dick Cheney, who say they believed in the cause of the war but felt themselves to have "other priorities" in their lives rather than fight it, or George W. Bush, who clearly employed his privileged position in society to ensure a series of cushy postings in the Air National Guard that he then did not even bother to fulfill? Leaving moral questions aside, moreover, the presence of so little genuine military experience among the Iraq War planners on the Bush team was significant *not* because of any implication that those who have not served in the military do not have the right to chart policies for those who do: civilian leadership is a fundamental precept of modern democracy. Rather, it was significant because the experience of war tends to teach a lesson that can be learned no other way, and it is this lesson—the reality of combat—that is perhaps most essential to understand when planning a military venture. As General William Tecumseh Sherman said after the Civil War: "It is only those who have neither fired a shot nor heard the shrieks and groans of the wounded who cry aloud for blood, more vengeance, more desolation."[9] That America's misadventure in Iraq was planned almost exclusively by those who had seen combat only on television, if at all, was one of the most important reasons it was so predictably doomed to failure.

The list of prominent right-wing "chickenhawks"—those who support the use of force as an instrument of policy but were unwilling to serve on active duty themselves—includes President George W. Bush, Vice President Dick Cheney, top presidential adviser Karl Rove, Iraq War planners Paul Wolfowitz, Douglas Feith, Richard Perle, Elliott Abrams, I. Lewis Libby, and John Bolton, and many more. In the conservative congressional "chickenhawk" caucus we find most of the 2002–6 congressional leadership, including Senate majority leader Bill Frist, Senate majority whip Mitch McConnell (R-KY), third-ranking Republican in the Senate Rick Santorum, and former majority leader Trent Lott; in the House, Speaker Dennis Hastert, House majority leader Tom DeLay, former Speaker Newt Gingrich, House majority whip Roy Blunt, former House majority leader Dick Armey, and virtually every other prowar Republican. Among prominent political pundits who demanded war, almost none could claim the wisdom and experience that even a brief enlistment in the military might have provided. Added together, the collective time served in the army, navy, and air force by the likes of armchair warriors Rush Limbaugh, Bill O'Reilly, George F. Will, Bill Bennett, Paul Gigot, Michael Savage, Michael Medved, Sean Hannity, Jonah Goldberg, Rich Lowry, William Kristol, Fred Barnes, Andrew Sullivan, Christopher Hitchens, Tony Blankley, or—no reason to be sexist about this—Mary Matalin, Ann Coulter, Condoleezza Rice, and Michelle Malkin, comes to a grand total of zero.[10]

Conservatives have a difficult time admitting these facts, particularly to themselves: in a July 2007 *Weekly Standard* cover story, Dean Barnett, a blogger at HughHewitt.com, complains: "Sadly, the excesses of Woodstock became the face of the Boomers' response to their moment of challenge. War protests where agitated youths derided American soldiers as baby killers added no luster to their image. Few of the leading lights of that generation joined the military. Most calculated how they could avoid military service, and their attitude rippled through the rest of the century."[11] Barnett does not explain how some, like a number of hawkish writers and editors associated with the magazine upon whose cover his essay appeared, for instance, managed to avoid both service in the war they supported as well as any engagement with the counterculture he so blithely blames. Meanwhile, Rush Limbaugh went so far as to accuse war hero John Kerry, who served in Vietnam, of being "with the enemy" and having "met with them, lied for them before a Senate committee." (He did this accompanied by a graphic with a photo of Osama bin Laden that identified him as "D-Afghanistan.")[12] In fact, whether boomers or not, liberals and Democrats, it turns out, are far more likely to have served in the military, even when the war in question is one they personally did not support. Among the veterans who regularly receive lectures on patriotism from conservative chickenhawks are:

- David Bonior: staff sergeant, air force, 1968–72
- Tom Daschle: first lieutenant, air force, 1969–72
- Al Gore: enlisted in August 1969; sent to Vietnam in January 1971 as an army journalist in the 20th Engineer Brigade
- Bob Kerrey: lieutenant j.g., navy, 1966–69; Medal of Honor, Vietnam

- Daniel Inouye: army, 1943–47; Medal of Honor, Purple Heart, 442nd Regimental Combat Team (the most highly decorated unit in American military history), World War II
- John Kerry: lieutenant, navy, 1966–70; Silver Star, Bronze Star with Combat V, Purple Hearts
- Charles Rangel: staff sergeant, army, 1948–52; Bronze Star, Korea
- Max Cleland: captain, army, 1965–68; Silver Star and Bronze Star, Vietnam; paraplegic from war injuries
- Ted Kennedy: army, 1951–53
- Tom Harkin: lieutenant, navy, 1962–67; naval reserve, 1968–74
- Jack Reed: army Ranger, 1971–79; graduate, West Point; captain, army reserve, 1979–91
- Pete Stark: air force, 1955–57
- George McGovern: Silver Star and DFC, World War II
- Jimmy Carter: graduate, U.S. Naval Academy; seven years in the navy
- Walter Mondale: army, 1951–53

No less impressive than the sheer size of the conservative chickenhawk brigade is the imaginativeness and energy some employed to avoid putting on a uniform—or at least one that might get dirty. We may never know exactly what strings were pulled to keep young George W. Bush out of Vietnam, or to allow him to avoid being drafted or even to finish his tour at his cushy Air National Guard post, but we do know that Dick Cheney enjoyed four student deferments, and when those ran out, a fifth deferment for married men with children, in order to pursue what he termed "other priorities" than the war he claimed to support. Georgia senator Saxby Chambliss, who defeated Max Cleland, a man who lost three limbs to a grenade in Vietnam, by questioning his patriotism, managed to stay out of the military with five separate student deferments plus a medical deferment for a football-related knee injury. (While that may sound impressive, in the student deferment department it is hardly a record: former Bush administration attorney general John Ashcroft enjoyed six.) No wonder, given this culture of contempt for actual military service, that so many Republicans at their 2004 New York convention felt justified in mocking John Kerry's three Purple Heart awards by wearing them as Band-Aids, as so few of them had apparently ever seen a real one.

CONSERVATIVES AND THE MILITARY II

Tools for Nation-Building. Conservative disrespect for the military features a far more deadly aspect than mere personal hypocrisy. While often eager to risk the lives and limbs of our fighting men and women in war, they are notoriously stingy when it comes to protecting their lives there, or even the institutions they serve. Nowhere is this more evident than in the Bush administration's management of the invasion of Iraq. The Bush team chose its course without bothering to do its due diligence on what their invasion plans might mean for the men and women they were sending to fight and die. As retired four-star U.S. Marine Corps general Anthony Zinni, who formerly headed the Central Command in the Middle East and was appointed by President Bush as his special emissary to the Israel-Palestine negotiations there, would observe:

> In the lead-up to the Iraq war and its later conduct, I saw at a minimum true dereliction, negligence and irresponsibility; at worse, lying, incompetence and corruption; false rationales presented as justification, a flawed strategy, lack of planning, the unnecessary alienation of our allies, the underestimation of the risk, the unnecessary distraction from real threats, and the unbearable strain dumped on our overstretched military. All of these caused me to speak out, and I was called a traitor and a turncoat by civilian Pentagon officials.[13]

Among the most egregious of the many mistreatments of the men and women of the military by this conservative administration has been its cavalier misunderstanding of and disdain for the expertise and professionalism of the U.S. military. Presidential candidate George W. Bush spoke dismissively of the practice of nation-building. "I think what we need to do is convince people who live in the lands they live in to build the nations," he explained. "Maybe I'm missing something here. I mean, we're going to have kind of a nation-building corps from America? Absolutely not." And yet, running out of justifications for the catastrophe it had caused in Iraq, the Bush team finally fell upon not only nation-building but one of the most difficult and dangerous nation-building missions ever undertaken in human history. As Leon Hadar of the libertarian think tank the Cato Institute observed, "A conservative administration is now suggesting that all you need is, yes, government—a few days and nights of aerial bombing, 140,000 U.S. troops, bureaucrats with good intentions and economic aid from Washington—and, voilà! We have 'nation building.'"[14]

Perhaps Bush and his neoconservative boosters were serious when they predicted that Iraq might become, in war architect Paul Wolfowitz's words, "the first Arab democracy." The deputy secretary of defense also predicted that even modest democratic progress in Iraq would "cast a very large shadow, starting with Syria and Iran but across the whole Arab world." Weekly Standard editor and Republican strategist William Kristol went so far as to argue before the Senate Foreign Relations Committee that "reconstructing Iraq may prove to be a less difficult task than the challenge of building a viable state in Afghanistan"; a rather modest prediction, it turns out, but still a failed one.[15]

Yet the Bush administration had enough expert analysis accessible to gauge just how difficult democracy would be to export under the best of circumstances. Study after study, easily available to U.S. military planners, provided ample warning of just how daunting a task lay in store.[16] Indeed, just before the war was precipitately launched, a secret CIA report judged the administration's goal to be, in all likelihood, "impossible."[17]

The problems were as complicated as they were obvious. Noting that "Iraqi political values and institutions are rooted in a tortured history that must be understood before it is possible to consider the rehabilitation of Iraqi society," the CIA report summarized hundreds of years of that violent tribal history before concluding, "The establishment of democracy or even some sort of rough pluralism in Iraq, where it has never really existed previously, will be a staggering challenge for any occupation force," particularly given a society "where anti-democratic traditions are deeply ingrained."[18] This view was corroborated by a study published by the soldier-scholars at the U.S. Army War College, whose authors warned, "U.S. policymakers sometimes assume that a democratic government will be friendly to U.S. policies in the Middle East. This cannot," the report states, "be assumed in the case of Iraq."[19]

Even less credible than the administration's belief in the emergence of a generation of Iraqi Thomas Jeffersons and James Madisons was the intimation that much of the rest of the Arab world was poised to embrace democracy as well. David Frum, Bush's admiring ex-speechwriter, expressed this naive faith in his memoir, The Right Man: "American-led overthrow of Saddam Hussein—and a replacement of the radical Ba'athist dictatorship with a new government more closely aligned with the United States—would put America more wholly in charge of the region than any power since the Ottomans, or maybe the Romans." This, presumably, would lead to what administration officials claimed would be a "democracy domino effect" with "tyrannies collapsing on top of one another." Echoing William Kristol, Richard Perle suggested that the U.S. invasion had "the potential to transform the thinking of people around the world about the potential for democracy, even in Arab countries where people have been disparaging of their potential."[20]

The cynicism of the administration's policy was revealed when, in the summer of 2005, investigative reporter Seymour Hersh exposed the right-wingers' plot—after all their rhetoric about democracy—to subvert the Iraqi elections: "A Pentagon consultant who deals with the senior military leadership acknowledged that the American authorities in Iraq 'did an operation' to try to influence the results of the election. 'They had to,' he said. 'They were trying to make a case that Allawi was popular, and he had no juice.' A government consultant with close ties to the Pentagon's civilian leaders said, 'We didn't want to take a chance.'"[21] A few months later, the Washington Post reported that the

Bush administration was significantly lowering expectations of what could be achieved in Iraq, adding, "The United States no longer expects to see a model new democracy, a self-supporting oil industry or a society in which the majority of people are free from serious security or economic challenges." The report quoted a senior official involved in policy since the 2003 invasion admitting, "What we expected to achieve was never realistic given the timetable or what unfolded on the ground. We are in a process of absorbing the factors of the situation we're in and shedding the unreality that dominated at the beginning."[22]

The Bush administration never did take the job of Iraqi reconstruction particularly seriously. Instead of appointing trained professionals or individuals with knowledge of the region and its people to oversee the vast tasks of rebuilding the country, it placed the responsibility entirely on the shoulders of untrained political hacks whose only apparent qualification was a publicly professed loyalty to the administration itself. Among those chosen by the Pentagon to assist the Iraqi Provisional Government were a twenty-four-year-old who had never worked in finance but who, after applying for a White House job, was sent to reopen Baghdad's stock exchange; and the daughter of a prominent neoconservative commentator who, along with a recent graduate from an evangelical university for home-schooled children, was tapped to manage Iraq's $13 billion budget, even though neither had any training in accounting. Almost no one hired for these crucial jobs was asked if he or she possessed any professional experience or expertise in the relevant areas. But more than one of them was asked if he had volunteered to demonstrate against a fair count of Florida's votes in the 2000 election or disagreed with the Supreme Court's decision in *Roe v. Wade*.[23]

Needless to say, the men and women of the U.S. military have been forced to bear the brunt of this misguided fantasy, as they are being called upon to perform political, police, civil, and training tasks that might be considered impossible by those who have devoted their lives to acquiring the skills necessary to implement them. Expecting the military to provide guidance for the creation of a political democracy among people with no experience of it and little or no cultural basis or necessarily even a demonstrated desire to embrace such a system demonstrates disrespect for both the individual soldiers and the institutions they serve. It is a sacred trust granted to an American president to send soldiers off to fight and die. George W. Bush and his conservative supporters have treated this trust with contempt.

CONSERVATIVES AND THE MILITARY III

Soldier, Defend Thyself. Another deadly manifestation of the conservative contempt for the military was the Bush administration and Republican Congress's unwillingness to provide U.S. troops in Iraq with appropriate protection. In his speech accepting his party's nomination in August 2000, candidate Bush warned, "Our military is low on parts, pay, and morale. If called by the commander in chief today, two entire divisions of the army would have to report . . . 'not ready for duty.' This administration had its moment. They had their chance. They have not led. We will."[24] And yet, years into a murderous insurgency deploying roadside bombs and suicide crash vehicles, America's soldiers continued to travel in Iraq in vulnerable Humvees, while any number of nations do manufacture safer armored cars. Soldiers were even reduced to duct-taping old flak jackets to the sides of their Humvees to provide protection and putting sandbags on the floors of their vehicles. In fact, a stronger, better-protected vehicle was available to the Pentagon throughout this period, but while it did order some for the Iraqi armed forces, U.S. soldiers remained stuck in the vulnerable Humvees. An internal report by Roy McGriff III, then a major, produced for the Marine Corps School of Advanced Warfighting in Quantico, Virginia, noted in 2003: "Currently, our underprotected vehicles result in casualties that are politically untenable and militarily unnecessary. . . . Failure to build a MRAP vehicle fleet produces a deteriorating cascade of effects that will substantially increase" risks for the military while "rendering it tactically immobile. . . . Mines and IEDs will force U.S. troops off the roads," he wrote, "and keep them from aggressively attacking insurgents." But the Bush administration, in the person of the defense secretary, had ruled that this would be a quick war; remember that Bush famously declared, "Major combat operations in Iraq have ended" on May 1, 2003. Two years later Vice President Cheney announced that the Iraqi insurgency was "in its last throes." And Rumsfeld's strategy called for faster, less-well-protected vehicles to allow many such invasions when it suited the administration's strategic purposes. Five years after the invasion began and the need was identified, our soldiers were still dying in their Humvees.[25]

The body armor problem demonstrates a similar insouciance with regard to the lives of the men and women on the battlefields. One secret Pentagon study discovered that as many as 80 percent of the marines who had been killed in Iraq from wounds to the upper body could have survived if they had been given extra body armor. Such armor has been available since 2003, but until early 2005, the Pentagon declined to supply it to most troops, despite calls from the field for additional protection, according to military officials.[26] In fact, the United States went to war with Iraq equipping only around thirty thousand soldiers with body-armor protection, as troops "experienced shortages of force-protection equipment such as up-armored vehicles, electronic countermeasure devices . . . weapons and communications equipment," according to an unclassified summary of a still-secret report. "As a result, service members were not always equipped to effectively complete their missions."[27]

Meanwhile, as suicide bombers and snipers stepped up their deadly attacks, and the need for greater protection became clearer, the administration failed to take any measures to free the Pentagon from the lengthy (albeit often necessary) process of peacetime procurement. Nor did the Republican-controlled Congress initiate so much as a single bill that might have encouraged the Pentagon to act with greater alacrity in its acquisition efforts. By contrast, when other nations' forces in Iraq required more bulletproof vests, they ordered them directly from a U.S. manufacturer, who began supplying them within twelve days.[28]

The net result was that soldiers' hometowns—indeed, even some of their families—banded together to buy soldiers the vests, at least until the army barred the use of privately purchased body armor. Meanwhile, the outsourcing of many of the tasks of providing for the troops to private companies—consistent with the administration's business-first ideology—had resulted in poor living conditions, contaminated drinking water, and substandard food for the troops.[29]

In late 2004 Defense Secretary Donald Rumsfeld made a surprise visit to Camp Buehring, Kuwait, on the eve of a group of soldiers' deployment into Iraq, and got a big surprise when, with the network cameras rolling, army specialist Thomas Wilson complained: "We're digging pieces of rusted scrap metal and compromised ballistic glass that has already been shot up, dropped, busted—picking the best out of this scrap to put on our vehicles to go into combat. We do not have proper armament vehicles to carry with us north." As Wilson's fellow soldiers cheered loudly, a startled Rumsfeld could only deflect this question with an oddly inappropriate rhetorical—almost existential—response: "As you know, you go to war with the army you have, not the army you might want or wish to have at a later time." In addition to his inability to speak to the soldier's specific complaint, this strange quip ignored the entirely elective aspect of almost every facet of the administration's decision to attack Iraq.[30] To be fair, we can always expect a lag time in the deployment of proper military equipment in wartime. Americans went into combat in 1941 and 1942 with inadequate armor, poor (compared to that of the enemy) aircraft, and substandard torpedoes, for example. But in those cases, conditions improved over time. By the conflict's third year, our soldiers were equipped with top-of-the-line weaponry, including the famous P-51 fighter, the Sherman tank, and a host of technological innovations at sea. The war in Iraq has already lasted longer than America's role in World War II and yet the conservative Bush administration has continually refused to address this matter.

Meanwhile, back at home, the Bush administration was also quietly slashing veterans' benefits over the next decade by nearly $29 billion, leaving them to languish in a system that demands that they wait weeks or months for mental-health care and other appointments; fall into debt as VA case managers study disability claims over many months; and hire help from outside experts just to understand the VA's arcane system of rights and benefits. In one all-too-representative case, reported by *Newsweek*, a soldier who was severely wounded by flying shrapnel from a mortar explosion on his base, and was even visited at his bedside by President Bush, was forced to see his schoolteacher mother take a second job flipping burgers at McDonald's to help support him while he waited for treatment.[31]

The conditions were no secret to anyone who cared to look. On February 17, 2005, Sergeant First Class John Allen, who had been injured in Afghanistan in 2002, testified before top Pentagon officials about the "dysfunctional system" at the military hospital system's crown jewel, Walter Reed Hospital, where, he said, "soldiers go months without pay, nowhere to live, their medical appointments canceled." Allen added: "The result is a massive stress and mental pain causing further harm. It would be very easy to correct the situation if the command climate element suppressed it." These same complaints were also well known to top officials, as Mark Benjamin reported on *Salon*, because "the Defense Department had been conducting monthly focus group discussions with soldiers treated at Walter Reed since before the wars in Afghanistan and Iraq had even begun, and . . . it continued to do so as wounded veterans of those conflicts arrived at the facility." And money was not to blame. "Let me just say, this is not a resource issue," said Dr. William Winkenwerder Jr., the assistant defense secretary then overseeing military medicine, just a day before the White House announced he would be leaving his post.[32] Rather than bothering to do anything to improve the vets' care, the administration put a premium on managing the media. Soldiers' complaints were ignored; some complainants were threatened, and truth-tellers like Dr. Winkenwerder were dismissed. When the *Washington Post* initially exposed these condition at Walter Reed—where the wounded were housed in a former prostitution hotel among mice, mold, rot, and cockroaches—the Bush administration's initial reaction was to instruct patients to refuse to answer reporters' inquiries. Finally, as the outrage over the stories continued to build, and after a few low-level staffers were thrown to the wolves, those responsible were finally forced to resign, and a complete investigation was ordered.[33] Bush would later refer to the scandalous treatment of wounded veterans there as merely "some bureaucratic red-tape issues."[34]

CONSERVATIVES AND THE MILITARY IV

Insufficient Troops, Forced Rotations, and Depleted Reserves. As a presidential candidate, George W. Bush echoed the complaints of many conservatives that the Clinton administration had both abused and misused the men and women of the armed forces. "This administration wants things both ways: to command great forces, without supporting them, [and] to launch today's new causes with little thought of tomorrow's consequences," Bush declared at the Citadel military academy in September 1999. A better description of his own administration's manpower miscalculation in Iraq would be hard to imagine.

Part of the problem was clearly the result of political manipulation. Prior to the invasion, when they were still making their misleading case, war supporters did everything possible to downplay the likely costs and negative consequences of the venture. When the army chief of staff, General Eric K. Shinseki, offered his estimate to the Senate Armed Services Committee that the occupation of Iraq would likely require "something on the order of several hundred thousand soldiers," he was hardly exaggerating. If the model under study had been the most recent experience of military occupation—that of NATO in Kosovo—the requisite troop requirement would have risen to 526,000.[35] In 1999 the Pentagon set up an Iraq war game called Desert Crossing, which recommended a force of 400,000 troops to stabilize the country in the war's aftermath.[36] But Secretary Rumsfeld and his neoconservative advisers, who were eager to keep troops available for future military adventures, as well as to downplay the costs of the Iraq War itself, rejected this exercise and the lessons gleaned from it. The war's primary ideological architect, a man with no actual military experience whatsoever, Deputy Defense Secretary Paul Wolfowitz, thereafter ridiculed General Shinseki's estimate as being "wildly off the mark," adding, "It's hard to conceive that it would take more forces to provide stability in post-Saddam Iraq than it would take to conduct the war itself and secure the surrender of Saddam's security forces and his army."[37] Of course Wolfowitz also professed to believe that the Iraqis would "greet us as liberators, and that will help us to keep requirements down."[38]

This combination of ignorance, arrogance, and purposeful dishonesty proved deadly. President Bush's special envoy to post-Taliban Afghanistan, James Dobbins, has observed, "The highest levels of casualties have occurred in the operations with the lowest levels of U.S. troops." He added, "Only when the number of stabilization troops has been low in comparison to the population"—such as in Somalia, Afghanistan, and now Iraq—"have U.S. forces suffered or inflicted significant casualties." By contrast, in Germany, Japan, Bosnia, and Kosovo—where troop levels were high—Americans suffered no postwar combat deaths.[39] But pressure from the defense secretary's office to keep the force small enough for the U.S. military to move from war to war at will, according to one army officer, ensured that the occupation would be undermanned.[40] Deputy Undersecretary of Defense Douglas Feith acknowledged as much when he admitted that the decision to limit the number of troops was "strategic and goes far beyond Iraq. This is part of his [Rumsfeld's] thinking about defense transformation. It's an old way of thinking to say that the United States should not do anything without hundreds of thousands of troops. That makes our military less usable."[41]

Ultimately, according to Larry Diamond, who advised the Coalition Provisional Authority in Baghdad from January to April 2004 before moving to the conservative Hoover Institution, Bush and the neoconservatives "squandered the soldiers' stunning military victory." As Diamond observed, "By operating in a manner that was so often arrogant, imperial, ill-informed, isolated from Iraqi realities, and simply incompetent, we lost the confidence of the Iraqi public, and we fed a violent resistance that was probably inevitable but became much more extensive, deadly, and crippling as a result of our mistakes."[42] A total of six thousand U.S. soldiers were in Baghdad when the city fell on April 9, 2003, and they controlled a mere 15 percent of a city of over five million people.[43]

Beginning with the circus of looting and lawlessness that immediately followed the city's liberation, administration incompetence proved the rule, rather than the exception, in the U.S. occupation of Iraq. "If we had had 250,000 troops, the targets of looting might have been secured," explained ex-marine Lou Cantori, formerly of the faculty of West Point, the U.S. Air Force Academy, and the U.S. Marine Corps University. "We were shorthanded because of the Rumsfeld team's preconceptions, and therefore the troops stood around and watched as the infrastructure of Iraq was destroyed."[44]

The Bush administration conservatives who inexcusably abused the trust of our soldiers have done so without any sense whatsoever of personal accountability—a value that we are frequently led to believe is the bedrock of conservative philosophy. "Those in highest authority," one frequent chronicler of the war noted in the *New Yorker*, "have been kept in office (Dick Cheney), promoted (Gonzales, Condoleezza Rice), honored with medals (Tenet, General Tommy Franks, Paul Bremer), or sent off with encomiums (Wolfowitz, Rumsfeld)."[45]

And yet as the situation in Iraq has continued to deteriorate, the stress these failures place on the fighting men and women has grown ever more burdensome. In theory, soldiers expect a year between Iraq rotations, but in this war, the time between rotations was only six months. Owing to "stop-loss orders"—which involuntarily extend active-duty tours—these same soldiers would also be forced back into combat nine months after their enlistment had already expired, and these tours were later extended to fully fifteen months.[46] "There's never been anything close to this much demand on the all-volunteer military in its 30-year history," observed Brookings's Michael O'Hanlon, a war supporter, even before the additional forced rotations into Iraq were announced in the winter of 2007. "Even in wartime, with conscription, we didn't send people overseas on two tours of duty. Certainly in Vietnam, if you did your one tour, you were done."[47]

Naturally, as word got out about all of the above, recruitment grew more difficult.[48] With the military facing its worst enlistment crisis since the all-volunteer army began in 1973, the manpower shortfall became so

acute that, beginning in 2005, military leaders felt forced to accept significant numbers of new recruits with criminal records and pending criminal
charges—and to offer them enlistment bonuses ranging from $14,400 to
$20,000, plus $70,000 in college loans. To retain the elite enlisted soldiers
in the oft-deployed Special Forces, the army was compelled to come up
with as much as $150,000 per soldier. The Pentagon also asked Congress
to lift the age of military recruits to forty-two, a full six years older than it
had been three years earlier.[49] And yet, even with all these inducements,
all three services continued to miss their recruiting missions.[50] In 2004,
the army lost more young officers, particularly graduates of West Point
and other educational institutions, than it had in sixteen years, as more
than a third of those trained for a military career at taxpayer expense decided to bail out at their first contractual opportunity.[51] In early 2007 a
congressional commission judged nearly 90 percent of army National
Guard units in the United States as "not ready"—largely as a result of
shortfalls in billions of dollars' worth of equipment—jeopardizing their
capability to respond to crises at home and abroad.[52]

What makes these sacrifices most painful to bear for those who have
closely examined the details of debates over the planning for the war is
the fact that not only was so much of what came to pass predictable, but
it was actually predicted—and not by the opponents whom the right-
wingers in the Bush administration treated with undisguised contempt,
but by the very people who attacked the patriotism of those who raised
the issue. Long before Iraq was on the table, the neocons at the *Weekly
Standard* published an editorial calling on Rumsfeld and Wolfowitz to
resign in protest at what they predicted would be "the impending evis-
ceration of the military." Indeed, they went even further, warning, "In
practice, assembling a heavy armored force of even four divisions to defeat Saddam's army and then occupy Iraq would require every heavy
unit based in Korea, Europe and the United States." And yet they signed
on to the program anyway, first for the tax cuts and then for the undermanned invasion. The neocons would regret this, naturally, when the
entire adventure went sour. "Those of us who expressed concern about
the Bush administration's shorting of the military were told not to

worry," the *Standard*'s editors wrote. "Bush had to pass his tax cut first. Then the damage would be repaired in the [fiscal year] 2002 and FY 2003 budgets. But that's not the way things have turned out." As Jonathan Chait translates this passage, it really reads: "We thought Bush was just lying to the American public, but now we discover he was lying to us also!"[53] For such shenanigans have thousands of American soldiers lost their lives and limbs.

CONSERVATIVES AND THE MILITARY V

No Shared Sacrifice. President Bush has spoken on the importance of national sacrifice to win the "war on terror," musing, "Amid all this violence, I know Americans ask the question: Is the sacrifice worth it? It is worth it, and it is vital to the future security of our country."[54] What was unclear from his remarks was just who, besides the soldiers and their families, was making any sacrifices. "Nobody in America is asked to sacrifice, except us," said one officer upon returning from a yearlong tour in Iraq. "For most Americans," said another officer with a year's experience in Iraq, "their role in the war on terror is limited to the slight inconvenience of arriving at the airport a few hours early." Indeed, Bush is the first president in American history to combine commitment to a war with the simultaneous granting of a massive tax cut to the wealthiest Americans—or indeed any Americans. The president also encouraged Americans to shop and offered further tax breaks for gas-guzzling SUVs. As part of its political strategy to keep the war from interfering with its domestic agenda, the administration established another precedent by refusing to allow the coffins of returning soldiers to be photographed, thereby preventing Americans from honoring their war dead. (The flights carrying wounded soldiers to U.S. military hospitals also arrived at night to discourage photographers.) Again ignoring precedent, George W. Bush attended no military funerals. He also refused numerous requests that he personally deliver a recruitment speech, despite the desperate need for new enlistees. Sergeant David Thomas, a Tennessee National Guard gunner with a Purple Heart and an amputated leg, even found himself left off the guest list for a summer presidential ceremony honoring a fellow amputee after he said he would be wearing shorts, not pants, when occupying a seat in the first row.[55]

Asked by a journalist what sacrifices nonmilitary Americans were making for the war, Bush answered by explaining that Americans "sacrifice peace of mind when they see the terrible images of violence on TV every night." Asked about this issue by NBC's Ann Curry on the *Today* show in April 2007, Laura Bush responded, "No one suffers more than their president and I do."[56] Suffice it to say that few soldiers serving in Iraq—nor the family members of those who paid the ultimate sacrifice for the administration's folly—would be likely to embrace either Bush's definition.

CONSERVATIVES AND THE MILITARY VI

Sunshine Patriotism. When Senator Chuck Hagel, a Republican, voiced misgivings about the Pentagon's strategy for victory, Donald Rumsfeld compared him to those who "at the height of World War II . . . praised Stalin . . . [when] Communism was very much in vogue."[57] Around the same time that Rumsfeld made this absurd remark, a full 90 percent of Americans polled were telling pollsters that they supported the right of Americans to protest the war, while eight straight monthly Gallup polls had found that a majority of Americans questioned believed that the Iraqi invasion had been a mistake, dishonestly undertaken.[58] And yet conservatives never let up on their equation of dissent and disagreement with treason. As late as July 2007, when virtually everyone outside the declining band of die-hard Bush loyalists had come to view Iraq as a disaster that demanded some sort of exit strategy, if only to maintain the cohesion of badly overstretched U.S. military forces, President Bush was still misinforming the public and threatening his opponents. "Those who justify withdrawing our troops from Iraq by denying the threat of al-Qaeda in Iraq and its ties to Osama bin Laden ignore the clear consequences of such a retreat."[59] Going the president one better,

Undersecretary of Defense Eric Edelman, a former top aide to Vice President Cheney, insisted that "questions about how the U.S. plans to eventually withdraw from Iraq boosts enemy propaganda."[60] At the time Edelman made his poisonous comments, the Pentagon itself was engaged in drawing up exactly these plans; it was only democratic discussion about the issue to which he and his fellow neocons objected.[61] With a degree of audacity that is shocking, given the context of the history of the Iraqi catastrophe, William Kristol wrote, "Having turned against a war that some of them supported, the left is now turning against the troops they claim still to support," adding, "The left slanders them. We support them." Even so, the McCarthyite accusations continued fast and furious. *National Review* pundit Jonah Goldberg even went so far as to accuse liberals of responsibility for a future Iraqi "genocide."[62]

Ironically, when it came to Kosovo—a war in which the conservatives were divided—the Republican-led House of Representatives refused even to pass a resolution supporting American troops in combat. Leading conservatives consistently dismissed the war and sought to undermine the commander in chief's authority. Then–House majority whip Tom DeLay, for instance, referred to the multinational operation in Kosovo as "the Clinton war," while other Republican leaders took to calling it "the Democratic war"; former House Speaker Dennis Hastert even described U.S. military personnel involved in the NATO operation as "his [Clinton's] forces."[63] None of this could have been supportive of military morale, as those men and women were undoubtedly under the impression that they were fighting for the United States of America, rather than one of its politicians or political parties.

CONSERVATIVES AND THE MILITARY VII

Torturous Logic. Yet another demonstration of the hollow content of so much right-wing promilitary rhetoric is the unwillingness of so many conservatives to support the military when they need it most: when internal threats to its cohesion and professionalism threaten to corrupt it from within. Just as many conservatives rallied around the mass murderer Lieutenant William Calley and his accomplices following the massacre in the village of My Lai in Vietnam in 1968, they actively encouraged those soldiers who shamed their uniforms and nation by supporting or participating in the torture-chamber activity at places such as the Abu Ghraib prison in Iraq or Guantánamo Bay in Cuba (which is under the jurisdiction of the United States). The most notorious of these was Rush Limbaugh.

When the shocking photos taken at Abu Ghraib were published, Limbaugh volunteered his enthusiastic agreement with a caller that what was done at the prison was no worse than "a college fraternity prank that stacked up naked men." Limbaugh replied: "Exactly my point! This is no different than what happens at the Skull and Bones initiation and we're going to ruin people's lives over it and we're going to hamper our military effort, and then we are going to really hammer them because they had a good time. You know, these people are being fired at every day. I'm talking about people having a good time, these people, you ever heard of emotional release? You ever heard of the need to blow some steam off?"

Limbaugh returned to this theme frequently, seeking to trivialize these violations of the military code of conduct in a manner designed to encourage more such gruesome incidents, calling the pictures "good old American pornography" and comparing the photographs to "anything you'd see Madonna, or Britney Spears do on stage . . . and get an NEA grant for something like this. I mean, this is something that you can see on stage at Lincoln Center from an NEA grant, maybe on *Sex in the City*."[64] On another program, Limbaugh, who has never served in the military but is carried on Armed Forces Radio, praised the torture as "a brilliant maneuver" and termed the reaction to it "an example of the feminization of this country."[65] Incredibly, Limbaugh even went into business to make money making fun of the torture, selling souvenirs such as mugs and bumper stickers for what he joshingly called "Club Gitmo," and joked about selling "Soap on a rope."[66]

Whether out of fear, calculation, or genuine protorture conviction one cannot say, but White House press secretary Scott McClellan specifically refused to repudiate Limbaugh's remarks. Perhaps this should not be so surprising when one considers the power and influence Limbaugh wields in the contemporary conservative movement. William Bennett, who frequently decries the loss of standards of decency and civility among liberals, calls Limbaugh "possibly the greatest living American" and "extremely sophisticated, extremely smart. . . . He's very serious intellectually." Limbaugh sat with Barbara Bush in the presidential box for the 1991 presidential State of the Union address. Dick Cheney is a frequent guest on Limbaugh's radio show, and Limbaugh has been invited to join the *Meet the Press* roundtable as an honored and respected commentator by NBC's Tim Russert, invited to air his views on Katie Couric's *CBS Evening News* broadcast, and quoted as an expert on politics and race relations by Jake Tapper of ABC News.

(History appeared to repeat itself in September 2007 when Limbaugh, again demonstrating his contempt for the men and women who put their lives on the line to serve in the nation's military, referred to servicemen and Iraqi war veterans who have publicly disagreed with the Bush administration's failed policies there and concurred with the majority of Americans on the advisability of a U.S. withdrawal as "phony soldiers."[67] Even though George W. Bush had only recently condemned a liberal newspaper ad that questioned the veracity of the testimony of General David Petraeus, using a silly pun on his name, as "disgusting," not a peep of disapproval of Limbaugh was heard from the vicinity of 1600 Pennsylvania Avenue. This was the case when Limbaugh went so far as to compare one of the veterans who did voice his displeasure to an Iraqi suicide bomber.)[68]

Limbaugh's Abu Ghraib remarks were frequently echoed among other conservatives. *Weekly Standard* editor Jonathan Last chimed in that "worse things happen in frat houses across America." Talk show and cable host Oliver North felt that the torture represented "the kind of thing that you might find on any college campus nowadays."[69] And on MSNBC's *Imus in the Morning*, right-wing radio host Jay Severin criticized President Bush for calling the Abu Ghraib prisoner-abuse scandal "a mistake." He explained:

"We took terror prisoners, and we treated them essentially to a week in Las Vegas. I have to pay good money to have that done to me."[70]

What all of the pundits quoted above share is not merely a lack of experience within the military but also a lack of understanding of the importance of discipline in its hierarchy of values and traditions. Military historian and Seventh Cavalry officer Major Bob Bateman—now Lieutenant Colonel Bateman—complained that Limbaugh and others like him did "not realize that with his careless and thoughtless words that he's making things tougher on us soldiers, not easier." Bateman explained:

> Limbaugh is out there, making excuses for the prison guards, and in the process making it that much more likely that there will be a "next time." How? By making what they did excusable. By minimizing it. By saying that it's not so bad, and that he can see how it's just like a fraternity hazing. What Limbaugh apparently does not even realize is that in the process of saying that he is de facto slamming the officer corps of the U.S. Army and calling us incompetent. . . . It was Army officers who proffered the charges for court martial against the prison guards, and Limbaugh is making a mockery of our processes and decisions. In effect it seems to me that he's trying to make a criminal behavior into a political one, and I detest that when it's applied to the military from the right or the left. . . . By denigrating our decision to court-martial these soldiers, Limbaugh is undercutting our moral authority to control and contain violence so that it is used only in the right way . . . on the battlefield. He's giving all his listeners (and all the people who they, in turn, influence) the impression that this sort of thing is okay, despite what we officers in the Army are saying.[71]

Of course it would be easier to ignore even Limbaugh and his cronies were their arguments in conflict with those of the unofficial head of the conservative moment in the United States, President George W. Bush. The president elevated White House counsel Alberto Gonzales to the position of U.S. attorney general, the highest law enforcement office in the government (with unanimous approval from Senate Republicans), after Gonzales defended the use of torture techniques by the U.S. military in what Yale Law School dean Harold Koh described as "perhaps the most clearly legally erroneous opinion I have ever read." These regulations were adopted over the objections of Judge Advocate General (JAG) Corps lawyers, who warned that "'concern for [U.S.] servicemembers is not reflected' in the rationales given by Justice Department lawyers for abusive interrogations." Brigadier General Kevin Sandkuhler, staff judge advocate to CMC, also predicted a potential breakdown in uniformed "pride, discipline and self-respect."[72] Rear Admiral Michael F. Lohr, the navy's chief lawyer, termed the practices "inconsistent with our most fundamental values." The deputy judge advocate general of the Air Force, Major General Jack L. Rives, advised the investigative task force that several of the "more extreme interrogation techniques, on their face, amount to violations of domestic criminal law" as well as military law.[73]

Civilian officials were also willing to insist that these policies be carried out absent any evidence that they would likely be effective. On the same day Bush sought to legally authorize the CIA to conduct torture, the military flatly stated that such coercive practices were counterproductive. Army Deputy Chief of Staff for Intelligence John Kimmons explained, "I am absolutely convinced [that] no good intelligence is going to come from abusive practices. I think history tells us that. I think the empirical evidence of the last five years, hard years, tell us that." As a result, the military has released a new field manual banning such practices. Kimmons added, "Our most significant successes on the battlefield have been—in fact, I would say all of them, almost categorically all of them, have accrued from expert interrogators using mixtures of authorized humane interrogation practices." He concluded, "We don't need abusive practices in there. Nothing good will come from them."[74]

But the Bush administration remained unconvinced, and left its administrative instructions unchanged. So committed was it to its belief in the value and utility of torture that it even refused to compromise when the Republican-dominated Senate, led by Vietnam veteran John McCain (R-AZ), attempted to secure legislation that would have barred the U.S. military from engaging in "cruel, inhuman or degrading treatment" of detainees—in language modeled on wording in the U.S.-ratified UN Convention Against Torture—from hiding prisoners from the Red Cross, and from using interrogation methods not authorized by a new army field manual. McCain, fearful of the likely effect this disagreement would have on his nascent presidential plans with conservative voters, eventually caved.[75] This not only sent a message to the military endorsing unprofessional conduct, it also served as a de facto invitation to America's enemies to torture our own soldiers should they get the chance. After all, when one side in a conflict announces that it does not consider itself bound by the agreed-upon laws of warfare, why should the other exercise the moral fastidiousness necessary to refrain as well?

* * *

We wouldn't be honest if we didn't acknowledge that despite all of the lies, misperceptions, and insults detailed above, liberals do have a real problem with the military. During the 2004 election, according to one poll published in *Military Times,* Bush led Kerry among active-duty military personnel by a staggering 73 to 18 percent. Roughly 60 percent of all military personnel described themselves as Republicans, with just 13 percent calling themselves Democrats.[76] These findings are consistent with previous data, including a detailed 1999 study by the Triangle Institute for Security Studies, which found that twenty-first-century military officers "have largely abandoned political neutrality and have become partisan Republicans."[77] In 2006, however, a potentially significant shift appeared: the number of active-duty service members declaring themselves to be Republicans in the *Military Times* poll fell to just 46 percent, reversing a thirty-year trend. Undoubtedly the significant increase in the number of veterans—particularly those coming home from Iraq and Afghanistan—who ran on the Democratic ticket in 2006 made an impression on their fellow soldiers, as did the Bush administration's horrific handling of the war itself. (*Military Times* found that only 35 percent of active-duty military personnel approved of Bush's leadership.)[78]

Still, that Democrats had so far to go demonstrates the cost of what has been for nearly four decades an almost reflexive revulsion toward

liberals and liberalism within the military. Aside from the conflict between the basic values of the officer corps—"loyalty, obedience, discipline,
and responsibility"—and those of liberals—"independence, individualism,
equality, and self-expression"—the ordeal of Vietnam, and its inspiration
of an antiwar movement that at times veered into deliberate anti-
Americanism and flirted with supporting the enemy, bred a culture of
mutual distrust between liberals and the uniformed military that continues to color the relationship to this day. Vietnam still stings; it remains a
powerful cultural memory, and one that is uncomfortable for liberals
to address. Todd Gitlin does so more honestly than most when he writes,
"The most powerful public emotion of our lives was rejecting patriotism."[79] Its association with recreational drug use and sexual experimentation, coupled with its rejection of traditional social and societal
hierarchies, could hardly have offended the sensibilities of the officer
corps more if it had been invented expressly for that purpose. These excesses, continually trumpeted by the right and repeated, often mind-
lessly, by the mainstream media, continue to haunt liberalism today and
have interfered with liberals' efforts to forge a relationship of mutual respect with the military, where such patriotism is taken as a given. Some
aspects of the conflict are based on pure myth. For instance, though the
accusation is tossed around as a matter of faith, and proved a staple
of early coverage of the Iraq War, a study of the role of the media in
Vietnam, officially published by the U.S. Army War College at Carlisle
Barracks, specifically exonerates reporters and editors from any role
whatever in the U.S. defeat there.[80] Even so, apparently insignificant but
unquestioned details of the behavior of the antiwar movement—that
some of its members may have spit on returning vets, for example—do
not rest on a single verifiable piece of evidence, according to one
extremely detailed study.[81]

Even though antipatriotic, antimilitary values no longer characterize
the liberal mainstream—if they ever did—liberals do bear a measure of
responsibility for their estrangement from the military. Democratic defense specialist Heather Hurlburt argues that liberals "suffer from a genuine ignorance of and indifference to military affairs." She attributes a

portion of this attitude to Vietnam and to the "gut-level distrust of the military" that so many liberals retain. Younger liberals, meanwhile, evince a lack of interest in military issues and receive little encouragement from their elders should they by some chance happen to develop one. Liberalism is perceived among the politically active to be concerned with abortion, health care, and poverty, rather than Scuds, MIRVs, or Apache attack helicopters. Liberals who do evince an interest in foreign affairs tend toward "softer" issues, such as global poverty, human rights, and environmental threats.[82] For these reasons among others, Al Gore's 43 percent of the vote among those who ranked defense or foreign affairs as their number-one issue turned out to be a high-water mark for Democratic presidential candidates in the past three decades.[83]

Clearly, liberals need to address this issue in language their intended audience appreciates. To do so, they need to encourage soldiers and their families to overcome their distrust and identify their own self-interest. The Bush administration's unconscionable treatment of our soldiers in Iraq and Afghanistan, coupled with the choice by record numbers of veterans to run as Democratic candidates for office in 2006, provides an obvious entry point. (Fifty-five military veterans were contenders for House seats alone.) It's also up to liberals to demonstrate their respect and admiration for the patriotism and dedication of those who answer their nation's call to duty, regardless of our respective differences of opinion. Ideally, a bargain might be struck between the military's demand that it be allowed to continue to discriminate against gays and a number of universities' insistence that so long as the military insists on this right, they be enjoined from recruiting on the campuses of the Ivy League and other elite northeastern institutions. The current impasse serves no one save those who exploit the resentment that it causes on both sides. Liberals will have to learn to agree to disagree, respectfully, about this and other divisive issues and commit themselves to accepting necessary compromises to prevail against a common enemy: contemporary conservatives.

6

Why Do Liberals Always Blame America First?

Speaking at the 1984 Republican convention, then–UN representative Jeane Kirkpatrick won considerable applause from those assembled and in the larger media for her attacks on those "San Francisco Democrats" whose first instinct was always to "blame America first."[1] More than twenty years later, in July 2005, *Weekly Standard* editor Fred Barnes published an essay about Bush's liberal Iraq critics entitled "They Still Blame America First."[2] Indeed, the conservative pundit Mona Charen managed to write a best-selling book on the topic entitled *Useful Idiots: How Liberals Got It Wrong in the Cold War and Still Blame America First.*

Even by the standards of conservative rhetoric, liberals are guilty of none of the crimes of which they are accused in this area. Take the case of 9/11, for instance. It is well-nigh impossible to find a single prominent American liberal who expressed anything but public outrage and condemnation of the attacks. Liberals also overwhelmingly supported taking military action against the perpetrators as well as their sponsors. Polling data demonstrates that 84 percent of self-described liberals, two weeks after the attacks, supported "military action" against the terrorists, and 75 percent of them supported "going to war with a nation that is harboring those responsible."[3]

"Blame America first" was, in fact, the response of the prominent right-wing preachers Jerry Falwell and Pat Robertson, who together, on one of Mr. Robertson's television programs in the immediate aftermath of the 9/11 terrorist attacks, explained that we had offended God and therefore had it coming, with Falwell saying, "The abortionists have got to bear some burden for this because God will not be mocked. And when we destroy 40 million little innocent babies, we make God mad. I really believe that the pagans, and the abortionists, and the feminists, and the gays and the lesbians who are actively trying to make that an alternative lifestyle, the ACLU, People for the American Way, all of them who have tried to secularize America, I point the finger in their face and say: you helped this happen." Robertson only added, "Jerry, that's my feeling" and "Well, I totally concur."[4]

Under considerable pressure from the White House, the two men apologized, but until his death in May 2007, Falwell could hardly be considered beyond the mainstream of conservative debate. Like Robertson, he was a ubiquitous presence on cable TV, and Republicans regularly traveled to see both men during presidential primaries to kiss their proverbial rings. When Supreme Court justice Sandra Day O'Connor announced her retirement, Falwell reported that the White House had called him asking for his "input" on Bush's choice.[5] When CNN sought a knowledgeable expert analyst on the Middle East peace process, they ignored people who actually knew something about the region and turned instead to Robertson, whose belief in Jewish conspiracies and biblical prophecies of Armageddon were apparently among his qualifications.

Views like those of Falwell and Robertson are hardly unique among conservative Christians. In March 2002 conservative Republican senator James Inhofe gave voice to almost identical sentiments, insisting that America got what it deserved on 9/11, which he viewed as a divinely sanctioned retribution for George W. Bush's insufficiently pro-Israel foreign policy. "One of the reasons I believe the spiritual door was opened for an attack against the United States of America," he explained, "is that the policy of our government has been to ask the Israelis, and demand it with pressure, not to retaliate in a significant way against the terrorist strikes that have been launched against them."[6]

Bob Jones, host to both Bush and John McCain at his notoriously racist, anti-Catholic university, wrote a letter to the president reading in part: "In your re-election, God has graciously granted America—though she doesn't deserve it—a reprieve from the agenda of paganism. . . . Don't equivocate. Put your agenda on the front burner and let it boil. You owe the liberals nothing. They despise you because they despise your Christ."

The Reverend Fred Phelps, pastor of Westboro Baptist Church in Topeka, Kansas, operates the Web site GodHatesFags.com, which asserts that America's soldiers "voluntarily joined a fag-infested army to fight for a fag-run country now utterly and finally forsaken by God who Himself is fighting against that country."[7] More anti-American statements—as well as more ignorant ones—than these would be a challenge even to imagine.

It's not just the most outlandish fundamentalist Christians who endorse views like these. The conservative talk-show host Michael Savage declared that, owing to the arrival of what he terms "post-Christian times" in which "the churches are emptying out, the bathhouses are filling up, the sex-change operations are speeding up, the lesbian fertility clinics are increasing around the country," God wants to show "you boys in Hollywood and you girls in New York City" that he does "exist" through acts of catastrophe like the terrorist attacks of September 11, 2001: "Down came the World Trade Centers. That was God speaking."[8] Dinesh D'Souza, a conservative intellectual of good standing at Stanford's Hoover Institution, argues in his 2007 book *The Enemy at Home* that "the left has produced a moral shift in society that has resulted in a deluge of gross depravity and immorality. This deluge threatens to engulf our society and is imposing itself on the rest of the globe. The Islamic radicals are now convinced that America represents the revival of pagan barbarism in the world and 9/11 represents their ongoing battle with what they perceive to be the forces of Satan."[9] D'Souza's argument differs from Falwell's and Jones's in the singular respect that he does not believe that the terrorists are agents of God's wrath; he does think that terrorism against American citizens is the logical outcome of "the scandalous sexual mores that they [religious Muslims] see in American movies and television," as well as "the sight of hundreds of homosexuals kissing one another and taking marriage vows." They are also "horrified," in D'Souza's estimation, by Hillary Clinton.[10] The idea that these right-wing "blame America" views represent genuine patriotism is one that most Americans would find to be curious, and one that can only reveal the hypocrisy of the conservative attack on liberal patriotism for what it is.

7

But Aren't Liberals Awfully Cavalier
about Protecting Our National Security?

One of the unchallenged assumptions of American politics is that conservatives are not merely more patriotic than liberals, but also far more attentive to protecting America from physical threats to its security. This, too, is a myth perpetrated by conservatives in the media that collapses with even rudimentary scrutiny. In the first place, it arbitrarily ignores certain significant threats in favor of others. Here the Enlightenment motto of "Dare to Know" serves to prepare liberals to face threats in a far more realistic fashion than the ideologically inclined right. Many conservatives, including those in the Bush administration, advocate willful ignorance of the threat of global warming, up to and including doctoring the evidence to convince Americans that it poses no danger. A secret 2004 report commissioned by an internal Pentagon think tank and reported on in the British newspaper the *Observer* warned that climate change over the next twenty years could result in a global catastrophe costing millions of lives in wars and natural disasters, and argued that "climate change should be elevated beyond a scientific debate to a US national security concern."[1] Nearly three years later, former national coordinator for counterterrorism Richard Clarke acknowledged, "The world's scientists and many national leaders worry that the world has passed the point of no return on global warming. If it has, then human damage to the ecosphere will cause more major cities to flood and make the planet significantly less conducive to human habitation—all over the lifetime of a child now in kindergarten."[2] Nevertheless, according to Drew Shindell, a physicist and climatologist at NASA's Goddard Institute for Space Studies, the agency's press releases about global warming "were watered down to the point where you wondered, Why would this capture anyone's interest?" Once, he notes, when he issued a report predicting rapid warming in Antarctica, the document ended up announcing, in effect, "that

Antarctica has a climate."[3] James Hansen, director of the Goddard Institute and one of the world's leading climate scientists, was frequently censored by Bush administration political appointees and prevented from telling the truth about the threat: that, without U.S. leadership in the area, global warming "would eventually leave the earth a different planet." Officials warned Hansen of "dire consequences" if he continued to make such statements, and he was instructed—by a twenty-four-year-old department press aide named George Deutsch, who was later discovered to have lied on his résumé about even having graduated college, but who had previously worked in the 2004 Bush campaign "war room" operation—to cancel an NPR interview. Hansen's example was the rule rather than the exception for federal scientists working on sensitive areas, as more than three-quarters of those surveyed reported they had personally experienced at least one incident of inappropriate political interference.[4]

Philip Cooney, former chief of staff at the White House Council on Environmental Quality, acknowledged at a House hearing in March 2007 that he purposely doctored the information he received from government scientists on climate change before releasing it, "to align these communications with the administration's stated policy."[5] Even after these outrages against both science and the security of the United States were brought to light, and the Intergovernmental Panel on Climate Change concluded that the evidence for global warming was "unequivocal," the American Enterprise Institute could be found offering grants of $10,000 (plus travel and expenses) or more to scientists who would be willing to try to undermine it.[6] The potential risks were reinforced by another report authored by several former senior U.S. military officers who warned that climate change "poses a serious threat to America's national security" and could be a tipping point that would further destabilize fragile regimes: "In already weakened states, extreme weather events, drought, flooding, sea level rise, retreating glaciers and the rapid spread of life-threatening diseases will themselves have likely effects: increased migrations, further weakened and failed states." Even so, the Bush White House sought to weaken language in a June 2007 G-8 summit communiqué that encouraged countries to reduce their greenhouse gas emissions.[7]

At the same time, Republicans in Congress were arguing that U.S. intelligence agencies should not even be asked to study the political, social, economic, and agricultural risks of global warming in the National Intelligence Estimate.[8] They did so over the objections of Michael McConnell, director of national intelligence, who judged the task to be "entirely appropriate."[9] In this matter, as in many others, one could easily conclude that conservatives were not simply ignorant of nonmilitary threats to our security, they were actively working to allow them to worsen.

The media has all too often served as the willing handmaiden of conservative attempts to minimize the seriousness of this imminent threat. As former vice president Al Gore has noted, a ten-year University of California study found that while there was essentially no disagreement among peer-reviewed scientific journal articles that global warming exists, another study found that 53 percent of mainstream newspaper articles disputed the global warming premise.[10] Quite a few conservative pundits appear eager simply to reject global warming either because they believe the propaganda they are peddling or because they think that such a politics would prejudice Americans against their agenda. For instance, National Review's Jonah Goldberg argues, with impressive solipsism, "There is no such thing as a 'reasonable' movement to prevent climate change because climate changes by definition. Saying we can prevent climate change is like saying we can prevent tides, tectonic drift, or rain. And no one would say any movement to stop rain is 'reasonable.'"[11]

One could say much the same about the conservative dismissal of the continuing crisis in and around the Horn of Africa. As Richard Clarke (among others) points out, the horrific humanitarian crisis in Darfur is but one "of a pox of conflicts that, together with HIV/AIDS, are depopulating parts of Africa and robbing it of potential wealth from mineral, oil and gas deposits. Wars have also raged in Chad, Congo, Liberia, Sierra Leone and Somalia."[12] But since the end of the Cold War, Africa barely registers in the conservatives' calculations. (The one exception would be the Christian conservatives who do seek to alleviate the AIDS crisis, but have objected to the most effective means of preventing its spread: condoms and family planning.) The idea that the AIDS epidemic, which is killing millions of people and creating a continentwide refugee crisis, has implications for the material well-being of the United States is outside the narrow parameters of the right-wing conception of national security. The result of conservatives' insistence on ignoring these threats—and others too numerous to mention—is nothing but an invitation to what would have been a preventable catastrophe. And one can say the same of all too many comparable issues.

To take the right-wingers on even their own narrow definitional terms of what constitutes patriotism does them little favor either. Consider how some of America's most prominent conservatives behaved in the now-infamous Niger yellowcake/Valerie Plame case, which so preoccupied Washington for nearly two years.

- *Vice President Cheney* instructed his aide I. Lewis Libby to destroy the credibility of former U.S. diplomat Joseph Wilson. Wilson had been sent by the CIA to the African nation of Niger after Cheney's own office had requested that such a mission be undertaken, in order to investigate claims that Niger had sold uranium to Iraq, but he did not return with the answer Cheney desired.

- *George W. Bush* commuted Libby's prison sentence to no time whatsoever in July 2007, only the fourth such sentence he had commuted since taking office nearly seven years earlier, having denied some four thousand other pleas. Regarding these cases, Bush had written—or to put it more accurately, Karen Hughes had approved Bush's ghostwriter's prose to be published under Bush's name—in his 1999 "memoir," *A Charge to Keep:* "In every case, I would ask: Is there any doubt about this individual's guilt or innocence? And, have the courts had ample opportunity to review all the legal issues in this case?" According to a study of these cases published by the *Atlantic Monthly,* Bush allowed executions to go forward in Texas that frequently failed to meet this standard.[13] And yet none of these conditions could be said to apply to I. Lewis Libby. Bush neither questioned the verdict nor gave any indication he believed him to be innocent. (Bush himself had appointed Judge Reggie B. Walton, whose sentence he overturned.) What's more, in order to prevent Libby from having to spend a night in jail, he intervened in the process before the courts could complete their review of Libby's appeal.[14] In doing so, Bush also ignored his own Justice Department, whose standards for "Consideration of Clemency Petitions" explicitly states: "Requests for commutation generally are not accepted unless and until a person has begun serving that sentence. Nor are commutation requests generally accepted from persons who are presently challenging their convictions or sentences through appeal or other court proceeding." Perhaps intending to be ironic, Bush used the debased language of Fox News to defend his action, calling it "a fair and balanced decision."[15]

- *Karl Rove*, an assistant to President Bush, likewise leaked Plame's name and CIA status to journalists, but was able to escape indictment.
- *Robert Novak*, the conservative journalist, was alone among the at least six professional journalists approached by Bush officials to prove willing to reveal Plame's identity and CIA status. Bill Harlow, the agency's spokesperson at the time, later testified to special counsel Patrick Fitzgerald that at least three days before Novak's column was published, he warned Novak, in the strongest possible terms, that Plame's name should not be made public. Novak ignored him and published anyway.[16]

Recall that it was George W. Bush's own father who, speaking at CIA headquarters in 1999, said, "I have nothing but contempt and anger for those who betray the trust by exposing the name of our sources. They are, in my view, the most insidious of traitors."[17] That view is consistent with that articulated by Defense Secretary Donald Rumsfeld, who told reporters, "Leaks put people's lives at risk. And I think that the people in any branch of government have an obligation to manage their mouths in a way that does not put people's lives at risk. Folks that leak and put people's lives at risk ought to be in jail."[18]

But of course, when it comes to conservative situational ethics, there are good leaks and bad leaks, even with regard to the most sensitive matters of national security. When Bush and company decided early on in their administration that investigative reporter Bob Woodward could be counted on to offer a sympathetic rendering of their war planning, the president gave him and his coauthor, Dan Balz, ninety minutes of interviews, often speaking candidly about classified information, and providing him with notes and minutes of National Security Council proceedings. "Certainly Richard Nixon would not have allowed reporters to question him like that. Bush's father [former president George Bush] wouldn't allow it. Clinton wouldn't allow it," Woodward observed at the time.[19] Why did they do it? Was it an attempt to cover up larger crimes by higher-ups? As the columnist E. J. Dionne asked once the indictment of Libby was announced, "Has anyone noticed that the cover-up worked?"[20] During his October 2005 announcement of Libby's indictment, special prosecutor Patrick Fitzgerald bemoaned the fact that his key witnesses, including Libby, delayed their testimony for over a year. But of course, October 2004 would have been before Bush was reelected.

Neither George W. Bush nor, indeed, any prominent American conservative condemned any of these actions. The *Wall Street Journal* editorial page announced that Karl Rove "deserves a prize" for being a "whistle-blower." The *Weekly Standard* decried in Libby's indictment what it termed a "strategy of criminalization . . . implemented to inflict defeat on conservatives," despite the mass of contrary evidence.[21] The editor in chief of the *New Republic*, neoconservative Martin Peretz, joined Libby's legal defense team and argued his case on the once-liberal magazine's weblog. Robert Novak retained his esteemed positions on the *Washington Post* editorial page and the allegedly liberal CNN, until he lost his composure on the latter and uttered profanities before walking off the set while the show was still on the air. (He was quickly picked up by Fox News.) The most influential members of the punditocracy attempted to shrug off both the actions of the guilty men and their implications. Pundit "dean" David Broder called it "a tempest in a teapot." When "all of the facts come out in this case, it's going to be laughable because the consequences are not that great," suggested Bob Woodward. Novak himself complained that the controversy was based on "little elitist issues that don't bother most of the people."[22] Any fair examination of the case reveals the fact that it wasn't "elitism" that motivated those in the CIA and elsewhere to demand the truth in the Plame investigation, but patriotism.

Why Are Liberals So Damn Elitist?

As Robert Novak's self-serving comment in the previous chapter suggests, undoubtedly the most frequent charge one hears against liberals in America today is that of "elitism." It is not that the charge lacks any truth; some liberals are indeed "elitists." But what, one wonders, is ultimately so bad about elitism? Do conservatives really mean to argue that the functioning of a society of roughly three hundred million people does not require elites to help manage its affairs? And shouldn't these elites have certain qualifications—or some form of expertise—to help them to guide their fellow citizens in areas where they enjoy a particular competence? Many liberals do believe in contributing their talents to improve society; as early as 1935 John Dewey argued for the need for liberalism "to assume the responsibility for making it clear that intelligence is a social asset."[1] Though it can be easily abused, as can almost any political ideal, the notion itself hardly seems objectionable on its face.

Was there any other principle more dear to the founders of this nation's republican government than what Thomas Jefferson called "an aristocracy of the mind"? Conservatives pretend not to understand what John Judis has called the "paradox of American democracy": the fact that to function properly it requires effective, disinterested elites. Elites work best when they are visible and influential, and they are indeed often privileged and well connected. But if they can stand above the fray of clashing interests and parties, they can provide a democratic nation with a dose of pragmatism, pluralism, and, in some cases, legitimacy to accomplish politically difficult but necessary tasks.[2]

Consider the alternative. Look, for instance, at the way that cronyism, in the absence of qualification, undermines decency in governance. The

Bush administration is rife with such examples in virtually every cabinet department, but let's look at one such appointment. Before Monica Goodling resigned and took the Fifth Amendment before Congress, she rose to be the third most powerful person in the U.S. Justice Department at the age of just thirty-three. Though she had never worked a day as a prosecutor, she was given the responsibility of assessing the job performance of all ninety-five U.S. attorneys. "How do you get to be such a top dog at thirty-three?" asks the comedian/commentator Bill Maher. "By acing Harvard, or winning scholarship prizes? No, Goodling did her undergraduate work at Messiah College—and then went on to attend Pat Robertson's law school."[3]

Goodling was indeed one of more than 150 graduates of Robertson's Regent University (which shares a campus with Robertson's Christian Broadcasting Network studios and was originally named after it) working in the federal government under George W. Bush—making his administration, as Maher noted, the first to be populated by so many graduates of a school founded as an adjunct to a television network. Regent's brochure promises to provide "Christian leadership to change the world," but it ranks "fourth-tier" in *U.S. News & World Report*'s annual assessment of U.S. colleges. Goodling apparently took the charge to "change the world" seriously enough to ensure that only right-wing hacks—regardless of qualification—were considered eligible to enforce the laws of the United States. Questions Goodling was known to ask potential U.S. attorneys included "Which Supreme Court justice do you most admire and why? Which legislator do you most admire and why? And which president do you most admire and why?" Not to mention "Have you ever cheated on your wife?" She also complained when staff members in Puerto Rico used rap music in a public service announcement intended to discourage gun crime because "that kind of music glorifies violence."[4]

If you find yourself wondering how Iraq happened, how Katrina was botched, or how U.S. economic and environmental policies were so profoundly mismanaged by the Bush administration, imagine a government staffed by all too many Goodlings, "Brownies," and Doug Feiths—whom former chief of U.S. Central Command General Tommy Franks termed "the fucking stupidest guy on the face of the earth"—serving the Bushes, the Cheneys, and the Rumsfelds.[5] Perhaps a more useful question would be why it is that the ultimately contentless accusation of elitism—a quality that is usually considered complimentary in the worlds of, say, baseball, law, medicine, and so on—can be so confidently hung around the necks of liberals when conservatives are every bit as—if not more—attached to the very same "elitist" advantages they so decry in liberals. One of my own favorite examples of this tendency is a minor-league right-wing pundit named Russ Smith, whose wealthy family bought him a small, alternative newspaper in New York called the *New York Press*. Before losing millions on the project and being forced to sell, Smith wrote a press column under the pseudonym "Mugger" and developed a kind of obsession with the author of this book, whom he inevitably referred to as a "wealthy liberal," or a "wealthy left-wing pundit," or even a "foie gras devotee." Are my political views somehow less reliable because of my alleged culinary tastes? And what, for goodness' sake, is the otherwise unemployable scion of a wealthy publishing family doing attacking the alleged "wealth" of a liberal writer who earns his own modest living, as if that living somehow undermined the validity of his views? The idea appears to be that liberals have no right to live above the poverty level, lest their work be infected by elitism. Still, somehow, that idea continues to work.

The contemporary conservative obsession with the "liberal elite" has its origin, as Geoffrey Nunberg reminds us, in the campaign of 1964, when Ronald Reagan crisscrossed the country in support of Barry Goldwater's presidential aspirations, accusing liberals of believing that "an intellectual elite in a far-distant capital can plan our lives for us better than we can plan them ourselves." Richard Nixon took up the cudgel in his second State of the Union speech, complaining that "a bureaucratic elite in Washington knows best what is best for people everywhere." But it was Nixon's vice president, Spiro Agnew, who, aided by speechwriters Pat Buchanan and William Safire, showed right-wingers what political potential lay in this line of attack, with his orgies of alliteration regarding the evildoings of various "pusillanimous pussyfooters," "hopeless hysterical hypochondriacs of history," "nattering nabobs of negativism," and "effete corps of impudent snobs," to pick just a few of his favorite epithets for liberal opponents in the media and academia.[6]

Since then, no right-wing campaign has been complete without some form of repudiation of what former vice president Dan Quayle named the liberal "cultural elite," whose avowed purpose is to undermine all that is admirable and virtuous in Middle America, or as Quayle termed it, "the rest of us."[7] (Asked to define the evildoers, Quayle responded, "They know who they are.")[8] Quayle's addition of the word *cultural* to *elite*, coupled with his attack on a popular television character, single mom/anchorwoman Murphy Brown, was a stroke of genuine genius, as it allowed conservatives to continue to feel themselves oppressed even as they gained control of virtually all of the levers of political power in the United States and much of the news media. Liberals' power, conservatives continue to insist, trumps political power because we allegedly control the "culture." Today it is all but impossible to hear the word *liberal* without the word *elite* attached.

It's hard to know exactly what conservatives mean by the accusation of elitism, as it appears to fit almost any occasion. As Michael Kinsley once noted of Newt Gingrich, conservatives tend to use the term as an all-purpose epithet. For Gingrich it appeared to convey

> little more than someone or something he doesn't like. Just since the election he has applied the term to directors of art museums ("self-selected elites using your tax money and my tax money to pay off their friends"), to the Bipartisan Entitlement Reform Commission ("driven by elite values"), to people who send e-mail messages supportive of President Clinton ("urbanites make up the Internet elite," according to a Gingrich spokesman) and, of course, time and again, to the "elite media" or "media elite."[9]

If you examine the definitions offered by elitism's accusers, the crime is apparently one of mind, akin to such offenses as "bourgeois sentimentality" or "rootless cosmopolitanism" in the Stalinist Soviet Union. Rush

Limbaugh posited his own success as an example of what he termed "middle America's growing rejection of the elites," which he defines as "professionals'" and "experts," including "the medical elites, the sociological elites, the education elites, the legal elites, the science elites . . . and the ideas this bunch promotes through the media."[10] Former Watergate criminal G. Gordon Liddy, who likes to instruct his talk-show listeners on the most effective manner in which to murder U.S. government agents—"head shots, head shots," he suggests—explains the "elitist/rest of us" divide thusly:

> There exists in this country an elite that believes itself entitled to tell the rest of us what we may and may not do—for our own good, of course. These left-of-center, Ivy-educated molders of public opinion are concentrated in the mass news media, the entertainment business, academia, the pundit corps, and the legislative, judicial, and administrative government bureaucracies. Call it the divine right of policy wonks. There people feed on the great American middle class, who do the actual work of this country and make it all happen. They bleed us with an income tax rate not seen since we were fighting for our lives in the middle of World War II; they charge us top dollar at the box office for movies that assail and undermine the values we are attempting to inculcate in our children.[11]

The conservative pundit Peggy Noonan identifies "America's elite" as "the politicians, wise men, think-tank experts, academics, magazine and editorial-page editors, big-city columnists, TV commentators" who had the temerity to oppose Bush's ruinous war in Iraq. The qualities of the "big and real America," from which George W. Bush (of Harvard, Yale, and Andover) hails, are those that liberal elites would recognize only as native to "another America, and boy has it endured. It just won a war. [Noonan was writing in early 2003, before the catastrophe that Iraq has become was apparent to all.] Its newest generation is rising, and its members are impressive. They came from a bigger America and a realer one—a healthy and vibrant place full of religious feeling and cultural energy and Bible study and garage bands and sports-love and mom-love and sophistication and normality."[12]

Conservatives did not, of course, wish to do away with "elites." They merely wanted to replace them with their own. As John Judis pointed out in his book-length study, "The new groups, in contrast to the old, did not seek to be above class, party and ideology. On the contrary, they were openly pro-business and conservative. . . . They did not seek to mediate conflicts but to take one side. They had no ties to labor unions or to the environmental, consumer or civil rights movements that had emerged in the sixties, but only to the business counteroffensive against them. They did not seek to produce objective results by means of social science. On the contrary, they were willing to use social science to achieve partisan results . . . they undermined what it meant for a country to have an elite."[13]

Back in 1943, the philosopher Sidney Hook warned against an analogous tendency he discerned in fanatical fascists and Communists:

> The "truth" is regarded as possessing the same legitimacy as the considered judgment that finds no evidence for the feeling and uncovers its root in a personal aberration. After all is it not the case that every heresy-hunting bigot and hallucinated fanatic is convinced that there is a truth in the feelings, visions and passions that run riot within him? Hitler is not the only one for whom questions of evidence are incidental or impertinent where his feelings are concerned. If the voice of feeling cannot be mistaken, differences would be invitations to battle, the ravings of an insane mind could legitimately claim to be prophecies of things to come. It is not only as a defense against the marginally sane that we need the safeguards of critical scientific method. Every vested interest in social life, every inequitable privilege, every "truth" promulgated as a national, class or racial truth, likewise denies the competence of scientific inquiry to evaluate its claims.[14]

In observing the members of the conservative elite denouncing "elitists," it can be difficult to tell your players without the proverbial score-card. For instance, the radio talk-show host and former conservative cable host Laura Ingraham has written an entire book about the dangers posed by liberal elites, entitled *Shut Up & Sing: How Elites from Hollywood, Politics, and the Media Are Subverting America.* In it, this daughter of a Connecticut lawyer, and graduate of Dartmouth and the University of Virginia Law School, who now lives in an expensive home in Washington, D.C., distinguishes between liberal elitists and those whom she terms "true Americans." She begins her treatise by explaining who these "elite Americans" are and what they think: "They think we're stupid. They think our patriotism is stupid. They think our churchgoing is stupid. They think having more than two children is stupid. They think where we live—anywhere but near or in a few major cities—is stupid. They think our SUVs are stupid. They think owning a gun is stupid. They think our abiding belief in the goodness of America and its founding principles is stupid."

In Ingraham's case, as in many others, one detects a strain of anti-Semitism in her insistent elite-bashing. During the flap over Mel Gibson's *Passion of the Christ*—more about which below—Ingraham announced, "I want to see any movie that drives the anti-Christian entertainment elite crazy."[15] Presumably Ingraham did not mean to imply that this "anti-Christian entertainment elite" was mostly made up of Muslims, Hindus, Sikhs, or Scientologists.

Ingraham is joined in her crusade by another ex-MSNBC pundette, the second-generation Connecticut lawyer and Cornell University alumna Ann Coulter, who rhapsodizes about red-state denizens, as Nunberg notes, "with the effusiveness of a fifth-grader reporting on a zoo visit." "I loved Kansas City! It's my favorite place in the world. . . . It's the opposite of this town. They're Americans, they're so great, they're rooting for America!" "I love Texas Republicans! . . . Americans are so cool!"[16] "Queens, baseball games—those are my people. American people."[17] Like Ingraham, Coulter distinguishes between "us" and "them" on the basis of attitude, rather than income, though the multimillionaire does allow that "the whole point of being a liberal is to feel superior to people with less money." She continues:

> They promote immoral destructive behavior because they are snobs, they embrace criminals because they are snobs, they oppose tax cuts because they are snobs. Every pernicious idea to come down the pike is

instantly embraced by liberals to show how powerful they are. Liberals hate society and want to bring it down to reinforce their sense of invincibility. Secure in the knowledge that their beachfront haciendas will still be standing when the smoke clears, they giddily fiddle with the little people's morals.[18]

John Podhoretz, the son of neoconservatism's second couple, Norman Podhoretz and Midge Decter,[19] who attended elite private schools and the University of Chicago before his father's political connections helped him secure jobs in the media empires of Sun Myung Moon and Rupert Murdoch, also professes to see America through rose-hued glasses. "Bush Red is a simpler place," he explains, on the basis of a visit to Las Vegas. It's a land "where people mourn the death of NASCAR champion Dale Earnhardt, root lustily for their teams, go to church, and find comfort in old-fashioned verities."[20] His comrade-in-anti-intellectual-arms, former CBS News reporter Bernard Goldberg, who has spent a career working within what conservatives would call the "liberal media elite" and who wrote a book comparing his former friend Dan Rather to a "prison bitch," has sworn off all association with liberals even when he agrees with them, he says, "because of their elitism. They look down their snobby noses at ordinary Americans who eat at Red Lobster or because they like to bowl or they go to church on a regular basis or because they fly the flag on the Fourth of July."[21]

Michael Ledeen, Washington-based *National Review* contributor and neoconservative think-tank denizen, offered up a classic of the genre in September 2007, when he bragged of a road trip he took with his wife "to Indianapolis for a Toby Keith concert, where [they] partied with something like 25,000 happy rednecks." Ledeen paid tribute to Keith as a "a wonderful performer," not least because of his deeply moving patriotic songs like "American Soldier," "Courtesy of the Red, White and Blue," "The Taliban," and so on, but he could not help adding how "great" it was to be among "rednecks, a.k.a. real Americans," and "to see Toby say 'don't ever apologize for your patriotism,' and then lift the middle finger of his right hand to the skies and say, 'F*** 'Em!'" This profanity-laced salutation proved a particularly welcome antidote in the Ledeen household to what he diagnosed as the "disgusting anti-Americanism in Washington," and so he recommended to his conservative readers, "You ought to try it. Does wonders for the spirit."[22] Alas, what nobody told the American Enterprise Institute resident scholar was the fact that "happy redneck" Toby Keith was actually a proud, card-carrying Democrat and a committed opponent of the wars championed by Ledeen and company in the AEI's decidedly inner-Beltway offices.

In red-state America, explains the slumming blue stater David Brooks, "the self is small"; whereas in blue-state America, "the self is uncommonly large."[23] Unlike the citizens of the states that voted for Al Gore, according to Andrew Sullivan, they can even be trusted not to betray their country on behalf of Islamic terrorists. While unelite America is wonderful in every way, it's just not a place where a Laura Ingraham or Rush Limbaugh or Bernard Goldberg or Ann Coulter or John Podhoretz or Newt Gingrich or Peggy Noonan or Andrew Sullivan or Michael Ledeen or David Brooks would ever choose to live.

An additionally telling aspect of the conservatives' attack on liberal elitism is their intense attachment to the very same elite liberal academic institutions they profess to detest. When George Bush tried to nominate his personal lawyer, Harriet Miers, a graduate of Southern Methodist University Law School, to the Supreme Court, conservatives had a collective conniption fit over her meager credentials. *National Review*'s Ramesh Ponnuru called her "an inspiring testament to the diversity of the president's cronies." Former Bush speechwriter David Frum complained that for his old boss "to take a hazard on anything other than a known quantity of the highest intellectual and personal excellence" was "simply reckless."[24] It was "an unserious nomination," whined John Podhoretz.[25] "I'm beginning to think that this appointment was an expression of the president's contempt for the conservative intelligentsia," Andrew Sullivan complained. To top it all off, Robert Bork, the Yale man whose extremist views kept him off the Court in 1987, called the nomination "a slap in the face to the conservatives who've been building a conservative legal movement for 20 years."[26]

No complaint was heard from these same firebreathers, however, when Bush caved in to their demands and dumped Miers for Princeton and Yale Law alum Samuel Alito. (This was the same president, you'll recall, who nominated Ben Bernanke, a Princeton economist, to be chairman of the Federal Reserve and later chose John G. Roberts of Harvard College and Harvard Law School to be chief justice of the United States.) Other commentators have noticed that in the antielitist Bush administration, the plum positions are dominated by graduates of Swarthmore, Stanford, Harvard, Yale, and Andover. One can see exactly the same dynamic at work on Bush's national security team. When Bush finally admitted the catastrophic direction his war plans had taken in Iraq, he kept Condoleezza Rice (PhD, Stanford University), fired Donald Rumsfeld (BA, Princeton) and put Robert Gates (PhD, Georgetown University) in his place, and named General David H. Petraeus head of U.S. forces there. The latter earned a PhD from Princeton. He was joined by Colonel Michael J. Meese (ditto) and what Carter Malkasian, who has advised Marine Corps commanders in Iraq on counterinsurgency and himself holds an Oxford doctorate (with a degree in the history of war), noted was the most "highly educated" set of advisers a U.S. commander had ever assembled—at least in Malkasian's recollection.[27] According to conservative antielitist prejudices, such educational contamination should disqualify a man from service, rather than recommend him.

Given the transparent hypocrisy of the "liberal elitist" charge, coupled with its shifting but always not quite definable content, one cannot help but be awed by the effectiveness with which it is wielded. The simplest explanation is that "elitism" has come to be perceived as a legitimate attack word by the right, without anyone really being able to define why. Remember: It's not about where you live, how much money you have, how many security guards you regularly employ, where you summer, what you drive, what you drive when you're driving whatever else you drive when you're not driving that, where you went to school, or where you think people should have gone to school. Conservatives are as one with the people they so disdain on all of those scores. Rather, it has simply become a contentless cudgel with which to beat back one's political opponents, without the trouble of engaging their arguments. Geoffrey Nunberg notes that right-wingers have had remarkable success in pigeonholing liberalism as a "white upper-middle-class affectation."

> Just look, for example, at the way liberals are referred to in the media, even in the New York Times and the Los Angeles Times. Wherever you look, the liberal label is almost exclusively reserved for middle-class whites. Phrases like working-class liberals, Hispanic liberals, and black liberals are virtually nonexistent, though conservative is frequently used to describe members of all those groups. When the media are referring to members of the working class or minority groups who vote left-of-center, they invariably describe them as Democrats, with the implication that their political choices are shaped by economic self-interest or traditional party loyalty, rather than by any deep commitment to liberal ideals. It's as if you can't count as a liberal unless you can afford the lifestyle. Liberalism is treated less as a political credo than the outward expression of a particular social identity, like a predilection for granite counter-tops and bottled water.[28]

It's quite a trick these right-wingers have pulled off, one that might even impress George Orwell. When they dislike a position, they deride it as "elitist," irrespective of the fact that it is supported by a majority of Americans. Personally, they enjoy exactly the same advantages as liberal elitists, but they insist that this does not matter, because they think about them differently. When asked to define just what is so awful about the way liberals think, they fall back on a series of unproven—and ultimately unprovable—accusations of the kind made by totalitarian regimes against their dissidents. Somehow they've manage to convince the so-called liberal media to repeat these same accusations, despite the rather inconvenient fact that they make no sense. In the meantime, they've managed to discredit virtually all of the people to whom they can successfully attach their wholly meaningless tag. It may not make much sense, but as the folks at American Express have taught us, success is its own reward.

9

Why Do Liberals Love
Hollywood Smut Peddlers?

Conservative disgust at liberals in particular and Democrats in general for their embrace of the entertainment industry is truly a wonder to behold. Nothing seems to goose their gander quite so much as a picture of some liberal politician poolside with Warren Beatty or Sharon Stone. No matter that these horrible Hollywood heathens automatically morph into admirable political visionaries just as soon as they become Republicans. Ronald Reagan, it turns out, was not the exception to the rule, but its template. Arnold Schwarzenegger is now revered as a political phenomenon and potential president (despite a constitutional prohibition against naturalized and foreign-born Americans holding that office). Ron Silver, who supported Bush, was not only given a speaking spot at the Republican convention, but appointed to a position in the country's national security apparatus.[1] Another Republican actor/politician, Fred Thompson, ran for president in 2008 and actually announced his candidacy in Hollywood on *The Tonight Show,* to say nothing of the hallowed position occupied by Charlton Heston. Even Sonny Bono managed, somehow, to make himself kosher for conservatives.

And yet consider the hysterical language conservatives routinely employ when pontificating about Hollywood. L. Brent Bozell III, of the conservative Media Research Center in Washington, complains of "political dilettantes . . . leftist celebrities" who are "America-haters" and jokes about "congressional leaders lauding their faxes from 'advisers' whose qualifications for office include starring in *Hello Dolly* and *The*

Prince of Tides." When it was revealed that Al Gore consulted with the extremely knowledgeable former actor Rob Reiner before giving a speech on Iraq, columnist Charles Krauthammer joshed that while Bush was relying on the likes of Cheney, Powell, Rice, and Rumsfeld, Gore was "huddling with Meathead." Andrew Sullivan complained that "the Hollywood Left" lost the election for John Kerry. The level of vituperation can become so extreme that one begins to wonder what the issue really is. *Wall Street Journal* media critic Dorothy Rabinowitz denounces the world of Hollywood political liberalism as one of "elitist scum" who "live in . . . an alternate revolting universe." Bill O'Reilly goes her one better, comparing Hollywood liberals' access to the "profitable and pervasive" "celebrity media" to that of a "Leni Riefenstahl Third Reich propaganda proposition, where what they say and do is put in everybody's face."[2] Back in 1996 Bob Dole tried to make this argument a centerpiece of his presidential campaign. "Our popular culture," he complained just as the fight was getting under way, "threatens to undermine our character as a nation."[3]

According to the logic of this argument, it is the liberals' embrace of Hollywood that has doomed their hopes of earning the trust of the public at large. Immediately following the 2004 elections, the *Wall Street Journal* editorial page asked, "Who are George Soros, Michael Moore, Tim Robbins, Susan Sontag, Teresa Heinz Kerry and all these other self-anointed spokespersons for everything good and true? And what does a party that is dominated by a loose coalition of the coastal intelligentsia, billionaires with too much spare time, the trial lawyers' association, the Hollywood Actors' Guild, rock stars and unionized labor have in common with what's quaintly known as Middle America? The majority's answers were (a) not us; and (b) not a whole lot."[4] Writing in the *Boston Globe,* reporter Scot Lehigh offers up the selfsame conventional wisdom. In a column entitled "Say Goodbye to Hollywood," Lehigh insisted, "The attitudes and behavior of the film-industry elite are out of sync with much of the country, and linking the party with the West Coast glitterati makes national Democrats suspect with too many voters. . . . Now, the celebrities' contempt may well mirror the sentiment of confirmed Democrats. But it was hardly the way to win undecided votes. The sooner the Democrats come to realize those points, the better their future prospects will be."[5]

The constant refrain that Hollywood is "out of sync" with, and filled with "contempt" for, regular folk is evidence of a profound difference between its political participation and that of other wealthy communities like Wall Street, Grosse Point, or even Silicon Valley. Yes, Barbra Streisand's life bears little resemblance to yours or mine. But this is less a function of her location than of her celebrity and economic power. And conservatives, the vast majority of whose life experiences are no closer to those of "average Americans" than are Ms. Streisand's, suffer from no reticence in the exploitation of their own celebrity or economic power. Hollywood political life is, in fact, dominated by liberals, but no more so than, say, Houston's is dominated by conservatives. Where the disjunction between wealthy Hollywood political players and wealthy non-Hollywood political players does exist, it redounds, I think, to the moral benefit of the former, as Hollywood is almost alone in American political life in giving away its money to the candidates in whose visions it believes, regardless of economic self-interest. The mainstream media has a difficult time comprehending the distinction. In reporting on the power of political contributions during the 2004 elections, *Business Week*, for instance, cited Hollywood environmental activist Laurie David's seeking "tougher anti-pollution laws if Kerry wins in November" versus "Wall Street lobby[ing] for new retirement savings plans if Bush triumphs," and concluded, "in any case, the special interests can be expected to call in their chits one way or the other." In fact, the term *special interest* actually becomes oxymoronic when applied to lobbying for clean air and water, particularly when compared with congressionally created retirement plans designed to line the pockets of Wall Street contributors. Precisely why so many people in the media believe that Americans find it less objectionable for the CEO of GM to lobby for relaxed auto-emission standards than for an actor or director to contribute to a campaign for clean air is not immediately apparent.

Part of the confusion arises from the fact that Americans' insatiable fascination with all things celebrity creates a curious amalgam of conundrums for both those who wish to practice politics and those whose job it is to report and explain it. While even C-list stars can cause a mini-panic in a Capitol Hill hearing room, "Hollywood," the industry, is routinely reviled there. Conservatives have good reason to demonize the industry, not only because of their cultural objections to the messages they believe they see purveyed regarding so-called traditional values but also because of the money it is pouring into the other side's coffers. In this regard, Hollywood celebrities perform a function similar to that of unions and trial lawyers, the other two pillars of Democratic fund-raising. Those in the media would have a stronger case for objecting to Hollywood politicking were it not their own institutions that are providing the breathless coverage of the star in question's latest pronouncement. As the British actor Daniel Day-Lewis complains, "The media are sick and tired of people in my profession giving their opinion, and yet you're asking me my opinion. And when I give it, you'll say, 'Why doesn't he shut up?'"[6]

The real problem the right wing has with Hollywood is the fact that its cultural and financial center of gravity is liberally located (just as the analogous axes of Houston or Dallas turn rightward). Because these same liberals are also wealthy and pampered and not always perfectly well informed on all the issues upon which they opine—much like the rich everywhere else—they are supposed to embrace the right-wing politics that would benefit their economic self-interest and leave the opinion business to the professionals. (The vast majority of American Jews, who—as the saying goes, "earn like Episcopalians but vote like Puerto Ricans"—are also a problem for conservatives for exactly this reason; and the Jewishness of Hollywood is hardly irrelevant to either side of this equation. More on this below.)

It is true that, Hollywood's wealth notwithstanding, its politics are by and large liberal. Like an Ivy League humanities department or a folk-singers' convention, Hollywood attracts those kinds of people. They give their dollars to protect the environment, to secure a woman's right to choose, to promote the rights of gay people to enjoy the same rights as the rest of us, to help prevent the spread of AIDS in Africa, and to oppose virtually every aspect of President Bush's foreign policy. By mainstream American political standards, the groups that compete with one another to be *the* group in Hollywood—the National Resources Defense Council, the American Civil Liberties Union, People for the American Way, Artists for a New South Africa—are all also quite liberal. In Hollywood circles, though, supporting such groups is no more controversial than heading up a campaign for a cancer clinic in Nashville or for the Museum of Modern Art in New York. To many in the media—and certainly to conservative critics—this fact alone inspires fear and loathing. Part of the reason is pure professional laziness. It doesn't exactly require Bob Woodward to find a Hollywood star whose dumb remarks about politics can provide endless fodder. (Among my own favorites in this category was the pop singer Jessica Simpson's comment to Gale Norton, who had been introduced to her as the secretary of the interior: "You've done a nice job decorating the White House," though this is closely rivaled by Britney Spears's advice to Americans that we should take on trust anything said by President George W. Bush.) But since when are current-events quizzes required to make political donations or even political pronouncements? Do conservatives give their fund-raisers such examinations? Perhaps uniquely among the tiny percentage of Americans who do contribute large amounts of money to political campaigns—and the number who give a thousand dollars or more to any candidate hovers around one-quarter of 1 percent of the population—Hollywood's contributions do not buy the giver anything, at least nothing so concrete as a tax break or a regulation relaxation.[7] A March 2004 report by Public Citizen found that of the 416 Bush campaign "Rangers" and "Pioneers"— donors who had raised $200,000 and $100,000 respectively—90 percent represented the special interests of America's most powerful corporations. The top six, CEOs all, enjoyed an average additional income of $270,000 each in 2003 alone, merely on the basis of their personal tax reductions. No fewer than sixty-one of Bush's top moneymen enjoyed direct benefits for their businesses owing to the twin boondoggles of the 2003 Medicare prescription-drug bill and the giant 2004 energy bill.[8]

Former Clinton adviser Paul Begala recalls, however, that during all his time in the White House, meeting with hundreds if not thousands of powerful contributors, "Nine-nine point five percent of them were asking me for something designed to put money in their own pockets. Hollywood people were the only big givers who never asked for anything but that we try to make America a better country, as they saw it." Billionaire entertainment mogul David Geffen, for example, raised in the neighborhood of $20 million for the president and his party during the Clinton years, perhaps as much as anyone in the United States. He threw large fund-raisers at his home as well as small, billionaire-only dinner parties, where he would provide access to Clinton to various entertainment-industry moguls. After the dinners Geffen would frequently call his guests for contributions. According to his biographer Thomas King, two such dinners, which included just twenty-four guests, raised a total of $2 million. But instead of seeking special favors from the president, they actually lobbied him not to give them any. One night at Geffen's Malibu beach house, Geffen brought nine or ten of these guests together to tell the president not to cut the capital gains tax: "We've already got enough. We don't need this too."[9] Have we become so cynical a society that altruism is itself reason for contempt?

Liberals do, indeed, pay a political price for the media's insistence on using Hollywood celebrities as emblems of liberalism. As Thomas Frank points out, this too is counterproductive. When tied to movie stars who go to charity balls for causes like animal rights and the environment, all the while instructing "real people" how to behave, liberalism becomes a politics "of shallow appearances, of fatuous self-righteousness." A politics in which "the beautiful and the wellborn tell the unwashed and the beaten-down and the funny-looking how they ought to behave, how they should stop being racist or homophobes, how they should be better people," is not a politics likely to be attractive to large numbers of people.[10] (In mocking this tendency, a wonderful Tom Tomorrow cartoon features the likeness of yours truly, as a stand-in for a textbook liberal elitist, declaring, "Barbra Streisand is my president.") This problem is part of the larger one of the division of liberals' primary constituencies: working-class people and well-educated, affluent professionals. It is also in some measure a result of the fact that elections in America are fantastically expensive, and that money has to be found somewhere. Hollywood has it, and liberal candidates need it. The story is no different for Republicans and the oil and gas industry, save for the fact that they do not provide such fascinating subjects for journalists. A sensible campaign-finance reform law would largely solve this problem, since liberal candidates could communicate with their constituencies without having to find millions of dollars to do so. Not surprisingly, the liberals in Hollywood would support it. I've been invited to speak on this very topic at the home of some people who enjoy outsize influence in politics owing to their wealth. My assigned topic was "Reducing the power of money in politics."

10

When Will Liberals Stop Undermining America's Values and Poisoning the Minds of Its Youth?

Complaints about Hollywood's—and therefore liberalism's—introduction of cultural pollution into the national ecosystem reached a comic crescendo following "Super Sunday" 2004. Experiencing what would soon become the most famous "wardrobe malfunction" since Lady Godiva, thirty-six-year-old singer Janet Jackson had her top ripped off at the end of a musical number by the younger pop star Justin Timberlake, revealing her breast—though not her entire nipple, which was covered by a silver shield—and thus setting off a political firestorm. Then–New York Times conservative columnist William Safire termed it "the social-political event of the past year," and it certainly did get the media excited. TiVo's technology revealed a 180 percent spike in viewership, a far greater number than was inspired by the commercials on the same program (including those that featured horse flatulence, bestiality, and a dog biting a man's penis). A second, albeit smaller, cultural crisis—also by coincidence considered shocking to football viewers—took place one Monday evening during a preview for ABC's Desperate Housewives, when one of its stars, Nicollette Sheridan, dropped her towel in a team's locker room. Her back was to the camera and her backside off-camera, but she did this for the enjoyment of a black man, NFL wide receiver Terrell Owens.

As with Ms. Jackson's barely visible nipple, the NFL locker-room commercial was rebroadcast around the clock, presumably shocking everyone over and over and over again. Rush Limbaugh, noted a bemused Frank Rich, "taking a break from the legal deliberations of his drug rap and third divorce, set the hysterical tone. 'I was stunned!' he told his listeners. 'I literally could not believe what I had seen.'" He then recommended that his audience stun themselves: "At various places on the Net you can see the video." "People were so outraged they had to see it ten times," joked then–CNN anchor Aaron Brown.[1] In 2006 it was announced that the Jackson incident was the "Most Searched in Internet History," and was cited as the "Most Searched for News Item" in the *Guinness Book of World Records*.[2]

Meanwhile the FCC, led by its chairman, Michael Powell, did a total turnaround on the issue of alleged "obscenity." After network fines for Ms. Jackson's performance were levied at $550,000, FCC fines for dirty words and exposed butt cheeks skyrocketed to nearly $8 million in 2004, up from just $440,000 the year before and only $48,000 in 2000. Powell told a congressional committee that the change was necessitated by a "dramatic rise in public concern and outrage about what is being broadcast into their homes," and cited an exponential increase in the number of complaints the FCC had received, reaching 240,000 in 2003 and more than a million in 2004, up from just 400 two years earlier.[3]

At the same time, conservative censors were diligently defending Americans from the threat of off-screen lesbians visited by animated PBS bunnies. Early in George W. Bush's second term, Education Secretary Margaret Spellings—who hadn't even been officially sworn in to the cabinet yet but apparently sensed a need for emergency action—bravely threatened public television with a sharp cut in funding if it proceeded to broadcast a planned episode of the children's cartoon *Postcards from Buster,* in which an anthropomorphic animated rabbit paid a visit to a pair of mothers—who never actually appeared on-screen—while traveling to Vermont to learn how to make maple syrup. In previous episodes, Buster had dropped in on the homes of Muslims, Mormons, Orthodox Jews, and Pentecostal Christians, but the gay couple—even when not identified as such to the audience—proved to be a matter of alarm to the secretary of education. "Many parents would not want their young children exposed to the lifestyles portrayed in this episode," Ms. Spellings wrote in her threatening letter to then–PBS chief Pat Mitchell.[4] From a personal standpoint, however, it was an odd campaign for Spellings, a single mother of two, to undertake. It was also difficult to defend from a scientific standpoint. While President Bush has explained to the nation that "studies have shown that the ideal is where a child is being raised by a man and a woman," as the New York Times reported, "There is no scientific evidence that children raised by gay couples do any worse."[5]

But daring to know the scientific data was apparently not on Spellings's personal or political agenda. The powerful right-wing preacher James Dobson, who heads up Focus on the Family, has often complained of the "brainwashing of children by homosexual advocacy groups." Robert Knight, director of Concerned Women for America's Culture and Family Institute, also protested "children homosexualized in the name of 'education,'" and Fox anchor Bill O'Reilly joined in, naturally, comparing the bunny couple to "a bigamy situation in Utah" or "an S&M thing in the East Village [of New York City]."[6]

PBS has also advised member stations to air a bowdlerized version of a Frontline documentary about the war in Iraq because the uncut version featured soldiers swearing.[7] At around the same time, sixty-five ABC affiliates refused to show Saving Private Ryan despite the fact that the film had been aired—unedited—in 2001 and 2002. (In its stead they programmed Return to Mayberry.) The episode recalled one four years earlier in which conservative Republican congressman (now senator) Tom Coburn of Colorado attacked NBC for encouraging "irresponsible sexual behavior" and taking "network TV to an all-time low with full frontal nudity, violence and profanity being shown in our homes." The offense? Televising Schindler's List.[8] In the aftermath of these attacks, Fox felt compelled to pixilate a baby's bare bottom in a rerun of the cartoon series Family Guy. Even NBC's presentation of the 2004 Olympics, which featured actors in body suits to simulate ancient Greek statues, became the target of an FCC investigation.[9]

The conservative reaction to the PBS threat has recently gone beyond even censorship to McCarthyism. In July 2006 a young woman named Melanie Martinez, who hosted a kids' program called The Good Night Show, found herself fired because, six years earlier, she had appeared in two funny but decidedly nonpornographic videos spoofing abstinence education.[10]

It's not merely bad words, body parts, imaginary cartoon bunnies, and privately made satires that offend the new censors; it's science itself. The *New York Times* has reported that some Imax theaters—even those in science centers—will no longer show Darwinian documentaries like *Galápagos* or *Volcanoes of the Deep Sea* for fear of antagonizing faith-based activists who find evolution offensive.[11] When New York's American Museum of Natural History presented its historic Charles Darwin exhibition in 2005, it could not find a single corporate sponsor. Meanwhile, near Cincinnati, the "Creationist Museum," which explains the creation of the universe according to a literal interpretation of the Bible, announced that it had raised $7 million in donations.[12] The effects of these campaigns are unknown, as we have no means to measure the losses derived from works unproduced or even unimagined owing to the ill winds blowing from Washington.

Artists in America receive precious little corporate support from the major media in their battle for free expression because these same companies are petitioning the very same FCC commissioners to allow them to expand their respective empires. While media companies are otherwise eager enough to race one another to the bottom of the barrel with regard to the exploitation of titillating sex and violence, at the same time they have no desire to anger the members of the FCC, the Bush administration who appointed them, or the conservative movement that sponsored the anti-indecency crusade. When the broadcast corporations asked the FCC for consistency regarding the limits on free expression, the commission refused to spell out its policies—like obscenity, it deemed indecency to be whatever it deemed it to be. When at the 2003 Golden Globes, Bono termed U2's winning of Best Original Song from a film "fucking brilliant," the FCC ruled originally that the words were not indecent, because they did not refer to sex. Six months later, however, it changed its mind and decided that using the F-word was objectionable, and the fine was levied. "Well, that's democracy," you might say, and you might be right . . . save for one more inconvenient truth: unknown to most Americans, the movement to bring "decency" to broadcast entertainment is a right-wing Potemkin production. An enterprising reporter for *MediaWeek* noted that according to the FCC's own records, 99.8 percent of the complaints brought in 2003 were filed by a single right-wing pressure group, the Parents Television Council (PTC), a conservative activist group founded by L. Brent Bozell III, who also serves as president of the far-right Media Research Center.[13] Despite its minuscule membership and ideological extremism, the PTC has harnessed technology it calls the "Entertainment Tracking System," which logs "every incident of sexual content, violence, profanity, disrespect for authority and other negative content," and includes "even those minor swears," as its staffers proudly explain. The PTC also claims an e-mail list of 125,000 "online members," and its Web site offers complaint form letters and streaming video clips of TV episodes so that visitors can watch them, find them offensive, and then, with a mouse click, send off an outraged letter.[14] Although the PTC has a loud voice, the size of its actual constituency is debatable at best. In 2004, when in response to viewer complaints the FCC levied its largest TV fine ever—$1.2 million against Fox for an episode of the reality show *Married by America*—the commission said the broadcast had generated 159 letters of complaint. But a Freedom of Information Act request to obtain copies of these letters yielded mail from just twenty-three separate individuals, twenty-one of whom used Bozell's preprinted complaint forms.[15]

Ironically, the would-be censors of the far right are not opposed to all indecency, or even public endorsements of lesbianism. It's just *liberal* lesbianism that offends them. Mary Cheney, perhaps the most prominent Republican lesbian in America and a former gay and lesbian marketing liaison for the conservative Coors corporation, appeared frequently with her partner, Heather Poe, in public and on TV during the presidential campaign of 2004, campaigning for her father, who supports civil unions for gays. But of course this kind of personal hypocrisy pales when compared to that of Rupert Murdoch's empire. Among recent successes in the News Corporation family are books such as Jenna Jameson's *How to Make Love Like a Porn Star* and the Vivid Girls' *How to Have a XXX Sex Life*, both of which were frequently promoted on Fox News. There are "real fun parts and exciting parts," anchor Rita

Cosby gushed to Jameson on Fox News' *Big Story Weekend* during a Saturday-morning broadcast, a time when America's living rooms were filled with children channel-surfing between cartoons. It was another Fox program, *Married by America,* recall, that earned the $1.2 million fine, owing to an episode of this heterosexual-marriage–promoting reality show that included scenes in which "partygoers lick whipped cream from strippers' bodies," and two female strippers "playfully spank" a man on all fours in his underwear. Another Fox show, the short-lived *Keen Eddie,* included a scene where a woman, described as a "filthy slut," was hired to "extract" semen from a horse. (She lifted her skirts and the horse keeled over.)

All this attention to public morality came together in the strange episode when, in November 2006, Fox sought to employ a bit of corporate synergy on behalf of O. J. Simpson, for the purposes of exploiting the very murders for which he was tried. (The victims included the mother of his children, Nicole Brown.) Murdoch's News Corporation sought to sell the public both a book—published through one of its subsidiaries—and a lurid television interview in which Simpson would, in exchange for millions of dollars paid to his estate, explain how he *would* have committed the murders, *if* he "did it." For once, the public outcry was so extreme that it upset the careful balance between moralism and exploitation that Murdoch and company had so cannily perfected. Fox's own Bill O'Reilly called it "simply indefensible, and a low point in American culture." The offense was egregious, as was the fact that O'Reilly felt compelled to lie to his audience about his own network's relationship to the corporation responsible. "For the record, Fox Broadcasting has nothing to do with the Fox News Channel," he insisted to viewers. In fact, O'Reilly's boss, Roger Ailes, is head of both Fox News Channel and Fox Television Stations, which are both owned by Murdoch's News Corporation, and which regularly share both programming and personalities. When Murdoch and company finally realized the magnitude of their error, they canceled the program and issued a two-sentence explanation in Murdoch's name, noting, "I and senior management agree with the American public that this was an ill-considered project," but the company did not in any way apologize or even acknowledge any breach of public etiquette, much less morality.

The Murdoch smut- and scandal-producing machine can make for odd bedfellows. Pat Robertson may enjoy every opportunity to condemn liberals for the promotion of casual sex and alternative lifestyles at the expense of society's bedrock social institutions like marriage and courtship, but Mr. Robertson has no more powerful and influential adversary in this regard than his Fox Family Channel business partner, Rupert Murdoch. In the spring of 2000 the network that had invented *Studs*, a dating show with male strippers, managed to shock even its most vociferous critics with *Who Wants to Marry a Multi-Millionaire?* Here, women were invited to debase the institution of marriage for the greater glory of Fox's Nielsen ratings. (It almost didn't matter that the program's producers went about this task entirely incompetently, as the alleged "multi-millionaire" was no such thing, but did have a few restraining orders in his past. The marriage was never consummated, but the "bride" did subsequently pose naked in *Playboy*.) A year afterward, Fox somehow managed to outdo itself in the cultural debasement category with the debut of *Temptation Island*, in which four "committed" couples were dumped on an island and filmed "canoodling" in ever shifting combinations.[16]

From the outset, the Fox network's "news" programs demonstrated a similarly fluid interpretation of the term *family values* when it came to reeling in viewers (and hence profits). Its original flagship, *A Current Affair*, erased much of the journalistic rule book. As one of its top producers, Burt Kearns, later recounted in *Tabloid Baby*, in order to get a copy of a tape alleging to show the actor Rob Lowe having sex with two underage women at the 1988 Democratic convention in Atlanta, the producers lifted footage from an Atlanta station and claimed it as its own, paid a club owner for the sex tape even though he had no legal ownership, and physically destroyed the evidence in the face of a lawsuit. As Kearns puts it, "The Rob Lowe tape was a milestone for the show and tabloid television. Sex, celebrity, politics, crime, morality and America's obsession with home video cameras were all rolled into one. . . . We were the fucking champions of the world." (In fact, the events caught on tape did not really take place in Atlanta but were filmed in France. There were no underage girls involved and hence, no story. None of those details ever made it onto Fox, however.)[17] Inconvenient truths aside, Kearns was right: Roger Ailes, the former Republican strategist who was promoted in 2005 to head up the entire News Corporation Television Group, does not believe that such programming requires a defense. "News is what people are interested in," he explains. "We're just getting the same girls to dance around shinier poles."[18] Indeed, even these poles were not as "shiny" as Ailes might have liked to believe. EchoStar Communications, of which Murdoch was a part owner, deployed its fleet of satellites to sell more porno videos than did the Playboy Corporation.[19]

Despite this rather equivocal track record on family values, when Murdoch debuted Fox News Channel in 1996 with Ailes at the helm, conservatives fell all over themselves to praise it. "If it hadn't been for Fox, I don't know what I'd have done for the news," Trent Lott gushed during the Florida election recount.[20] George W. Bush extolled Bush I aide-turned-anchor (and later Bush II press secretary) Tony Snow for his "impressive transition to journalism" in a specially taped April 2000 tribute to Snow's Sunday-morning show.[21] The right-wing Heritage Foundation had to warn its staffers to stop watching so much Fox News on their computers, lest the entire system crash.[22] These conservatives were well aware of Fox's role in purveying the kinds of "indecency" they professed to oppose.

As should be obvious to anyone paying attention, Murdoch is hardly the only conservative who likes to take perversion public when it looks to be profitable. What follows are a number of excerpts from books published by prominent right-wingers, who believe, with Ecclesiastes, that to everything there is a season, including what most conservatives say they consider to be sexual perversion: Scooter Libby (from *The Apprentice*, 1996):

> At age ten the madam put the child in a cage with a bear trained to couple with young girls so the girls would be frigid and not fall in love with

their patrons. They fed her through the bars and aroused the bear with a stick when it seemed to lose interest. Groups of men paid to watch. Like other girls who have been trained this way, she learned to handle many men in a single night and her skin turned a milky white. . . . Then, they trained the young whore in all of the finest ways to pleasure men. They gave her wooden penises and taught her how to handle them. They taught her how to sing out in the night and move to finish off her customers quickly. . . . They taught her how to draw pubic hair on her mound . . . because she was still too young to have any of her own.

Bill O'Reilly (from *Those Who Trespass*, 1998):

Robo used his "product" only occasionally, but tonight was special. He had two fifteen-year-old girls who would do anything for the drug, and he was determined to exploit the situation.

"Say, baby, put that pipe down and get my pipe up," Robo said to one of the girls. She was so intoxicated she had trouble standing, but Robo was her sugar daddy, and as he sat in a filthy, imitation leather couch, there in the living room of a run-down three-room apartment, she obediently performed oral sex on him.

Five feet away, the other teenage girl sat on a mattress on the floor and watched, greedily sucking on the crack pipe Robo had passed to her. Edgar looked over and grinned, showing yellow, decaying teeth. Obviously, he preferred oral sex to oral hygiene.

"You're next, girl, and I want you to do her too," he ordered.

As Robo took the crack pipe back, the girl groggily nodded her consent. Inhaling deeply, Robo blew the cocaine smoke out through his nose and mouth. The bitter taste left him feeling powerful, energized, and free of worry. He was bad and he was flush.[23]

Lynne Cheney, from her book *Sisters*, 1981:

Sophie opened it, thinking she should thank Adah, but when she saw what was inside, she was speechless. There were several small sponges, each in a silken net with a string attached. There were packets labeled "Preventive Powders" and lined up in neat rows with several dozen condoms. "There are all these things, you know?" Adah was saying. "But the sheaths really are the best. Sometimes men don't like them."

"Why do we stay? I have no reason beyond a few pupils who would miss me briefly, and your life would be infinitely better away from him. Let us go away together, away from the anger and imperatives of men. We shall find ourselves a secluded bower where they dare not venture. There will be only the two of us, and we shall linger through long afternoons of sweet retirement. In the evenings I shall read to you while you work your cross-stitch in the firelight. And then we shall go to bed, our bed, my dearest girl."

To recap: that's a ten-year-old in a cage with an aroused bear being masturbated with a stick; a crack dealer receiving oral sex from two fifteen-year-olds; and "sisters," doing things, well . . . let's just say it's not what most people have in mind when they hear the phrase *family values*.

11

Why Do Liberals Deny That America
Was Founded as a Christian Nation?

In his book *The Myth of the Separation*, religious conservative David Barton argues that America's founders simply did not support the separation of church and state. Indeed, he maintains, the United States is a Christian nation founded by Christian men who very much wanted the government to support religion. Fully 62 percent of white evangelical Protestants say that the Bible should be the guiding principle in making laws, even when it conflicts with the will of the people; the same percentage believe it to be the literal word of God.[1] Similar arguments can be found in books like Dee Wampler's *Myth of Separation between Church and State*, D. James Kennedy's *What If America Were a Christian Nation Again?*, and Gary Demar's *American Christian Heritage*. The right-wing Web site WorldNetDaily.com sells a special print magazine called *The Myth of Church-State Separation*. Newt Gingrich complained at Jerry Falwell's Liberty University that "a growing culture of radical secularism declares that the nation cannot publicly profess the truths on which it was founded."[2] Former two-time Republican senatorial candidate and U.S. ambassador Alan Keyes refers to the "so-called doctrine . . . that the courts created out of thin air," while his fellow Republican senatorial candidate, ex-representative Katherine Harris, goes so far as to call the very idea that a separation of church and state was intended "a lie." These same evangelicals and their political allies draw strength from their oft-stated belief that America was founded as a "Christian nation" inspired by, and in the service of, God's will.[3]

They're all wrong. In the first place, apart from its prohibition against religious tests for public office in Article 6, and the First Amendment's refusal to allow the countenancing of an established religion "or prohibiting the free exercise thereof," the U.S. Constitution makes no reference whatsoever to God. This was clearly a conscious choice on the part of the document's authors, as it broke with virtually all known precedent, including the Articles of Confederation and nearly every state constitution. God is also barely mentioned in the eighty-five Federalist Papers by James Madison, Alexander Hamilton, and John Jay, written in support of the Constitution, and the deity receives only two mentions in the Declaration of Independence. Isaac Kramnick and R. Lawrence Moore, authors of *The Godless Constitution*, observe, "The framers erected a godless federal constitutional structure, which was then undermined as God first entered the U.S. currency in 1863, and the federal mail service in 1912, and finally the Pledge of Allegiance in 1954." The Reverend John M. Mason, a hellfire-and-damnation-style eighteenth-century New York minister, declared the absence of God in the Constitution "an omission which no pretext whatever can palliate" and warned that Americans would "have every reason to tremble, lest the Governor of the universe, who will not be treated with indignity by a people more than by individuals, overturn from its foundation the fabric we have been rearing, and crush us to atoms in the wreck." No less an authority than the Reverend Timothy Dwight, president of Yale College, lamented, in 1812, "The nation has offended Providence. We formed our Constitution without an acknowledgement of God; without any recognition of His mercies to us, as a people, of His government or even of His existence. The [Constitutional] Convention, by which it was formed, never asked even once, His direction, or His blessings, upon their labours. Thus we commenced our national existence under the present system, without God."[4]

The likely fundamentalist response to this evidence would be that the founders were so steeped in their religious beliefs at the time that they felt it unnecessary to state these commitments in explicit form. Alas, like so many right-wing interventions in contemporary American politics, such an argument would rest far more on faith than evidence. Once the founding documents were approved and the first national government was formed, its representatives made its lack of religious underpinnings manifest. In 1797 it accepted the "Treaty of Peace and Friendship between the United States of America and the Bey and Subjects of Tripoli of

Barbary," now known simply as the Treaty of Tripoli. Article 11 of the treaty contains these words:

> As the Government of the United States of America is not, in any sense, founded on the Christian religion; as it has in itself no character of enmity against the laws, religion, or tranquillity of Musselmen; and as the said States never have entered into any war, or act of hostility against any Mahometan nation, it is declared by the parties, that no pretext arising from religious opinions, shall ever produce an interruption of the harmony existing between the two countries.

The treaty document was endorsed by Secretary of State Timothy Pickering and President John Adams. It was then sent to the Senate for ratification; the vote was unanimous. Journalist Brooke Allen notes that this vote was particularly significant because "although this was the 339th time a recorded vote had been required by the Senate, it was only the third unanimous vote in the Senate's history. There is no record of debate or dissent. The text of the treaty was printed in full in the *Pennsylvania Gazette* and in two New York papers, but there were no screams of outrage, as one might expect today."[5]

The fact is, contemporary conservative Christians could hardly be less in sympathy with the political sentiments of America's founders if they converted to cannibalism. While America's founders lived in deeply religious times, and were, with some important exceptions, Christians themselves, it is almost impossible to find a founder who played a significant role in the creation of the republic who shared conservative Christian views on the role of God and politics; and this includes the evangelical community of the day. America's founders possessed a panoply of religious beliefs, many of them syncretic, and not given to standard Christian categories. They also—no less predictably—differed on the role of religion in politics. What almost all did share, however, was a profound distaste for the interference of religious hierarchies in temporal affairs. Like so many of the Puritans who founded the New England colonies, they were deeply suspicious of a European pattern of governmental involvement in religion. As Jon Butler, a historian of early America, writes in his seminal study *Awash in a Sea of Faith: Christianizing the American People,* the founders "were deeply concerned about an involvement in religion because they saw government as corrupting religion." As Butler notes, "Most of the wars from 1300 to 1800 had been religious wars and the wars that these men knew about in particular were the wars of religion that were fought over the Reformation in which Catholics and Protestants slaughtered each other, stuffed Bibles into the slit stomachs of dead soldiers so that they would eat, literally eat, their words, eat the words of an alien Bible and die with those words in their stomachs. This was the world of government involvement with religion that these men knew and a world they wanted to reject."[6]

Whatever their political or religious orientation, the founders sought to separate these beliefs from their conduct in public life. According to David L. Holmes, author of *The Religion of the Founding Fathers,* Thomas Paine and Ethan Allen were non-Christian Deists and scorned Christianity, which is not to say they scorned faith itself. Paine could write, in *Common Sense,* that "the Almighty hath implanted in us these inextinguishable feelings for good and wise purposes." But with respect to organized religion, he once said, "Of all the systems of religion that ever were invented, there is none more derogatory to the Almighty, more unedifying to man, more repugnant to reason, and more contradictory in itself than this thing called Christianity." Although George Washington and John Adams were sometimes regular churchgoers, neither man appeared to evince a powerful connection to any particular Christian denomination. Patrick Henry, Samuel Adams, and John Jay, meanwhile, not only attended church but accepted the divinity of Jesus, and so are classifiable as orthodox Christians. Ben Franklin, who did not attend church and does not appear to have believed in the divinity of Jesus, nonetheless thought religion was a healthy sociological phenomenon. "Franklin," writes Holmes, "was also among those Deists who remained open to the possibility of divine intervention or special providence in human affairs"—a view shared by most of the founders, especially Washington. Thomas Jefferson was another matter, however. Like Thomas Paine, Holmes writes, "He had a visceral contempt for organized religion and for clergymen, believing that they were always in alliance with despots against liberty." "To this effect," he said, "they have perverted the purest religion ever preached to man, into mystery and jargon unintelligible to all mankind and therefore the safer engine for their purposes." The Trinity was nothing but "Abracadabra" and "hocus-pocus . . . so incomprehensible to the human mind that no candid man can say he has any idea of it." In a letter to John Adams in 1823, he wrote: "The day will come when the mystical generation of Jesus . . . will be classed with the fable of the generation of Minerva in the brain of Jupiter." Jefferson believed, by 1822, that "there is not a young man now living in the United States who will not die a Unitarian."[7]

While the antireligious zealot Jefferson drafted the Declaration of Independence, he played no role in authoring the U.S. Constitution. Alas, unfortunately for the right-wing argument about the religious convictions of the founders, the "father" of America's Constitution, James Madison, is on record as expressing sentiments no less hostile to Christianity. In 1785 he wrote, "What have been [Christianity's] fruits? More or less in all places, pride and indolence in the Clergy, ignorance and servility in the laity; in both, superstition, bigotry and persecution."[8]

What is particularly inconvenient for the fundamentalists (and ironic for the rest of us) is the fact that among the strongest voices for keeping God and Christianity out of the Constitution was the eighteenth-century evangelical Christian community. As Beliefnet's Steven Waldman points out, "It was the eighteenth-century evangelicals who provided the political shock troops for Jefferson and Madison in their efforts to keep government from strong involvement with religion." For instance, in 1784 Patrick Henry, at the time the most popular local political leader, campaigned in Virginia for a state law that would tax citizens to support the promotion of Christianity. The bill was quite fair-minded for its kind, even providing an opt-out provision for people who did not share these beliefs and would have preferred to target their tax dollars toward nonreligious education. Called "A Bill Establishing a Provision for Teachers of the Christian Religion," the law gained wide support from most of Virginia's founders, save Madison. The measure passed but was eventually overturned as the state's evangelical community swung into opposition. The state went even further, sanctioning Jefferson's famous statute on religious freedom, which enjoined not only the establishment of a formal state religion, but also the employment of any government monies for the purpose of aiding any religious practice. "To compel a man to furnish contributions of money for the propagation of opinions which he disbelieves, is sinful and tyrannical," it declared. A similar dynamic can be found in the ratification battle over the Bill of Rights. Jefferson was correct in his famous 1802 letter to the Baptists of Danbury, Connecticut, in which he claimed that the First Amendment of the federal Constitution erected a "wall of separation between Church & State," though, ironically, his allies in this interpretation were less his own Deists and antireligious brethren than the evangelicals themselves.[9] The evangelicals stood with Jefferson and Madison not only to prevent the establishment of official churches but also because they believed deeply in the separation of the spiritual and secular, as the latter could only corrupt the former. "Religious freedom resulted from an alliance of unlikely partners," explains historian Frank Lambert in his study *The Founding Fathers and the Place of Religion in America.* "New Light evangelicals such as Isaac Backus and John Leland joined forces with Deists and skeptics such as James Madison and Thomas Jefferson to fight for a complete separation of church and state."[10]

A few contemporary right-wing Christians share this concern. Pundits Cal Thomas and Ed Dobson, both formerly employed by the Moral Majority, argued in 1999 that religious right-wingers had "confused political power with God's power." Modern conservative Christians are certainly within their rights in attempting to employ our political system to try to obtain taxpayer dollars for their religious activities, and prevent the rest of us from freely practicing our own religious (or nonreligious) beliefs. But as Waldman points out in the *Washington Monthly,* "They should realize that in doing so they have dramatically departed from the tradition of their spiritual forefathers."[11] It wasn't liberals who ensured that the separation of church and state would remain a fundamental precept of American politics; it was America's founders, with the men (and women) of God on their side.

12

Why Won't Liberals Admit That America
Is Suffering from a Crisis in Moral Values?

One unquestioned maxim of contemporary conservative discourse is that morally speaking, America is heading to hell in a handbasket at NASCAR velocity. Conservative morals czar William Bennett warned a 1995 audience at the Heritage Foundation: "Current trends in out-of-wedlock births, crime, drug use, family decomposition, and educational decline, as well as a host of other social pathologies, are incompatible with the continuation of American society as we know it. If these things continue, the republic as we know it will cease to be."[1] Indeed, American civilization, writes Robert Bork, is in peril of "slid[ing] into a modern, high-tech version of the Dark Ages." In *Slouching towards Gomorrah: Modern Liberalism and American Decline*, Bork declares, "There are aspects of almost every branch of our culture that are worse than ever before and the rot is spreading." That rot derives from the nation's "enfeebled, hedonistic culture," its "uninhibited display of sexuality," its "popularization of violence in . . . entertainment," and "its angry activists of feminism, homosexuality, environmentalism, animal rights—the list could be extended almost indefinitely." Bork closes out his account by insisting that the country is "now well along the road to the moral chaos that is the end of radical individualism and the tyranny that is the goal of radical egalitarianism. Modern liberalism has corrupted our culture across the board."[2]

As Bork would have it, things have gotten so bad that he was willing to participate in a November 1996 symposium entitled "The End of Democracy?" sponsored by the theoconservative journal *First Things*, in which the contributors addressed themselves to the proposition that "we [America] have reached or are reaching the point where conscientious citizens can no longer give moral assent to the existing regime."[3] It was *First Things'* editor, Father Richard John Neuhaus, who did more than anyone else to push the tone of the symposium beyond what most of us would consider the limits of responsible discourse. In an unsigned editorial, Neuhaus, who like David Horowitz moved from being a youthful left-wing revolutionary to settling in as a middle-aged right-wing revolutionary without stopping to rest anywhere in between—adopted the actual language of the Declaration of Independence to lament the judiciary's "long train of abuses and usurpations" and to warn darkly about "the prospect—some might say the present reality—of despotism" in America. In Neuhaus's view, what was happening in the United States could only be described as "the displacement of a constitutional order by a regime that does not have, will not obtain, and cannot command the consent of the people." Hence the stark and radical options confronting the country, ranging "from noncompliance to resistance to civil disobedience to morally justified revolution."[4] While these sentiments caused some consternation among fellow conservatives at the time, they have hardly disappeared. As recently as May 2007 Thomas Sowell, one of America's most honored and admired conservative intellectuals—in movement circles, in any case—went so far as to muse in *National Review,* "When I see the worsening degeneracy in our politicians, our media, our educators, and our intelligentsia, I can't help wondering if the day may yet come when the only thing that can save this country is a military coup."[5]

Now transpose these radical, revolutionary assumptions to the rough-and-tumble of American electoral politics. In Ohio, for instance, a movement called the Ohio Restoration Project trains thousands of "Patriot Pastors" to turn out right-wing religious voters at the polls. Its leader, Russell Johnson, the senior pastor of the Fairfield Christian Church in suburban Columbus, attacks public schools as "secular jihadists" that have "hijacked" America in order, among other things, to prevent schoolchildren from learning that Hitler was "an avid evolutionist." Similarly condemned are those he terms the "pagan left," and those of us who seek to use "homosexual rights" to welcome "a flood of demonic oppression." Another of the Restoration Project's architects is the popular

Columbus televangelist Rod Parsley, who sits atop a $40-million-a-year television ministry broadcast on 1,400 stations and boasting a staff of 350. Terming himself a "Christocrat" battling "the very hordes of hell in our society," he considers the separation of church and state to be "a lie perpetrated on Americans—especially believers in Jesus Christ" and seeks to "restore Godly presence in government and culture; as a wall buster he will tear down the church-state wall." At political rallies he has been known to scream, "Let the Revolution begin," as his flock repeats his words back to him.[6] Invoking Martin Luther, he calls for a spiritual army to "track down our adversary, defeat him valiantly, then stand upon his carcass."[7]

Why do these people matter? Because, as the television journalist Bill Moyers first noted, if you go now to the Web site of an organization called America 21, "there, on a red, white, and blue home page, you find praise for President Bush's agenda—including his effort to phase out Social Security and protect corporations from lawsuits by aggrieved citizens. On the same home page is a reminder that 'There are 7,177 hours until our next National Election. . . . ENLIST NOW.' Now click again and you will read a summons calling Christian pastors 'to lead God's people in the turning that can save America from our enemies.'" Recalling Falwell and Robertson, the site explains: "'One of the unmistakable lessons [of 9/11] is that America has lost the full measure of God's hedge of protection. When we ask ourselves why, the scriptures remind us that ancient Israel was invaded by its foreign enemy, Babylon, in 586 B.C. . . . [and] Jerusalem was destroyed by another invading foreign power in 70 A.D. . . . Psalm 106:37 says that these judgments of God . . . were because of Israel's idolatry. Israel, the apple of God's eye, was destroyed . . . because the people failed . . . to repent.' If America is to avoid a similar fate, the warning continues, we must 'remember the legacy of our heritage under God and our covenant with Him and, in the words of Chronicles 7:14: "Turn from our wicked ways."'"

The fine print at the bottom of the site explains that "America21 is a not-for-profit organization whose mission is to educate, engage and mobilize Christians to influence national policy at every level. Founded in

1989 by a multi-denominational group of pastors and businessmen, it is dedicated to being a catalyst for revival and reform of the culture and the government."[8] Ohio, recall, is the state that decided the last presidential election. In October 2005, Parsley promised that during the next four years his campaign would bring a hundred thousand Ohio voters to Christ, register four hundred thousand new voters, and lead the state through "a culture-shaking revolutionary revival."[9]

These are the shock troops of the Christian conservative "revolution" to whom Republican candidates have been, and will continue to be, beholden for future victories. Indeed, they have already to a considerable degree taken over the Republican Party. Supreme Court justice Antonin Scalia, who helped hand the 2000 election over to George W. Bush, argues that the American "government derives its moral authority from God" and that "the reaction of people of faith to the tendency of democracy to obscure the divine authority behind government should not be resignation to it, but the resolution to combat it as effectively as possible."[10] Former House majority leader Tom DeLay explained his mission on behalf of the party as the promotion of a "biblical worldview" and even justified his pursuit of the impeachment of Bill Clinton on that basis.[11]

In fact, little if any evidence can be found for the "crisis" that these conservatives purport to detect in America's value system, even by their own highly questionable criteria. Many of the problems that so motivate right-wing Christian activism improved significantly during the Clinton administration, despite the fact that the country was ruled by a man many regarded as little less than a soldier of Satan. For instance, during that period the teen birth rate fell seven years in a row, by 18 percent from 1991 to 1998, reaching its lowest rate on record. The administration required the installation of V-chips in all new televisions and encouraged schools to adopt school-uniform policies to deter violence and promote discipline; Clinton signed Megan's Law and the Jacob Wetterling Crimes against Children and Sexually Violent Offender Registration Act, requiring states to set up sex offender registration systems and mandating community notification when sex offenders are released from prison.[12]

But even if you believe that evil lurks in the heart of all things Clinton, the root of America's "values" problem cannot be found in any appreciable decline in the kinds of issues about which theoconservative Christians profess to care. As the scholar Wayne Baker explains in his 2005 book *America's Crisis of Values*, during the two decades covered by the World Values Surveys of sixty developed and developing nations on six continents, America's values did not appreciably change between 1981—when we were among the most traditional people in the world, especially for an economically advanced democracy—and 2001. According to these surveys, Americans espouse values far more traditional than the values of almost any advanced industrial society and even a few that aren't. America's social attitudes, cultural values, and religious beliefs are likewise not as polarized as the fundamentalists would have us believe. According to these consistent sets of survey data, Americans share a multitude of attitudes, values, and beliefs, and are united when it comes to core issues, a finding that is supported by the studies of other social scientists employing different sets of data.[13]

What does plague us, however, is an increase in moral absolutism of the kind currently animating both the contemporary conservative movement and the Republican Party. Despite their religiosity, a supermajority of Americans see no conflict between a belief in God and a liberal embrace of the Enlightenment. According to the Barna Group, which conducts extensive research on religion and American life, a mere 5 percent of Americans endorse what they term a "Biblical worldview."[14] The sociologist Alan Wolfe interviewed hundreds of Americans for his study *One Nation, After All,* and concluded, "Clearly, most middle-class Americans take their religion seriously. But very few of them take it so seriously that they believe that religion should be the sole, or even the most important, guide for establishing rules about how other people should live."[15]

Fewer than 20 percent of Americans tell pollsters that "changes to how the federal courts handle moral issues" is an issue they find to be "extremely important."[16] Our country's problem is the fact that those 20 percent seek to run the lives of the rest of us. For instance, in a poll taken by Greenberg Quinlan Rosner Research in June 2006, Robert

Borosage notes, "Independents (63 percent to 32 percent) and moderates (71 percent to 26 percent) preferred a government that would promote 'scientific inquiry and personal freedom and let individuals make up their own moral choices' over one that would 'promote morality and restrict abortion and limit science where it violates the sanctity of life.' Conservatives (51 percent to 45 percent) stood alone in preferring the latter."[17] In the area of foreign policy, the Bush administration has undoubtedly alienated majorities in almost every country on earth with its various manifestations of unilateralism, militarism, arrogance, ideological extremism, and incompetence, and most Americans share the views of these same majorities. Even leaving aside the catastrophe of Iraq, where again opposition to Bush policies began to reach supermajority levels in 2005, a study of the available opinion data in 2004 by political scientists Ronald Asmus, Philip P. Everts, and Pierangelo Isernia argues that "the real gap across the Atlantic is between American conservatives and the European mainstream." They point to "the existence of a strong 'hawk' minority centered in the Republican Party that believes that military power is more important than economic power and that war is, at times, necessary to obtain justice." Also in nearly perfect contrast to the position of these Republican right-wingers is the finding that more than 80 percent of both Democrats and Republicans surveyed believed it would be "a good thing . . . if the European Union becomes as powerful as the U.S."[18]

While their desire to exclude those who do not share their religious beliefs draws on historical tendencies that hearken back to the Puritans, the theoconservative mode of politics is actually a much more recent phenomenon in American life. Writing in 1956, the sociologist Daniel Bell observed that while religious fanaticism had manifested itself historically through temperance campaigns, censorship, book burnings, and the like, it had rarely injected itself into politics. Yet in the early 1950s, this began to change, largely due to the actions of ex-Communist "McCarthyite" politicians and intellectuals who viewed politics through a Manichean prism of their own "good" and everyone else's evil. What Bell termed "the rise of the intellectual apologists for a reactionary right" was the result of the fact that "many of these men were Communists or near Communists" who embraced anticommunism with the same ideological fervor and intensity with which they had practiced their original faith, acting "as if all politics were only two-sided, in this case, McCarthy and the Communists."

This was a devastating development for the health of our body politic, for as Walter Lippmann observed, "A nation, divided irreconcilably on 'principle,' each party believing itself to be pure white and the other pitch black, cannot govern itself." Politics, as Edmund Wilson described the view of Theodore Roosevelt, "is a matter of adapting oneself to all sorts of people and situations, a game in which one may score but only by accepting the rules and recognizing one's opponents, rather than a moral crusade in which one's stainless standard must mow the enemy down."[19] Indeed, the man who inspired the modern conservative movement with his failed 1964 presidential run, Barry Goldwater, found just a few years later that his campaign had unleashed a fundamentalist Frankenstein. "I'm frankly sick and tired of the political preachers across this country telling me as a citizen that if I want to be a moral person, I must believe in 'A,' 'B,' 'C,' and 'D,'" Goldwater complained in 1981. "Just who do they think they are? And from where do they presume to claim the right to dictate their moral beliefs to me?"[20]

The prophetic warning of James Madison, in Federalist Paper No. 10, that "a religious sect may degenerate into a political faction" has come to fruition 200 years later in the contemporary conservative movement.[21] Bush himself told a group of religious editors and writers that "the job of a president is to help bring about change," and that the government can help effect such change by "standing with those who have heard the call to love a neighbor, and changing society one soul at a time."[22] This is, apparently, exactly what Bush and his fellow theoconservatives have in mind. In 2002 Bush's Justice Department established a "religious rights" unit within the Civil Rights Division that focused not on racial or ethnic discrimination but what Bush and company interpreted as religious discrimination. What this meant in practice was that organizations like the Salvation Army would henceforth be allowed to violate federal antidiscrimination laws by requiring employees to embrace Jesus Christ to keep their jobs, and the government would support their right to receive millions of taxpayers dollars to do so.[23] President Bush's only veto during his first six years was against a congressional compromise on stem-cell research.

The right's crusading fundamentalism on these issues takes a particularly worrisome tack when it comes to the use of America's military, for what ought to be an obvious reason: we live in a world where most people do not share our values, and the conflict between those values has the potential to destroy our respective societies.

Let two examples suffice. To oversee our government's efforts to track the actions of our adversaries and potential adversaries, and recommend action against them, in the autumn of 2003 President Bush chose as his deputy undersecretary of defense for intelligence General William "Jerry" Boykin. What were his qualifications? Boykin had already achieved worldwide fame for comments like: "Now ask yourself this. Why is this man [George W. Bush] in the White House? The majority of Americans did not vote for him. Why is he there? I tell you this morning he's in the White House because God put him there for such a time as this. God put him there to lead not only this nation but to lead the world in such a time as this." As far as his capacity to understand the complexities of intelligence matters, Boykin, who claims to have heard God speak out loud directly to him, asserts that these are not so important. In a slide lecture he gives frequently to church groups, he explains: "Well, is he [slide of bin Laden] the enemy? Or is this man [slide of Saddam Hussein] the enemy? The enemy is none of these people I have showed you here. The enemy is a spiritual enemy. He's called the principality of darkness. The enemy is a guy called Satan."[24] After he led the failed "Black Hawk Down" raid in Mogadishu in 1993, Boykin flew over the city taking photographs. The photos revealed black smears on the landscape, which Boykin concluded represented "a demonic presence in that city, and God revealed it to me as the enemy that I was up against in Mogadishu." He remembered, in the same context, the horror he first experienced in that non-Christian nation: "I could feel the presence of

evil. . . . The demonic presence is real in a place that has rejected God."
His task was not simply to defeat an enemy force, but to carry Jesus to
the benighted: "It is a spiritual enemy that will only be defeated if we
come against him in the name of Jesus."[25] As Garry Wills notes, "When
General Edwin Walker began to promote the John Birch Society to his
NATO troops, President Kennedy removed him. What happened to
General Boykin after he went around calling Muslims Satanic? He was
not silenced, demoted, removed, or even criticized."[26] In a similar vein,
as recently as December 2006, Republican congressman Robin Hayes
from North Carolina suggested that the best way to solve Iraq's sectar-
ian conflict was for the U.S. military to engage in "spreading the message
of Jesus Christ," as "everything depends on everyone learning about the
birth of our savior."[27]

With attitudes like Boykin's and Hayes's popular among leading conservatives, events like those that took place at the U.S. Air Force Academy
in Colorado Springs, Colorado, in 2004 should not surprise us. The school
became engulfed in a climate of intimidation and bigotry directed against
nonevangelicals in general and Jews in particular. The crisis came to light
when Cadet Curtis Weinstein informed his father, "I think I'm going to get
into trouble. Dad, I'm going to beat up the next one who calls me a 'fuckin'
Jew' or says that we killed Jesus." Weinstein's father, who graduated from
the academy and served in the Reagan administration, put together 117
charges of religious coercion or discrimination, of which only 8 came from
Jews. When a group from Yale Divinity School got involved, together
with Americans United for Separation of Church and State, they reported
on a series of incidents involving faculty and seniors regularly using their
power to proselytize for conservative Christianity. Students who refused
to attend chapel during basic cadet training were marched back to their
dormitories in what was called a "heathen flight"; worshippers were told
by the school's top chaplain to proselytize to their classmates or "burn
in the fires of hell"; students were encouraged by faculty members to become born again; a banner was hung in the football team's locker room
that declared, I AM A CHRISTIAN FIRST AND LAST; I AM A MEMBER OF TEAM JESUS
CHRIST; faculty and upperclassmen used their classrooms to proselytize

and attack the unconverted. Students were pressured to see Mel Gibson's anti-Semitic film *The Passion of the Christ*. Large crucifixes were erected in the cadet area outside the chapel; flyers were placed under doors on Easter morning celebrating the reincarnation of Jesus; and video projections of Bible verses were shown on screens in the dining hall during mandatory meal formations.

Upon the release of the report, Democratic representative David Obey called for an investigation into the situation, but to Republican conservatives like John Hostettler, even examining these events constituted a chapter in what he termed "the long war on Christianity" and the "denigration and demonizing" of Christians, which, he insisted, "continues unabated with aid and comfort to those who would eradicate any vestige of our Christian heritage being supplied by the usual suspect, the Democrats." Others joined in on the House floor, demanding that the evangelical Christians be allowed to "practice their faith."[28] A week later, the theoconservative leader James Dobson hosted Hostettler on his radio show, and announced: "Liberal forces in this country want to squelch the freedoms of evangelical Christians throughout the culture, but now it's popped up at the Air Force Academy." He praised Hostettler for having "the courage to stand up and be counted."[29] Following the release of a detailed report by Americans United for Separation of Church and State in the spring of 2005, the air force announced the creation of a task force to address the issue, but the fact of its having arisen at all—coupled with so many conservative Christians portraying themselves as the victims in this story—points to a pervasive problem for America that can only grow worse.

Though he no longer tells people, as he once did, that Jews and other non-Christians can plan on an afterlife of everlasting hellfire and damnation, George W. Bush has manifested many of the same political tendencies as his fanatic fundamentalist supporters. As the authors of the Web site thinkprogress.org reported in detail, when George W. Bush was desperate to defend his nominee for the Supreme Court, Harriet Miers, from a conservative revolt, he told reporters, "People are interested to know why I picked Harriet Miers. Part of Harriet Miers's life is her religion." Bush's comments came on the same day that James Dobson said he had received assurances from Deputy Chief of Staff Karl Rove that "Harriet Miers is an evangelical Christian [and] . . . she is from a very conservative church, which is almost universally pro-life." As the Reverend Barry Lynn, executive director of Americans United for Separation of Church and State, would ask, "Did Bush pick Miers because of her religious viewpoint instead of her legal qualifications? If he did, that is a disservice to the Constitution and the diversity of the American people." As Rich Lowry, editor of the right-wing *National Review,* could not help but notice, Bush's references to Miers's religion "display a touching faith in the power of hypocrisy, double standards, and contradictions to see his nominee through."[30]

The current climate in the White House is an almost perfect mirror image of that which characterized the administration of America's first Catholic president, John F. Kennedy. In 1960 Kennedy, the Democratic liberal, promised America that he would not allow his religious beliefs to impinge on his political actions. Forty-five years later, Bush touted conservative Catholicism as his Supreme Court nominee's most significant political qualification. Bush is joined in this view, moreover, by no less crucial a conservative than Antonin Scalia. The man who provided the model, according to the president, for his Supreme Court choices explains that he believes the U.S. Constitution permits "disregard of polytheists and believers in unconcerned deities, just as it permits the disregard of devout atheists."[31]

Despite its limited appeal, its extremist orientation, and its contradiction of the tenets of our Constitution, right-wing religious orthodoxy so dominates our political discourse that many in the media seem to be unaware of any other tradition. For instance, even on the allegedly liberal CNN—the network that right-wing Republicans call the "Communist News Network"—Wolf Blitzer, covering the death of Pope John Paul II with right-winger Robert Novak and liberal Paul Begala, observed: "I'm sure Bob is a good Catholic; I'm not so sure about Paul Begala." In fact, Novak was a Jew until not very long ago, but Begala, understandably, demanded of Blitzer, "Well, now, who are you to pass moral judgment on my religion, Mr. Blitzer?" Blitzer tried to laugh the whole thing off as a joke, but Begala, appropriately, took umbrage. He cautioned, "The Holy Father is liberal. And in fact, when [CNN contributor] Carlos [Watson] was speaking [earlier in the program], I was in the green room. Underneath, some producer had written, 'Many Catholic doctrines are conservative.' Absolutely correct. Many are liberal as well. The Holy Father bitterly opposed President Bush's war in Iraq. He came to St. Louis—and I was there—and he begged America to give up the death penalty. President Bush strongly supports it, as did President Clinton and others. Many of the Holy Father's views—my church's views—are extraordinarily liberal. The Pope talked about savage, unbridled capitalism, not Bob Novak's kind." Blitzer urged Begala not to "be so sensitive."[32]

Virtually the only kind of religious presence to which most television viewers are ever exposed is the fire-breathing, damn-all-the-liberals theocratic variety. In a winter 2005 survey of the subject, *Time* magazine concluded that religious Americans were "unlikely to be seduced" by Democrats so long as the party stuck to its "core positions," as if some obvious and fundamental conflict existed between the two that did not even warrant definition.[33] On his MSNBC program, *Tucker,* Tucker Carlson concurred with his guest *Weekly Standard* editor Andrew Ferguson's off-the-cuff observation about liberal Protestants that "they believe in everything but God," and later added, "I have never met anybody less sincere than the religious left."[34]

Media Matters did a study of this practice, released in late May 2007, that revealed:

- Combining newspapers and television, conservative religious leaders were quoted, mentioned, or interviewed in news stories 2.8 times as often as were progressive religious leaders.
- On television news—the three major television networks, the three major cable-news channels, and PBS—conservative religious leaders were quoted, mentioned, or interviewed almost 3.8 times as often as progressive leaders.

- In major newspapers, conservative religious leaders were quoted, mentioned, or interviewed 2.7 times as often as progressive leaders.[35]

This not only devalues the religious experiences of tens, perhaps hundreds, of millions of Americans, it is willfully blind to centuries of cultural and religious history. The actual data on religious belief and observance in America illuminates a picture at odds with the media's representation. According to a 2006 survey by the Center for American Values in Public Life, only 22 percent of Americans are traditionalist in their religious beliefs, whereas a full 50 percent can be classified as centrist in their religious orientation, 18 percent as modernist, and 10 percent as secular or nonreligious.[36] Other religious factions certainly have articulate spokespeople. For instance, black ministers represent a deeply religious and culturally quite conservative constituency, albeit one that is also politically quite liberal. Because of this latter fact, undoubtedly, they are invited on television and elsewhere only as "civil rights" leaders rather than as Christian spokespeople. Instead, the typical representative of Christian religion is the likes of Pat Robertson, perhaps the most popular of televangelists and founder of the Christian Coalition of America and host of the Christian Broadcasting Network's *700 Club*, who announced with murderous mischief that God had personally informed him, "I will remove judges from the Supreme Court quickly, and their successors will refuse to sanction the attacks on religious faith."[37] Another favorite is Focus on the Family's James Dobson, who, though not even an ordained minister, is treated as if he has a direct pipeline to the Almighty by many members of the media. One day he divined that Vermont senator Patrick Leahy was a "God's people hater" because he "has been in opposition to most of the things that I believe."[38] (*Newsweek*'s Howard Fineman, writing in 2006, nevertheless referred to Dobson, together with Falwell and Robertson, as the Republican Party's "three Kingmakers."[39] And then there's Bob Jones III, president of Bob Jones University and Republican power broker, who explained that the election of 2004 provided "a reprieve from the agenda of paganism."[40] Conservatives are often heard to complain that National Public Radio is biased on behalf of liberals, but when its program *Morning Edition* offered listeners "a look at how Democratic candidates are reaching out to religious voters" in early 2007, its only expert guest turned out to be Michael Cromartie, the vice president of the Ethics and Public Policy Center, a right-wing think tank that, in its own words, is "dedicated to applying the Judeo-Christian moral tradition to critical issues of public policy." The interviewer, Renee Montagne, and Cromartie employed the terms *religious* and *evangelical* interchangeably and spoke of religious values as if they were the exclusive province of the far right.[41]

Theoconservatives have grown so powerful in conservative circles that the right's leading intellectuals now pay them tribute, even when it means embracing the "relativist" arguments of their professed enemies and making a mockery of their own respective commitment to the pursuit of truth. Consider the battle over whether American schoolchildren should be taught the scientifically based theory of evolution or the religious myth of "intelligent design." When queried by an enterprising reporter whether they believe that a doctrine they understand to be nonsense should be taught in public schools, many of the right's most respected thinkers could not bring themselves to say a discouraging word about the intellectual hokum being perpetrated on certain students in the name of religious fundamentalism. It is not enough that, according to a 2001 National Science Foundation survey, 47 percent of Americans think humans were created instantaneously, and, incredibly, 52 percent believe that humans and dinosaurs shared the earth simultaneously.[42] Fundamentalists wish to perpetuate this ignorance in young people, owing either to clear cowardice or an alleged "respect" for the wisdom of the (conservative) common man, however ridiculous those beliefs may be.

Former Bush speechwriter and *National Review* pundit David Frum explained, for instance, that he did not "believe that anything that offends nine-tenths of the American public should be taught in public schools. . . . I don't believe that public schools should embark on teaching anything that offends Christian principle." His *National Review* colleague Jonah Goldberg took the same brave stand: "I see nothing [wrong] with having teachers pay some attention to the sensitivities of other people in the room. I think if that means you're more careful about some issues than others, that's fine. People are careful about race and gender; I don't see why all of a sudden we can't be diplomatic on these issues when it comes to religion." And then there's the remarkable solution offered by James Taranto of the *Wall Street Journal*'s Web site "Best of the Web": if parents are offended by scientific knowledge, let's just ignore it. "One possible solution might be," he advises, "just take it out of the curriculum altogether."[43]

In public, this kind of self-subjugation to conservative Christian dogmatism is, sadly, the rule rather than the exception among conservatives. Behind closed doors, however, the embraces by nonfundamentalist Christians of their religious brethren appear to have all the earmarks of a cynical political ploy. This was certainly the experience of David Kuo, a deeply committed evangelical supporter of George W. Bush and the former deputy director of the White House Office of Faith-Based and Community Initiatives, which channels federal dollars to religious charities. According to Kuo, "National Christian leaders received hugs and smiles in person and then were dismissed behind their backs and described as 'ridiculous,' 'out of control,' and just plain 'goofy,' in the White House." That mockery, he added, included the Reverend Pat Robertson being called "insane," the Reverend Jerry Falwell being called "ridiculous," and comments that Focus on the Family's Dobson "had to be controlled." Kuo's criticism reflected that of his predecessor, John Di-Iulio, who complained that the Bush conservatives were far more interested in exploiting the Christian leadership than in working to achieve its goals; their efforts, as he explained it, were meant to "satisfy certain fundamentalist leaders and beltway libertarians 'but bore' few marks of 'compassionate conservatism.'"[44] In fact, while Bush promised Theocons $8 billion for their faith-based programs during his first year, they received barely $80 million over two years. It was, as is typical of the Bush administration, part of a shell game. The funds, as Kuo explained to a befuddled George W. Bush, were actually drawn from "existing dollars where groups will find it technically easier to apply for grants. But faith-based groups have been getting that money for years."[45] Kuo suggests that "evangelical Christians should take a fast from giving their money to political causes and from giving much of their time as well. Take that money that is currently fueling all those wonderful hate-filled ads, the hundreds of millions being spent, and spend that money on the poor and inner-city kids."[46]

The net result of the above trends is, as the Reverend Michael Livingston, president of the National Council of Churches of Christ USA, explains, that "mainline Protestant and Orthodox churches have been pounded into irrelevancy by the media machine of a false religion; a political philosophy masquerading as gospel; an economic principle wrapped in religious rhetoric and painted red, white and blue."[47] More to the point, the theocrats' position is not even acceptable to all conservative Christians. Brian D. McLaren, the founding pastor at Cedar Ridge Community Church in Gaithersburg, Maryland, worries that "you cannot say the word 'Jesus' in 2006 without having an awful lot of baggage going along with it. You can't say the word 'Christian,' and you certainly can't say the word 'evangelical' without it now raising connotations and a certain cringe factor in people. Because people think, 'Oh no, what is going to come next is homosexual bashing, or pro-war rhetoric, or complaining about 'activist judges.'" The Reverend Gregory A. Boyd, who leads the five-thousand-member Woodland Hills Church in suburban St. Paul, opposes reproductive choice, gay marriage, and the rest of the liberal litany, but like so many of America's founders, he thinks that involvement in partisan politics debases the church. "America wasn't founded as a theocracy," he explains. "America was founded by people trying to escape theocracies. Never in history have we had a Christian theocracy where it wasn't bloody and barbaric. That's why our Constitution wisely put in a separation of church and state." "All good, decent people want good and order and justice," he adds. "Just don't slap the label 'Christian' on it."[48]

13

If Liberals Are So Peace-Loving,
Why Do They Want to Murder the Unborn?

The problem of abortion is a complex one, to put it mildly. It is complex whether viewed in moral, psychological, political, legal, religious, or even gynecological terms. Its complexity leads politicians to posture for constituents over it, and therefore invites the courts to hammer out the actual policies that define women's choices. It would be hard to find a more egregious example of such irresponsibility than that contained in the 2004 Republican Party platform. It calls for "legislation to make it clear that the 14th Amendment's protections apply to unborn children," and for the appointment of judges who believe likewise. As Michael Kinsley points out, "If fetuses are 'persons' under the 14th Amendment, which guarantees all persons 'equal protection of the law,' abortion will be illegal whether a state or Congress wants to legalize it or not. More than that: There could be no legal distinction between the rights of fetuses and the rights of human beings after birth. So, just for example, a woman who procured an abortion would have to be prosecuted as if she had hired a gunman to murder her child. The doctor would have to be treated like the gunman. If the state had a death penalty, it would have to apply to both." Perhaps not so surprisingly, this same platform insists that all of the above is actually already the case; Republicans need only pass legislation to "make it clear" and appoint more judges to enforce it.[1]

While these ideas are clearly absurd, and unlikely ever to be legislated into law—much less survive a constitutional challenge—they make for smart politics nevertheless. In part because many of them are driven by genuine religious fervor, and in part because they believe themselves to be preventing the equivalent of legally sanctioned mass murder, many abortion opponents are an atypically dedicated bunch. They not only vote in primaries but work together throughout the year to gain control of their local Republican Party machinery. Energized by their regular protests—including the harassment of young women seeking legal abortions and of medical personnel willing to brave their threats to perform them—in 1992, notes Thomas Frank, "this populist conservative movement conquered the Kansas Republican Party from the ground up: in Johnson County, in Sedgwick County (Wichita), and in all the other heavily populated parts of the state, they swamped the GOP organizations with enthusiastic new activists and unceremoniously brushed the traditional Kansas moderates aside. In Sedgwick County, some 19 percent of the new precinct committee people responsible for throwing out the old guard actually had arrest records from the Summer of Mercy."[2]

These cadres of activists are inspired primarily by a sense of victimization. Republican strategies base their playbook on the activation of "anger points" in the electorate, and rhetoric like that concerning abortion in the party's political platform serves to do just that. As for the potential political cost of this kind of extremism, well, who pays attention to party platforms save journalists and activists, anyway?

To be honest, "choice" advocates have only exacerbated this unhappy situation. As the outspoken liberal evangelical pastor Jim Wallis complains, many moderate and progressive Christians cannot cooperate in any way, politically, with those who refuse to respect their views on a question they define to be absolutely fundamental to their personal and religious identities. Liberals who focus on abortion as purely a question of "rights" fail to appreciate not only the issue's legal complexity but also its emotional intensity, as well as the tragic toll it often takes on young women. I am hardly the first writer to note that if pro-choice advocates put as much energy into passing policies that sought to make abortions unnecessary—and did so explicitly under this rubric—they would find considerable common ground with religious Americans. Wallis suggests that pro-choice and pro-life constituencies unite to support programs that reduce teen pregnancy—and, failing that, adoption reform—while offering real support and meaningful alternatives for women at greater risk for unwanted pregnancies, particularly low-income women.[3] As a society, we were actually making considerable progress on helping to do just this with regard to the most vulnerable members of society: teens. Pregnancies between the ages of fifteen and seventeen fell 35 percent beginning in the early 1990s, with most of that drop attributable to increased use of contraception, together with reduced teen sexual activity. It was, according to Bill Albert of the National Campaign to Prevent Teen Pregnancy, "a really remarkable achievement." Alas, beginning in 2001, Bush administration conservatives instituted their purposefully misinformative "abstinence only" sex-education policy. Evidence indicates that a massive educational undertaking on exactly these issues would be far more effective.[4] But even in the face of the evidence, conservatives are unlikely to embrace such a plan, however effective, which is a pity. But even if those parts are made dependent on parental consent, such a campaign could emphasize health care and child care; combating teenage pregnancy and sexual abuse; improving poor and working women's incomes; and supporting what Wallis terms "reasonable restrictions on abortion, like parental notification for minors (with necessary legal protections against parental abuse)."[5] The latter part of the program is certain to be controversial with some, but most of Wallis's suggestions would be broadly supported by the vast majority of Americans and many liberals, and a compromise here might be highly productive in retaining the right for others. Hillary Clinton took a major step in the correct rhetorical direction when in January 2005 she appeared before a group of New York State family-planning providers and explained: "I believe we can all recognize that abortion in many ways represents a sad, even tragic choice to many, many women. Often, it's a failure of our system of education, health care, and preventive services. It's often a result of family dynamics. This decision is a profound and complicated one; a difficult one, often the most difficult that a woman will ever make. The fact is that the best way to reduce the number of abortions is to reduce the number of unwanted pregnancies in the first place."[6]

Meanwhile, even the most dedicated choice advocates need to give some thought to the best means to protect the right they believe to be embodied in the Constitution. While the rhetoric of Christian conservatives gives the impression that America is awash in abortions, the fact is, while in most places in the United States abortions are technically legal, they are nearly impossible to obtain. A mere 13 percent of counties in the nation now offer the service. This number can only decrease, as every one of the more than four hundred or so federal judges appointed by George W. Bush will seek to reduce it to zero.[7] Even where abortions are available, getting one can be such an ordeal that it's difficult to imagine many women actually going through with the process.

The state of Mississippi, for instance, home to nearly three million people, has a single abortion clinic. It also boasts the highest infant-mortality rate in the nation and ranks forty-third among the fifty states in the number of women who have health insurance. In 2004 Mississippi failed to meet national standards on the length of time it took to restore foster children to their birth families and to place a child for adoption. Meanwhile, the state's counseling provisions also require that patients be told that abortion may increase the risk of breast cancer, despite the fact that the National Cancer Institute, the British medical journal the *Lancet,* and faculty members of the Harvard Medical School have found no such link.[8] Mississippi is also one of only two states that require a minor to get the consent of both parents to have an abortion (though if the minor has been impregnated by her father, she needs only the consent of her mother). Not surprisingly, it boasts the highest teen birth rate in America, which continues to increase, including particularly girls under the age of fifteen.[9] Is this really the "right" choice advocates insist on defending to the death?

Mississippi may appear to be an extreme example, but, in fact, it is not unusual: as of the end of 2005, it came in at eighth place on the honor roll of states that "defend life," according to the rankings of the pro-life organization Americans United for Life.[10] Elsewhere in America, Medicaid funding has for nearly thirty years restricted abortions for low-income women, and eleven states now restrict abortion coverage in insurance plans for public employees. Forty-three states require parental consent or notice before a minor obtains an abortion. Thirty-one states demand that women receive "counseling" before an abortion, and eighteen offer it only in a misleading and frequently inaccurate form designed to scare them into changing their minds. Six states insist that this "counseling" be provided in person, ensuring at least two visits to the clinic. In addition, over a dozen states have so-called TRAP laws, which force abortion doctors and clinics to adopt especially difficult regulations. Former attorney general John Ashcroft subpoenaed hospitals for their files on hundreds of women who had undergone abortions, apparently looking for a means to harass both the women who had undergone abortions and the doctors who performed them.[11]

Liberals' insistence on the court-ordered "right" to abortion has also weakened their ability to make their broader case to the public in a democratic fashion. Kinsley makes the point that the judicial doctrine of *Roe v. Wade*, to which nearly all Democratic candidates for the Supreme Court—and the presidential candidates who wish to appoint them—must swear fealty, is, legally speaking, "a muddle of bad reasoning and an authentic example of judicial overreaching." While the same is undoubtedly true of any number of judicial decisions that have advanced our constitutional freedoms, *Roe* has turned out to be a political disaster for liberals. More than any other judicial decision, it has sustained the fervor of religious conservatives to remain in the political arena, and it may have prematurely ended a trend toward increasing the availability of legalized abortion on a state-by-state basis. Ruth Bader Ginsburg, who was in 1973 a prominent feminist attorney in New York, later said that lawsuits like *Roe* had "halted a political process that was moving in a reform direction." By 1972, sixteen states with 41 percent of the nation's population had liberalized their abortion laws, and the Republican platform did not even mention the subject, as George F. Will notes: "In 1976 the Republican platform protested the court's decision," recommended "continuance of the public dialogue on abortion," and endorsed a constitutional amendment "to restore protection of the right to life for unborn children." Today, this energized conservative constituency controls the executive and judicial branches of the U.S. government.[12]

The sad truth of American political life is that abortions, like narcotics, will always be relatively riskless for the well-to-do; it's the poor whose lives require such protections, and they require a lot more than theoretical access to abortion to improve their lives and share in the beneficence of America if the cost is the empowerment of an entire right-wing agenda. Should the Roberts Court wholly overturn *Roe,* liberals will once again be forced to fight for the now-attenuated right to choice in America, and with it, many of the causes that have died with it. Abortion rights won democratically will be far stronger and more stable than those secured only by what many consider to be judicial fiat, as they would be protected by the will of the majority and the politicians sent to defend them.

14

Why Do Liberals Believe in
Marriage Only for Homosexuals?

While perhaps not quite as weighty as that of abortion, the issue of gay marriage has also proven in recent times to be a political burden for liberals. Although gays have gained increasing acceptance as individuals, their collective rights remain a political hot potato. Once a series of court cases in Massachusetts, Vermont, and California put the issue of gay marriage front and center, with photos of mass marriages on the steps of San Francisco's City Hall broadcast on every television station in America, "public opinion," notes Thomas Edsall, "which had for several decades been trending in an increasingly liberal direction on the subject of gay rights, abruptly shifted rightward." Poll after poll reported sharp drops in backing for gay marriage, while opposition grew no less precipitately. In 2004 over 40 percent of voters insisted that they would not vote for a candidate who disagreed with them on this issue, no matter what. These numbers were higher than those for either abortion or gun control, two issues previously acknowledged to be at the vortex of the American culture wars.[1] Moreover, gay marriage is a no-cost contest for conservatives. Most reliable estimates put the gay population at somewhere between 2 and 4 percent of the U.S. population. "Targeting homosexuality harvests much greater popular support than any attempt to outlaw or reduce the incidence of divorce—which, in terms of its impact on 'traditional families,' is far more significant," observes Edsall. "In effect, the conservative crusade against homosexuals is a means of uniting the Christian evangelical troops, and protesting the deregulation of sexual norms in general, without requiring much moral effort from the right-of-center heterosexual Christian electorate."[2]

The issue attracts the attention of working-class Catholics, who tend to hold the political balance in national elections. Pope Benedict's pronouncements represent a hardening of even his predecessor's tough line against not only gay marriage but all activities associated with homosexuality. In his 1986 "Letter to the Bishop," then-Cardinal Ratzinger declared what he called "the homosexual condition" to be "a more or less strong tendency ordered toward an intrinsic moral evil," and "an objective disorder."[3] No doubt in response to intense campaigning by members of the church hierarchy on this point, in 2004 the Catholic candidate John Kerry lost the Catholic vote to the Baptist George W. Bush, whose position on gay marriage (and abortion) was closest to that of the church. Moreover, not only did Bush markedly improve his percentage of the Catholic vote, but Catholic turnout increased by 11 percent.[4]

Clearly, gay marriage has been a loser for liberals; but that doesn't necessarily imply that they should therefore capitulate. Pandering to public opinion can easily boomerang politically. John Kerry's presidential campaign had any number of credibility problems, but one glaring one was his position on gay marriage. Kerry opposed its legalization, but hardly anyone believed him, and with good reason: it would be difficult to find a single Massachusetts liberal who did not think that gay people should enjoy the same rights to civil marriage as straight people. It's certainly possible that Kerry was speaking from his heart when he rejected this position, but it undoubtedly struck voters as a great deal more likely that he was pandering to majority sentiment in the electorate. The net effect was that few Americans were convinced that the candidate shared their values, while many had good reason to question his authenticity and willingness to stand up for his beliefs, making the issue a loser twice over.

One strategy would be to try to table the subject for now, asking gays to please wait patiently while the political views of the majority catch up to the norms of social reality. Most gays are also liberals and rational people, and could probably see the value of putting aside this particular demand for the time being. The number of Americans favoring gay civil unions reached a majority in 2006, with fewer than a third embracing the conservative Christian position in favor of a constitutional amendment that would ban gay marriage.[5] When given a choice between civil unions or nothing at all, the percentage in favor rises to 65 percent.[6] More important, surveys of people under age twenty-five demonstrate significantly higher support for a live-and-let-live policy toward gays, including issues of marriage and civil unions, than among the older population[7]—a finding that suggests that winning this issue is probably just a matter of patience.

Consider, for instance, the progress of acceptance of gays in other aspects of American life. Edsall notes that in the late 1980s, voters by a margin of 51 to 42 percent believed that "school boards ought to have the right to fire teachers who are known homosexuals." Today voters disagree, 66 to 28. In 1987 voters found themselves roughly evenly divided over whether "AIDS might be God's punishment for immoral sexual behavior." Today voters disagree, 72 to 23.[8]

Capitulation on this subject is, in any case, impractical. In the first place, the courts have decided that the issue is upon us, as evinced by the justices in Massachusetts, Hawaii, and New Jersey who have ruled on its legality, so it's going to happen anyway. Second, there will always be ambitious politicians who seek to solidify their reputations for "bravery" and "vision," and many in the conservative and tabloid-driven media will seize on these individuals and blow their positions up into national controversies. Conservative Republicans will naturally do the same, for when the topic dominates the headlines, it not only removes the proverbial spotlight from a whole host of issues where their positions are well beyond the national consensus but puts liberals in exactly the same bind in which candidate Kerry found himself. This explains why the Republicans continue to bring up the subject on the floor of Congress just before every election, but ensure that they lose whatever vote it happens to take. If they won, the issue would go away, which is the last thing they want. Instead, continual defeats on gay marriage—which is already illegal virtually everywhere in America—allow them to appeal to the sense of persecution that so many conservatives enjoy, even while controlling two of the three branches of the federal government, most state legislatures, and much of the media.

Gay marriage is a nearly perfect "anger point" for right-wingers. As the data indicate, "gay marriage is a make-or-break voting issue only to the opponents of that idea; supporters of gay marriage generally say a candidate's stance would not affect their vote."[9] All this is one reason we find U.S. senators like Tom Coburn of Oklahoma warning that "the gay community has infiltrated the very centers of power in every area across this country, and they wield extreme power. . . . That agenda is the greatest threat to our freedom that we face today. Why do you think we see the rationalization for abortion and multiple sexual partners? That's the gay agenda."[10] The Supreme Court's legalization of consensual homosexual sex led then–Pennsylvania senator Rick Santorum to sound the alarm against the imminent arrival of "you know, man on child, man on dog, or whatever the case may be."[11] It also found U.S. Supreme Court justice Antonin Scalia writing in his dissent that the decision would inspire "the end of all morals legislation" banning "bigamy . . . adult incest, prostitution, masturbation, adultery, fornication, bestiality, and obscenity."[12] And finally, recall Louisiana Republican senator David Vitter, who, speaking after Hurricane Katrina had devastated the lives of hundreds of thousands of his constituents and all but destroyed the largest city in the state, nevertheless insisted that new legislation preventing the already outlawed practice of gay marriage was the single most "important" issue facing the nation.[13]

Liberals' only conceivable response given all of the above is to argue for what they truly believe. What they lose on the question itself, they win back on the question of authenticity, and since the issue is trending their way, it will eventually cease to carry a political cost. Already, liberals and moderates agree that "homosexuality is a way of life that should be accepted by society," while conservatives still believe, by 64 percent to 29 percent, that it is something that should be "discouraged."[14] Homophobic conservatives are not going to be voting for liberals anyway. Indeed, many on the right are so committed to their intolerant beliefs that they support the policy of firing gay Arabic translators from the military at a time when the nation is desperately seeking to increase our ability to monitor terrorist communications. These bigots, as one fired gay translator told Stephen Colbert, would prefer to be blown up by al-Qaeda than to be saved from an attack by a gay man or woman.

Meanwhile, liberals will demonstrate their ability to fight, unapologetically, for an unpopular cause, which can yield untold dividends, virtue being the child of necessity. George W. Bush's most effective argument in 2004, according to numerous pollsters and political analysts, was the line, "You may not always agree with me, but you'll always know where I stand." Even his strongest supporters—outside of his immediate family—would not have made the same argument vis-à-vis John Kerry, in part precisely because of his unwillingness to endorse civil marriage for gays. There can be no harm, likewise, in making the case in the context of a strong pro-family argument. We all recognize the value of families, both to children and adults; the difference between liberals and conservatives is that the former are not going to tell you who's allowed to be a part of yours.

15

Why Are Liberals Educating
Our Children to Be Perverts?

Sex education has long required a careful juggling act on the part of American politicians. In a nation that retains much of its Puritan heritage, the combination of sex and children remains particularly explosive politically. Talking about sex with kids can make almost any adult uncomfortable. Ideally, parents would pass along to their children before they reached the age of sexual maturity the knowledge they need to behave in a sexually responsible fashion. In practice we know this does not always happen. Many parents, even the ones who approve of the idea, cannot bring themselves to carry it out. They prefer to live in a fantasy world where other people's children may be sexually active, but not their own. Unfortunately, the cost to society of this fantasy is not merely hurt feelings or unwanted pregnancies for teenagers, but potentially death. In the age of AIDS, as well as other resistant strains of sexually transmitted diseases, society cannot afford to indulge these parents.

Americans long ago decided that sex education was a necessary part of a teenager's academic education, but they have never agreed on its content. Liberals tend to argue that children, once they reach a certain age, should receive all the information necessary to conduct happy and healthy sex lives, with the understanding that their moral education is the responsibility of their families, churches, and so on. Conservatives, meanwhile, tend to prefer that children be drilled on the lessons of the Bible, and on what pundits call "traditional morality." That means they are to be taught nothing about birth control, and urged to reject heterosexual sex outside of marriage, and homosexuality under any circumstances. During the past decade, conservatives have employed their political dominance to force on schools an "abstinence-only" curriculum designed to instruct teenagers to refrain from all sexual activities, sometimes even including masturbation. Alas, these programs are not merely ineffective but counterproductive. According to one study done in George W. Bush's home state of Texas, teenagers in twenty-nine high schools became increasingly sexually active, mirroring the overall state trends, after implementation of the abstinence-only curriculum. The study revealed that before receiving abstinence education, about 23 percent of ninth-grade girls, typically thirteen to fourteen years old, had had sex. After taking the course, 28 percent of the girls in the same group said they had had sex.[1] In a larger study by the Centers for Disease Control, researchers found that although teenagers who take "virginity pledges" may wait longer to initiate sexual activity, they are more likely to enjoy oral and anal sex, and they are just as likely as other students to be infected with sexually transmitted diseases. Eighty-eight percent eventually have premarital intercourse. While abstinence-only programs show little evidence of sustained effect on a student's sexual activities, they do reduce the use of contraception, including condoms, when sex does take place.[2]

The failure of these program is at least partially attributable to the fact that they are purposely, indeed transparently, dishonest. Of the thirteen federally funded programs studied, just two provided students with accurate medical and scientific information. In the rest, students learned such "facts" as:

- Half the gay male teenagers in the United States have tested positive for the AIDS virus.
- Touching a person's genitals "can result in pregnancy."
- A forty-three-day-old fetus is a "thinking person."
- HIV, the virus that causes AIDS, can be spread via sweat and tears.
- Condoms fail to prevent HIV transmission as often as 31 percent of the time in heterosexual intercourse. (In fact, the rate is less than 3 percent, according to the Centers for Disease Control.)
- Women who experience abortions "are more prone to suicide," and as many as 10 percent of them become sterile.

According to the conservative Christians in the Family Research Council, however, the relative failure of their lessons merely indicates that even more of the same may be needed. Upon the announcement that yet another study, this one congressionally mandated and published by Mathematica Policy Research Inc. in the spring of 2007, had demonstrated the ineffectiveness of such education, the group insisted that these very same failed "programs must be intensive and long-term, so that the knowledge, attitudes, and skills needed to reject sex before marriage are constantly reinforced—particularly in the pivotal high school years."[3] No wonder, then, that nine states—at the time of this writing—have chosen to forgo federal matching funds to which they would be entitled rather than submit their children to the dishonest, propagandistic programs of conservative abstinence-only ideologues.[4]

In keeping with the conservative Christians' "don't ask, don't tell" attitude toward nearly all forms of sexual activity, in November 2006 Bush appointed Dr. Eric Keroack to the post of deputy assistant secretary for population affairs, overseeing a number of Health and Human Services programs, including the Office of Family Planning and what is called "Title X," a Nixon-era program that distributes contraceptives to poor or uninsured women. A favorite guest speaker of the National Right to Life Committee and one of the administration's "experts," who insists that federally funded abstinence-education programs must mention contraceptives only in relation to their failure rates, Keroack teaches that there is a physiological cause for relationship failure and sexual promiscuity that he calls "God's Super Glue," which results in a hormonal cause and effect that can be short-circuited only by sexual abstinence until marriage. And though he enjoyed the position of full-time medical director for A Woman's Concern, a chain of Boston-area crisis pregnancy centers that regards the distribution of contraceptives as demeaning to women, he was not even a certified obstetrician-gynecologist at the time of his appointment.[5] (Keroack resigned this post shortly after the Massachusetts Office of Medicaid announced an investigation into his private practice.)

Still, Keroack may have looked like a slam-dunk appointment for the right when posed beside George W. Bush's choice for the President's Advisory Committee for Reproductive Health Drugs in the Food and

Drug Administration. That nominee, Dr. W. David Hager, who played a lead role in the FDA's long delay in approving the so-called morning-after pill, tells audiences that "God has called me to stand in the gap . . . not only for others, but regarding ethical and moral issues in our country." But according to his wife of thirty years and coauthor, Linda Carruth Davis, Hager repeatedly sodomized her without her consent for a period of seven years. She termed the sexual incidents "painful, invasive," and "totally nonconsensual."[6]

In June 2007 Bush chose as the nation's surgeon general Dr. James W. Holsinger Jr., who belongs to a church that offers a ministry to "cure" gays, and who was the author of a 1991 paper that compared human genitalia to pipe fittings in making the argument that homosexuality was both unnatural and medically unhealthy. "When the complementarity of the sexes is breached, injuries and diseases may occur," wrote the man whom George W. Bush thought should be America's most important and influential medical officer.[7]

He was to replace Richard H. Carmona, a former professor of surgery and public health at the University of Arizona, who told a congressional panel in the summer of 2007 that Bush political appointees frequently vetted speeches for politically sensitive content and blocked him from speaking out on public health matters such as stem-cell research, abstinence-only sex education, and the emergency contraceptive Plan B.

"Anything that doesn't fit into the political appointees' ideological, theological or political agenda is often ignored, marginalized or simply buried," he said. "Much of the discussion was being driven by theology, ideology, [and] preconceived beliefs that were scientifically incorrect," he explained. This was particularly true with regard to sex. Carmona said that when the administration touted funding for abstinence-only education, he was prevented from discussing research on the effectiveness of teaching about condoms as well as abstinence. "There was already a policy in place that did not want to hear the science but wanted to just preach abstinence, which I felt was scientifically incorrect," Carmona said.[8] But it was not true only with regard to sex; it was true with regard to pretty much everything. When, for instance, in 2006, the surgeon general wished to release a report that was compiled by government and private public-health experts from various organizations—including the National Institutes of Health, the Catholic Medical Mission Board, and several universities—addressing the problems of global health that were related to intense poverty, and suggesting that multinational corporations could play a role in addressing these problems, its publication was blocked by William R. Steiger, a Bush family friend who had no scientific or medical background but had somehow been charged by the Bush administration to run the Office of Global Health Affairs in the Department of Health and Human Services. Carmona later admitted that he was "called in and again admonished . . . via a senior official who said, 'You don't get it.'" He said a senior official told him that "this will be a political document, or it will not be released." One of the issues upon which the report focused, naturally, was the prevention of a global pandemic of AIDS and educational means of combating it.[9]

Why do right-wingers promote the lies of such sources, whose express purpose is to misinform young people and deny them the knowledge they require to conduct their inevitable sexual experiments safely? The answer is that conservatives place significant social value on hypocrisy, particularly in matters of sex, and particularly when it comes to the less fortunate members of society. For instance, the editors of the *Wall Street Journal* argued that while elites could be trusted to enjoy a wide variety of sexual stimulation, the "weaker or more vulnerable" require social "guardrails," as they are not "exceedingly sophisticated, neither thinkers nor leaders, never interviewed for their views, they're held together by faith, friends, fun and, at the margins, fanaticism." It may be true that "most of the teenage girls in the Midwest who learn about the nuances of sex from magazines published by thirtysomething women in New York will more or less survive," the editors continued, but "some continue to end up as prostitutes on Eighth Avenue. . . . These weaker or more vulnerable people, who in different ways must try to live along life's margins, are among the reasons that society erects rules."[10] The *Journal* editors, together with the Bush administration, might be interested to learn that, in an extensive 2006 survey of the literature based on twenty years of National Survey of

Family Growth polling by the Alan Guttmacher Institute, a New York City–based nonprofit organization that studies reproductive and sexual health data, fully 95 percent of American adults said that they had had premarital sex, 93 percent of them by the age of thirty. (The *Journal* editors notwithstanding, with nearly 150 million females in America, the number of those who end up as "prostitutes on Eighth Avenue" would appear to be statistically insignificant.) Given that federal government guidelines for the millions of dollars it offers for abstinence-only programs now target unmarried adults up to age twenty-nine, the ludicrousness of the hypocrisy involved becomes ever more stark.[11] The funds are in effect attempting to restrict something that 93 percent of Americans—voting with their bodies—think is just fine. The taxpayer—so beloved by the *Wall Street Journal* when it comes to preventing government expenditures that actually benefit poor people—is expected to fund this nonsense because, in the area of sex as in so many others, conservative hypocrisy trumps common sense.

What is perhaps most infuriating, however, is that conservatives rarely insist that their own elites play by the rules they insist on for others. Personal sexual scandals are hardly unknown to the *Wall Street Journal* editorial writers, and yet none of them has ever been lectured about the danger his low moral standards poses to the nation at large. The same is true of some of America's most prominent "virtuecrats." Conservative pundits Bill O'Reilly and John McLaughlin have both paid massive amounts of money to settle sexual harassment suits leveled by their employees. Fire-and-brimstone preachers Jim Bakker, Jimmy Swaggart, and Ted Haggard led secret sex lives that would impress almost anyone. Randall Tobias, the Bush administration official who championed abstinence-based international AIDS funding, lost his job for apparently failing to abstain all those times he paid "to have gals come over to the condo to give me a massage."[12] In addition to Tobias, the activities of Messrs. Gingrich, Hyde, Livingston, Vitter, and Foley also raise questions about the bona fides of conservatism's leading lights to lecture the rest of us in this context. These politicians are hardly statistical outliers.

When we examine the statistics on their personal behavior, we find that for all of their moralizing about the wicked lives led by the rest of us, conservative Christians are really in no position to lecture anyone about any of the issues they consider fundamental to morality. The evidence from extensive polling of evangelicals, laments evangelical theologian Michael Horton, "presents survey after survey demonstrating that evangelical Christians are as likely to embrace lifestyles every bit as hedonistic, materialistic, self-centered, and sexually immoral as the world in general." In a 1999 national survey, the Barna Group found that the percentage of born-again Christians who had been divorced was slightly higher (26 percent) than that of non-Christians (22 percent). In Barna's polls since the mid-1990s, that number has remained nearly consistent. Barna also found in one study that 90 percent of all respondents who divorced did so after they accepted Christ. In many parts of the Bible Belt—where the number of conservative Christians is highest—the divorce rate was discovered to be "roughly 50 percent above the national average," while the number of couples living "in sin" also increased far faster than the national average.[13] If it's liberals who are trying to corrupt our nation's notions of right and wrong when it comes to matters of family and sexuality, and to turn our children into "perverts," they're doing something wrong. They could easily take a lesson from Christian conservatives.

16

Why Do Liberals Hate Religion?

Missing from almost all discussions of the role of religion in public life is what William James famously termed the "varieties of religious experience." The right wing's hijacking of religion's public role in our political discourse is as undeniable as it is inappropriate, and represents one of liberalism's most serious problems. And while all of the problems discussed above certainly interfere with liberals' ability to make their case to religious Americans, they, too, must share some degree of responsibility for their failure. Whereas a generation ago Americans found themselves inspired by such liberal religious figures as Dorothy Day, Reinhold Niebuhr, Abraham Joshua Heschel, Michael Harrington, and, of course, Martin Luther King Jr., the prophetic voice has been, in recent days, in decidedly short supply in American liberalism. Also largely AWOL from the liberal barricades are the mainline Protestant churches that made up the backbone of the middle-class civil rights and antiwar movements.

In the 2006 election, when Democrats scored a signal victory by almost any standard, and while the Republican Party was weighted down with homosexual sex scandals involving congressional pages and accusations of betrayal from the White House liaison to the evangelical community, the losing team, according to exit polling, still carried 60 percent of voters who say they attend religious services more than once a week, a figure that remained consistent with findings from the 2002 and 2004 elections. A majority (53 percent) of those who attend church at least once a week also support Republicans.[1] An earlier 2006 poll by the same organization, the Pew Forum on Religion and Public Life, found that barely more than a quarter of voters—26 percent—regarded the Democratic Party as "friendly to religion," roughly the same number that thought that liberals had gone too far in keeping religion out of government and schools.[2] This is a political catastrophe in a country where more than half the citizens questioned tell pollsters they attend religious services at least once a week, and nearly three-quarters say they pray at least once a day.[3]

While the number of Americans who have become alienated from organized religion appears to be increasing, particularly among young people, roughly 90 percent of Americans continue to tell pollsters that they consider themselves to be believers of one sort or another.[4] About 80 percent identify with some Christian faith, 79 percent believe in the virgin birth, 78 percent say Jesus physically rose from the dead, and 48 percent claim to have had a "born again experience."[5] This is one area in which Americans differ quite markedly from Europeans, and indeed, from the people of every other major industrial democracy. More than 60 percent of Americans state that belief in God is necessary in order "to be moral and have good values," which is about twice the number of Germans and six times the number of French who say they feel similarly.[6] As Barack Obama points out, "Substantially more people in America believe in angels than they do in evolution."[7]

Liberals, particularly religious liberals, have done a poor job of communicating their own bedrock values to America's religious majority. Following the 1960s the left made the politically suicidal choice of cultural radicalism, which succeeded, over political and economic radicalism, which failed. As religion reporter Peter Steinfels observes, "American liberalism has shifted its passion from issues of economic deprivation and concentration of power to issues of gender, sexuality, and personal choice. . . . Once trade unionism, regulation of the market, and various welfare measures were the litmus tests of secular liberalism. Later, desegregation and racial justice were the litmus tests. Today the litmus test is abortion."[8] Liberals, as Michael Kazin put it, have morphed in the public imagination "from people who looked, dressed and sounded like Woody Guthrie to people who look, dress and sound like Woody Allen."[9]

This historic mistake can, in fact, be easily rectified. Liberal lion Franklin Roosevelt felt no compunction in proclaiming that the "Almighty God has . . . given our people stout hearts and strong arms with which to strike mighty blows for freedom and truth. He has given to our country a faith which has become the hope of all peoples in an anguished world." During World War II, FDR's War Department provided every member of the armed forces with a Bible accompanied with a message from the president that read, "As Commander in Chief, I take pleasure in commending the reading of the Bible to all who serve in the armed forces of the United States. Throughout the centuries, men of many faiths and diverse origins have found in the Sacred Book, words of wisdom, counsel and inspiration. It is a foundation of strength and now, as always, an aid in attaining the highest aspirations of the human soul." Religious liberals responded in kind. *Commonweal* magazine informed readers that FDR's 1932 victory was "likewise the Catholic opportunity to make the teachings of Christ apply to the benefit of all." The Christian journalist and editor Stanley Hoflund High, who organized the pro-FDR Good Neighbor League to rally religious support that year, argued, "This is the first time in modern history when a Government in any nation has set out to give practical application to the principles of the Sermon on the Mount."[10]

FDR's successor, the famously plainspoken Harry S. Truman, was not averse to announcing, "We believe that all men are created equal because they are created in the image of God. From this faith we will not be moved." John F. Kennedy invited his fellow Americans to embrace "the same revolutionary beliefs for which our forebears fought," those that were "still at issue around the globe: the belief that the rights of man come not from the generosity of the state, but from the hand of God."[11] Certainly historian James T. Kloppenberg is correct in arguing that it would be as "impossible to understand the civil rights movement without Reverend King or Vernon Johns or the antiwar movement without the Reverend Robert Drinan or William Sloane Coffin as it would be to try to comprehend earlier American reform movements in isolation from the religious activists who helped give them their shape and their energy."[12]

Should contemporary liberal rationalists experience some discomfort in engaging the spiritual realm, we turn to no less an authority than John

Dewey, who praised the crusading fundamentalist Christian reformer William Jennings Bryan as "the backbone of philanthropic social interest, of social reform through political action, of pacifism, of popular education." Indeed, as Bryan's biographer Michael Kazin notes, the Great Commoner transformed his party from a bulwark of conservatism into a bastion of anticorporate progressivism. Speaking of nineteenth-century America (and it only slightly overstates the case as it applies to the following century), Kazin argues that "American progressive reform has never advanced without a moral awakening entangled with notions about what the Lord would have us do."[13]

American liberals need to remember what the great German philosopher Jürgen Habermas has frequently argued: not only must believers tolerate others' beliefs, including the credos and convictions of nonbelievers, but disbelieving secularists must likewise appreciate the convictions of religiously motivated fellow citizens.

Liberals actually have many points of confluence with many cultural conservatives—at least those who reject biblical literalism. You don't need to be a Christian conservative to object to the kinds of cultural messages regularly communicated to children and teens by American entertainment culture. For instance, when Justin Timberlake ripped off Janet Jackson's top at the Super Bowl performance, liberals tended to mock conservative hysteria over a single barely exposed breast. I did so myself. But far more objectionable was the fact that Timberlake ripped off Jackson's clothing in what the liberal social critic Robert Wright described as "an act of stylized male sexual aggression, an apparent preamble to rape."[14] This ought to offend all of us, particularly liberals, and especially parents. As a parent I find myself constantly bombarded with messages explicitly designed to corrupt the values of my child for the purpose of corporate gain. In addition to being a cesspool of right-wing racism, much of talk radio is also a free-fire zone for verbal violence against women. Recall that after the "shock jocks" Opie and Anthony were kicked off terrestrial radio for reporting, live, an alleged sex act in St. Patrick's Cathedral, they moved to satellite radio, where they featured a guest who joked about performing an anal rape on Secretary of

State Condoleezza Rice and other unspeakable acts on Laura Bush. (The penalty for this offense was a thirty-day suspension.)[15]

Liberal politicians, like all politicians, are no strangers to high-minded condemnation of things that all sensible people reject; would it be so difficult to pay more attention to the outrages against what used to be called "common decency" by those who profit in our culture from encouraging attacks on our wives, daughters, and mothers? Similarly, the disrespect for women, and for our collective humanity, in so much "gangsta rap" need not be censored but does require condemnation, at least by those of us who do not wish to live in a society that regards women as "hos" and "bitches" and celebrates rape and genuinely disgusting forms of sexual violence.[16] Hollywood producers and rap artists who exploit the violent denigration of women should be condemned by liberals every bit as much as the racism, homophobia, and sexism that are so frequently purveyed on right-wing talk radio.

The same is true for corporations that deliberately glorify antisocial behavior in teens and other impressionable people. Cigarette companies are in many ways the worst and most obvious offenders, but why, for instance, do liberals fail to protest when clothing companies selling to teens plaster the subways with posters for the "State Property" line, which distinguishes itself from other brands by featuring hidden pockets and gun holsters, as if to teach teens to admire jailed drug-dealing thugs and murderers? Why do we not object when the fashion industry promotes not only anorexia in young girls but also the deliberately spaced-out junkie look, or when the media obsessively covers sexualized preteens who continually make headlines with their vulgar and spoiled behavior? John Stuart Mill wrote in *On Liberty* of the use of "moral disapprobation in the proper sense of the term as a useful check on antisocial behavior." (His example was a father's squandering his family's food money.)[17] Where, today, is that liberal voice of "moral disapprobation," directed where it might not only be most useful but could find common ground with cultural conservatives?

A second avenue open to liberals who seek to reach religious and culturally conservative Americans would be to employ a moral vocabulary when discussing political and economic issues. There is nothing to prevent making a moral case, for example, that it is objectionable to give huge tax cuts to the rich while cutting social programs for the poor and working class when that gap is already at its widest in an entire century. Liberal arguments for universal health care and education are also fundamentally moral arguments, and need not be defended entirely in terms of economic efficiency—though they can be. CEOs who rob their corporations and stockholders need to be held up to public disapproval in the manner that right-wingers condemn drug dealers and violent criminals. According to a 2005 poll of more than ten thousand voters conducted by Zogby International for the Center for American Progress, 64 percent of voters chose either greed and materialism or poverty and economic justice as the most urgent moral problems facing America, compared to only 27 percent who answered abortion and same-sex marriage. Fifty-one percent of voters said the conservative focus on social issues made no difference to their vote, and 56 percent of Catholic voters said efforts to make abortion and gay marriage, quote, "non-negotiable" had no influence on their vote.[18] And yet where is their voice? Who is their champion? Just what is preventing liberals from joining their cause?

Perhaps it is true, as the liberal and devout Catholic E. J. Dionne concedes, that conservatives have a number of natural advantages when seeking to link religious devotion to politics. They have claimed the word *tradition* as their own, for one thing. And as Russell Kirk pointed out in his 1953 book *The Conservative Mind*, the canons of conservatism tend naturally to appeal to the faithful: conservatives, he wrote, believe in "a transcendent order, or body of natural law, which rules society as well as conscience." Their attachment to "custom, convention and old prescription" provides a check on "man's anarchic impulse and upon the innovator's lust for power." Liberalism, on the other hand, arose in revolt against many of these same customs and conventions, particularly the oppressive power of the church.[19] Conservative Christians are also cohesive in their beliefs. While Americans who identify themselves as "liberal or progressive Christians" outnumber self-described evangelical Christians by a 32 to 24 percent margin, the former belong to different religious traditions and disagree almost as often as they agree on a number of key political and social issues, and as such could not be organized to act as a political bloc even if anyone were to give it a serious try.[20]

Liberals do enjoy one proverbial ace in the hole when it comes to the marriage of religion and politics, and that is Christianity itself, properly understood. Liberal evangelical Jim Wallis correctly points out that the issue the Bible raises most often is not abortion or gay marriage but "how you treat the poorest and most vulnerable in your society. That's the issue the prophets raise again and again, and Jesus talks about it more than any other topic, more than heaven or hell, more than sex or morality. So how did Jesus become pro-rich, pro-war and only pro-American?"[21] In fact, evangelicals are finally becoming more sensitive to issues of environmental and global justice, and recent surveys by the evangelical Barna Group demonstrate a definite trend on the part of younger "born-again" Christians toward more acceptance of homosexuality and less opposition to gay rights. (The same is decidedly not true, however, when it comes to abortion.)[22]

Certainly liberals have much in common with the theology of those like the modern best-selling evangelical leader Rick Warren, the pastor of a huge 22,000-member church in Orange County, California. Warren is, after Billy Graham, America's most famous evangelical preacher, a conservative on matters relating to abortion and gay marriage, but critical not only of his church but also of himself for focusing exclusively on these issues at the expense of those relating to the social gospel. Warren chooses not to speak about politics from his pulpit. "I have been so busy building my church that I have not cared about the poor," he confessed to his fellow pastors. "I have sinned, and I am sorry."[23] Warren's *The Purpose-Driven Life*—which happens to be one of the best-selling books ever written, with a reported twenty-five million copies in print—calls upon Christians "to attack the five global, evil giants of our day. . . spiritual emptiness, corrupt leadership, poverty, disease, and illiteracy." He has scandalized some of his fellow evangelicals by signing the February 2006 evangelical statement to combat global warming, by condemning the Bush administration's eagerness to torture prisoners, by visiting

America's adversaries in Syria, and by issuing an invitation to none other than Barack Obama to appear at his church's second global AIDS conference.[24]

Indeed, as Warren's own evolution suggests, it ought not to be too taxing for any religious Christian to commit to memory a few of the Bible's more poetic phrases that have no place in a Karl Rove playbook, much less a Rush Limbaugh rant. There is, for instance, the Gospel that explains, "He has cast down the mighty from their thrones, and has lifted up the lowly. He has filled the hungry with good things, and the rich he has sent away empty!" (Luke 1:52–53). The prophet Isaiah commands us to "undo the heavy burdens . . . let the oppressed go free." Martin Luther King Jr. frequently drew on the prophet Amos to insist, "We will not be satisfied until 'justice rolls down like waters, and righteousness like a mighty stream.'" Jesus demanded we feed the hungry and clothe the naked and tells us we will be judged by how we treat the "least of these my brethren." Fully 92 percent of churchgoing Christians tell pollsters that their pastor has addressed the congregation on the topic of poverty and homelessness, which is 50 percent more than those who've sermonized on abortion and nearly twice as many as those who say they've been instructed on the hot-button topic of gay marriage.[25] Clearly most churchgoers—in contradistinction to their largely self-anointed conservative spokespeople—keep the focus of Christianity where Jesus himself established it.

The "key," if there is one, is not merely to say the passages, but to say them with genuine conviction. If liberals cannot do this, then they resign themselves to losing, always, in America. This is a free country, but also a deeply religious one. There can be no more Sisyphean battle than to ignore this or try to wish it away. For liberals, this fact should be a blessing, not a curse. Where we differ from conservatives ought not to be in the degree of our religious commitment, or in the belief that politics and religion are largely inseparable. For liberals, religious beliefs provide personal inspiration rather than dogmatic direction. Our Enlightenment legacy mitigates any claims of absolute truth, particularly one deriving from a literalist interpretation of a particular religious text. Let justice flow, as Dr. King preached, like a mighty river. But while rivers flow in only one direction, they can have many tributaries and many uses. As liberals, we do not enforce our own understanding of the word of God on others who might not share it. But that does not mean we cannot hear it in our hearts, speak its truths, and allow it to inspire us once again, someday, to overcome.

17

Why Do Liberals Hate the Jews?

"Contemporary empirical realities demonstrate one undeniable fact," according to the right-wing Web magazine Frontpagemag.com, published by David Horowitz. "The primary source of the hatred of Jews now emanates from the Left. In fact," the magazine's managing editor, Jamie Glazov, continues, "anti-Semitism has evolved into a cultural code and even a rallying cry for progressive radicals throughout the world."[1] Many conservative and even centrist media figures take this case even further, attacking liberal bloggers for alleged anti-Semitism in their opposition to the senatorial candidacy of Joe Lieberman or for providing space on their blogs where anti-Semites and other lunatics occasionally post comments, until they are noticed, taken down, and condemned. When an instance of this occurred on the Web site of the liberal organization MoveOn.org, one writer, Marshall Wittmann (now Lieberman's spokesman), asked, "The question is why Democratic leaders continue to collude with the anti-Semitic appeasing left." Actually it's not such a tough question to answer, and a blogger responded immediately: in this context, "collude" means that Democratic leaders work with people who run a Web site on which some readers have posted some allegedly anti-Semitic material. Wittmann, in contrast, worked directly for the extremist anti-Semite Pat Robertson as he was in the process of disseminating the familiar ideology of the far right: a conspiracy theory blaming wars and revolutions on a secret cabal of Jewish bankers, Freemasons, Illuminati, atheists, and internationalists. Wittmann's complaint was nevertheless picked up by William Kristol on the *Wall Street Journal* editorial page, the *Washington Times*, and all over the right-wing media and blogosphere, and yet, strangely, no one thought to point out the irony.[2] (In fact, the entire extent of the offense on MoveOn's part was to have a bulletin board where anyone could post; as soon as the offending comments were discovered, they were immediately removed.) The Lieberman campaign continued to traffic in this kind of unsupported allegation, however, and was rarely checked in doing so by mainstream reporters. Lieberman's adviser and later communications director Dan Gerstein insisted during the campaign of the existence of "a growing tolerance" in the "progressive community" of a "perhaps anti-Semitic" faction. The *New York Times* printed his accusation, again without providing any evidence, context, or even dissenting voices.[3]

As the Wittmann/Robertson/MoveOn.org case indicates, given the context of what the rest of us experience as "reality," the equation of liberalism with anti-Semitism is one of the oddest and least explicable of right-wing obsessions in recent decades. While it is not impossible to find expressions of anti-Semitism on the left, it is espoused almost exclusively by the most marginal of political figures: Al Sharpton back when he was causing riots in Harlem, or the *Nation's* crackpot Communist crank, Alexander Cockburn, perhaps. As with the charge of a media dominated by liberals—which for many on the right is a code word for "Jews"—most such complaints are undertaken on behalf of some unspoken agenda on the part of the accuser.

What may be the chef d'oeuvre of this particular form of performance art took place on a December 2004 edition of the MSNBC program *Scarborough Country*. I include it as an example of both how this topic makes some conservatives crazy, and also how divorced from any kind of recognizable reality the accusations against liberals have grown. Recall that MSNBC is a mainstream cable-news network that is actually considered "liberal" by the standards of the medium. That night's discussion concerned the alleged media campaign of character assassination against Mel Gibson and his film *The Passion of the Christ*. William Donohue, president of the Catholic League for Religious and Civil Rights, happened to be making one of his twenty-three 2004 cable appearances. As he explained to guest host Pat Buchanan, "Hollywood is controlled by secular Jews who hate Christianity in general and Catholicism in particular. It's not a secret, okay? And I'm not afraid to say it. . . . Hollywood likes anal sex. They like to see the public square without nativity scenes. I like families. I like children. They like abortions."

When another panelist, Rabbi Shmuley Boteach—author of the book *Kosher Sex* and a spiritual adviser to Michael Jackson—tried to jump in to put a halt to the nakedly anti-Semitic comments, Buchanan—a conservative who defends accused Nazi war criminals and refers to Congress as "Israel's Amen corner"—interceded on Donohue's behalf to tell Boteach to "stop the personal insults." So, too, did another guest on this estimable panel: Jennifer Giroux, founder and director of SeeThePassion.com, and a member of Buchanan's splinterite Reform Party, who was making one of her fourteen separate *Scarborough Country* appearances in just nine months. The following exchange occurred in the wake of Donohue's secular Jews–anal sex observation:

> *Boteach*: Stop the anti-Semitic garbage, OK?
>
> *Donohue*: Who's making the movies? The Irishmen?
>
> *Boteach*: Michael Moore is certainly not a Jew. Let me speak here.
>
> *Donohue*: I didn't question that.
>
> *Boteach*: Hollywood has become a cesspit because it's secular, period. Don't tell us—don't tell us that it's secular Jews.
>
> *Donohue*: So the Catholics are running Hollywood, huh. . . . They're not Rastafarians. They're Jews. . . . You're going to tell me that the Chinese don't live in Chinatown, right?
>
> *Giroux*: Yes. All I can say, Rabbi, is, you've got to concede the fact—and it's difficult because we all at times in life have to say, I'm sorry, I was wrong—we cannot go back and make it that the Hawaiians killed Christ.[4]

Reading that exchange, one is hard pressed to put one's finger on just what is oddest about it. Remember, the exchange occurred on MSNBC, with conservative Pat Buchanan sitting in for the conservative Joe Scarborough. The conservative Mr. Donohue's contention that the secular Jews who run Hollywood both "hate Christianity" and "like anal sex" was never once contradicted by the show's host. Another guest, also a conservative, unabashedly blames the Jews for killing Christ, and again, no one disagrees. The only person who does take up the defense of Jews is a rabbi who writes sex manuals and hangs out with an accused child molester at his "Neverland" ranch.

And yet the debate on this edition of *Scarborough Country*—while a classic of its kind—was hardly beyond the pale during the controversy over Gibson's film. Gibson himself assessed the situation in comparable terms when he complained, "The *L.A. Times*, it's an anti-Christian publication, as is the *New York Times*."[5] He denounced particularly *New York Times* pundit Frank Rich, who had taken note of Gibson's father's writings denying the Holocaust—as well as Gibson's explicit refusal to disassociate himself from his father's views or from the extremist church of which he is a member: "I want to kill him. I want his intestines on a stick. . . . I want to kill his dog."[6]

This is not the place to debate the whethers and whys of alleged anti-Semitic themes in Gibson's film, in which the writer-director not only portrays Jews as plotting and scheming to manipulate the Romans into killing Jesus, but even adds scenes to the story in which, as Katha Pollitt notes, "the Jewish guards who arrest Jesus whip him with chains, throw him over a bridge and dangle him over the water, choking, for fun."[7] One would have had to be an especially indulgent Jew to grant Gibson the likelihood of mere coincidence. Charles Krauthammer—a writer who is otherwise sympathetic to Gibson's right-wing agenda—adds:

> When it comes to the Jews, Gibson deviates from the Gospels—glorying in his artistic vision—time and again. He bends, he stretches, he makes stuff up. And these deviations point overwhelmingly in a single direction—to the villainy and culpability of the Jews. The most subtle, and most revolting, of these has to my knowledge not been commented upon. In Gibson's movie, Satan appears four times. Not one of these appearances occurs in the four Gospels. They are pure invention. Twice, this sinister, hooded, androgynous embodiment of evil is found . . . where? Moving among the crowd of Jews. Gibson's camera follows close up, documentary style, as Satan glides among them, his face popping up among theirs—merging with, indeed, defining the

murderous Jewish crowd. After all, a perfect match: Satan's own people.[8]

Gibson did respond to some of the criticism of the film by Jews. Before its release, he announced that he had cut the scene where a Jewish mob yells for the blood of Jesus to descend on the heads of its children (a scene that occurs in only one of the four contradictory Gospels). In fact, the scene remained, but without its English subtitles. (The film's dialogue was spoken in Hebrew, Latin, and Aramaic.) In other countries, where Christian and Islamic anti-Semitism is rampant, the calumny remains. This was presumably one of the changes Gibson says he made, reluctantly, because, "They'd be coming after me at my house, they'd come to kill me"[9] Gibson did not elaborate on who "they" in the scenario might be, but presumably he meant the Jews. During the controversy, Gibson defended himself by arguing that he blames many people, not just Jews, including "a cabal of secularists, so-called humanists, trial lawyers, cultural relativists, and liberal, guilt-wracked Christians—not just Jewish people. . . . They are liberal by definition, and they proclaim their liberal values."[10]

The right in America embraced Gibson as a true, brave voice in the wilderness. Talk-show host Hugh Hewitt explained, "I do not understand the accusations of anti-Semitism," arguing that merely quoting Jesus in a film was "a guarantee that the maker of *The Passion of the Christ* is in for a rough go of it, as well as its cast and crew. If anyone knows Mel Gibson, please pass along my thanks."[11]

Some of Gibson's defenders traded on their own Jewishness to add credibility to their defense of his motives. Longtime Stalinist of both the left and right David Horowitz insisted, "There is no finger-pointing at Jews in the film, and it is unsustainable to suggest that this will provoke Christians into violence against Jews." The Jewish talk-show host Michael Medved, who shared Gibson's views about the "vicious and despicable article" by Frank Rich, went on to argue that Gibson was "being attacked because he's a charitable guy who has spent hundreds of thousands of dollars of his own money to build a church."[12] The right-wing rabbi

Daniel Lapin, whose activities received funding from Gibson, joined in the attack on his critics: "Surely it is now time to analyze the vitriolic loathing demonstrated by various Jewish groups and their leaders toward Mel Gibson over the past six months. This analysis might help forestall some similar ill-conceived and ill-fated future misadventure on the part of self-anointed Jewish leadership. At the very least it might advance human understanding of destructive group pathologies."[13]

This case became considerably more difficult to defend, however, when, during the summer of 2006, he exploded across the headlines with a drunken rampage during which, after being pulled over for speeding, he abused a group of Malibu police by telling them that "the Jews are responsible for all the wars in the world," and then asked the deputy: "Are you a Jew?" But even then, he managed to retain much if not all of his right-wing cheerleading section. *National Review*'s John Derbyshire argued, "As little as I care for Mel and his splatter-fest Brit-hating oeuvre, though, I care even less for the schoolmarmish, prissy, squealing, skirt-clutching, sissified, feminized, pansified, preening moral vanity of the vile and anti-human Political Correctness cult." On Fox News' *Hannity & Colmes,* David Horowitz demonstrated remarkable compassion toward Gibson, explaining, "As a Jew, I feel much more threatened by people like Jimmy Carter." Horowitz added that the anger over Gibson's comments was "all about politics" and that "a lot of the people who are jumping all over Mel Gibson see him as some kind of a conservative or as a Christian. There's a lot of hatred of Christians in this country."[14] And Bill O'Reilly went back to the anti-Semitic well one last time: "I was right in the middle of that attack on Mel Gibson," he told Geraldo Rivera. "And it was brutal. . . . It wasn't all Jewish people behind the attacks. But it was Frank Rich, who's Jewish, at the *New York Times* and other people. . . . That doesn't condone it, but it does explain it, does it not?"[15]

As befits a profitable Hollywood production, the controversy over *The Passion* was something of a sequel to a previous episode in organized right-wing anti-Semitism, the 1988 debate over the Universal film *The Last Temptation of Christ.* Based on a novel by Greek Orthodox author

Nikos Kazantzakis, adapted by Calvinist Protestant screenwriter Paul Schrader, and directed by Italian Catholic Martin Scorsese, the film— which attributes human qualities and physical desires to Jesus—inspired a Christian conservative hate campaign against Jews. At a demonstration organized outside the late Universal president Lew Wasserman's home, demonstrators chanted, "Jewish money, Jewish money!" That same week the late Reverend Jerry Falwell predicted that the film would "create a wave of anti-Semitism," and the Reverend Donald Wildmon sent out a half-million letters to his American Family Association members terming Universal a "company whose decision-making body [is] dominated by non-Christians." Meanwhile, the Reverend R. L. Hymers Jr. and members of his fundamentalist Baptist Tabernacle picketed Universal Studios, accompanied by a small airplane flying overhead that carried a banner reading WASSERMAN FANS JEW-HATRED W/"TEMPTATION." The problem, as Hymers explained it, was that "these Jewish producers with a lot of money are taking a swipe at our religion." Hymers also staged a demonstration in which Wasserman was represented nailing Jesus to the cross. (Demonstrators also marched outside the Wilshire Boulevard Temple, to which they mistakenly believed Wasserman belonged.) Twenty-five thousand people also rallied outside Universal headquarters, with many carrying anti-Semitic signs. In the mainstream media, columnist Pat Buchanan accused Wasserman and company of "assaulting the Christian community in a way it would never dare assault the black community, the Jewish community or the gay community."[16]

The protests achieved many of their intended aims. A week before the rescheduled premiere, two theater chains—United Artists and General Cinema Corporation, representing a combined total of some 3,300 screens—announced that they would not show the film. *The Last Temptation* was also banned in Savannah, Georgia; Montgomery, Alabama; and New Orleans, Louisiana. When it was finally released on DVD, Blockbuster Video also refused to distribute it. (The movie eventually did open to considerable critical acclaim in nine cities, and proved to be a modest hit, earning back Universal's investment and then some.) As the film historian J. Hoberman observed, "*The Last Temptation* was indeed a godsend that served to energize the Christian right at a critical time—arriving, as it did, in the wake of the demoralizing sex scandals that, earlier in the year, had disgraced the televangelical superstars Jim Bakker and Jimmy Swaggart. The movie turned moral indignation back on Hollywood; by providing a particular artifact around which to organize religious and political protest, it anticipated what soon came to be called the "'culture wars.'"[17]

Of course it's hardly possible to claim coincidence in such cases, given how much of the right's rhetorical firepower is focused on an industry that happens to be dominated by Jews. For many, the imputation of Jewish plots to subvert America's moral fiber—for fun and profit—is an added bonus. The degree of lunacy required to fit their arguments into this mind-set can be breathtaking to watch, as for instance when Rush Limbaugh opined that a letter to President Bush from Iranian president Mahmoud Ahmadinejad—the very same leader who had previously advocated "wiping Israel off the map," referred to Israel as a "rotten, dried tree," and dismissed the Holocaust as a "myth"—contained, in Limbaugh's scholarly view, "some liberal Hollywood Jewish people talking points."[18] The notion that pushy, arrogant, money-hungry, and sexually deviant Jews are ruining the world for God-fearing Christians has been a common enough leitmotif in conservative complaints that it hardly appears to be an anomaly any longer.

As with its obsession with Hollywood's Jewish character, much of the right wing's campaign against the mainstream media has an undercurrent of anti-Semitism as well. This is particularly true of its attacks against the *New York Times*, where the very words *New York* conjure up Jewishness for many Americans, and given the fact that the paper has been owned by a prominent Jewish family for over a century. Many of its best-known editors and columnists are also Jews, a fact that rarely escapes those who criticize the paper for its alleged "elitism" and putative liberal bias. But the *Times* is hardly alone in being vilified. The conservative talk-show host Michael Savage—hired and fired by MSNBC—complained that the media didn't cover the story of Sulejman Talovic, an eighteen-year-old Bosnian immigrant who reportedly killed five people and wounded four at a Salt Lake City shopping center, "because of one reason . . . the 'M' word"—presumably a reference to the fact that the boy was a Muslim. Savage stated that "had the shooter been blond haired and blue-eyed . . . why, then, all of the boys with the curly hair and the large glasses in the newsrooms of America—'Stop the presses! We have a white boy, a Christian, to crucify!'" In fact, a number of media outlets did identify Talovic as a Muslim, and an FBI agent investigating the case explained that there was no reason to believe that "religious extremism" or "terrorism" was involved. In any case, the accusation of Jews being eager to protect Muslims but wishing to "crucify" Christians boggles the mind with its sheer illogic.[19] This followed a previous outburst by Savage against Richard Cohen, a Southern Poverty Law Center attorney, who filed suit to remove a monument to the Ten Commandments from an Alabama courthouse. Savage put forth his objections as follows:

> A guy like Cohen, who is obviously a Jew from New York, is going after a decent Christian man. What am I supposed to do? Sit here and take crap from him? I think he is a vile human being who ought to be arrested for a hate crime. And I am not going to mince words. And I guarantee you that he says "goy" behind the scenes. . . . That's next, isn't it? From these verminous Brooklyn College lawyers, isn't it? Go down South and have a tee-hee over the goyim. Laugh at the goyim. Go down there and take away their crosses and they can't touch you, huh, Mr. Cohen? Mr. Cohen, and you wonder where anti-Semitism comes from. . . . It comes from situations like this, when you have a New York Jew like Cohen going down South into the heartland of Christianity and stealing the religious symbol from Christians.[20]

While Savage's views are admittedly extreme, they are not entirely out of sync with those of mainstream attitudes within cable-news networks. In the world of American cable television, Christianity is viewed as a chronically beleaguered religion, particularly when you consider that, as Bill O'Reilly insists, "more than 90 percent [sic] of American homes celebrate Christmas." The problem, according to O'Reilly, is the Jews and the networks they control. But "the small minority that is trying to impose its will on the majority is so vicious, so dishonest—and has to be dealt with." When a Jewish caller attempted to explain to the talk-show host that he had, in fact, grown up in a "not very Jewish area . . . with a resentment because I felt that people were trying to convert me to Christianity," O'Reilly exploded: "You have a predominantly Christian nation. You have a federal holiday based on the philosopher Jesus. And you don't wanna hear about it? Come on, [caller]—if you are really offended, you gotta go to Israel then." O'Reilly also described the B'nai Brith Anti-Defamation League, which exposes and protests examples it finds of anti-Semitism, "an extremist group that finds offense in pretty much everything," and labeled its president, Abraham Foxman, "a nut."[21] He insists that George Soros is the movement's "moneyman" and also frequently attacks the Jewish Jon Stewart as one of its putative leaders.

Indeed, the degree of attention that O'Reilly pays to this "war" is truly astounding. "There is a very secret plan," he explains, "to diminish Christian philosophy in the U.S.A." He compares the people and groups he holds responsible—including Soros (a Holocaust survivor) and the American Civil Liberties Union—to Hitler and Stalin, who also "wiped out religion." He seeks to protect America against this scourge by listing, on his Web site, department stores' policies regarding the greeting "Merry Christmas." The Web site also contained a poll asking, "Will you shop at stores that do not say 'Merry Christmas'?" Following suit, conservative organizations like the American Family Association vigilantly report on their Web sites which stores wish their customers "Happy Holidays" and which used the preferred "Merry Christmas" in their corporate advertising. (Unmentioned on either one were coconspirators George and Laura Bush, who sent out 1.4 million holiday cards that made no mention of Christmas.)[22]

No matter what outrage against which the Christian right is busy fulminating, the media not only reports it but does so quite credulously. Geoffrey Nunberg observes:

"No," said the Plano, Texas, Independent School District, we didn't bar students from wearing green and red to school during the Christmas season, as O'Reilly reported. And after Jerry Falwell denounced a Wisconsin school for changing the lyrics of "Silent Night" to "Cold in the Night," a charge repeated on Fox and MSNBC, the *Washington Post* reported that the offending carol was sung by a tree in a school play called "The Little Tree's Christmas Gift," written by the music director at Ronald Reagan's former church, which was performed along with "Angels We Have Heard on High" and other Christmas songs. As for that school that banned the Declaration of Independence, the incident turned out to involve a teacher who had given students a handout entitled "What great leaders have said about the Bible," which included not just a passage from the Declaration of Independence, but quotations from Jesus Christ.[23]

Falwell also claimed that "seven high school students in Westfield, Mass., have been suspended solely for passing out candy canes containing religious messages," which led him to argue, "The fact is, students have the right to free speech in the form of verbal or written expression during non-instructional class time. And yes, students have just as much right to speak on religious topics as they do on secular topics—no matter what the ACLU might propagate." In fact, the late Mr. Falwell might have been interested to learn that it was the ACLU that submitted a friend-of-the-court brief in the case defending the students on the grounds that, as the organization's attorney said, "students have a right to communicate ideas, religious or otherwise, to other students during their free time, before or after class, in the cafeteria, or elsewhere."[24]

The conservative response to the alleged threat to Christmas provides yet more evidence to make one wonder whether American politics has collectively taken leave of its senses. Sean Hannity and Michael Medved put out a CD complaining of "the recent onslaught of cultural attacks against the Christian aspects of Christmas." Paul Weyrich, speaking on Fox News, which offered viewers no fewer than fifty-eight separate segments on the "War on Christmas" in the five days between November 28 and December 2, 2005, alone, told listeners that he imagined himself as a victim of thugs who want to "get back at God."

On the conservative Web site Townhall.com, a project of the Heritage Foundation, an author named Burt Prelutsky connected the dots for those conservatives who required more guidance: "When it comes to pushing the multicultural, anti-Christian, agenda," he argued,

> you find Jewish judges, Jewish journalists, and the ACLU, at the forefront. . . . But the dirty little secret in America is that anti-Semitism is no longer a problem in society; it's been replaced by a rampant anti-Christianity. For example, the hatred spewed towards George W. Bush has far less to do with his policies than it does with his religion. The Jews voice no concern when a Bill Clinton or a John Kerry makes a big production out of showing up at black Baptist churches or posing with Rev. Jesse Jackson because they understand that's just politics. They only object to politicians attending church for religious reasons.
>
> . . . It is the ACLU, which is overwhelmingly Jewish in terms of membership and funding, that is leading the attack against Christianity in America. It is they who have conned far too many people into believing that the phrase "separation of church and state" actually exists somewhere in the Constitution. . . . I happen to despise bullies and bigots. I hate them when they represent the majority, but no less when, like Jews in America, they represent an infinitesimal minority.
>
> I am getting the idea that too many Jews won't be happy until they pull off their own version of the Spanish Inquisition, forcing Christians to either deny their faith and convert to agnosticism or suffer the consequences.[25]

The Christmas campaign enjoyed institutional support as well. As author Michelle Goldberg reported, in 2005 the right-wing Catholic League for Religious and Civil Rights initiated a brief boycott of Wal-Mart, charging the company with "insulting Christians by effectively banning Christmas." The American Family Association announced a Thanksgiving-weekend boycott of Target because of the chain's purported refusal to use the phrase "Merry Christmas" in its advertising, though Target denied having any such policy. A few days later Jerry Falwell announced that he was combining his efforts with the right-wing Christian legal group Liberty Counsel's "Friend or Foe Christmas Campaign," for the purposes of suing any public official who sought to limit religious Christmas celebrations in schools or other public places. James Dobson's Alliance Defense Fund organized more than eight hundred lawyers to defend the holiday against its enemies. "It's a sad day in America when you have to retain a lawyer to wish someone a merry Christmas," explained its senior legal counsel, Mike Johnson.[26]

These same conservatives have gone so far as to imagine not merely a liberal war on Christians' favorite holiday but a war on Christians themselves. When in 2006 right-wing radio commentator Rick Scarborough convened a two-day conference in Washington on the "War on Christians and the Values Voters" in 2006, he attracted not just the typical nutcases but former House majority leader Tom DeLay (R-TX), Senators John Cornyn (R-TX) and Sam Brownback (R-KS), and conservative Christian leaders Phyllis Schlafly, Rod Parsley, Gary Bauer, Janet Parshall, and Alan Keyes. Among the complaints about America—the most deeply religious Christian country on earth—was Tom DeLay's observation that it "often treats Christianity like some second-rate superstition." Attendants were congratulated by former Republican White House official Michael Horowitz, a senior fellow at the conservative Hudson Institute, because: "You guys have become the Jews of the 21st century."[27] The sentiments aired at the conference were typical of those that regularly dominate coverage of this phony war in the mainstream media. When Democrats criticized a Bush district court nominee named Leon Holmes for equating pro-choice groups with Nazis and his insistence that "a wife is to subordinate herself to her husband," conservatives complained that opponents were "not only bigoted, but unconstitutional."[28] When Democrats considered a filibuster, the Family Research Council organized a protest telethon under the slogan "The filibuster was once used to protect racial bias and now it is being used against people of faith."[29] As the always perspicacious Nunberg notes, "On the face of things, the contention that radical secularists have a 'secret plan' to eradicate Christianity so they can 'pass secular progressive programs like legalization of narcotics, euthanasia, abortion at will, [and] gay marriage,' as Bill O'Reilly argues, appears on par with the black-UN-helicopter fantasies of the fruitcake right. But taken with the rest of the right's campaign against 'anti-Christian discrimination,'" within the topsy-turvy world of cable TV and American electoral politics, it some-how works.[30]

Lest anyone conclude that this "war on Christmas" or even the "war on Christians" is just too silly to take seriously, let us note that such fan-tasies are not the exclusive province of Christian conservatives, nor are they isolated incidents. The liberal billionaire philanthropist George Soros, who stands at number eight on an inflation-adjusted list of all-time American philanthropists through his charitable donations of more than $5.4 billion, has been the target of several malicious conservative campaigns, a number of which trafficked in traditionally anti-Semitic tropes. Bill O'Reilly denounced him as a "committed atheist."[31] Accord-ing to the Richard Mellon Scaife–funded magazine *NewsMax,* Soros is the leader of "a new semi-secret establishment he has built to take over many East European countries," masking his "efforts to realize his vision of a world without God." He has made "billions from undermining Brit-ain's economy and now he could do the same thing to America."[32] A writer in Sun Myung Moon's *Washington Times* complained that "the Hungarian native anointed himself a major player in American politics." Then–RNC chair and ex–Enron lobbyist Ed Gillespie laments that Soros, a champion of campaign finance reform, is using what the RNC's Christine Iverson calls "an unregulated, under-the-radar-screen, shad-owy, soft-money group" for his nefarious purposes.[33] *Washington Times* pundit and former Newt Gingrich flack Tony Blankley went furthest. Speaking to pundit Sean Hannity, he attacked Soros as "a robber baron," "a pirate capitalist," and "a Jew who figured out a way to survive the Holocaust." Along with others, I called attention to this incredible out-burst on my Web site, Altercation, and one of my readers contacted Blankley about it. The pundit responded with an e-mail that read: "Soros and his family converted from their Jewish faith and survived the Holo-caust (there was speculation that they may have collaborated with the Nazi's [*sic*])." (Blankley later apologized in a faxed letter to the author about the last comment, when asked about it, and expressed "regret" that his statement on *Hannity & Colmes* was "both incomplete and pregnant with a malicious implication I did not intend.")[34] Yet Blankley continued to circulate this outrageous tale—as he did in the e-mail he sent to my Altercation correspondent—long after he had time to rethink the comments. It is hard to imagine a more immoral strategy to use against a Jewish opponent than to insinuate that his family were Nazi collaborators (not that a teenage George Soros would have had much say in the matter at the time). The outrageous slander—originally circulated by Lyndon LaRouche—had long been disproved by Soros biographer Michael Kaufman in his exhaustive study, *Soros: The Life and Times of a Messianic Billionaire*.[35] And yet, once again, the rest of the right-wing chorus joined in. Long after the charges were disproved, David Horowitz and Richard Poe published *The Shadow Party* in the summer of 2006— with the right-wing Christian publishing house Thomas Nelson—in which they libelously asserted that Soros was a Nazi "collaborator in fascist Hungary" and "survived [the Holocaust] by assimilating to Nazism" as a fourteen-year-old boy, a calumny later repeated (and withdrawn) by the *New Republic's* Martin Peretz, who also called Soros a "ruthless Jewish banker."[36] And it hardly stopped there. Bill O'Reilly accused Soros of being one of the "moneymen" behind a so-called "secret plan" to "diminish Christian philosophy in the U.S.A.," and attacked "the big left-wing loon who's financing all these smear sites, [who] shelters his money on the Caribbean island of Curaçao," adding, amazingly, "They ought to hang this Soros guy."[37]

Now, it is true that not all conservatives are right-wing religious extremists,[38] nor, it goes without saying, are all deeply religious people right-wingers. Though in October 2007, Ann Coulter apparently thought it wise to confuse much of the country on this point again, when, anointing herself as a spokesperson for all Christians, she explained to CNBC host Donny Deutsch, "We just want Jews to be perfected, as they say. . . . That's what Christianity is."[39] Coulter's professed mission is, in fact, one of the myths about normal, everyday Christians that theocons seek to perpetuate. However, it is not only the famously (and purposely) provocative Coulter but also members of this group who are the leading figures in the coalition that presently not only leads the conservative movement but also governs our nation. They do not believe in a live-and-let-live philosophy, and they are unalterably opposed to allowing the nation to continue on the separate-church-and-state path that has largely characterized the first 230 years of American history. And while they sometimes wrap themselves in the symbols of secular patriotism, they are actually seeking to subvert the constitutional arrangements that have so far sustained us—as well as the stated preferences of the vast majority of Americans. Merely by alerting their fellow citizens to the dangers these efforts pose, liberals can perform a Paul Revere function in the service of American democracy.

18

Why Are Liberals So Contemptuous of Individual Freedom?

Conservatives tend to define contemporary liberalism in terms of its alleged opposition to individual freedom, a definition that frequently finds its way into nonconservative conversation. A quick check on the day I'm writing this for the word *liberals* on the Yahoo! Answers Web site, for instance, yields the question "Why Are Liberals So Opposed to American Freedom?" A visit to the definition of the word *liberalism* on the Conservapedia—the conservative alternative to Wikipedia—turns up the following putative liberal credo:

- Support of political correctness
- Censorship of prayer in classrooms
- Compelled taxpayer funding of government schools for nearly all ages
- Government-controlled medical care
- Income redistribution, usually through progressive taxation

These are all poised in opposition to what its authors explain was the original meaning of *liberalism* in the classical sense. In the good old days, liberalism meant:

- Freedom of speech
- Freedom of religion
- The right to form political parties and vote
- Freedom to invest in and use private property
- Freedom to work as one chooses
- Freedom to enter into economic contracts
- Free trade and freedom of migration[1]

These definitions find an echo on the Web site of the libertarian Institute for Humane Studies at George Mason University, which explains,

"Liberals favor government action to promote equality, whereas conservatives favor government action to promote order. Libertarians favor freedom and oppose government action to promote either equality or order."[2]

And yet, when one looks at the actual performance of liberals and conservatives in power, the former actually outperform the latter when measured by libertarianism's own criteria. Liberals may want to live according to values that some Americans may find offensive, but they do not, as contemporary conservatives do, insist on the right to dictate the choices of others. No one in America was ever forced by a liberal politician to undergo an abortion or engage in a homosexual partnership. In this most intimate aspect of private lives, therefore, liberalism and libertarianism are as one. American conservatism, however, cannot claim as much, given its political alliance with an extremely interventionist Christian fundamentalism. To take just one salient example: during the 2005 argument over the fate of poor Terri Schiavo, conservative pundit William Bennett demanded that Florida governor Jeb Bush override the legal right of her husband and "order the feeding tube reinserted."[3] In Congress, the Republicans decided to intervene as well owing to what Senate majority leader Frist called "a unique bill passed under unique circumstances that should not serve as a precedent for future legislation." (Frist's language recalled yet another "unique circumstance" in which conservatives specifically instructed the country to pay no attention to the precedents they were setting: the legal case *Bush v. Gore*, in which the Court ignored its much-cherished philosophy of federalism and overruled Florida law.) The White House agreed that the Schiavo matter required a philosophical exception because "this case involves some extraordinary circumstances." The circumstances proved so "extraordinary" that some conservatives went so far as to suggest that government adopt tactics previously associated with the Gestapo or KGB. Fox News anchor John Gibson argued that the governor should "think about telling his cops to go over to Terri Schiavo's hospice, go inside, put her on a gurney and load her into an ambulance. They could take her to a hospital, revive her, and reattach her feeding tube. It wouldn't save Terri exactly; she'd still be in the same rotten shape she was in before they disconnected the feeding tube. But the point is, the temple of the law is not so sacrosanct that an occasional chief executive cannot flaunt it once in a while, sort of drop his drawers on the courthouse steps and moon the judges."

Keep in mind that all of these suggestions were responding to no public outcry whatsoever. According to a March 2005 CBS poll, 82 percent of those questioned opposed the intervention of Congress or the president in the case at all. A mere 13 percent of those polled thought the concern voiced for Schiavo was a sincere concern about her own good, while 74 percent believed that it was politically motivated.[4]

If conservatives demand the right of life or death over the wishes of a person's own family—and are willing to subvert the law in order to try to get their way—it's hard to imagine any meaningful limitations they would recognize in their willingness to use the power of the state to demand fealty to their own worldview. Nor can one credibly argue that the Schiavo case was unique. As Brink Lindsey of the libertarian Cato Institute cogently observed after the 2006 midterm election:

> Despite the GOP's rhetorical commitment to limited government, the actual record of unified Republican rule in Washington has been an unmitigated disaster from a libertarian perspective: runaway federal spending at a clip unmatched since Lyndon Johnson; the creation of a massive new prescription-drug entitlement with hardly any thought as to how to pay for it; expansion of federal control over education through the No Child Left Behind Act; a big run-up in farm subsidies; extremist assertions of executive power under cover of fighting terrorism; and, to top it all off, an atrociously bungled war in Iraq.

Lindsey goes on to make a convincing case that libertarianism has more in common with contemporary liberals than with the conservatives with whom it has traditionally been associated. Among the issues that unite the two, he notes, are support for a more open immigration policy, and a rejection of "the religious right's homophobia and blastocystophilia." Liberals and libertarians both support "rethinking the country's draconian drug policies" as well as preventing "gratuitous encroachments on civil liberties or extensions of executive power" in the name of national security. "And underlying all these policy positions," Lindsey wisely notes, "is a shared philosophical commitment to individual autonomy as a core political value."[5] Liberals are, indeed, far better at protecting the individual liberties upon which libertarians base their political philosophy than is the contemporary conservative movement, dominated as it is by censorious Christian fundamentalists, favor-seeking corporate CEOs, and neoconservative ideologues dreaming of a global empire. In early 2007 a group of longtime conservatives even tried to force their ideological compatriots to face up to this fact. Conservative activists like Reagan administration attorney Bruce Fein; mass-mailer maestro Richard Viguerie; Bob Barr, a former Republican congressman from Georgia; and David Keene, chairman of the American Conservative Union, found themselves so offended by the Bush administration's usurpation of extra-constitutional authority that they and others formed the American Freedom Agenda, in order to demand that every Republican 2008 presidential candidate pledge, if elected president of the United States, that he would "undertake the following to restore the Constitution's checks and balances: to honor fundamental protections against injustice, and to eschew usurpations of legislative or judicial power," as the "keystones of national security and individual freedom."[6] Clearly, from the standpoint of limited government, as many libertarians and even some conservatives have been forced to recognize, contemporary liberals are, at the very least, the lesser of two evils.

19

Why Do Liberals Love "Activist Judges"?

You know the rap: liberal judges "legislate from the bench." Liberals win in the courts what they can't win on Election Day. It is a topic that continues to excite fury among conservatives, with Newt Gingrich's complaint being typical: the U.S. Supreme Court has become an instrument through which "appointed lawyers can redefine the meaning of the U.S. Constitution and the policies implemented under that Constitution either by inventing rationales out of thin air or by citing whatever foreign precedent they think helpful." He adds that "this is not a judiciary in the classic sense, but a proto-dictatorship of the elite pretending to still function as a Supreme Court."[1] Robert Bork, perhaps the most influential conservative judicial intellectual in America, has remarked that he found himself agreeing with his wife when she dismissed the U.S. Supreme Court justices as a "band of outlaws." "An outlaw is a person who coerces others without warrant in law," he wrote. "That is precisely what a majority of the present Supreme Court does."[2]

Prominent conservatives have been known to take this critique even further. Speaking to a banquet of the Confronting the Judicial War on Faith conference in Washington, a constitutional lawyer named Edwin Vieira discussed the Supreme Court's majority opinion in *Lawrence v. Texas*, written by Associate Justice Anthony M. Kennedy, which struck down that state's antisodomy law. Vieira maintained that the judge had based his jurisprudence on "Marxist, Leninist, Satanic principles drawn from foreign law." What did Vieira believe to be the appropriate response? "Here again I draw on the wisdom of Stalin. We're talking about the greatest political figure of the 20th century. . . . He had a slogan, and it worked very well for him whenever he ran into difficulty. 'No man, no problem.' " The audience laughed a little, no doubt on the assumption that he was joking. So Vieira restated his point: "'No man, no problem.' This is not a structural problem we have. This is a problem of personnel." The full quote, had he had it handy, was: "Death solves all problems: no man, no problem."

Vieira is hardly a lone wolf in conservative circles, or even much of a radical. Frequent Republican senatorial candidate Alan Keyes was received no less enthusiastically at the same conference when he said, "I believe that in our country today the judiciary is the focus of evil."[3] Focus on the Family's James Dobson believes that "the biggest Holocaust in world history came out of the Supreme Court" with the *Roe v. Wade* decision. This followed an earlier speech by Dobson that compared the "black-robed men" to "the men in white robes, the Ku Klux Klan."[4] For good measure, Dobson also denounced Justice Kennedy as "the most dangerous man in America."[5] During the Terri Schiavo case Tom DeLay promised, "The time will come for the men responsible for this to pay for their behavior." What, exactly, was he implying? As he helpfully explained, "Judges need to be intimidated," adding that if they don't behave, "we're going to go after them in a big way."[6]

As usual when right-wingers start deploying such arguments, ironies abound. Judicial Activist Public Enemy Number One, Anthony Kennedy, was nominated to the Court by none other than the conservative Christian hero Ronald Reagan, and has most often sided with the conservatives in his opinions. More significantly, the phrase *judicial activism*, however disparaged, has rarely if ever been defined, and almost never coherently, and both liberals and much of the media have bought into this linguistic sleight of hand. Kennedy, for example, is an "activist" when he issues opinions that feel "liberal" to conservatives and a conservative when he doesn't. It was he who, in the spring of 2007, authored the opinion in *Gonzales v. Carhart*, the so-called partial-birth abortion case, in which he outlawed an extremely rare abortion process on the basis not of the right to life of the unborn but of the need for adult American women to be protected from the potential consequences of making their own decisions. "Respect for human life finds an ultimate expression in the bond of love the mother has for her child," Kennedy declared.

Concerned that women might learn the details of how the procedure is performed only after the fact, he wrote, "The State has an interest in ensuring so grave a choice is well informed."[7] Nevertheless, one is hard-pressed to locate a single prominent conservative who objected to this decision's rejection of previous precedent or its casting aside of the relevance of the right to privacy, not to mention its undeniable expansion of judicial authority. Meanwhile, it's difficult to imagine a more "activist" ruling than 2000's *Bush v. Gore,* in which the Court not only ruled on a matter strictly defined to be one of state jurisdiction but did so in clear contravention of its own frequently promulgated judicial philosophy of federalist devolution. Here, as scholar Richard Briffault noted, the Supreme Court "dramatically intervened in an area traditionally left to the states, rejected the efforts of a state supreme court to provide more vigorous protection of the rights of Florida voters whose ballots had not been tabulated by local ballot-counting machinery, and opened the door to nationalization of election administration."[8] And yet where was the conservative outcry about "judicial activism in this matter?"[9]

Two legal scholars have attempted to actually make this term quantifiable, and the data don't do much to bolster the right-wingers' case—in fact, just the opposite. Paul Gewirtz and Chad Golder of Yale derived a formula to measure "judicial activism" based on decisions to strike down legislation as "unconstitutional," an action, they declare, that is "the boldest thing a judge can do." In an 1867 decision, they note, "the Supreme Court itself described striking down Congressional legislation as an act 'of great delicacy, and only to be performed where the repugnancy is clear.'" Between 1791 (the year of the Court's founding) and 1858, this happened only twice; between 1858 and 1991 the Court struck down an average of one congressional statute every two years.

Obviously the Court has grown a great deal more "activist" in recent times. According to Gewirtz and Golder, the current Court, beginning in 1994, has upheld or struck down sixty-four congressional provisions during the first eleven years of its tenure. When applying the measurement to determine which judges were most likely to strike down the laws passed by Congress, Justice Clarence Thomas was clearly in the lead, followed by Justices Kennedy, Scalia, Rehnquist, O'Connor, Souter, Stevens, Ginsburg, and Breyer, in that order. In other words, all of the Republican-appointed justices were more "activist" than those appointed by Democrats, with the pair appointed by President Clinton overturning the fewest of all sitting justices. Justice Stephen Breyer, generally thought to be a liberal, had a rating of 28.3 percent, which was less than half of the more than 65 percent scored by Justice Clarence Thomas, whom conservatives, particularly Christian conservatives, profess to revere.[10]

If the Gewirtz-Golder criteria fail to convince, Thomas J. Miles and Cass R. Sunstein, of the University of Chicago Law School, have suggested measuring activism in a different way: "How often do justices vote to strike down acts of the executive branch?" They compiled more than five hundred votes from 1989 through 2005 and discovered that "the more liberal members of the Court were the most likely to vote to uphold the decisions of the executive branch. The most conservative members of the Court were the least likely to vote to uphold those decisions." The numbers are no less striking than those measuring justices striking down the laws of Congress. The authors note that "Justice Stephen Breyer voted in favor of the executive 82 percent of the time— the highest pro-executive voting rate on the Court. Justices David Souter, Ruth Bader Ginsburg, and John Paul Stevens were next, with an average voting rate in favor of the executive of 75 percent," while "Justice Antonin Scalia voted the least often for the executive (52 percent), and Justice Clarence Thomas was close to him (54 percent). Former Chief Justice William Rehnquist showed a somewhat higher pro-executive rate (64 percent)." Consistent with their reputations as the moderate-to-conservative Court center, "Justices Sandra Day O'Connor and Anthony Kennedy were exactly in the middle (around 67 percent)." These results correlated with the ideological inclinations of the right-wingers. For instance, Rehnquist, Scalia, and Thomas voted with the executive branch 47 percent of the time under a Democratic administration but 65 percent under a Republican one. Breyer, Souter, Stevens, and Ginsburg, on the other hand, showed no statistically significant difference in their views regardless of administration.[11]

So is the problem liberal "judicial activism"? Or is it the fact that right-wingers are prone to object to the outcomes of certain cases? Once again, as soon as the evidence is examined, the conventional wisdom collapses in a heap of conservative misinformation, which is parroted by the press and prevents any possibility of a genuine debate on the complex issues involved.

20

When Will Liberals Stop
Crying "Racism" at Every Opportunity?

One of the most interesting—and perhaps bedeviling—linguistic transformations that has taken place in American politics is conservative
adoption of the vocabulary of antiracism. They have done so, however,
in ways that, when used in the past by liberals, led conservatives—with
some justification—to accuse their opponents of "playing the race card."
When George W. Bush nominated the extreme right-wing judge Miguel
Estrada to the U.S. Court of Appeals for the District of Columbia in 2003,
Republican senator Charles Grassley warned Democrats that to reject
this one nominee "would be to shut the door on the American dream of
Hispanic Americans everywhere." Later, in Bush's second term, when
he put Alberto Gonzales up to be attorney general, Grassley's colleague,
conservative Republican senator Orrin Hatch, took the same tack, declaring, "Every Hispanic in America is watching."[1] When this appointment proved a castastrophe, to the point of Gonzales's becoming a
national punch line, Rush Limbaugh lashed out that Gonzales was 'under fire by white liberal racists in the Senate.' "[2] Conservative claims such
as these—and they were heard during the nominations of African American Condoleezza Rice for secretary of state and Italian American Samuel Alito for the Supreme Court—represent exactly the kind of "If you
disagree with me, you're a racist" moral bullying that so many people
rightly criticized in liberals for so many years. It reduces a complex individual to a single characteristic, and privileges that characteristic above
all others. Ironically, it is itself a deeply racist way of looking at things,
which is one reason it can be so infuriating.

No less frequently, however, the conservative attitude toward the ongoing discrimination on the basis of race in America can be summed
up with the phrase, "Shut up already." (The Bush administration has

actually redirected much of the work of the Justice Department's Civil Rights Division to cases of alleged religious prejudice—almost always involving members of its fundamentalist base.)[3] A typical example of the right-wingers' attitude toward racial bias can be found in a column by *U.S. News & World Report* pundit Michael Barone, who wrote following the 2004 election that he was "struck" by how black Americans were "motivated not by ideas about how to change the future, but by something like nostalgia for the past." The 88–11 percent margin for Kerry over Bush among black voters in the 2004 Election Day Data Survey Poll, Barone noted, was roughly equivalent to the margin by which blacks favored Lyndon Johnson over Barry Goldwater in 1964, and every Democratic candidate since. While Goldwater opposed the Civil Rights Act, Barone notes, "That was a big issue, then. . . . But the Civil Rights Act has long since become uncontroversial, racial discrimination disapproved and integration of schools, workplaces and public accommodations widely accepted. Yet 40 years later, the image of the Republican Party as unsympathetic to equal rights for blacks seems to persist. Black voters seem still focused on a moment in history 40 years ago."[4]

Like so many conservatives and media pundits, Barone seems to think that racism in our society is an issue that is no longer relevant, now that the Civil Rights Act has become part of law; black Americans and other minorities simply need to get with the program and stop whining so much. "The premise that racial discrimination has been erased and that the remaining reason for differences in the relative earnings of blacks and whites is a difference of skills has become an article of faith among conservatives," notes educational scholar Richard Rothstein.[5] As Princeton sociologist Douglas Massey explains, however, "Strong social scientific evidence exists showing that relatively high rates of discrimination persist in markets for housing, lending, and employment—by far the most important markets for achieving socioeconomic mobility in the United States."[6] And yet even when confronted with such evidence, conservatives imagine that their own experiences are somehow more significant. When Bill O'Reilly faced a scholar on his program who was able to cite studies of systemic prejudice against blacks and Hispanics in the United States, the host retorted: "I don't believe it. I think your documentation is anecdotal. . . . It doesn't matter whether they're studies or not. It's anecdotal." Again, O'Reilly provides a perfect illustration of the purposeful know-nothingism that he and so many right-wing pundits have made their personal calling cards. During the same broadcast, O'Reilly also complained that when he first "was in [news] corporations," the executives allegedly decided they were "not gonna let O'Reilly anchor" because O'Reilly "was from Levittown [New York], a working-class Irish—they call them shanty Irish—background." According to O'Reilly, "they" decided to give "anchor" positions to "Stone [Phillips] or Forrest [Sawyer]," which was "bigotry against" O'Reilly because he was "better than those people."[7]

As both individuals and corporations grow more sophisticated in their ability to mask deliberate discrimination, racism becomes harder to demonstrate as a matter of law, or even journalism. But almost every day, those of us who are impressed by evidence find ourselves confronted by extremely worrisome examples of pervasive racial and ethnic prejudice in the United States. Absent the continuing power of institutional racism, Florida Republicans would never have been able to disenfranchise black voters during the 2000 elections by, in Douglas Massey's words, "systematically allocating older, error-prone voting machines to black precincts; by illegally purging black voters from registration rolls through a variety of ruses; by systematically blocking the access of African Americans to polling places through police activity; and by blanketing black precincts with direct mail and fliers announcing that it was illegal for anyone arrested for a 'crime' (as opposed to convicted of a felony) to vote and that 'illegal' voting would be prosecuted to the fullest extent of the law (thus frightening many would-be voters)."[8] And again, absent the continuing power of both personal and institutional racism, would the Equal Employment Opportunity Commission, staffed by Bush appointees, have found that Kodak was paying black workers less than similarly situated whites, promoting them less frequently, and, should they complain, either harassing or firing them? Author Andrew Hacker notes that in studies of black and white job-seekers with identical résumés who apply for publicly advertised jobs, we find incontrovertible evidence of "systemic discrimination that cannot be attributed to differences in skills between comparably educated blacks and whites." One study, undertaken by the Urban Institute in Chicago and Washington, D.C., in the early 1990s, went to the time and expense of training applicants for jobs with nearly identical résumés to present themselves in exactly the same way in their interviews. The result: black males were three times as likely to be rejected as white males. Other studies have found that among applicants who were offered jobs, whites were offered higher salaries. Another study discovered that whites' applications were more successful than blacks' even when the whites had criminal records, and the otherwise identical blacks did not.[9] And when we read an account of, say, a sorority at DePauw University in Greencastle, Indiana, ejecting every single black, Korean, and Vietnamese (and overweight) member from their group residence, does anyone really think that racism plays no significant role in the lives of its potential victims?[10]

And even that story appears rather mild when compared with one that took place in September 2006, in the town of Jena, Louisiana, where a group of African-American high school students asked the school for permission to sit under a "whites only" shade tree. The following day, students were greeted upon their arrival at school by the sight of three nooses hanging from the tree. They were color-coordinated to match the school's colors. While the boys who had done the deed did receive a short suspension for what was termed a prank, the town's black population reacted angrily. After fights broke out at the school, the local district attorney, Reed Walters, came to class and instructed the black teenagers that he could "end their life with a stroke of the pen." Other incidents followed. Black students were beaten up when they showed up at white parties. A Caucasian man pointed a loaded rifle at three black teenagers at a nearby convenience store. An attempt was made to set fire to the school, and when a major fight finally broke out, Walters charged six black students with attempted murder, pushing for maximum charges, which would carry sentences of eighty years in prison.[11]

Not surprisingly, statistical evidence demonstrates continuing legacies of racism in virtually every aspect of our education system. Black
and Hispanic high school students, for instance, continue to read and do
arithmetic at only the average level of whites in junior high school, a gap
that has remained despite the implementation of the so-called No Child
Left Behind law.[12] Unless one is willing to embrace the racist pseudo-
science of the likes of Charles Murray, which posits the intellectual infe-
riority of blacks and Hispanics to whites (and particularly Jews), then
one has to ask what factors are at work here. And while no liberal would
argue that cultural patterns within communities of color—including particularly absentee parenthood, the lack of positive role models in ghetto
communities, and the glorification in rap music of antisocial behavior—
do not constitute significant factors, one cannot escape the conclusion
that the contemporary manifestation of hundreds of years of white racism continues to play an important role in the achievement gap. It's no
coincidence, after all, that the schools with the largest minority student
bodies are also the ones with the weakest tax base and the children of the
poorest families attending.

Views like those expressed by Michael Barone also do not allow for
consideration, for instance, that it might be appropriate to address the
question of black median family income, which is now 62 percent of
white income, up only slightly from 58 percent thirty years ago. Nor
would he deem it a matter of public policy that the median net worth of
black families is still only 8 percent of whites'. Nor is it an issue for Barone
that a part of the reason for this difference is undoubtedly the fact that
many lenders, both public and private, do not lend to blacks for the purpose of buying homes in America's suburbs, where much of the wealth
that sets the families there apart from the poor has been accumulated. It
might interest Mr. Barone to learn that black families are over six times
more likely to file for bankruptcy than whites, or that far fewer are covered by employer-sponsored health care or private pension plans.[13] Lest
the reader think the problem lies exclusively with blacks, we should note
that while net worth increased 17 percent for white households from
1996 to 2002, it increased only 4 percent for Hispanic homes, to about a

mere $7,900. This is a better outcome than that for blacks, whose average net worth actually fell by 16 percent during the period, to roughly $6,000, but it hardly bespeaks anything remotely representative of the American dream of equal opportunity for all.[14]

The obvious long-term answer to these problems would appear to be a series of educational affirmative-action programs designed to raise the achievement level of blacks and Hispanics to that of whites, along with consistent enforcement of antidiscrimination laws. But this is exactly what we have tried to do for the past four decades, and it has proved woefully inadequate to the scale of the problem. In addition to the myriad personal, psychological, and social complications that inevitably arise when people are believed to have been given "special treatment" owing to their race—as well as the insulting implication that black students need to sit next to whites to be able to learn effectively in school—affirmative action affects only a small and usually privileged sliver of the minority population. As early as 1967, the famed sociologist Kenneth B. Clark observed, "The masses of Negroes are now starkly aware of the fact that recent civil rights victories benefited a very small percentage of middle-class Negroes while their predicament remained the same or worsened." But the solution adopted—race-based affirmative action—has turned out to benefit these same better-off minorities: those who enjoyed the largest combination of the key building blocks for economic success in America, such as family stability, financial means, peer groups, and good schooling.[15] Not surprisingly, a 2004 study discovered that while affirmative action triples the representation of black and Latino students at the nation's 146 most selective colleges and universities, it offers minimal benefits to low-income and working-class students. This was confirmed in another study of elite schools by ex–Princeton president William Bowen.[16] The net result is that poor people, in which minorities are unhappily overrepresented, are shut out of America's elite colleges. Another massive aspect of America's racial problem that affirmative action does not begin to touch is the problem of the various pathologies of the black and Hispanic ghetto, where young people grow up with little education and virtually no (legitimately) marketable skills.[17]

Within what William Julius Wilson named "the truly disadvantaged"—the ghetto underclass—problems such as "poverty, joblessness, family breakup, educational retardation in inner-city public schools, increased welfare dependence, and drug addiction" continued to worsen.[18]

Whether liberals choose to support race-based affirmative action or not is rapidly becoming an academic—in the sense of irrelevant—question, as almost all affirmative-action programs are in the process of disappearing anyway. When the U.S. Supreme Court decided in a 5–4 ruling on the final day of its 2006–7 term to all but eliminate race as a legally acceptable criterion for school admission, its decision proved the culmination of a pattern that had been progressively narrowing the applicability of race-based affirmative action in education for more than a quarter of a century.[19] Moreover, even when judges do not find race-based affirmative-action plans unconstitutional, voters find them uncongenial. Since 1996, ballots cast by about a quarter of the U.S. population have banned all racial preferences for minorities and women in public universities and state governments. At the same time, no state has passed a single affirmative-action measure. During the 2006 midterm election, the relatively liberal state of Michigan passed a ban on affirmative action quite easily, despite electing two female Democrats to the statehouse and the U.S. Senate, and despite the opposition of virtually the entire state political establishment, plus most businesses, labor unions, civil rights, religious, and education leaders, and both the Republican and Democratic gubernatorial candidates. Affirmative-action proponents even enjoyed a three-to-one spending advantage, but it made no difference.[20]

The views that motivate many to oppose affirmative action are frequently based on misinformation. According to an extensive poll by the Kaiser Family Foundation, between 40 and 60 percent of all whites believe that blacks are now doing as well as or better than most whites in area of employment, income, education, and access to health care. Given that mind-set, they naturally oppose any and all measures to address the problem of racism. Whites who do have accurate views of black circumstances show far greater sympathy for political solutions designed to address these issues, including efforts by the courts and law enforcement to ensure that laws are followed.[21] Part of the misperception, to be sure, can be attributed to the media's portrayal of racial issues. As Robert M. Entman and Andrew Rojecki demonstrate at length in their study *The Black Image in the White Mind,* a sampling of the network news drawn from 1997 reveals that blacks are featured in basically three ways: "entertainer, sports figure or object of discrimination." A more detailed study of ABC News in particular found that the network "mainly discusses Blacks as such when they suffer or commit crime, or otherwise fall victim and require attention from government." As a result, "The news constructs African Americans as a distinct source of disruption." The authors note that since Caucasians are rarely featured in this manner, relative to the number of times they appear, "The news can easily imply a baseline or ideal social condition in which far fewer serious problems would plague the society if only everyone in the United States were native-born whites."[22]

It may be that America will never be able to address the legacy of its Original Sin, and must seek to transcend it instead. Still, any charge that liberals are overly concerned with race—when the inequities of skin color remain so profound in the nation—is fundamentally false. It is one thing to try and fail to solve a problem and quite another to deny its existence. Racism in America remains real in the post–civil rights era, but it has proven a kind of poisoned chalice for any liberal who makes it the center of his or her platform. Despite an increasingly multicultural population, the fact remains that according to 2004 exit polling, white Americans made up 78 percent of voters.[23] Whatever one thinks of the alleged fairness or unfairness of any given policy, alienating over three-quarters of voters with race-based appeals that exclude them is a surefire formula for political failure.

Fortunately, at least the affirmative-action aspect of this problem has a relatively simple, pragmatic solution that can be isolated from the dilemma of race—at least rhetorically and as a matter of law. As Wilson has argued, "Many white Americans have turned, not against blacks, but against a strategy that emphasizes programs perceived to benefit only racial minorities." What liberals need to do, says Wilson, is "promote new policies to fight inequality that differ from court-ordered busing, affirmative action programs, and antidiscrimination lawsuits of the recent past."[24] As the liberal education expert Richard D. Kahlenberg explains, forty years of studies have demonstrated that the socioeconomic status of the school a child attends is, after family economic status, the single most significant factor in determining future success in school. As he puts it, "Blacks don't do better sitting next to whites; poor kids do better in middle-class environments." The value of a "middle-class school environment," in other words, rather than the particular races of the children attending a given school, is the primary reason why racial desegregation often improves black grade scores and the like. Kahlenberg adds that he finds "powerful evidence that even the widely discussed phenomenon in black communities of denigrating academic achievement as 'acting white' is, in fact, a phenomenon more deeply rooted in class—common among low-income students of all races," and finds that in places where students are desegregated by class rather than race, performance increases are often much easier to locate.

Looking at class rather than race is not only far more politically palatable than reverse racial discrimination, it brings us closer to the nub of the problem. According to a study conducted in 2003–4 by the Civil Rights Project at Harvard University, 76 percent of predominantly minority schools were high poverty, compared with only 15 percent of predominantly white schools.[25] Students who are admitted to the most competitive schools come overwhelmingly from the wealthiest quartile of the population, where educational opportunities already abound. (Just 3 percent come from the poorest quartile.) Class-based affirmative action would likely boost the combined representation of black and Latino students from the 4 percent who would be admitted based strictly on grades and test scores by 250 percent, to 10 percent. And while this is slightly less than the current 12 percent representation that is now achieved with race-sensitive admissions at the 146 selective colleges, it seems a small price to pay for eliminating all of the political, social, and racial animosities that race-based affirmative action inevitably inspires.

Those students who are admitted under a class-based program are more likely to succeed. At UCLA Law School, which used a class-based affirmative-action program that considered wealth among other factors, African Americans were sixteen times as likely to be admitted as through the normal race- and class-blind admissions process.[26]

Making class, not race, the centerpiece of an appeal to Americans' sense of fairness would do wonders for poor Americans of all races, while simultaneously opening up the debate on fairness and equality more generally. After all, no one but an avowed racist or a crackpot would argue that black and Hispanic children are mentally disadvantaged relative to whites, as no scientifically credible evidence has ever emerged to support this contention.[27] Few people would argue, either, that the members of the more than one million black American families who earn over $100,000 a year ought to be given special help denied to a white, Hispanic, Asian (or whatever) family member who must live on a fraction of that amount.[28] Are we, in America today, really arguing that it is the job of today's poor white students to pay for the wrongdoings of generations past? Make no mistake: if we moved from race-based to class-based affirmative action, the children of the wealthy would suffer. At Harvard, Walter Benn Michaels notes, almost 90 percent of students come from the top economic half of the population, and nearly three-quarters from the top fifth. A class-based affirmative-action policy might cost as many as half of those students their spots. David Brooks claims that "the rich don't exploit the poor, they just outcompete them." But as Michaels aptly answers, if "outcompeting people means tying their ankles together and loading them down with extra weight while hiring yourself the most expensive coaches and the best practice facilities, [Brooks is] right."[29]

Ironically, the secular saint most closely associated with America's struggle for racial justice, the Reverend Martin Luther King Jr., was coming around to just this view before the assassin's bullet ended his journey to what he called "the Mountaintop." "We must recognize that we can't solve our problem now until there is a radical redistribution of economic and political power," he preached. And King called for a "massive assault upon slums, inferior education, inadequate medical care [and] the entire culture of poverty."[30] "Long before William Julius Wilson spoke of the 'declining significance of race,'" observes the historian William Chafee, "King recognized that maldistribution of wealth and income was as central to America's problems as the color of one's skin."[31]

Liberals' misguided obsession with identity politics spawned a decades-long wild-goose chase in pursuit of an antiracist, multicultural utopia as it simultaneously blinded them to the effects of a vicious class war conducted against those in our society least able to bear it. Minorities don't need their cultural heritages respected, their speech patterns legitimized, and their sense of self uplifted. They need more money, more opportunity, and a dependable ladder to educational and professional improvement. As the contemporary civil rights leader Bill Fletcher Jr. aptly notes, though class is the fault line of U.S. society, race is merely its "trip wire."[32]

21

Why Are Liberals So Soft on America's Enemies?

In his memoir, Bill Clinton looked back at some of the most difficult decisions of his presidency and concluded that Americans prefer leaders who appear "strong and wrong" to those that are "weak and right."[1] This dynamic presents a diabolical dilemma for American liberals. Being "strong and wrong," as George W. Bush has repeatedly demonstrated in the aftermath of the 9/11 attacks, is not so tall an order. Perhaps no president in all of American history has had more words like *strong, resolute, firm, unswerving, unwavering, constant, steadfast,* and *determined* applied to him, when, given the results of the policies in question—be they in Iraq or for the U.S. economy, environment, health care system, and so on—far more accurate descriptions might have been *stubborn, obstinate, inflexible, mulish,* and *impervious to reality.* Until quite late in his presidency, most members of the media tended to treat Bush's proclivity to put the pedal to the floor when approaching the cliff's edge with enormous equanimity, taking the increasingly alarming warning signs alongside the long and winding road to the catastrophe of Iraq as an expression of manly character. The power of the concept of "manliness," is, however, almost impossible to overestimate. In a story almost too tasteless to credit but whose symbolism is too powerful to ignore, presidential historian Robert Dallek relates the tale of a meeting between President Lyndon B. Johnson and a group of journalists who were inquiring as to why he insisted on sticking to his failed but deadly policy in Vietnam. Johnson, according to Dallek, "unzipped his fly, drew out his substantial organ, and declared, 'This is why!'"[2]

Consider too, Gordon Liddy's observation to Chris Matthews forty years later, following George W. Bush's touchdown on an aircraft carrier and speech delivered below a massive, and now sadly inaccurate, MISSION ACCOMPLISHED banner following the initial incursion into Iraq.

"After all, Al Gore had to go get some woman to tell him how to be a man. And here comes George Bush. You know, he's in his flight suit, he's striding across the deck, and he's wearing his parachute harness, you know—and I've worn those because I parachute—and it makes the best of his manly characteristic. You go run those—run that stuff again of him walking across there with the parachute. He has just won every woman's vote in the United States of America. You know, all those women who say size doesn't count—they're all liars. Check that out." Much of the analysis of Bush in his phony flight suit focused on related issues that were barely less juvenile, but equally telling:

- *Chris Matthews:* "That's the president looking very much like a jet, you know, a high-flying jet star. A guy who is a jet pilot. Has been in the past when he was younger, obviously. . . . He won the war. He was an effective commander. Everybody recognizes that, I believe, except a few critics. . . . Here's a president who's really nonverbal. He's like Eisenhower. He looks great in a military uniform. He looks great in that cowboy costume he wears when he goes West."

- *Chris Matthews:* "We're proud of our president. Americans love having a guy as president, a guy who has a little swagger, who's physical, who's not a complicated guy like Clinton or even like Dukakis or those guys, McGovern. They want a guy who's president. Women like a guy who's president. Check it out. The women like this war. I think we like having a hero as our president."

- *Ann Coulter to Matthews:* "It's stunning. It's amazing. I think it's huge. I mean, he's landing on a boat at 150 miles per hour. It's tremendous. It's hard to imagine any Democrat being able to do that. And it doesn't matter if Democrats try to ridicule it. It's stunning, and it speaks for itself."

- *Brian Williams:* "And two immutable truths about the president that the Democrats can't change: He's a youthful guy. He looked terrific and full of energy in a flight suit. He is a former pilot, so it's not a foreign art form to him. Not all presidents could have pulled this scene off today."

- *Morton Kondracke:* "That was great theater."
- *David Broder:* The president's "physical posture" communicated "authority and command."
- *Joe Klein:* "That was probably the coolest presidential image since Bill Pullman played the jet fighter pilot in the movie *Independence Day*. That was the first thing that came to mind for me. And it just shows you how high a mountain these Democrats are going to have to climb."
- *Laura Ingraham:* "Speaking as a woman, and listening to the women who called into my radio show, seeing President Bush get out of that plane, carrying his helmet, he is a real man. He stands by his word. That was a very powerful moment."[3]

Now, compare these raptures over the president's alleged manhood with the manner in which pundits treat his liberal counterparts. Once again we get punditry as locker-room juvenilia, but here it's not the adulation of the football captain but the harassing of the math nerd. Ann Coulter refers to Bill Clinton as a "latent homosexual," Al Gore as "a total fag," and John Edwards as "a faggot." John Kerry, says Coulter, "can't even stand up to his wife," and has "girlish hands." Liberals as a whole "throw like girls." Barack Obama's rhetoric, says the bow-tied pundit and *Dancing with the Stars* contestant Tucker Carlson, is "kind of wimpy." This has "turned him into Oprah" and makes him "seem like kind of a wuss." His guest, producer William Geist, wondered if Obama would be hosting "mani-pedi parties."[4] Later in the week, Carlson added the observation that watching Hillary Clinton on television forced him to "involuntarily cross [his] legs."[5] Meanwhile, Rush Limbaugh nominated Edwards as, potentially, "the first woman president." As usual, when Coulter and Limbaugh go too far, mainstream pundits are all too happy to follow, albeit at a distance. Fox News anchors go on and on about John Kerry's alleged enjoyment, "unlike most men," of the occasional manicure. Maureen Dowd, Chris Matthews, and Joe Scarborough, among many others, have dubbed John Edwards "the Breck Girl." ("He don't play in West Virginia" was the way macho man Scarborough analyzed Edwards's alleged problem.)[6] When Edwards received two $400 haircuts in the spring of 2007, which he mistakenly charged to his campaign, and then paid for out of his own funds, the story ran in virtually every media outlet in America. As Eric Boehlert pointed out, CNN aired more references to John Edwards's haircut than it did to his reaction to the Supreme Court's decision to uphold the ban on so-called partial-birth abortions.[7] Months later, the media could not let go of it. During a Republican presidential debate, former Arkansas governor Mike Huckabee quipped, "We've had a Congress that's spent money like John Edwards at a beauty shop," a comment that was celebrated by many in the media. Politico executive editor (and ex–*Washington Post* reporter) Jim Vande-Hei praised Huckabee's "great timing," adding that the dig at Edwards was "great for that red meat audience. I mean, they love making fun of . . . sort of the masculinity of Democrats, and they love to take pokes at people—Democrats who spend a lot of money. You know, they're elites, and . . . that's the message they're trying to pound home."[8] (Naturally, the GOPUSA deployed the phrase "Spending like John Edwards at a Beauty Shop" as its debate roundup title, too, though it needn't have bothered.) Fox pundit Sean Hannity, a man who makes his living in a midtown Manhattan television studio as a perfectly coiffed, albeit tough-talking, TV personality, made the nonsensical point explicit: calling Edwards the "$400 haircut man," he insisted, somehow, that Edwards was "not really viewed as somebody that is up to the task of understanding the nature of the battle in the war that's being waged against us."[9] As late as mid-July 2007, the *Washington Post* felt that the story remained sufficiently important and compelling to weigh in with a 1,288-word investigation of the fateful haircut, replete with an in-depth interview with the hair stylist in question. Bizarrely, the reporter, John Solomon, mused early in his article on whether it was "some kind of commentary on the state of American politics that as Edwards has campaigned for president, vice president and now president again, his hair seems to have attracted as much attention as, say, his position on health care."[10] It apparently did not occur to him that mention after mention, in articles published months after the fact by allegedly reputable newspapers, may have had something to do with this unhappy phenomenon. This was, after all, at least the fifteenth such mention in the *Post* of said haircut, and a Nexis search undertaken in September 2007 turned up more than a thousand such mentions. During that same month, the AP's Ron Fournier was still wondering aloud whether Edwards was somehow a "phony" owing to what the reporter termed "the Three Hs—haircut, house and hedge fund. Edwards' $1,250 haircuts, his new 28,000-square-foot estate in North Carolina and his consulting work with a hedge fund that caters to the super rich undercut his everyman image." Fournier also judged Edwards's "excuse" for his making so much money to be "lame."[11]

One of the above mentions, Jamison Foser notes, came courtesy of NBC Pentagon correspondent Jim Miklaszewski in the form of a speech to the Greater Providence Chamber of Commerce, a conservative, pro-business group that opposes Edwards's economic policies, and for which Miklaszewski was paid $30,000. As Foser observes, some Americans might have found it odd for a wealthy journalist to take money from a conservative organization to bash a liberal candidate.[12] But to virtually everyone in the mainstream media who mentioned it, the problem was Edwards's haircut—and his house and his personal wealth—rather than the fact that his policy proposals were never going to get a fair hearing.

This obsessiveness, much of it just plain silly rather than malevolent, is obviously not as objectionable as Ann Coulter calling Edwards a "faggot," but ultimately serves a similar purpose: the feminization of a male candidate as a means of insinuating that he is unqualified for the "man's job" of the presidency.

Apparently, the same qualities that once made for a successful caveman are also those that the leading lights of the punditocracy now believe determine a successful American president. It's not only dressing up in uniform that gets the pundits all hot and bothered. In contemporary American political debate, manliness is likewise associated with the will to kill—or at minimum, torture—people whom we call "terrorists." It doesn't matter if these "terrorists" are, actually, terrorists; in fact, even caring too much about accuracy in such matters is considered unmasculine. (George W. Bush proudly brags that he doesn't "do nuance.") Anyone who looks vaguely Middle Eastern, or happens to have a name that sounds like it might be Arabic, is fair game for murder, torture, lifetime imprisonment without resort to habeas corpus, or some combination of the three. Jonah Goldberg of *National Review,* CNN, and the *Los Angeles Times* admiringly quotes his colleague Michael Ledeen on the salutary aspects of war for its own sake: "I'm not sure my friend Michael Ledeen will thank me for ascribing authorship to him and he may have only been semi-serious when he crafted it, but here is the bedrock tenet of the Ledeen Doctrine in more or less his own words: 'Every ten years or so, the United States needs to pick up some small crappy little country and throw it against the wall, just to show the world we mean business.'"[13]

Naturally, a policy based on such problematic precepts can cause the occasional disaster, in addition to the death of a great many innocent people, which in turn generates an anger that feeds into a vicious and all-but-endless cycle of death and destruction for all concerned. This has, indeed, been exactly the effect of the Bush administration's policies in Iraq, as testified to by sixteen of the United States' own intelligence agencies, according to the official 2006 National Intelligence Estimate.[14]

Still, being prowar (in the abstract), not to mention protorture, is considered to be good politics, because no matter what the result—and it's an intellectual challenge even to imagine a worse set of outcomes than those resulting from America's invasion of Iraq—it still qualifies as "strength" within the context of American political debate, and such assumptions, even when unstated, underlie virtually all media coverage. For instance, two *Los Angeles Times* staff writers observed of the April 2007 Democratic presidential debate, "Even as they roundly attacked President Bush's policies on Iraq, the leading Democratic candidates for president sought to burnish their credentials Thursday as tough leaders who would defeat terrorists." They also asserted that the Democrats face a "challenge" because they "must woo antiwar primary election voters while fending off Republican attempts to paint them as weak on defense." The writers did not bother to explain why, in a nation where nearly 70 percent of the country then disapproved of the president's war in Iraq and where most gave the Democrats higher marks than Republicans on national security, they discerned a contradiction between criticizing the Bush administration's war and presenting oneself to this same public as a "tough leader who would defeat terrorists" and was not "weak on defense."[15]

Because our political system values macho pigheadedness pretty much as a prerequisite for the presidency, it is all but impossible for liberals to address this topic critically. Examine almost any American election campaign, and you'll probably see the more conservative candidate accuse the more liberal one of being "soft"—in other words, unmanly— with regard to one threat or another. Today that threat is terrorism. For decades the charge was leveled with regard to communism, though often in tandem with something else like pornography or, depending on the decade, drugs, immigration, homosexuality, integration, juvenile delinquency, and so on. In none of these cases did those leveling the charges feel compelled to defend the effectiveness of any program they employed to address the problem. Did the war in Vietnam, for instance, succeed in improving America's security vis-à-vis communism any more than the Iraq War has helped us protect ourselves from terrorists? Of course not. Did Ronald Reagan's illegal mining of Nicaragua's harbors protect the people of the United States in any meaningful way? The discussion almost never reaches the point of rationality, but rather becomes a way of signaling to voters that one is "strong," "tough," and sufficiently "masculine" to allow them to feel "safe" in pulling the lever for your side. This gambit has worked for conservatives for fifty years, and there is no sign that its effectiveness will ebb anytime soon. Even though they won World War II, rebuilt Europe through the Marshall Plan, created NATO, and faced down the Soviets in the Cuban missile crisis—or at least appeared to do so—poll after poll for nearly fifty years has demonstrated that liberals inspire little credibility with most American voters. In 1960, for instance, Richard Nixon outpolled John F. Kennedy on foreign policy by a margin of five to one.[16]

Sadly, owing to Americans' limited attention span for politics along with their limited body of knowledge about issues, they remain extremely easy prey for dishonest politicians and their manipulative consultants, who deal in evocative imagery designed to deceive rather than enlighten the average voter. Election discourse rarely delves beneath the airiest of glittering generalities, discussed entirely in symbolic terms. They are important, as a wise wag once said, merely for the "character" signals they send off about their holder. Say something "tough," and that makes you tough—at least, that's how the thinking goes. It's possible to be too "tough," as Barry Goldwater proved with his loose talk about turning North Vietnam into "a parking lot" in 1964, but Lyndon Johnson had to demonstrate just the right amount of "toughness" by taking the nation into a needless and destructive war in that same country on the basis of a dishonestly promoted "attack" on American warships that never actually took place. In other words, if what a politician needs to stave off an attack on his manliness is a Gulf of Tonkin incident—to say nothing of taking out his private parts and showing them to reporters—it becomes hard to see how liberals can win this contest at an acceptable cost to their own beliefs.

The degree to which waging war (and its attendant policies of torture, the suspension of habeas corpus, the creation of secret prisons, domestic wiretapping, and so on) can be taken as an exemplar not only of "strength" and "toughness" but also of simple patriotism at the very pinnacle of political debate is illustrated clearly in the following description of the alleged split between what top conservative columnist, editor, and think tank strategist William Kristol, writing in the *Weekly Standard*, terms "Dick Gephardt liberals and the Dominique de Villepin left":

The Gephardt liberals are patriots. They supported the president in the run-up to this war, and strongly support the war now that it has begun. . . . The other group includes the Teddy Kennedy wing of the Senate Democrats, the Nancy Pelosi faction of the House Democrats, a large majority of Democratic grass-roots activists, the bulk of liberal columnists, the *New York Times* editorial page, and Hollywood. These liberals—better, leftists—hate George W. Bush so much they can barely bring themselves to hope America wins the war to which, in their view, the president has illegitimately committed the nation. They hate Don

Rumsfeld so much they can't bear to see his military strategy vindicated. They hate John Ashcroft so much they relish the thought of his Justice Department flubbing the war on terrorism. They hate conservatives with a passion that seems to burn brighter than their love of America, and so, like M. de Villepin, they can barely bring themselves to call for an American victory.[17]

The distinctions Kristol draws here deserve to be unpacked in some detail. The author is not a provocateur at the level of an Ann Coulter, Rush Limbaugh, or David Horowitz, who barely even pretend to believe their own incitements to torture and mass murder. Kristol, on the other hand— the founding editor in chief of the *Weekly Standard,* the right's most influential opinion magazine; a founder of the Project for the New American Century, one of the think tanks where plans for the Iraq attack first originated; the most important strategist in both the first Bush administration and the Republican Congress during the Clinton administration; a former contributor to ABC's *This Week,* before moving to Fox News; a columnist for the *Washington Post* and, during 2007, *Time* magazine; and America's most prominent neoconservative publicist and the son of the original "godfather" of the movement, Irving Kristol—speaks for the absolute highest traditions of contemporary conservatism. And what is Kristol, arguably America's most important conservative intellectual, and certainly the media's most popular one, saying about liberals? Well, those who "supported the president in the run-up to this war, and strongly support the war now" are "patriots." Those who think the war was a mistake or, worse, that the United States "was committed to war illegitimately" are something else. Because they cannot possibly have the best interests of the nation at heart, the only explanation for their hesitation to embrace Bush's dishonestly promoted and incompetently executed war as well as Donald Rumsfeld's counterproductive military strategy and John Ashcroft's unconstitutional assault on American civil liberties is not only that they are wrong, but that they are illegitimate, unpatriotic, and possibly traitorous.

Kristol's list of those kinds of liberals he seeks to read out of patriotic political debate—at least by category—included at the time of his writing about half the Democratic Party, those few outspoken liberals with jobs in the mainstream media, and all of Hollywood. But unhappily for Kristol, he issued his ideological diktat during what might be termed neoconservatism's false dawn. Back then, his list of the ideologically impure was large but manageable, at least for a political movement that sought to rule American politics unimpeded. Four years later, however, the vast majority of American voters had come to embrace the very views Kristol all but called treasonous.

The fact remains: liberals are never going to succeed in a machismo contest with America's right wing. As it happens, the reason Bush refused even to fire Donald Rumsfeld and replace him with James Baker, as was recommended by his chief of staff and his closest foreign policy adviser (and, reports Bob Woodward, his secretary of state and his own wife), was because "Vice President Cheney and Karl Rove, his chief political adviser, [said] that it would be seen as an expression of doubt about the course of the war and would expose Bush himself to criticism."[18] In other words, Bush was willing to pursue a failed strategy on the war led by a discredited defense secretary because replacing him with someone more capable would be perceived as weakness. The president was willing to see tens, perhaps hundreds, of thousands of people die and to send hundreds of billions of dollars down a hopeless sinkhole because he preferred this to admitting a mistake.

It is no less a paradox than the fact that the draft-evading, truth-evading George W. Bush managed to defeat the war hero John F. Kerry on issues relating to foreign policy in poll after poll, while at the same time these very same voters expressed strong disapproval of the actual actions Bush had taken in this area. Even on Election Day 2004, according to the exit polls, a 49–44 percent plurality of voters told questioners that the war in Iraq had made the country less safe than before. The war was the administration's central endeavor in the area of national security, and yet somehow this failure translated into the commanding 18 percent lead on questions relating to security that gave him his tiny margin of victory.[19]

The great Duke basketball coach Mike Krzyzewski likes to tell his players that people remember 30 percent of what they hear, 50 percent of what they see, and 100 percent of what they feel.[20] Former Republican pollster Frank Luntz made this point in typical Republican fashion when he instructed GOP officeholders, "A compelling story, even if factually inaccurate, can be more emotionally compelling than a dry recitation of the truth."[21] This disjunction is well known to every viewer of *The Daily Show* or *The Colbert Report*.

Liberals have had little luck in trying to square this circle so far, both because the world is a great deal more complicated than it "feels" to most people—and most political pundits—and because to try to do justice to this complexity is to embrace the kind of "wimpiness" with which liberalism is already almost universally associated. Substantively, conservative foreign policy arguments are often unsophisticated. When dealing with the problems and issues that inevitably arise in relations between nations, few conservatives will admit to the slightest concern about what Thomas Jefferson called "the good opinion of mankind." In a column entitled "To Hell with Sympathy," Charles Krauthammer attacked what he called "the world," which he insisted "apparently likes the US when it is on its knees. From that the Democrats deduced a foreign policy—remain on our knees, humble and supplicant, and enjoy the applause and 'support' of the world."[22] Bill O'Reilly put the problem similarly when complaining of a lack of support for Bush's policies: "Everywhere else in the world lies."[23] This attitude, while typical of conservatives, actually overstates their level of interest in the views of non-Americans. In 1998 then–House majority leader Dick Armey explained, "I've been to Europe once. I don't have to go again." The House Appropriations Subcommittee on Foreign Operations chair at the time, Republican representative Sonny Callahan, summed up his view of foreign aid to Middle Eastern nations—the very nations whose poverty and lack of economic opportunity help breed the kind of people who threaten our security—by saying: "Every time somebody walks in the White House with a turban on his head . . . the president says, 'Let me give you a little bit of money.'"[24]

While both of the above quotes are self-evidently silly, they are well within the mainstream foreign-policy debate in Congress, on cable TV and talk radio, and even within the nation's most prestigious op-ed pages, where, for instance, Krauthammer regularly appears and even wins Pulitzer Prizes. In that realm, liberals are basically sunk. A liberal foreign policy necessarily involves some mixed measure of diplomacy, foreign aid, breadth of knowledge—attention to transnational threats like global warming, refugee migration, and famine—and so forth: all issues useful to those who would tar those proposing them as "soft." When liberals try to play on the conservative field, they often forfeit the game even before the first coin toss. One tactic that is certain to fail is Me-Tooism. The calamities caused by the Republican foreign policy in the Middle East and elsewhere have provided a political opening, but until liberals can articulate their own series of foreign policy principles and stick to them, they will continue to fall prey to the same syndromes that have crippled them in the past. It is liberalism's inability to explain itself when it comes to protecting and defending America that offers conservatives the opportunity to win elections no matter how incoherent their ideas or incompetent their implementation. Literally, nothing is more important to the long-term political success of liberals than their ability to combine their humanitarian and environmental foreign policy principles with a strong, clear, and "tough" articulation of their willingness to protect and defend the United States from its genuine adversaries, so as to earn the trust of Americans who, alas, will likely continue to prefer "strong and wrong" to "weak and right," particularly in periods of perceived peril. Still, the central argument of this book is no less true here than in any other aspect of policy making. Since the end of the Vietnam War, liberals have moved rightward and the vast majority of Americans leftward enough that once again, it is the liberal foreign policy agenda that meets with supermajority approval. Liberals, like most Americans, prefer diplomacy to war, desire to protect the environment, and embrace multilateralism whenever possible and unilateral power only when absolutely necessary. They reject the neoconservative doctrine that embraces unilateral war and empire as the primary means of assuring national security. While divided on trade, liberals nevertheless believe that American workers deserve a helping hand from the government when it comes to competing with underpaid foreign workers in nations that ignore both labor rights and environmental sustainability.

By abusing the trust of the military, alienating our allies, encouraging terrorism, and increasing America's insecurity, the Bush administration has offered liberals a wide-open field to define a national security policy that defends U.S. interests while securing the trust and respect of the rest of the world, which is so necessary in facing up to collective threats to our security and prosperity. A doctrine that embraces toughness, realism, and respect both for our own military and for the multiplicity of threats we face, whether from genuine enemies or from the spillover effects of potential ecological disaster and political catastrophe, requires a kind of American political and diplomatic leadership that has few precedents in world history. Liberalism must, as pundit and social critic E. J. Dionne has observed, offer up a doctrine to Americans that "convey[s] a clearer sense that it knows how to preserve social justice in a globalized economy and how to respond to a growing impatience with government. It must figure out how to preserve civil liberties, protect immigrants and foster an inclusive sense of national solidarity at the same time."[25] This is no easy task, given the complexity of the challenges, but not since the disaster of Vietnam have liberals been so well poised and prepared to do so—through both their own hard work in discarding some of the shibboleths of previous eras and the spectacular incompetence their political adversaries have demonstrated when entrusted with these same solemn responsibilities.

22

Why Do Liberals Love to Tax and Spend?

Well, this one's true: liberals are guilty as charged, as most of them really do embrace a political philosophy of "taxing and spending." The truth is, however, that everyone who deals with real politics must embrace a policy of taxing and spending, too. Conservatives love it no less than liberals, but as with sex, they evince considerably more discomfort in admitting this, particularly to themselves. Liberals, however, can and should acknowledge their love, and indeed should shout it from the proverbial rooftops. A society's ability to tax itself to provide for the common good lies at the very foundation of liberal philosophy, and pretty much any philosophy that deals with politics and the proper distribution of resources. The devil, per usual, rests snugly inside the details: to tax whom, how much, and for what purpose? As a philosophical matter, conservatives cannot credibly claim to disagree with those parameters.

And yet liberals remain on the defensive today even with regard to so fundamental an aspect of their self-definition. It can hardly be considered coincidence that the heyday of American liberalism—the New Deal and Fair Deal eras—coincided with the pinnacle of liberal self-confidence when it came to just this aspect of governance. The problem with a focus on spending and taxation policies is not, as the *Wall Street Journal* editorial page editors would have us believe, that "the tax-spend-elect formula does not work so well in an age of growing affluence and sophistication. Too many people feel the taxes; too many people have learned the meaning of inflation."[1] Rather, the problem is that its fruits have been too unevenly—even capriciously—distributed. Taxing and spending worked just fine when Americans felt that both were fairly and judiciously applied. The rich and the middle class paid and received their fair shares, respectively, and the poor received emergency assistance and the occasional leg up to the higher rungs of the economic system. It was only when so many Americans came to feel that both taxes and spending failed their test of fairness and assaulted their sense of themselves as decent, nonracist, nonsexist, nonimperialistic individuals that such policies grew to be politically unsustainable. This violation of Americans' basic sense of fairness—which began to appear in tandem with race-based affirmative-action policies—was followed by a subsequent destructive double helix of rising inflation and unemployment that helped to discredit the entire philosophy in the minds of millions. But the political miscalculations of a particular group of politicians during the 1960s and '70s can hardly be said to represent the entire philosophy. Nor, in fact, can conservatives argue that their own brand of redistributionary politics has proven any more effective. The difference, I would argue, is that when it comes to economics, conservatives are quite comfortable insisting on their principles while ignoring them in practice, while too many liberals lack the courage to defend their fundamental convictions, regardless of circumstance.

Historically, American conservatives have, virtually without exception, argued on behalf of small government, balanced budgets, and fiscal prudence. At the dawn of the so-called Republican Revolution of 1994, then–House majority leader Dick Armey announced that most government programs do nothing "to help American families with the needs of everyday life," and that "very few American families would notice their disappearance." He went on to insist that "there is no reason we cannot, by the time our children come of age, reduce the federal government by half as a percentage of gross domestic product." Armey and company failed on their own terms; as the economist Paul Krugman points out, federal outlays other than interest payments and defense spending comprised 14.8 percent of GDP in fiscal 2006, compared with 13.8 percent in fiscal 1995, when Armey initially did his crowing.[2]

Meanwhile, under President Bush, tax collections fell to 16 percent of the GDP, while overall spending rose from 18.5 percent to 20.3 percent. Taken together, this imbalance creates a massive structural deficit that coming generations must somehow make up. (During the Clinton years, federal spending actually fell as a share of GDP, from 21.4 percent in 1993 to 18.5 percent in 2001.) Republican fiscal irresponsibility in this regard dwarfs that achieved during the "taxing and spending" heyday of liberal Democrats, and yet it masks a case of even worse fiscal malfeasance that lurks barely beneath the surface: the entitlement budget. Social Security, Medicare, and Medicaid, for instance, which today consume 7 percent of GDP, are slated to rise to 13 percent in 2030, at which time, according to present projections, they will represent 25 percent of the entire U.S. economy, or an unthinkable $700 billion a year in higher taxes.[3] Current accounting practices allow these numbers to remain hidden to most journalists, and therefore most Americans, but the fact is, if the federal government were forced to adopt the standard accounting rules of corporate America, the 2006 federal deficit would have been more than $1.3 trillion, rather than the $248 billion claimed by the Bush administration. As of May 2007, U.S. taxpayers owed a rapidly rising $59.1 trillion in liabilities, or the equivalent of more than half a million dollars for every household.[4]

How have the conservatives in the Bush administration and the Republican Congress sought to address this problem? True to form, they've sought to exacerbate it. Bush's plan to partially privatize social security, for instance, would have added as much as $80 billion in deficits to his final two budgets plus nearly $700 billion more to those of his successors. But these costs pale in comparison to the trillion-plus-dollar bill of Bush's corporate-friendly Medicare legislation. Representative John M. Spratt Jr., the then–ranking Democrat on the House Budget Committee, put the cost of the first full ten years of the program at $1.4 trillion, rising to $3.5 trillion in the second decade. These obligations were, in addition to the massive Bush tax cuts, advertised to total approximately $1.7 trillion at the time, but given the likelihood that at least some of them will remain in place, rather than end on December 31, 2010, they will likely cost at least an additional $1.1 trillion beyond that.[5]

While George W. Bush enjoys the dubious distinction of presiding over perhaps the largest negative budget swing in American history—from a surplus of $236 billion in 2000, the year he was elected, to a deficit of $412 billion, or 3.6 percent of GDP, four years later[6]—he could not have accomplished this without the collusion of the conservative-controlled Congress. When Bush pretended to set a serious cost limit of $6.7 billion for tax breaks in his energy bill, Congress came back with one that would reach roughly twice that much.

The notion that these are fiscally conservative values at work is clearly preposterous. The 1,752-page Bush–Republican Congress transportation bill, for instance, turned out to be the single most expensive piece of public works legislation in U.S. history, replete with 6,376 earmarked pet projects by individual legislators.[7] Back in 1987, when the president contemporary conservatives most revere, Ronald Reagan, vetoed what he considered an unconscionably pork-laden highway and mass transit bill, the offense had been a mere 152 earmarks.[8] To try to appreciate the level of fiscal irresponsibility on display here, consider the size of the burden it has left for future generations. Technically, the U.S. government, like any business, is responsible for the projected value of all future expenditures. Unless it embarks on an inflation-inspiring money-printing craze, it must cover these obligations with its income from future receipts. What lies between these two numbers is a gap that by 2003 had already reached $44.2 trillion or so, on its way to roughly four times the size of the entire GDP. What is perhaps most alarming about that figure—calculated by the economists Jagadeesh Gokhale and Kent Smetters in a study commissioned by then–treasury secretary Paul O'Neill, but later disowned by the U.S. government—is that it is actually based on the government's own, sometimes laughably optimistic, projections.[9]

"Liberalism's goal of achieving greater equality of condition," argues George F. Will, "leads to a larger scope for interventionist government to circumscribe the market's role in allocating wealth and opportunity."[10] But clearly, as the apostate conservative Kevin Phillips observes, "the Bush Administration is not against big government." What it opposes is merely that "portion of it that regulates business and requires tax increases, against a welfare system. When it's the latter, they're against big government, but when it's big government that takes care of the oil industry or bails out financial institutions or pumps money into the Pentagon, then they tend to be in favor of that."[11] As the economically conservative *Financial Times* of London observed after Bush's second round of tax cuts was passed, "On the management of fiscal policy, the lunatics are now in charge of the asylum."[12]

And yet this transformation in the real-world meaning of political conservatism has made little if any impact on popular thought. During the 2006 election Juan Williams, who passes at Fox News for a liberal, complained, "most people are telling pollsters that they trust the Democrats more on taxes than they do the Republicans." Indeed, even Republican pollster Frank Luntz admitted, "Democrats now hold a perceived advantage with voters not just on reducing deficits and balancing the budget but on an issue long seen as a GOP strength: ending wasteful spending." But Williams wouldn't buy it. "To me, that's crazy," he insisted.[13] "Crazy," too, was the assertion made by MSNBC's Chris Matthews when he claimed, "Republicans know from the polls they got two strengths right now"—terrorism and taxes—"whether the current polls back that up or not."[14] And when the *New York Times* invited the famously maverick Republican senator Chuck Hagel to sound off on the issue, he attacked his own party's profligacy by complaining, "In terms of the deficit, we have blown the top right off. We're a bunch of Democrats. . . . The Democrats are better because they are honest about it. They don't pretend. I admire that. They'll say: 'We want more money. We need more money.'"[15]

Hagel is wrong in his particulars but symbolically, at least, on target. No Democratic or liberal American politician of national significance would ever imagine proposing a fiscal program as financially irresponsible as that pursued by contemporary American "conservatives." But the larger point—that it is proper to pursue policies based on the government's power to levy taxes on certain kinds of enterprises in order to provide the variety of services that make up the myriad responsibilities of modern governance—is relevant to both conservatives and liberals. The appropriate question is: To what end? Both liberals and conservatives share the belief, expressed cogently by former French prime minister Lionel Jospin, "that the market is an instrument that is effective and important, but it is nothing more than an instrument."[16] The difference between liberals and conservatives is that the former admit this to be the case, while the latter pretend, for the purpose of tribute, that they disagree.

Unarguably, liberals made some horrifically misguided decisions regarding taxpayer monies during the 1960s, when it appeared that prosperity was the rule and the growth of the U.S. economy was all but limitless. Their attempt to fund a host of social programs under the rubric of Lyndon Johnson's Great Society at the same time that the Vietnam War raged on, unaccounted for in budget appropriations, upset the fiscal health of the nation for nearly a decade and saddled liberals with a reputation for fiscal profligacy that continues to burden them today. Yet these mistakes—as costly and irresponsible as they may have appeared at the time—pale in comparison to the fiscal and economic nightmare that so-called conservatives have intentionally inflicted on the nation.

Beginning in the early 1970s, the American productivity boom that fueled rising living standards in the postwar era came to an abrupt end; so too did rising real incomes for the middle class. Whatever improvements in living standards did occur for the majority of Americans during this period can be attributed to advances in technology and the entry of women into the workforce. Wages, meanwhile, have remained virtually flat for most people, and have even been subject to some decline. This is, alas, a phenomenon hardly limited to our own economy. In the decade since the passage of NAFTA, for instance, labor productivity in U.S. manufacturing rose between 70 and 80 percent, while real wages rose only 6 percent. In Mexico, productivity rose 68 percent, while real wages rose 2 percent. In Canada, the numbers are 34 and 3 percent, respectively.[17] The question for any democratic society is how to address this imbalance. In the United States we have done so by conducting what one conservative writer terms "a massive social experiment" in economic inequality. Over the last quarter century the portion of the national income accruing to the richest 1 percent of Americans has doubled. The share going to the richest one-tenth of 1 percent has tripled, and the share going to the richest one-hundredth of 1 percent has quadrupled.[18]

In 2005, the wealthiest 1 percent of the country earned 21.2 percent of all income, according to IRS data, while the bottom 50 percent of all Americans earned just 12.8 percent of all income, down from 13.4 percent, a year earlier. [19] Together, these two figures define a new postwar record for American economic inequality, which is believed by many economists to be greater today than at any other time since the 1920s.

For working people, wages and salaries now make up the lowest share of the nation's gross domestic product since the process of collecting this data began more than sixty years ago. [20] In the period since 2000 the number of Americans living below the poverty line has increased by nearly a third. [21] Meanwhile, the average CEO of a Standard & Poor's 500 company took home $13.51 million in total compensation in 2005, a year in which the top 1 percent of Americans earned nearly 22 percent of all income. [22] Believe it or not, by 11:02 A.M. of the first day of work on the first day of the year, one of these average CEOs will "earn" more money than a minimum-wage worker in his company will make for the entire year. [23] The media tends to treat these trends as merely the way the world works, but this is actually the essence of conservative ideology. As the political philosopher Michael Walzer pointed out in 1973:

> At the very center of conservative thought lies this idea: that the present division of wealth and power corresponds to some deeper reality of human life. Conservatives don't want to say merely that the present division is what it ought to be, for that would invite a search for some distributive principle—as if it were possible to make a distribution. They want to say that whatever the division of wealth and power is, it naturally is, and that all efforts to change it, temporarily successful in proportion to their bloodiness, must be futile in the end. [24]

One cannot help but ask: Why is this not the case in Europe or Japan? In fact, among major world economies, the United States in recent years has had the third-greatest disparity in incomes between the very top and everyone else; only Mexico and Russia are worse. [25] Only in the United States are the superwealthy so powerful, and their ideological interests so well tended and defended, that their interests have come to stand as "principles" in our political discourse. As the historian Eric Foner notes, according to Franklin Roosevelt, "individual freedom" could not be said to "exist without economic security and independence . . . for the average man which will give his political freedom reality." And his successor, Harry Truman, would still use the phrase *economic freedom* in his 1950 State of the Union address to mean "a fundamental economic freedom for labor." But by the time of Ronald Reagan's second inaugural, the same phrase had come to imply not the right to organize or achieve economic security and independence, but deregulation, tax cuts, and an attack on unions on behalf of powerful corporations and their wealthy owners and investors.[26]

By the second Bush presidency, following more than twenty years of conservative agitation, the ideological demands of the superrich had grown ever more extreme. For instance, Kenneth C. Griffin, who received more than a billion dollars in 2006 as chairman of a hedge fund, the Citadel Investment Group, explained to a *New York Times* reporter in the summer of 2007, "The income distribution has to stand," adding, "I am proud to be an American. But if the tax became too high, as a matter of principle I would not be working this hard."[27] Just what "principle" Mr. Griffin had in mind, he did not say. Meanwhile, this period in American history witnessed a pitched battle between members of the Democratic Congress and a Republican-supported group of private equity billionaires fighting to retain their tax privileges. These included, as Warren Buffett explained, the right to "pay a lower part of our income in taxes than our receptionists do, or our cleaning ladies, for that matter." They insisted on this right because to force billionaires to pay what bartenders must, would, according to wealthy Bush administration "pioneer" Wayne Berman, "disrupt thousands of partnerships around the country that provide the economic engine," and "punish innovators."[28] In no other democracy in the world were the wealthiest members of society so generously indulged. This argument, so patently absurd from the standpoint of basic fairness, was nevertheless sufficiently respectable for its adaptation by New York senator Charles "Chuck" Schumer, the third-ranking Democrat in the Senate leadership, one of the key architects of the 2006 electoral victory, and a self-described "progressive" politician (though not, in his own estimation, a "liberal").[29] Of course Schumer had good political reasons to go to bat for one of his most important sources of campaign funds, and one whose industry happens to be located in the state he represents. Even so, the mere spectacle of a prominent center-left politician agitating for a tax cut for plutocrats, without shame or apology, demonstrates just how influential the power of money has become in twenty-first-century America.

Yet this trend is not only fiscally unhealthy, but also politically dangerous. Conservatives insist that inequality is a nonissue; the economist Tyler Cowen wonders "why we should worry about inequality—of any kind—much at all." What matters, he argues, "is how well people are doing in absolute terms"—and not whether Smith makes ten times more than Jones. Bruce Bartlett, also a conservative, concurs: "If my real income does not fall, how am I hurt when Bill Gates makes another billion dollars?"[30] Such arguments are almost perversely naive. In the first place, as the economist J. Bradford DeLong notes, "an unequal society cannot help but be an unjust society. The very first thing that any society's wealthy try to buy with their wealth is a head start for their children. And the wealthier they are, the bigger the head start. Any society that justifies itself on a hope of equality of opportunity cannot help but be undermined by too great a degree of inequality of result."[31]

Additionally, in our political system money has been defined by the U.S. Supreme Court as political speech and therefore exercises political power as well. Whether "liberal" or "conservative," those Americans with sufficient resources to give $2,300 or more to a candidate share much in outlook. In his book *The Audacity of Hope,* Barack Obama notes that these wealthy donors, in his brief experience, exhibited "no patience with protectionism, found unions troublesome, and were not particularly sympathetic to those whose lives were upended by the movements of global capital." Obama discovered that if he was honest with himself, he recognized that the more time he spent hitting rich people up for cash, the more he, as a politician, became "like" them, "in the very particular sense that I spent more and more of my time above the fray, outside of the world of immediate hunger, disappointment, fear, irrationality, and frequent hardship of the population—that is, the people I'd entered public life to serve."[32] He suspects that this phenomenon is the case, "in one fashion or another . . . for every senator."

Indeed, Obama's concern is as welcome as his experience is universal in our money-driven political system. A report issued by the American Political Science Association in 2004, entitled "American Democracy in an Age of Rising Inequality," noted, "Skewed participation among citizens and the targeting of government resources to partisans and the well-organized ensure that government officials disproportionately respond to business, the wealthy." Indeed, a study by Princeton's Larry Bartels of the Senate's voting record between 1989 and 1994—when, we should note, Democrats were in control—found the people's representatives highly responsive to the demands of the top third of the income spectrum, rather less responsive to the middle third, and altogether uninterested in those put forth by the poorest third. This was particularly true, unfortunately, for those issues that affected poor Americans most directly. Bartels discovered, for instance, that minimum wages rose only when wealthy Americans supported the idea; those forced to work at these rates enjoyed "no discernible impact."[33] While this is true of direct influence, it is no less significantly so regarding indirect influence. Wealthy people and their corporations own newspapers and fund think tanks, public affairs television, university chairs, advertising campaigns, lecture series, and the like. Poor people do not. With few exceptions, these same organizations and institutions represent the views of the wealthy. "It's all very well to sympathize with the working man," William Raney Harper, the first president of the University of Chicago, once remarked. "But we get our money from the other side and we can't afford to offend them."[34]

With these trends pervasive in the economy, you'd think the last thing our democracy needs is policies designed to accelerate them. Yet the Bush administration has supported exactly such measures. According to the U.S. Internal Revenue Service, the only taxpayers whose share of taxes declined in 2001 and 2002 were those in the top 0.1 percent, or Americans who earn more than $10 million a year. The following year their tax share declined by another million.[35] These same lucky folks now pay a lesser share of their income in taxes than those making $100,000 to $200,000,[36] and this includes only legally reported income. The really rich are different from you and me; they have more tax shelters.

What is the purpose of depleting the treasury to further enrich those who already enjoy an unprecedented showering of riches? Broadly speaking, I can think of two. The Bush economic policies were deliberately designed to redistribute even more money to the extremely rich from the rest of us. Recall Vice President Cheney's response, quoted earlier, to Secretary O'Neill when the latter complained that new tax cuts would bust the budget: "We won the mid terms. It's our due." By "our" Cheney was clearly referring to the wealthiest swath of American society, particularly its corporate elite, who financed the political careers of the president, the vice president, and their political allies. Conservatives regularly mouth the nostrum that tax cuts for the richest Americans actually increase government revenues and eventually trickle down to poor and middle-class Americans. President Bush, for example, maintains that "you cut taxes and the tax revenues increase." Cheney adds, "The tax cuts have translated into higher federal revenues." On the basis of who-knows-what, Cheney has claimed, "The evidence is in, it's time for everyone to admit that sensible tax cuts increase economic growth and add to the federal treasury." He was joined by ex–majority leader Dr. Bill Frist, in possession of "a dirty little secret about tax-cut measures: When done right, they actually result in more money for the government." To Frist it's a secret, but to John McCain, it's something "we all know . . . starting with Kennedy."[37]

In fact, this is nonsense. Even the administration's own budget does not project that revenues will continue to grow at their 2005 rate or that the tax cuts will pay for themselves. Under the assumptions in the budget, real per-person revenues will grow by an annual average of 0.8 percent between 2000 and 2011, only about half the growth rate during the 1980s and less than one-fourth the growth rate during the 1990s.[38]

When the actual results of Bush's policy were finally tallied, the effect of the tax cuts was, unsurprisingly, to increase the deficit and enrich the

wealthy. According to Alan D. Viard, a former Bush White House economist who moved to the right-wing American Enterprise Institute, "Federal revenue is lower today than it would have been without the tax cuts.
There's really no dispute among economists about that." An analysis of
treasury data prepared by the Congressional Research Service estimates
that economic growth fueled by the cuts is likely to generate revenue
worth about 7 percent of the total cost of the cuts.[39]

Tax policy is hardly the only place that the Bush administration has
put the power of government at the service of the extremely wealthy. It
has purposely stood in the way of an increase in the national minimum
wage, which fell from well over one-third as much per hour as the wage
of an average worker to less than a quarter, before the Democratic Congress finally raised it in 2007. Its National Labor Relations Board has severely constricted labor unions' ability to organize and has ruled that
millions of workers are simply ineligible to join unions, despite meager
wages and virtually no power over their conditions of employment. Less
than 8 percent of the private-sector workforce is presently unionized,
compared with over 20 percent during the 1970s. Finally, the globalization of production, including particularly advances in telecommunica-
tion, has forced U.S. workers to compete with exploited Third World
workers—including some children who earn literally pennies a day. This
"global convergence of wages," as the former treasury secretary and
chair of Citigroup, Robert Rubin, put it, will act as a downward force on
U.S. workers' wages indefinitely, as a billion and a half new workers
from India, China, and elsewhere come on line to replace what were
once middle-class occupations for American citizens. Alan Blinder,
former vice chairman of the board of governors of the Federal Reserve
System, and a dedicated free-trader, estimates that as many as thirty to
forty million jobs are "potentially offshorable," including scientists and
mathematicians as well as clerks, telephone operators, and typists. The
administration has only encouraged the outsourcing of such positions,
going so far as to protect and defend tax breaks for companies that
shift jobs overseas. During the 2004 election campaign, George W. Bush
declared that the United States must act to "make sure there are more

jobs at home, and people are more likely to retain a job." But true to form, he called in his budget two years later for a cut in exactly this category: "Trade Adjustment Assistance" to workers displaced by foreign competition.[40]

Clearly, conservatives simply do not care about the impact on American workers as high-paying jobs travel overseas, never to return. Liberals, on the other hand, are concerned but divided about how to respond. Most reject "protectionism" but embrace programs that encourage retraining and vocational education. As more and more good jobs leave, though, many are demanding that the United States ask its trading partners to accept the same kinds of labor and environmental protections that safeguard U.S. workers as a means of evening out the playing field. Following an election that focused in many respects on trade policy, in May 2007 Democratic congressional leaders forced President Bush to demand that other nations guarantee workers the right to organize, ban child labor and prohibit forced labor, enforce environmental laws already on their books, and comply with several international environmental agreements.[41] Until Republican policies were clearly repudiated in 2006, such practices had continued unimpeded.

Back in the early 1980s Ronald Reagan's budget director, David Stockman, admitted that the purpose of the president's tax cuts had been ideological rather than economic in intent. Stockman sought to "put a tightening noose around the size of the government," as he told journalist William Greider.[42] Contemporary conservatives have embarked on a far more profligate course than Stockman had ever dreamed of, but they have done so with the same goal: to cripple the government's ability to act as a brake on the power of the wealthy to further enrich themselves at the expense of the rest of us. It is all but impossible to locate a single action undertaken by the Bush administration that is not in keeping with this principle.

Ultimately, the choice is not between one philosophy of government that supports policies of "tax and spend" and one that does not. Rather, it is between one that taxes and spends for the good of the wealthiest 0.1 percent of us or one that attempts to address the concerns of the other 99.9 percent. Following the 2006 election, *Weekly Standard* executive editor and Fox commentator Fred Barnes made the astonishing claim that despite all of the evidence cited above, Democrats and liberals wish to raise taxes on the richest Americans, "even though there's no reason except vindictiveness against the well-to-do for doing it." The issue, said Barnes, had become "theological" for Democrats, who had been driven "crazy [by the fact] that the top [federal income tax] rate is only 35 percent."[43]

It's hard to know what to say to a conservative who considers annual deficits approaching a half trillion dollars, to say nothing of even larger looming deficits deriving from the Medicare debacle, to amount to literally nothing compared to the alleged vindictiveness of "crazy" liberals who love to tax people. Then again, that such voices represent mainstream thinking in American politics is itself a significant part of the problem.

23

Don't Conservatives Do a Better Job of Promoting Economic Growth Than Liberals?

Even by the attenuated standards of what American liberals have been able to accomplish while working through the Democratic Party, constrained by both Republican and corporate opposition, they have managed to amass an economic record superior to that of Republicans, even when measured by conservatives' own standards. Take government spending, which since 1960 has increased by approximately $50 billion a year on average. If you examine just who is responsible for its relative increase (and assume a one-year time lag for a given president's policies to take effect), the net result is an average increase of $60 billion under Republican and just $40 billion under Democratic presidents. (If you eliminate the time lag, the Democratic spending figure drops to $35 billion.) If you begin your calculation in 1981, when President Reagan initiated the modern conservative campaign to cut federal spending and shrink the size of government, Democrats still enjoy the advantage, no matter which formula you employ. This tendency has, of course, mushroomed under Bush, as federal discretionary spending increased by 49 percent during his first six years in office.[1] The result of this is that if an average American worked 78.5 days to pay his federal taxes under Bill Clinton, that number rose to 86.5 days under Bush.[2] This is hardly a coincidence. A study by William Niskanen of the conservative/libertarian Cato Institute found that the conservative "starve the beast" strategy with regard to taxes actually has the opposite effect in the real world. Niskanen discovered to his shock and profound surprise that, beginning in 1981, tax cuts have tended to produce more spending, while tax hikes tended to produced less.[3]

While conservatives denounce the evils of deficit spending and sing the praises of fiscal responsibility, the historical record reveals once again just how cavalierly they treat their own rhetoric when in power. Michael Kinsley does the math and finds:

> Under Republican presidents since 1960, the federal deficit has averaged $131 billion a year. Under Democrats, that figure is $30 billion. In an average Republican year the deficit has grown by $36 billion. In the average Democratic year it has shrunk by $25 billion. The national debt has gone up more than $200 billion a year under Republican presidents and less than $100 billion a year under Democrats. If you start counting in 1981 or attribute responsibility with a year's delay, the numbers change, but the bottom line doesn't: Democrats do Republican economics better than Republicans do.

As for the Republicans' argument that decreased government debt increases overall economic growth, well, they may be right. But the fact is, the only examples we have to judge that contention in recent times can be found during Democratic administrations. Kinsley runs these numbers and discovers:

> From 1960 to 2005, the gross domestic product measured in year-2000 dollars (in other words, taking inflation into account) rose an average of $165 billion a year under Republican presidents and $212 billion a year under Democrats. Measured from 1989, or with a one-year delay, or both, the results are similar. And how about this one? The average annual rise in real per capita income (that's the statistic that puts money in your pocket): Democrats score about 30% higher.

The inflation numbers tell a similar story, as do the unemployment figures. Democratic presidents have a better record on inflation, Kinsley calculates (averaging 3.13 percent versus 3.89 percent for Republicans), and on unemployment (5.33 percent versus 6.38 percent). Unemployment went down in the average Democratic year, up in the average Republican one.[4] Armed with such statistics, if liberal pundits, politicians, and intellectuals cannot win this argument, then really, it's time to find another line of work.

— 24 —

But Why Are Liberals So Nasty?

We hear it over and over: Liberals are mean. Liberals are nasty. Peggy Noonan explains that for conservatives, what "lies at the heart of modern liberalism . . . is hate."[1] Liberals, they believe, hurt people's feelings for the sheer pleasure of it. Brian C. Anderson, author of the book *South Park Conservatives,* says nothing controversial when he writes, "It's hard not to notice that political discussion over the last decade has increasingly degenerated into name-calling—and that the insults most often come from the left: 'racist,' 'homophobe,' 'sexist,' 'mean-spirited,' 'insensitive.' It has become a habit of left-liberal political argument to use such invective to dismiss conservative beliefs as if they don't deserve an argument and to redefine mainstream conservative arguments as extremism and bigotry."[2] *National Review* writer Peter Wood complains that liberals engage in "a special kind of theater in which the performer enacts rage and attempts symbolically to annihilate his opponent," and cites in particular "Angry Left blogs such as the Daily Kos and Eschaton," *New Republic* writer Jonathan Chait, and *New York Times* columnist Paul Krugman."[3] (Indeed, one rarely sees the word *left* or *liberal* before *blog* without the word *angry* appended to it.)[4]

The accusation is not entirely unfounded, though much of the evidence put forward is quite silly, and most of the rest comes from people who are "liberals" by virtue of their positions in the entertainment industry, rather than politics. Sometimes conservative standards of "mean" are so elastic it's a challenge to figure out just what the offense might have been, and to whom it was addressed. Dinesh D'Souza, for instance, criticizes the "vehemence" of novelist Philip Roth's *The Plot against America*—a fictional counterhistory of a Lindbergh presidency during World War II—and quotes a reviewer who describes the book as "a cautionary tale about how easily the country could slide into fascism."[5] Just whose "vehemence"—Roth's or the reviewer's—and for what, exactly, D'Souza never explains. He is apparently offended merely by the plot itself, much in the way that Soviet and Cuban censors have reacted to fiction of which they did not approve.

It would be a mistake, moreover, to assume that mindless vituperation is the exclusive province of conservative provocateurs. Roger Cohen, for instance, has made quite a career for himself at the *New York Times*. Formerly the paper's foreign editor, he is currently the international affairs columnist of the (*Times*-owned) *International Herald Tribune,* and author of the "Globalist" column and "international writer at large" for the *Times,* plum assignments all. Yet to Cohen, writing on the *Times* Web site and in the *Tribune,* America was, at the close of 2006, under siege from "hyperventilating left-liberals [whose] hatred of Bush is so intense that rational argument usually goes out the window." Liberals were "so convinced that the Iraq invasion was no more than an American grab for oil and military bases" that they had "forgotten the myriad crimes of Saddam Hussein." What's more, liberals were made up of "America-hating, over-the-top rant[ers] of the left—the kind that equates Guantánamo with the Gulag and holds that the real threat to human rights comes from the White House rather than Al Qaeda." And for good measure, Cohen reported, they "equate the conservative leadership of a great democracy with dictatorship." Lest there be any confusion on the matter, Cohen wished the rest of us to know that he was sick of "sterile screaming in the wilderness, tired of the comfortably ensconced 'hindsighters' poring over every American error in Iraq, tired of facile anti-Americanism and anti-Semitism masquerading as anti-Zionism."[6]

To support these amazing charges, the veteran *Times*man quoted exactly one person: the Scottish MP George Galloway, who was last seen making an ass of himself on the TV reality show for washed-up gossip fodder *Celebrity Big Brother.* Galloway, who was thrown out of the Labour Party, is about as representative of the "left-liberals" here and abroad as, say, former KKK grand wizard and Holocaust denier David Duke would be of the right. Remember: this is not the *Weekly Standard,* the *New York Post,* or Fox News; this invective appeared in the news—not opinion—columns of the allegedly liberal *New York Times.*

To be sure, "liberal" potty-mouths are easy enough to find in a media that treats the topic obsessively. For instance, Jennifer Aniston of *Friends* once called George W. Bush "a fucking idiot," and the singer John Mellencamp termed him "a cheap thug." Cher called him "stupid and lazy," and Whoopi Goldberg made a lot of juvenile jokes about the word *bush* at a Kerry fund-raiser in New York. Alec Baldwin has said a few things he wishes he hadn't, no doubt, as has Barbra Streisand. The undeniable coarsening of the discourse that has taken place in the world of talk radio—often, but not always, resulting from conservative hate speech—has been indulged and sometimes even celebrated in the mainstream media. When Don Imus referred to black female college basketball players as "nappy-headed hos," it unleashed a media firestorm that ultimately led to his dismissal from MSNBC and CBS. But not only had these corporations enabled Imus's constant derogation of minorities and woman, he received the official seal of approval from those occupying the position of media referee. Howard Kurtz, the media cop for both CNN and the *Washington Post,* was himself termed by Imus to be "a boner-nosed, beanie-wearing Jew-boy." But Kurtz, who enjoyed Imus's promotion of his books on the air, says he "just shrugged it off as Imus's insult schtick." He later attempted to excuse the man's vicious racism by explaining, "Over the years, Imus made fun of blacks, Jews, gays, politicians. He called them lying weasels. This was part of his charm."[7] Naturally, if Imus was given permission to engage in this kind of abuse against groups and individuals, others felt free to do the same.

Imus's former employer MSNBC even once decided it would be a good idea to give a show to conservative hate-speech specialist Michael Savage. In what, in a just universe, would appear in the dictionary beside the word *chutzpah,* Savage—long after being fired by MSNBC for telling a gay caller that he was a "sodomite" who should "get AIDS and die"—took the occasion of a racist outburst by the comedian Michael Richards (famous for his *Seinfeld* character but possessing no known political affiliation) to make the following case against liberals: Richards's screaming of "nigger, nigger" at black hecklers "is what the sub-text of liberalism really is. Under the surface, if you got them in a room alone, I guarantee you they'd say the same kind of hateful things about Catholics and about Jews and about straights and about soldiers."[8]

When the purveyor of "liberal hate speech" is not an actor or a rock star, the offender is almost always someone nobody has ever heard of previously. How many times have we read about the idiotic views of Ward Churchill, the ex–University of Colorado professor who called the victims of September 11 "little Eichmanns," or Nicholas De Genova, the Columbia professor who loudly wished "a million Mogadishus" on American troops in Iraq? D'Souza has rounded up every conceivable ob-jectionable liberal statement he could following 9/11, and the Ameri-cans he cites are: Churchill, De Genova, the Yale historian Glenda Gilmore, Noam Chomsky, and the largely nonpolitical novelist Norman Mailer. Of this group, only Chomsky has a following on the left, mostly on col-lege campuses and among radicals who—like the Stalinist columnist Al-exander Cockburn—revile liberals more than they do conservatives. The rest, including especially the angry and often anonymous (and sometimes, no doubt, imaginary) posters of liberal political Web sites, owe their political notoriety entirely to conservative publicists who seek to misportray them as spokespeople for all of American liberalism.

Quite a few liberals and leftists did, presciently, object to the Bush administration's reaction to 9/11, though again, even here, D'Souza's "Enemies" list is heavily weighted not only with foreigners but also with showbiz types like Jane Fonda, Oliver Stone, Martin Sheen, Danny Glover, Spike Lee, and even Mumia Abu-Jamal.[9] On the basis of such a list D'Souza complains, "The left is serving as bin Laden's public rela-tions team in America and conservatives should not be afraid to say this."[10] D'Souza, who has previously written books in support of private-sector racism and who professes to admire Joe McCarthy, is regarded by most to be well within the conservative mainstream. Unlike, say, Ann Coulter, Rush Limbaugh, or David Horowitz, he is not considered a purposeful provocateur and has been honored with prestigious positions not only at the Hoover Institute but also at the American Enterprise

Institute. His books are published by respected publishers, rather than explicitly ideological ones. If his views do, indeed, represent the right's honest appraisal of who represents liberal America, then it is enough to say that it is no longer possible to expect an honest exchange of ideas about anything, much less "civility."

Conservatives are quick to exploit the perception of liberal "hate speech" for maximum political effect. As Geoffrey Nunberg observes, "During the primaries leading up to the 2004 elections, Republicans were trying to depict the Democrats' criticisms of President Bush as the expressions of pathological rage. 'So far all we hear is a lot of old bitterness and partisan anger,' George Bush said in a speech in February, 2004."[11] The Bush campaign not only mailed out a letter warning of a "venomous assault from rage-filled Democrats" but also produced an ad entitled "When Angry Democrats Attack." RNC chair Ed Gillespie explained to reporters, "The kind of words we're hearing now from the Democratic candidates go beyond legitimate political discourse—this is political hate speech."[12] Gillespie's only reference for his complaint was then presidential candidate Dick Gephardt's description of Bush's first term as "a miserable failure," which, as I write this, would strike most Americans who speak to Gallup or Harris pollsters as a reasonably accurate description of reality rather than "hate speech."

The fact is, while conservatives complain of "angry," "hateful," or "venomous" attacks by liberals on conservatives—or even on average, churchgoing, mind-their-own-business, middle-class Americans—hatred, abuse, and even incitement to violence are standard elements in right-wing discourse. While an entire book could be filled with examples, the following will suffice, and please note that none of them are culled from politically marginal individuals—there are no quotes from Mel Gibson or Charlie Daniels or Ted Nugent or even Charlton Heston. Consider, instead, the most popular talk-show host on cable TV, Fox's Bill O'Reilly. In addition to being a veritable font of misinformation, O'Reilly is also a source of never-ending vituperation. In May 2007 three University of Indiana scholars published a "propaganda" content analysis of O'Reilly's broadcasts based on the same criteria employed by the political scientist

Harold Lasswell in the early 1970s, and previously employed to examine the radio broadcasts of the demagogic FDR opponent Father Charles Coughlin, among others. The authors found that during one hundred consecutive "Talking Points Memo" portions of *The O'Reilly Factor* they examined, "O'Reilly employed name calling 8.88 times a minute, which is close to once every seven seconds." Among his favorites were: "calling academics who criticize the Bush war policy 'anti-American voices'" (February 8, 2005), and referring to French president Jacques Chirac sarcastically as "our pal" who "dislikes America too much" to help in the war on terror (February 21, 2006). In another commentary, O'Reilly labeled the estate tax, which Republicans were trying to eliminate, as the "death tax" and "un-American" (April 15, 2005). As far as calling large groups of people nasty names, the authors determined that, to O'Reilly, "foreigners, academics, and illegal aliens . . . were villains most of the time. Foreigners were less often villainous than academics. . . . Illegal aliens were never victims and they were presented in one of the strongest evil frames, only topped by terrorists."[13]

Had the authors expanded their research, they might have included O'Reilly's statements calling liberal philanthropist George Soros an "incredible imbecile,"[14] or his fantasy that "they'll never get it until they [Islamic extremists] grab Michael Kinsley out of his little house and they cut his head off. And maybe when the blade sinks in, he'll go, 'Perhaps O'Reilly was right,'"[15] or his belief that detaining all "Muslims between the ages of 16 and 45" for questioning "isn't racial profiling," but "criminal profiling."[16]

To be fair to everyone concerned, we must admit that even as far as the insult game goes, O'Reilly is a mere piker compared with some of his colleagues. Just take a look at some of the examples of conservative hate speech that were compiled by my colleagues at Media Matters for America.

On "Hate"

"I now find that I am infected with a hatred for the very quarter that inspired the rule—the deranged, lying left. . . . I detest them as among the most loathsome people America has ever vomited up. . . . I hate the executives at CNN. . . . I now hate Howard Dean. . . . I hate the Democrats."[17] —Paul Burgess, director of foreign-policy speechwriting at the White House from October 2003 to July 2005

On People Who Do Not Support
Rendition for the Purposes of Torture

"I hope it's your family members that die."[18] —Representative Dana Rohrabacher (R-CA), to American citizens who questioned the Bush administration's unlawful extraordinary rendition policies

On Hillary Clinton

"She's the stereotypical bitch."[19] —CNN/ABC host Glenn Beck

"An Orwellian Big Sister" and "There's just something about her that feels castrating, overbearing, and scary."[20] —MSNBC host Tucker Carlson

On Al Gore

"It looks as if Al Gore has gone off his lithium again."[21] —Charles Krauthammer

"It is now clear that Al Gore is insane. I don't mean that his policy ideas are insane, though many of them are. I mean that based on his behavior, conduct, mien and tone over the past two days, there is every reason to believe that Albert Gore Jr. desperately needs help. I think he needs medication, and I think that if he is already on medication, his doctors need to adjust it or change it entirely."[22] —John Podhoretz

On Gold Star Mother and Antiwar Protestor Cindy Sheehan

"A crackpot."[23] —Fred Barnes

"The poster child for surrender."[24] —Frank Gaffney

"A willing tool of anti-American forces in this country that want America to lose the war in Iraq and the war on terror generally . . . She is a disgrace to her brave son who gave his life for the freedom of ordinary Iraqis and the security of *his* countrymen. She has betrayed his sacrifice and embraced his enemies."[25] —David Horowitz

"A pretty big prostitute."[26] —Glenn Beck

On Princeton University Professor Cornel West

A "bloviating dummy" and a "black airhead" who "is blessed with these unearned and undeserved perks solely because he's black," and who "hasn't written a scholarly paper or book in twenty years (if ever)."[27] —David Horowitz

On Journalist Diane Sawyer

A "lying whore" who, "in essence, is agreeing that the Holocaust didn't occur."[28] —Michael Savage (following her February 2007 interview with Iranian president Mahmoud Ahmadinejad)

On the People of Washington, D.C.

"The people of Washington are morally repugnant, cheating, shifty human beings."[29] —George W. Bush's White House domestic policy chief, Karl Zinsmeister

On Jews

"That's why the department store dummy named Wolf Blitzer, a Jew who was born in Israel, will do the astonishing act of being the type that would stick Jewish children into a gas chamber to stay alive another day. He's probably the most despicable man in the media next to Larry King, who takes a close runner-up by the hair of a nose. The two of them together look like the type that would have pushed Jewish children into the oven to stay alive one more day to entertain the Nazis."[30] —Michael Savage

On Katrina Victims

"Scumbags . . . I didn't think I could hate victims faster than the 9/11 victims."[31] —Glenn Beck

On Moderate Republican Lincoln Chafee
"They shot the wrong Lincoln."[32] —Ann Coulter

On the New York Times
"My only regret with Timothy McVeigh is he did not go to the New York Times Building."[33] —Ann Coulter

* * *

So what is the point of this tally? Is it that conservatives are far nastier than liberals? Certainly, but the real question is, Why isn't this obvious to everyone? Figures such as Limbaugh, Hannity, and O'Reilly dominate much of what passes for political debate in the U.S. media, and they regularly make fun of people with life-threatening diseases; mock the sons, daughters, and even mothers of soldiers killed defending America; and wish for people they don't like to die in painful ways. Boortz and Beck were even invited to the White House for a meeting with President Bush together with Hugh Hewitt in late July 2007.[34] Not only is the right far nastier than the left, it pays no price in public opprobrium for its hate-filled rhetoric. And yet it is liberals—so frequently vilified as wimps who won't stand up for themselves—who must also take the rap for allegedly coarsening the culture with their nastiness.

What does this state of affairs imply? Well, either liberals *are* wimps, and are failing to defend their own side, or the debate is stacked against them in so many facets that they must defend themselves against charges of which they are largely innocent, and which are leveled against them by the guilty. Or both. Let us consider each one, in tandem.

Why Are Liberals Such Wimps?

The poet Robert Frost once famously accused liberals of being so broad-minded they would not stick up for their own side of an argument. Examples of this unhappy species continue to abound, particularly in the U.S. media. These individuals are often of the type who proudly proclaim themselves to be liberal for the sole purpose of undermining the liberal case. Throughout the media the spaces reserved for "liberals" in debate are often populated by those who embrace the conservative viewpoint, or what can be considered as such. When a number of famously liberal law professors, including such renowned figures as Laurence H. Tribe of Harvard, Akhil Reed Amar of Yale, and Sanford Levinson of the University of Texas, found themselves embracing an interpretation of the Constitution's Second Amendment that pleased not liberal gun controllers but right-wing gun enthusiasts—for what one assumes were intellectually honest and unimpeachable reasons—they, too, found their national profiles enhanced and their courage universally praised. "Contrarian positions get play," Carl T. Bogus, a professor at Roger Williams University School of Law, wrote in a 2000 study of Second Amendment scholarship. "Liberal professors supporting gun control draw yawns."[1]

It is a sad fact of political life that "liberals" are never so influential in American politics as when they mouth conservative pieties. Conservatives profess to see the same phenomenon in their own treatment, as perhaps the mainstream media's love affair with that "maverick" "straight-talker" John McCain might illustrate. To be fair, they have a point, though to argue that conservatives need to endorse liberal or centrist notions to be influential would be ridiculous, given the course of George W. Bush's presidency. Moreover, the political center of gravity has moved so far right within the insider and punditocracy debates of recent decades that what was conservative and centrist under, say, President Nixon has today become defined by what *Newsweek*'s "Conventional Wisdom Watch" column calls "dopey liberalism." The "I'm a liberal but even I agree" phenomenon is exactly what kept the *New Republic* so influential during the Reagan years and afterward as it simultaneously shed much of its influence among genuine liberals and forfeited roughly half of its subscribers. For nearly thirty years and counting, the magazine has advertised itself to be America's most influential liberal magazine, even as its owner and many of its top editors embraced conservative and neoconservative antiliberal calumnies. This process has become so stale after decades that former editor Michael Kinsley could joke in the May 2007 *New York Times Book Review* that "at *The New Republic* in the 1980s, when I was the editor, we used to joke about changing our name to 'Even the Liberal New Republic,' because that was how we were referred to whenever we took a conservative position on something, which was often. Then came the day when we took a liberal position on something and we were referred to as 'Even the Conservative New Republic.'"[2] Given that the magazine has supported every single military adventure embarked upon by a Republican president for the past three decades, manifested pathological hatred toward Bill and Hillary Clinton under two consecutive editors, celebrated Charles Murray's racist pseudoscience, helped kill the country's only hope for comprehensive health coverage during the past fifty years, and endorsed the liberal pariah Joe Lieberman for president in 2004, it hardly takes much imagination to accept Kinsley's latter designation over the former.

While unlike the *New Republic*, the *New York Times* can honestly be said to boast a genuinely liberal editorial page, it is not so liberal that it is not willing to go out of its way to endorse conservative Republicans on occasion, even when they have proven incompetent in the past. For instance the paper endorsed the state's Republican governor, George Pataki, for reelection over his capable, if unexciting, liberal Democratic African-American opponent, Carl McCall, in 2002. One of the most prominent liberals on its op-ed page is Nicholas Kristof. Though a brave and eloquent reporter, particularly with regard to the humanitarian crisis facing Africa, as a political pundit he shares with the editors of the *New Republic* the trait of embracing conservative positions in the name of liberalism, and thereby serving to help stigmatize genuine liberals as beyond the pale of respectable debate. In one 2004 column, for instance, his ideological commitment to "free trade" led him to equate the mistrust of some of the corporate-driven free-investment accords negotiated by the Bush administration, which was the position not only of the Kerry campaign but also of most Democrats by this point, with the Swift Boat Veterans' deliberate efforts to lie about John Kerry's war record. Kristof wrote, "I'm afraid that the dishonesty of politics has infected all of us if we're so partisan that we're willing to point out only the sins of the other side. Intellectual consistency requires a tough look first at one's own shortcomings. So Republicans should be denouncing the smear against Mr. Kerry's war record and Democrats should be denouncing their candidate's protectionist tone on trade."[3] How Kristof justified his equation of the Swift Boaters' slanderous lies with intellectual disagreements he happens to have with Democratic politicians, he never explained.

Three years later, he was angrily beating this same drum. This time, he was attacking the two Democratic presidential front-runners, Hillary Clinton and Barack Obama, for trying to "drag this country backward" with "cowboy diplomacy" in opposition to George W. Bush, who "has been steadfast on trade." Trade, the pundit explained, "is a particularly useful prism through which to look at politicians, for it offers a litmus test of political courage and economic leadership. That's because there are no political benefits to a candidate who supports free trade, but considerable benefits to the country."[4] Kristof did not address himself to counterarguments, or mention to his readers that many respected and admired economists, including such former free-trade stalwarts as Alan Blinder, Lawrence Summers, George A. Akerlof, Joseph Stieglitz, and even former treasury secretary Robert Rubin were in the process of questioning the relevance of the economic orthodoxy he was asserting. Nor did he note that many important economists, including Frank Taussig, Dani Rodrik, David Card, Dean Baker, Brad DeLong, James

Galbraith, and others associated with Washington's Economic Policy Institute had already created a significant body of work calling into question many of the claims of the free-traders and laying the groundwork for an alternative path. (Indeed, Mr. Kristof's own newspaper had covered this debate thoroughly just two weeks earlier in an article entitled "In Economics Departments, a Growing Will to Debate Fundamental Assumptions.")[5] Instead, he termed it a "litmus test of political courage and economic leadership" to defy the specific demands of the people who elected you; for if there was a single issue that united the Democratic victors in 2006 and separated them from their Republican opponents—many of whom also questioned the wisdom and competence of George W. Bush's military policies—it was the insistence that they would take a tougher line on trade—with China identified as the primary culprit. And yet to the liberal Kristof, all of these people were merely "staking out myopic positions for political calculations," and their arguments, like those of Ross Perot, "appealed to Know-Nothing nativists."[6]

The pundit is also not so crazy about environmentalists. Kristof writes that they are "too often alarmists," and "have an awful track record, so they've lost credibility with the public."[7] Kristof, moreover, did not join the vast majority of Americans in rejecting President Bush's transparent attempt to undermine Social Security—the proudest achievement of liberalism for perhaps the past seventy years. Once again, he embraced right-wing logic by congratulating himself on his bravery. "It's impolite to say so in a blue state, but President Bush has a point: there is a genuine problem with paying for social security, even if it isn't as dire as Mr. Bush suggests."[8] What else? Well, there's the continent of Africa, for starters. Kristof has done heroic reporting from there, and deserves our thanks for ensuring that the plight of millions does not remain invisible to the rest of us. But as a pundit, once again, his natural inclination is to blame his own side. "There's a liberal tendency in America to blame ourselves for Africa's problems," he writes.[9] Once again, he does not trouble readers with any examples of any actual liberals doing so. It is enough merely to caricature them for the purpose of attack.

To be fair, Kristof is a liberal cheerleader compared with his colleague Tom Friedman. Though he is frequently lumped together with liberals by conservatives and sloppy mainstream commentators, Friedman rarely mentions liberals save to impute traitorous thoughts into their heads. "Liberals don't want to talk about Iraq because, with a few exceptions," he charges, "they thought the war was wrong and deep down don't want the Bush team to succeed."[10] And what of the famously liberal Maureen Dowd of the *New York Times*? As the *American Prospect's* Michael Tomasky has noted, "Maureen Dowd: Liberal columnist, right? She's not a right-winger, so at least she's a liberal by default. So you'd expect that during the last election, she tossed most of her darts at George W. Bush, right? She didn't. I counted. Between Labor Day and Election Day 2000—when it mattered—she wrote about twice as many columns having sport with Gore (and Clinton) as with Bush. This is the sort of thing that constitutes the liberal side these days."[11]

None of the above charges would hold water if leveled by conservatives against conservatives. The *Wall Street Journal,* for instance, includes no liberals at all on its op-ed pages and attacks other conservatives only from the right, never giving credence to the liberal position on anything. The same is true of the *Weekly Standard,* the *National Review,* and, of course, the entire panoply of Limbaugh-inspired conservative talk-radio and TV hosts. As the conservative organizer Grover Norquist correctly observed, "The conservative press is self-consciously conservative," but the liberal press "sees itself as the establishment press. So it's conflicted."[12]

No, liberals are not "wimps." In fact, much of the perceived wimpiness on the part of liberals is the result of an inability—sometimes purposeful, sometimes not—to define properly whether the person professing to speak on behalf of liberals or liberalism has any right to do so. Too often in mainstream discussion, this is done so that a certain pundit or magazine editor might more effectively tar liberals with a position considered to be beyond the bounds of rational debate. What's more, in many respects, where some would attack a liberal unwillingness to fight conservative fire with fire, this is due to entirely admirable qualities in both historic and contemporary liberalism. Liberals' willingness to question the arguments of their own side, and to do so publicly without concern for who might be listening, indicates an admirable commitment to intellectual integrity. There is no conservative counterpart to the liberal law professors discussed above, who pursue scholarly and intellectual arguments that undermine their own deeply held political beliefs. I salute these scholars, and do my best to follow their example. But when bashing their own side, liberals must ask themselves whether the inspiration is honesty or a desire to appear relevant in a debate guided by right-wing assumptions. Too often, one fears, it's the latter, and we all pay the costs.

Conclusion

As I've indicated throughout this book, many problems facing contemporary liberalism have no simple or easily implemented answers. But the actual problems that face liberals today do not bear much in common with the accusations that are routinely leveled against them. Liberals are not more "elitist" than conservatives, nor any less patriotic. They are far more responsible and successful when entrusted to run the nation's economy or foreign policy, and a great deal more respectful of their opponents when it comes to debating these and other points. What's more, on issue after issue after issue, liberals, media contentions to the contrary, represent the views of the majority of Americans.

That America's political discourse rests on assumptions that are contradicted by these realities is a problem with many causes. Again, I hope I've explained in the preceding pages why and how this has happened. Some demand new thinking and new habits on the part of liberals, but many are beyond their control. Liberals cannot expect to even up the financial disadvantage they face with respect to conservatives; all but the most farsighted capital will always flock to the party that does its bidding. They cannot force people to recognize their own material self-interest, to vote their economic hopes over their cultural fears. They cannot simply repopulate the red states or redraw the political maps that lead them to waste millions of votes each election. Nor can they somehow force Rupert Murdoch and Roger Ailes to take seriously the universally accepted meanings of "fair," "balanced," or even "news." They cannot drive a stake through the heart of the right-wing propaganda machine or, barring the reinstatement of the "fairness doctrine," force cable, talk-radio, or even broadcast executives to give them a fair shake in the opinion media.

Many on the left believe, therefore, that the answer is just to let the right have its victory—not so much substantially as etymologically. In other words, we should give up on ever rejuvenating the term *liberal* as one of pride and honor in American politics and focus instead on building up a coalition of "progressives," since the right-wing slander machine apparently neglected to attach the same kinds of epithets to that term when it invested millions of dollars to dishonor the term *liberal*. One public opinion poll taken in late July 2007, after Hillary Clinton was asked for a self-definition during a CNN/YouTube–sponsored Democratic presidential debate, for instance, discovered what Rasmussen Reports termed "a huge swing, from a net negative of nineteen points to a net positive of seventeen points" in the views of Americans questioned when a politician switches from calling him- or herself a "liberal" to the term "progressive."[1]

Personally, I think this is a mistake. In the first place, as the political scientist Paul Starr points out, it "is a pointless dodge in the contest of ideas."[2] Moreover, leaving aside some troubling historical associations with the word *progressives,* it is unlikely to work. Politicians will still be confronted with variations of the "Are you now or have you ever been a liberal?" question, and only a yes or no will do. If no, then really, what will it mean to say that one is a "progressive" except that one is a dodgy politician who cannot be trusted to give a straight answer about anything, since the difference between the two terms is pretty much impossible to enunciate convincingly? Tim Pawlenty, the governor of Minnesota, for instance, told a reporter at the end of 2006 that his state "prides itself on a certain measure of populism, not to be confused with liberalism, but populism meaning stuff that helps people," as if there were any coherence to that notion. For emphasis, he adds, "That's what we've got to stand up for," as if it would be possible to find a politician anywhere, anytime, who would argue against "stuff that helps people."[3] As Irving Kristol said long ago of "neoconservatism," which was originally coined as a pejorative term when he and his allies first entered the scene: "The sensible course . . . is to take your label, claim it as your own, and run with it."[4]

If we cannot win this battle—particularly within the context of a discredited right wing—then we will forever find ourselves competing with one arm tied behind our collective back. As we've noted throughout this book, right-wingers have not been able to defeat liberals in the public mind on the actual issues. If they can no longer demonize those who support these ideas with just an unpopular label, they will be left only with their extremist positions and indefensible arguments.

What liberals can and must do, however, is to clear away the detritus of decades of mistakes and misunderstandings in order to give more Americans a chance to see who they really are and hear what they are actually saying, rather than relying on the definitions supplied by their ideological enemies and the lazy journalists who parrot them. After seven disastrous years, Americans have woken up to the fact that they have just experienced perhaps their nation's worst leadership ever. Its combination of gross incompetence, ideological extremism, and deeply embedded corruption has, at least temporarily, discredited conservatives as proper stewards of the nation's destiny and offered liberals their best opportunity in nearly half a century to make their case to the nation at large.

Liberals played a smart hand during the 2006 election, for once. Instead of focusing attention on the social and cultural issues that have traditionally proven so divisive within the Democratic Party and distasteful to so many people outside it, they swallowed their differences on these topics and reached out for a common position based on what looked to voters like a combination of populist economics and reality-based common sense. No one complained (much) when party leaders recruited candidates in certain areas who had conservative social positions, like Robert Casey Jr., the pro-life candidate for senator in Pennsylvania, or Heath Shuler, who ran successfully for Congress in North Carolina on a pro-gun, pro-life platform. Without selling out their political principles, they agreed to disagree with others in their party about gun control, abortion, and gay marriage and focus instead on those issues that united them and a broad swath of the American public. In achieving these goals, liberals demonstrated not only impressive political pragmatism but some newfound political muscle. John Dewey observed nearly eighty years ago that "the history of liberal political movements in this country is one of temporary enthusiasms and then steady decline. If liberals are 'tired,' it is chiefly because they have not had the support and invigoration that comes from working shoulder to shoulder in a unified movement."[5] The beauty of the Internet, however, is that it allows liberals to work shoulder to shoulder without ever having to leave their homes or offices. The blossoming of the liberal blogosphere, which barely existed two years earlier, coupled with increased sophistication on the part of candidates using the Internet to connect to their natural constituencies, has transformed the American political landscape in a manner that no one could have predicted, blunting traditional conservative advantages in fund-raising and within the insider media. As the blogger and activist Chris Bowers notes, during the 2006 election, "the average daily audience of the progressive blogosphere was more than twice its size in 2004, and twenty times its size in 2003." During the height of the campaign season, the netroots were reaching more than five million Americans every day. The effects of this new liberal ability to communicate with one another and create community while doing so have sent a seismic shock through American politics. For the first time ever, liberal congressional candidates were able to raise many millions of dollars through e-mail lists, campaign Web sites, and blogs, enabling them to match, advertisement for advertisement, and campaign worker for campaign worker, their corporate-funded conservative opponents. Bowers notes that "in 2004, a postelection study by MoveOn.org documented that their members gave more than $180 million to Democratic candidates in amounts greater than $200 from 2003 to 2004. (Had it been possible to measure all contributions, including those in amounts under $200, the totals would have been far greater.)" Two years later, the organization Act Blue recorded $16.8 million in donations to Democratic candidates during the 2004–6 election cycle, an increase of $16 million from 2003–4. This was almost entirely due to the agitation of the netroots. Bowers adds, "From Jeff Gannon to George Allen's 'Macaca' moment, the blogosphere and the netroots actually uncovered and pushed new Republican scandals into the more-established mainstream press."[6]

Before Web sites like Atrios, Digby, My DD, Josh Marshall's Talking Points Memo and its related Web sites, and the *American Prospect*'s Tapped—to say nothing of the millions of visitors to Daily Kos—liberals had nowhere to go not only to get a daily dosage of information they felt they could trust, but also to find a community of like-minded people with whom they could share a sense of camaraderie and conviction. What's more, until the creation of intellectual centers like the Center for American Progress, sophisticated and well-funded press watchdogs like Media Matters for America, and a whole host of institutions that support these new forms of Deweyite communication with verifiable facts and reliable analysis, conservatives in the media could bamboozle credulous reporters without any consequences for the respective reputations of either party.* Those days, thanks to the liberal blogosphere and the newly created and energized liberal intellectual- and opinion-oriented institutions, are over. And while the playing field may not have been perfectly leveled by this salutary and almost spontaneous political development, it has been enough to give liberals a kind of hope and enthusiasm they have not enjoyed since the movement's late-1960s collapse. For the first time in roughly two generations, liberals are working together cooperatively and effectively, with a sense of shared purpose and renewed solidarity and enthusiasm. What's more, in an especially encouraging and perhaps related sign, young people increasingly tell pollsters that they view politics through a more liberal lens, though the larger American public as well is, according to a careful reading of decades of polling data, more sympathetic to liberalism than almost any other moment in the past half century.[7] In this regard, and perhaps in this regard alone, George W. Bush has proven himself to be the "uniter" he promised to be on the campaign trail back in the election of 2000.

Yet even in an atmosphere of conservative crack-up, the political path ahead is far from obvious. True, the conservatives have laid the

* For the sake of disclosure, I should mention here that I have done my best to participate in this revival though the creation of my Web site, Altercation, which began in May 2002 on MSNBC.com and is now hosted by Media Matters at www.mediamatters.org/altercation; my media column in the *Nation;* my work as a senior fellow at the Center for American Progress, where I write a weekly media column called "Think Again"; and my books published during this period, including specifically *What Liberal Media? The Truth about Bias and the News* (2003), *The Book on Bush: How George W. (Mis)leads America* (2004), and *When Presidents Lie: A History of Official Deception and Its Consequences* (2004).

groundwork for the liberal case. The results of Bush's ideologically driven go-it-alone foreign policy have reminded Americans of the liberal virtues of burden-sharing, cooperation, and compromise, both with one's allies and, when possible, with one's adversaries. They have revived their patience with diplomacy and with the kinds of foreign policy tools that rest as much on carrots as on sticks. Similarly, the Katrina catastrophe provided a crash course in the value of government—so frequently derided by conservatives and so tepidly defended in recent years by liberals. It is hardly an accident, after all, that a president like Bill Clinton—ideologically committed to making government meaningful in people's lives—would insist on creating a Federal Emergency Management Agency (FEMA) that functioned properly and efficiently. True to the liberal political tradition, following Hurricane Andrew, Clinton appointed as FEMA head James Lee Witt, who directed the agency's efforts away from civil-defense efforts toward national disasters. Witt sought significant increases in resources for FEMA, instructed his staff to work closely with local officials to prioritize likely disasters and their optimum responses, and was even awarded cabinet status in order to allow him to secure the cooperation of the rest of the executive branch to implement his ambitious plans.

Upon winning the contest in the Supreme Court for the presidency, Bush turned FEMA over to his Texas campaign aide Joe Allbaugh, and then stripped it of its cabinet status, shunting it into the bureaucracy of the new Department of Homeland Security. Allbaugh then turned the agency over to Michael "Brownie" Brown, who had no more experience or competence with the agency than his predecessor. As Alan Wolfe has observed, Allbaugh and Brown "did not fail merely out of ignorance and inexperience. Their ineptness, rather, was active rather than passive, the end result of a deliberate determination to prove that the federal government simply should not be in the business of disaster management." As Allbaugh told a Senate committee in May 2001, "Many are concerned that federal disaster assistance may have evolved into both an oversized entitlement program and a disincentive to effective state and local risk management. . . . Expectations of when the federal government should be involved and the degree of involvement may have ballooned beyond what is an appropriate level."

The net result of the fact that neither Bush nor the men he appointed to run the agency believed in its mission—or indeed, in almost any aspect of the government's mission that did not benefit their far-right political base—was that they set about destroying FEMA. They purposely demoralized its staff and privatized many of its programs, removing the government from responsibility for its operation.

Repeatedly the agency ignored warnings about the insufficient levees protecting New Orleans. It cut preparatory funding by 44 percent and forced the New Orleans branch of the U.S. Army Corps of Engineers to impose a hiring freeze. (Many of these funds were—like the Louisiana National Guard—diverted to Iraq.) As Wolfe concludes, the conservatives' "ideological hostility toward government all but guaranteed that the physical damage inflicted by a hurricane would be exacerbated by the human damage caused by incompetence."[8] The performance was so pathetic that nearly two years into the Katrina rescue effort, the Bush administration could not even find a way to allow other nations to aid its victims. In the wake of the flood, U.S. allies offered $854 million in cash and in oil that was to be sold for cash, but the administration managed to collect barely 5 percent of that amount.[9] These blasé responses to desperately needed aid occurred as countless evacuees were forced to make do inside crime-ridden, geographically isolated hamlets made up of temporary tents and trailers, while the conservative ideologues inside the administration rejected a housing voucher program that would be both far less expensive and easier to implement, but would also have enlarged government programs to which they claimed to object.[10] The administration then purposely suppressed warnings from its own Gulf Coast field-workers regarding elevated levels of formaldehyde gas released in these same trailers in the hopes of dodging legal liability.[11] In other words, the administration's fatal incompetence, before and after the flood, was not merely predetermined; it was purposeful. Katrina provided Americans with an example of what happens when neat conservative rhetoric collides with messy reality: a teachable moment if ever there was one. It was matched by equally appalling performances regarding Iraq, Medicare, the nation's budget, and on and on.

The connivances and corruptions of congressional Republicans coupled with the veritable cornucopia of Bush administration–induced problems have provided liberals with a chance to make their case, much as the Great Depression did for FDR and company seven decades earlier. The question is not only one of disaster relief, but of the nature of government itself. Liberals believe that, when operated efficiently and honestly, democratic government contributes to the well-being of both the economy and of the polity, contrary to conservative dogma. Public expenditures on education, science and technology, health, and many programs for children are critical forms of investment, with a demonstrable history of long-term payoffs. Government also contributes to our wealth in other ways. Environmental protection allows us to ensure that our "natural capital" provides our children with a sustainable future. Financial regulation protects individual investors from dishonest market manipulators and helps to boost the efficiency of capital allocation, while preventing bad periods from becoming economic catastrophes. Finally, government provides us with the only means we have to buy what we must buy collectively: social insurance, national defense, transportation networks, emergency relief, and the like. It's not that hard a case to make when you focus on why government is necessary rather than what mistakes it tends to make. As the great liberal philosopher Adam Smith observed in 1776, it is the job of government to create public works and institutions "which it can never be for the interest of any individual, or small number of individuals, to erect and maintain . . . though it may frequently do much more than repay [the investment] to a great society."[12] The point is quite obvious when one considers the value of public schools, roads, defense, parks, clean air and water, and the like, but these values are largely taken for granted until a moment like the Bush administration's AWOL performance during the horror of Katrina reminds people of one of the primary reasons they need a government in the first place.

The sadly ironic legacy of two presidential terms of right-wing misrule has been the discrediting not only of what passes for conservatism in America today, but also of government itself. By 57 percent to 29 percent, Americans told pollsters in 2006 that government makes it harder for people to get ahead in life instead of helping them. More than 60 percent, according to the same extensive Pew Center survey, believe elected officials don't care what people like them think, and that all government programs are likely to be inefficient and wasteful.[13]

The attacks of September 11 were many things, but most of all, they were a shock to our system. In their wake, a confused and frightened citizenry placed its faith in the only leaders it had, trusting in their honesty and hoping for a display of wisdom, grace, and moral strength in the face of what appeared to be a historic blow to the nation's sense of self-confidence and security. Aided by a media establishment that forswore its traditional watchdog role in favor of that of a cheerleader, some confusing paper ballots in Florida, and the Republican-appointed majority on the Supreme Court, conservatives took history's driver's seat. These same conservative leaders used the opportunity presented by the trust bestowed upon them to pass far-reaching laws and start ambitious wars without anything remotely resembling the skepticism and scrutiny with which our democracy has traditionally greeted such radical proposals. As we all now know, moreover, they did so in a manner characterized by a degree of dishonesty, incompetence, ideological obsession, and stubborn refusal to face up to a reality whose depths might have proven unimaginable had we not witnessed it. Their net result has been, in the view of many American historians, the single most destructive presidency in our nation's history.[14]

Liberals are well positioned to lead America out of its current morass. The harsh lessons of the past thirty years of defeat and disappointment have forced a return to the most pragmatic aspects of a political philosophy that, after all, inspired America's founders to invent this nation. Liberalism is the natural political philosophy of our nation because it respects and encourages what is both good and great in all of us. It embraces freedom of thought rather than ideologically or theologically imposed certainty. It inspires the spirit of discovery in science and technology. It embraces the ideal of teamwork through its commitment to the common good, which allows us to make the best use of the wisdom of the many while at the same time respecting the sanctity of the rights and talents of the individual. As a political philosophy, it is both tough and realistic—tough enough to defeat both fascism and communism (which makes it more than tough enough to defeat violent fundamentalist Islam)—but sufficiently realistic to understand that it is just plain dumb to go around the world inspiring new enemies by insisting that everyone on earth must share our views. At the same time, liberalism surpasses other ideologies by combining this realism with a grounded form of idealism, one that embraces reform rather than revolution but insists that no matter how highly we may think of ourselves, we can always do better. American liberalism circa 2008 is a patriotic creed, but not one that is blind to our nation's flaws and limitations. We understand, as Reinhold Niebuhr put it, "the limits of man's wisdom and volition."[15] And perhaps most important, liberalism is open to its own evolution by reconsidering its nostrums, and reforming itself as conditions demand. Liberals do not have the answers to all of America's problems today, or even to all aspects of their own various political problems, but they have the capacity—as conservatives do not—to reform themselves and their philosophical foundations in the face of an ever-changing reality. In that respect, liberalism and America's political genius have proven themselves to be one and the same.

As the previous pages have demonstrated, most Americans are indeed liberals. They'd prefer to live in a society with increased equality of opportunity; greater access to health care for all; a more equitable system of taxation; a healthier respect for the environment; and a less belligerent and more cooperative foreign policy, one that not only protects and defends our nation from genuine threats without creating new ones, but also pays heed to Jefferson's "good opinion of mankind."

And thanks in roughly equal measure to their own newfound toughness and realism, and the unavoidable evidence of the ensuing catastrophe that befalls a nation that allows the hubris of Bush and the conservatives to so mislead it, Americans are ready to hear their message of hardheaded hope once again. The only thing we have to fear is fear itself.

Acknowledgments

This is my seventh book, so I hope I've learned a little something about the value of brevity in acknowledgments. In writing this book, I received invaluable help once again from my terrific team of agent Tina Bennett and editor Rick Kot. Thanks, too, to Laura Tisdel and all the people at Viking, and to Svetlana Katz and all the people at Janklow & Nesbit. My all-star readers, commenters, and correctors included, once again, Todd Gitlin, Michael Kazin, Kai Bird, and Michael Waldman, along with new teammates Tom Edsall, Lieutenant Colonel Bob Bateman, Danny Goldberg, Mike Tomasky, Jamison Foser, and Siva Vaidhyanathan. And thanks to Altercation reader Stephen Zeoli of Hubbardton, Vermont, for the suggestion on the paperback subtitle, as well as to all of those readers good enough to send in corrections and suggestions. During the four years spent writing and researching this book, I gratefully enjoyed the support and indulgence of my friends and colleagues at the *Nation,* the Center for American Progress, Media Matters for America, Brooklyn College, and the CUNY Graduate School of Journalism. The Century Foundation also graciously cosponsored a dinner series with CAP that allowed me to explore these topics with some great minds and great people. The Nation Institute also generously funded this book's fact-checking, which was meticulously undertaken by Tim Fernholz. Finally, I remain, as ever, in the debt of my parents, Carl and Ruth Alterman, and my girls, Diana Roberta Silver and Eve Rose Alterman, proud liberals all.

Notes

Introduction

1. Susan Page and Jill Lawrence, "Does 'Massachusetts Liberal' Label Still Matter?" *USA Today*, July 26, 2004, http://www.usatoday.com/news/politicselections/nation/president/2004–07–25-mass- liberal_x.htm.

2. Janet Hook, "Making 'Liberal' a Fighting Word Again," *Los Angeles Times*, October 15, 2004.

3. Eric Weiner, "Democrats, Republicans and the L-Word," *Day to Day*, National Public Radio, July 27, 2004.

4. Michael Kinsley, "Looney over Labels," *Washington Post*, July 25, 2004.

5. Todd Gitlin, "An Exercise in Futility," *American Prospect*, July 27, 2004.

6. *The O'Reilly Factor*, Fox News, May 31, 2005.

7. Media Matters for America, "ABC's Roberts: 'Disaster' for Party If Democrats Nominate Candidate Who Agrees with Americans on Iraq," http://mediamatters.org/items/200608060002.

8. David S. Broder, "'A Terrible Tug' for Democrats," *Washington Post*, July 30, 2006.

9. Jacob Weisberg, "Dead with Ned," *Slate*, August 9, 2006, http://slate.com/id/2147395/.

10. Martin Peretz, "Lieberman: The 'Peace' Democrats Are Back," *Wall Street Journal*, August 7, 2006.

11. Lanny J. Davis, "Liberal McCarthyism: Bigotry and Hate Aren't Just for Right-Wingers Anymore," *Wall Street Journal*, August 8, 2006.

12. David Brooks, "The Liberal Inquisition," *New York Times*, July 9, 2006.

13. "Headline News Anchor: 'Might Some Argue That Lamont . . . Is the al Qaeda Candidate?'" *Think Progress*, August 11, 2006, http://thinkprogress.org/2006/08/11/headline-news-lamont/.

14. Media Matters for America, "Fox's Gibson on Daily Kos and Michael Moore: 'Pol Pots,' 'Khmer Rouge Wing of the Democratic Party,'" http://mediamatters.org/items/200608100011.

15. *New York Times*/CBS News Poll, July 21–25, 2006, http://www.nytimes.com/packages/pdf/politics/20060726_poll.pdf.

16. Howard Dean interview by Chris Wallace, *Fox News Sunday*, Fox News Channel, November 12, 2006.

17. Associated Press, "Liberals Aim to Push Ideas through Congress: Hate-Crime Legislation, Reproductive and Gay Rights Top Wish List," MSNBC, November 19, 2006, http://www.msnbc.msn.com/id/15769199. "'It's exciting to get off the defensive,' said Cecile Richards, president of the Planned Parenthood Federation of America, expressing her hopes that the new Congress will stay away from debate on abortion restrictions and instead work on a

bipartisan basis to curtail unintended pregnancies. . . . 'What we've got is a new and respectful Congress that's open to our community, to learning the specifics of our issues,' [Human Rights Campaign president Joe Solmonese] said. 'To stress right now—"This is what we want and this is when we want it"—would be premature.' "

18. "Conventional Wisdom Watch: 2006 Edition; Cultural Learnings of America," *Newsweek*, December 25, 2006, 27.

19. Rick Perlstein, "Will the Progressive Majority Emerge?" *Nation*, July 9, 2007, http://www.thenation.com/doc/20070709/perlstein.

20. Geoffrey Nunberg, *Talking Right: How Conservatives Turned Liberalism into a Tax-Raising, Latte-Drinking, Sushi-Eating, Volvo-Driving, New York Times–Reading, Body-Piercing, Hollywood-Loving, Left-Wing Freak Show* (New York: Public Affairs, 2006), 41.

21. John Lukacs, "The Triumph and Collapse of Liberalism," *Chronicle Review*, December 10, 2004, http://chronicle.com/weekly/v51/i16/16b00901.htm.

22. Paul Waldman, *Being Right Is Not Enough: What Progressives Must Learn from Conservative Success* (New York: Wiley, 2006), 7.

23. American Presidency Project, "Speech of Vice President Richard M. Nixon, Grand Lodge Convention, International Association of Machinists, Kiel Auditorium, St. Louis, Missouri, September 15th, 1960," http://www.presidency.ucsb.edu/ws/index.php?pid=25372.

24. Jonah Goldberg, "L'Affaire Coulter," *National Review Online*, October 2, 2001, http://article.nationalreview.com/?q=Mm VhMGI5NGFjZjIxMjBmMTE5N2F1YzgzNGFmZTYz ZGQ= (accessed July 2007).

25. Ann Coulter, *Treason: Liberal Treachery from the Cold War to the War on Terrorism* (New York: Three Rivers Press, 2005), 289.

26. David Edwards and Ron Brynaert, "Coulter: 'Faggot' Not Offensive to Gays, It's a 'Schoolyard Taunt,'" *Raw Story*, March 6, 2007, http://www.rawstory.com/news/2007/Coulter_Faggot_not_offensive_to_gay_0306.html (accessed July 6, 2007).

27. David Horowitz, "Why Liberalism Has a Bad Name," Discover the Networks, http://www.discoverthenetworks.org/Articles/Why%20Liberalism%20Has%20A%20Bad%20Name.htm (accessed March 7, 2005).

28. David D. Kirkpatrick, "Latest Confirmed Nominee Sees Slavery in Liberalism," *New York Times*, June 9, 2005. See also Dave Denison, "Point Austin: What Molly Wrote," *Austin Chronicle*, February 8, 2007.

29. Richard K. Armey, *The Freedom Revolution: The New Republican House Majority Leader Tells Why Big Government Failed, Why Freedom Works, and How We Will Rebuild America* (Washington, D.C.: Regnery, 1995), 16.

30. Tom DeLay, *No Retreat, No Surrender* (New York: Sentinel, 2007). See also "Up Front: Zen Hammer," *American Prospect*, March–April 2007, 7.

31. Susan Milligan, "Santorum Resolute on Boston Rebuke, Insists Liberalism Set Stage for Abuse," *Boston Globe*, July 13, 2005.

32. Matt Corley, "Gingrich Blames Virginia Tech Tragedy on Liberalism," *Think Progress*, April 22, 2007, http://thinkprogress.org/2007/04/22/gingrich-liberalism-vatech/ (accessed July 8, 2007).

33. Media Matters for America, "Limbaugh Claimed *Media Matters* 'Fell for' His 'Liberal' Gunman 'Joke' 'Hook, Line and Sinker,'" http://mediamatters.org/items/200704230012. Limbaugh later claimed—not terribly credibly—to have been joking, though he added, "It was liberalism that got a hold of this guy and made him hate things."

34. Joel Whitney, "Infidel: An Interview with Ayaan Hirsi Ali," *Guernica*, February 2007, http://www.guernicamag.com/interviews/283/infidel/.

35. Shelby Steele, "Radical Sheik," *Wall Street Journal*, December 10, 2001.

36. Manuel Miranda, "Primum Non Nocere," *Wall Street Journal*, August 29, 2005.

37. Paul Starr, "Liberalism, Conservatism, and the Intellectuals," lecture, February 8, 1995, New York University Institute for the Humanities, http://www.princeton.edu/~starr/libcon.html.

38. Matt Taibbi, "The American Left's Silly Victim Complex," *Adbusters*, May–June 2007, http://adbusters.org/the_magazine/71.php?id=271#.

39. Mark Leibovich, "Talk of Pelosi as Speaker Delights Both Parties," *New York Times*, May 30, 2006.

40. Eric Alterman, "The Times, It Is A-Ragin'," *Nation*, August 15, 2005, http://www.thenation.com/doc.mhtml?i=20050815&s=alterman.

41. Nunberg, *Talking Right*, 32–33.

42. Media Matters for America, "Stephanopoulos Called Brownback 'Pro-Family' Because He Is a 'True Conservative,'" January 23, 2007, http://mediamatters.org/items/200701230002.

43. Nunberg, *Talking Right*, 32–33. In U.S. newspapers over the past twenty years, for example, references to working-class conservatives have outnumbered references to working-class liberals by better than seven to one.

44. Eric Alterman, *What Liberal Media? The Truth about Bias and the News* (New York: Basic Books, 2004), 54.

45. Media Matters for America, "CNN's Crowley on Dems' 'Old Message': '[W]e Don't Support the Troops and We're Not Tough on National Security,'" February 27, 2007, http://mediamatters.org/items/200702270013.

46. Paul Krugman, "Way Off Base," *New York Times*, April 16, 2007, http://select.nytimes.com/2007/04/16/opinion/16krugman.html, and http://mediamatters.org/columns/200704030007.

47. Robert Borosage, "Rejecting the Right," *American Prospect*, December 17, 2006, http://www.prospect.org/cs/articles?article=rejecting_the_right.

48. Ibid.

49. Todd Gitlin, *The Bulldozer and the Big Tent: Blind Republicans, Lame Democrats, and the Recovery of American Ideals* (New York: Wiley, 2007), 232–34.

50. These numbers are based on exit polls. The National Election Study (NES) suggests that the percentage of moderates has remained stable over the past three decades, while the percentage of both liberals and conservatives has risen modestly. Complex methodological debates among the authors in this volume cloud the conclusions we feel confident about drawing from these data. Suffice it to say that there has not been a huge swing away from the center since the 1970s.

51. "Political Labels: Majorities of U.S. Adults Have a Sense of What Conservative, Liberal, Right Wing or Left Wing Means, But Many Do Not," *The Harris Poll* no. 12, February 9, 2005, http://www.harrisinteractive.com/harris_poll/index.asp?PID=542.

52. Drew Westen, "Gut Instincts," *American Prospect*, November 19, 2006, http://www.prospect.org/web/page.ww?section=root&name=ViewPrint&articleId=12242.

53. Pew Research Center for the People and the Press, "Trends in Political Values and Core Attitudes, 1987–2007," March 22, 2007, http://pewresearch.org/pubs/434/trends-in-political-values-and-core-attitudes-1987–2007.

54. "Sex Education in America," National Public Radio/Kaiser Family Foundation/Kennedy School of Government poll, January 2004, http://www.npr.org/templates/story/story.php?storyId=1622610.

55. Center for American Progress, "Voters Deeply Concerned about Rising Materialism and Self-interest in American Society; Desire Government Focused on the Common Good and Basic Decency and Dignity of All," poll, June 5, 2006, http://www.americanprogress.org/kf/familyvaluesreport.pdf.

56. Heidi Przybyla, "Bush Faces Deepening War Opposition, Demand for Congress to Act," Bloomberg, January 18, 2007, http://www.bloomberg.com/apps/news?pid=20601070&sid=aDgGLrXB8vQA&refer=home; Ronald Brownstein, "Poll: Most Oppose Troop Buildup," Los Angeles Times, January 18, 2007.

57. Pew Research Center, "Trends in Political Values."

58. Michael Barone, The Almanac of American Politics, 2004, with Richard E. Cohen and Grant Ujifusa (Washington, D.C.: National Journal, 2003), 1287; Club for Growth, "RINO Watch," October 2, 2003, http://www.clubforgrowth.org/rino-03.php.

59. Barone, Almanac of American Politics, 1359.

60. Dan Balz, "Always the Party of What-Went-Wrong," Washington Post, June 11, 2006.

61. Jacob Hacker and Paul Pierson explain:

Figuring out what the American mood is, however, is not an easy task. It requires combining large numbers of opinion surveys in a way that allows reliable comparisons of aggregate opinion from year to year. Thankfully, this is exactly what the political scientist James Stimson has done in calculating his respected measure of the "national mood." Stimson uses nearly two hundred survey questions that have been asked every year for decades (about, for example, what people think the proper role of government should be). And what he finds belies the simple interpretation that Americans have been growing steadily more conservative. To the contrary, the index of the public mood that Stimson has developed suggests that Americans actually grew more liberal in the two decades after Reagan's election. When Reagan was elected in 1980, the public mood was more conservative than in any year since 1952. But by the time of George W. Bush's election in 2000, Americans had grown substantially more liberal, according to the measure. Indeed, their aggregate opinions were virtually identical to their aggregate opinions in 1972.

Whatever else these numbers indicate, they make clear that American opinion as a whole did not move sharply to the right in the lead-up to the Republican takeover of American politics in 2000. Nor, it seems clear from Stimson's data, are Americans markedly more conservative than they were a decade or two ago—even as their elected leaders have, of course, become much more conservative.

We do not need to rely on Stimson's data alone. The political scientist Morris Fiorina has recently conducted his own careful study of public views of left-right issues. And he has reached the same clear conclusion: "Americans are about as liberal or conservative as they were a generation ago." . . . Indeed, if these numbers are to be believed, Americans were more conservative when Bill Clinton was reelected in 1996 than when George W. Bush was reelected in 2004. But given the inevitable error and imprecision in any scale of this sort, we think the safest conclusion is that opinions have remained remarkably stable. They have certainly not shifted dramatically to the right.

Hacker and Pierson, Off Center: The Republican Revolution and the Erosion of American Democracy (New Haven, Conn.: Yale University Press, 2005), 37–38.

See also James A. Stimson, Public Opinion in America: Moods, Cycles, Swings, 2d ed. (Boulder, Colo.: Westview Press, 1998), updated data at http://www.unc.edu/~jstimson/time.html;

and Morris P. Fiorina, *Culture War: The Myth of a Polarized America*, with Samuel J. Abrams and Jeremy C. Pope (New York: Pearson, Longman, 2004).

1. Liberalism: A Crooked Branch of Timber

1. Quoted in John Cassidy, "The Ringleader: How Grover Norquist Keeps the Conservative Movement Together," *New Yorker*, August 1, 2005, 42.

2. Quoted in Jonathan Chait, "Fact Finders: The Anti-Dogma Dogma," *New Republic*, February 28, 2005, http://www.tnr.com/doc.mhtml?i=20050228&s=chait022805.

3. Lionel Trilling, *The Liberal Imagination: Essays on Literature and Society* (New York: Viking, 1951), xi.

4. For a learned and useful discussion of the ideas and influence of many of these thinkers, see Jonathan I. Isreal, *Enlightenment Contested: Philosophy, Modernity and the Emancipation of Man, 1670–1752* (New York: Oxford University Press, 2006).

5. I use the word *Marxism* here to connote not a tool of historical analysis, where it can be highly useful, but a program of economic organization.

6. Immanuel Kant, "An Answer to the Question: What Is Enlightenment?" 1784, http://www.english.upenn.edu/~mgamer/Etexts/kant.html.

7. Thomas Nagel, "Progressive but Not Liberal," *New York Review of Books*, May 25, 2006, http://www.nybooks.com/articles/19012.

8. Ronald D. Rotunda, *The Politics and Language of Liberalism as Word and Symbol* (Iowa City: University of Iowa Press, 1986).

9. Jo Ann Boydston, ed., *John Dewey: The Later Works, 1925–1953* (Carbondale: Southern Illinois University Press, 1991), 364–65.

10. Rotunda, *Politics and Language of Liberalism*, 18.

11. Ibid.

12. Dewey is quoted in David Chappell, *A Stone of Hope: Prophetic Religion and the Death of Jim Crow* (Chapel Hill: University of North Carolina Press, 2004), the first chapter of which can be found online at http://www.americanprogress.org/issues/2004/01/b100382.html. Note that Dewey's notion is consistent with that of "negative liberty" later put forth by the philosopher Isaiah Berlin, which might be called "freedom from coercion: Coercion implies the deliberate interference of other human beings within the area in which I could otherwise act. You lack political liberty or freedom only if you are prevented from attaining a goal by other human beings." See Isaiah Berlin, "Two Concepts of Liberty," in *Four Essays on Liberty* (Oxford, England: Oxford University Press, 1990), 118–72.

13. John B. Judis, "Structural Flaw: How Liberalism Came to the U.S.," *New Republic*, February 28, 2005, 20.

14. James P. Young, *Reconsidering American Liberalism: The Troubled Odyssey of the Liberal Idea* (New York: Westview Press, 1996), 171.

15. James L. Sundquist, *Dynamics of the Party System: Alignment and Realignment of Political Parties in the United States*, rev. ed. (Washington, D.C.: Brookings Institution, 1983), 210; Edgar Eugene Robinson, *They Voted for Roosevelt: The Presidential Vote, 1932–1944* (New York: Octagon, 1970), 4, 33.

16. Earl Black and Merle Black, *Divided America: The Ferocious Power Struggle in American Politics* (New York: Simon & Schuster, 2007), 5.

17. See Young, *Reconsidering American Liberalism*, 176. Note also that Republicans have wanted to destroy social security since the day it was instituted on August 14, 1935. Before FDR could even sign the act, almost every Republican in the House voted to kill it by sending

it back to committee. The 1936 GOP nominee, Alf Landon, called it "unjust, unworkable, stupidly drafted, and wastefully financed." Three years later, when social security benefits were extended to survivors, again, three-quarters of the Republicans voted against it. In 1950 social security was extended to the disabled, which drew nay votes from 89 percent of the Republicans.

18. Boydston, *John Dewey*, 284–85.

19. DeLong notes, "That is, with the exception of agricultural subsidies and the National Recovery Administration. They did little good—if any—at immense long-run cost." J. Bradford DeLong, "New Takes on the New Deal," post on *Wall Street Journal Econoblog*, February 7, 2007, http://online.wsj.com/public/article/SB117034177446995000-ypSGzvaEx_rLdzb7FZPZssWmJ4_20080207.html.

20. Cohen is quoted in Nelson Lichtenstein, *State of the Union: A Century of American Labor* (Princeton, N.J.: Princeton University Press, 2002), 27.

21. Hofstadter, quoted in Young, *Reconsidering American Liberalism*, 173.

22. Arthur Schlesinger Jr., "Liberalism in America: A Note for Europeans," in *The Politics of Hope* (Boston: Riverside Press, 1962), http://writing.upenn.edu/~afilreis/50s/schleslib.html.

23. Paul Goodman, quoted in Sam Tanenhaus, "The Buckley Effect," *New York Times Magazine*, October 2, 2005, 68.

24. Isaiah Berlin, "Two Concepts of Liberty," in *Four Essays on Liberty* (Oxford, England: Oxford University Press, 1990), 118–72.

25. Alonzo L. Hamby, *Liberalism and Its Challengers: From FDR to Bush*, 2nd ed. (Oxford, England: Oxford University Press, 1992), 121.

26. Alan Brinkley, *Liberalism and Its Discontents* (Cambridge, Mass.: Harvard University Press, 1998), ix.

27. Arthur M. Schlesinger Jr., *The Vital Center: The Politics of Freedom* (Boston: Houghton Mifflin, 1949).

28. Trilling, *The Liberal Imagination*, ix, 3–22.

29. Daniel Bell, *The End of Ideology: On the Exhaustion of Political Ideas in the Fifties* (New York: Free Press, 1966).

30. Steven Hayward, *The Age of Reagan: The Fall of the Old Liberal Order, 1964–1980* (New York: Forum, 2001), 11.

31. Richard Parker, *John Kenneth Galbraith: His Life, His Politics, His Economics* (New York: Farrar, Straus and Giroux, 2005), 245.

32. Arthur Schlesinger Jr., "Two Years Later: The Roosevelt Family," *Life*, April 7, 1947, 113; Eric Goldman, *Rendezvous with Destiny* (New York: Alfred A. Knopf, 1952), 405; Schlesinger, *The Vital Center*, xvii. For how FDR's death influenced the most important organization of liberals in the 1940s, Americans for Democratic Action, see Clifton Brock, *Americans for Democratic Action* (Washington, D.C.: Public Affairs Press, 1962), 39.

33. Fred Siegel, "Liberalism," in *The Reader's Companion to American History*, ed. John A. Garraty and Eric Foner (New York: Houghton Mifflin, 1991), 653–56.

34. "Truman's Blunder," *New Republic* 114 (June 3, 1946): 787.

35. Parker, *John Kenneth Galbraith*, 218.

36. Ibid.

37. Ibid., 240.

38. Kevin Mattson, *When America Was Great: The Fighting Faith of Postwar Liberalism* (New York: Routledge, 2004), 22–24.

39. Stevenson quoted in Jean Baker, *The Stevensons: A Biography of an American Family* (New York: W. W. Norton, 1996), 370.

40. Parker, *John Kenneth Galbraith*, 263.

41. William Leuchtenburg. *A Troubled Feast: American Society since 1945* (Boston: Little, Brown, 1973), 34; J. Ronald Oakley, *God's Country: America in the Fifties* (New York: Dembner/ W. W. Norton, 1986), 135.

42. Richard Hofstadter, *Anti-Intellectualism in American Life* (New York: Alfred A. Knopf, 1963), 225, 227.

43. William O'Neill, *American High: The Years of Confidence, 1945–60* (New York: Free Press, 1986), 181–83; Alonzo Hamby, *Beyond the New Deal: Harry S. Truman and American Liberalism* (New York: Columbia University Press, 1973), 497.

44. Richard Pells, *The Liberal Mind in a Conservative Age: American Intellectuals in the 1940s and 1950s* (New York: Harper & Row, 1985), 397. See also James T. Patterson, *Grand Expectations: The United States, 1945–1974* (New York: Oxford University Press, 1996), 252–53.

45. John F. Kennedy, "Acceptance of the New York Liberal Party Nomination," New York City, September 14, 1960, http://www.pbs.org/wgbh/amex/presidents/35_kennedy/psources/ps_nyliberal.html.

46. John F. Kennedy, quoted in Richard Goodwin, *Remembering America* (Boston: Little, Brown, 1998), 129.

47. Richard Reeves, *President Kennedy: Profile of Power* (New York: Simon & Schuster, 1993), 39, 126–33, 353–57.

48. Robert Dallek, *An Unfinished Life: John Kennedy, 1917–1963* (Boston: Little, Brown, 1988), 589.

49. Ibid., 604.

50. V. O. Key Jr., *Southern Politics in State and Nation* (New York: Knopf, 1949), 277.

51. Nicholas Lemann, *The Promised Land: The Great Black Migration and How It Changed America* (New York: Alfred A. Knopf, 1991), 83.

52. Quoted in Thomas Edsall and Mary Edsall, *Chain Reaction: The Impact of Race, Rights, and Taxes on American Politics* (New York: W. W. Norton, 1991), 48.

53. Edsall and Edsall, *Chain Reaction*, 182.

54. Mike Allen, "RNC Chief to Say It Was 'Wrong' to Exploit Racial Conflict for Votes," *Washington Post*, July 14, 2005.

55. Edsall and Edsall, *Chain Reaction*, 9.

56. Siegel, "Liberalism," 653–56.

57. Kenneth S. Baer, *Reinventing Democrats: The Politics of Liberalism from Reagan to Clinton* (Lawrence: University Press of Kansas, 2000), 15.

58. Dinesh D'Souza, *The Enemy at Home: The Cultural Left and Its Responsibility for 9/11* (New York: Doubleday, 2007), 257.

59. Eric Alterman, "Cruisin' with Miltie," *American Prospect*, November 16, 2006, http://www.prospect.org/cs/articles?article=cruisin_with_miltie.

60. Jefferson Cowie, "Nixon's Class Struggle: Romancing the New Right Worker, 1969–1973," *Labor History*, August 2002, 257.

61. Mark Schmitt, "The Legend of the Powell Memo," *American Prospect*, April 27, 2005, http://www.prospect.org/cs/articles?articleId=9606.

62. Robert Kaiser and Ira Chinoy, "How Scaife's Money Powered a Movement," *Washington Post*, May 2, 1999.

63. American Enterprise Institute, "AEI's Organization and Purposes," http://www.aei.org/about/filter.all/default.asp.

64. Heritage Foundation, "Our Mission," http://www.heritage.org/about/.

65. Quoted in Brendan Nyhan, "Creaky Foundation," *Salon*, May 10, 2002, http://dir.salon.com/story/politics/col/spinsanity/2002/05/10/heritage/index.html.

66. David Callahan, *$1 Billion for Ideas: Conservative Think Tanks in the 1990s* (Washington, D.C.: National Committee for Responsive Philanthropy, 1999), 22.

67. "About Brookings," Brookings Institution, http://brookings.edu/index/about.htm.

68. Urban Institute, "About UI," Urban Institute, http://urban.org/about/index.cfm.

69. Douglas S. Massey, "What Went Wrong with Liberalism?" *Altercation*, August 4, 2005, http://www.msnbc.msn.com/id/3449870/.

70. See Todd Gitlin, *Twilight of Common Dreams: Why America Is Wracked by Culture Wars* (New York: Metropolitan, 1995), 36; Richard Rorty, *Achieving Our Country: Leftist Thought in Twentieth-Century America* (Cambridge, Mass.: Harvard University Press, 1998), 73–107.

71. Eduardo Mendieta, ed., *Take Care of Freedom and the Truth Will Take Care of Itself: Interviews with Richard Rorty* (Stanford, Calif: Stanford University Press, 2006), 12, 40.

72. Thomas B. Edsall, *Building Red America: The New Conservative Coalition and the Drive for Permanent Power* (Basic Books: New York, 2006), 160.

73. John B. Judis, "Structural Flaw: How Liberalism Came to the U.S.," *New Republic*, February 28, 2005, 20.

74. William E. Leuchtenburg, *In the Shadow of FDR: From Harry Truman to Ronald Reagan*, rev. ed. (Ithaca, N.Y.: Cornell University Press, 1983), 249; and Parker, *John Kenneth Galbraith*, 553.

75. Nunberg, *Talking Right*, 43.

76. Leuchtenburg, *In the Shadow of FDR*, 257–58.

77. Ann Coulter, *Treason: Liberal Treachery from the Cold War to the War on Terrorism* (New York: Three Rivers Press, 2005).

78. E. J. Dionne Jr., *Why Americans Hate Politics* (New York: Simon & Schuster, 1991), 301.

79. Nunberg, *Talking Right*, 43.

80. James A. Barnes, "The Hard-Charger," *National Journal* 24, no. 3 (January 18, 1992): 129.

81. William J. Clinton, "The New Covenant: Responsibility and Rebuilding the American Community," speech at Georgetown University, Washington, D.C., October 23, 1991, http://www.ndol.org/ndol_ci.cfm?kaid=128&subid=174&contentid=2783.

82. William J. Clinton, speech in Springfield, Ohio, October 30, 1992.

83. John F. Harris, *The Survivor: Bill Clinton in the White House* (New York: Random House, 2005), 432.

84. John Micklethwait and Adrian Woolridge, "It Depends What the Meaning of 'Liberal' Is," *New York Times*, June 27, 2004.

85. Newt Gingrich, *To Renew America: On Principles and Values: Six Challenges for a Prosperous, Free, and Safe America* (New York: HarperCollins, 1996), 7–8.

86. Robert H. Bork, *Slouching towards Gomorrah: Modern Liberalism and American Decline* (New York: Regan Books, 1996), 13, 17.

87. Edsall, *Building Red America*, 190.

88. Lexington, "Hating Hillary," *Economist*, January 27, 2007, 32.

89. John F. Harris, "Truth, Consequences of Kerry's 'Liberal' Label," *Washington Post*, July 19, 2004.

90. Thomas Frank, "What's the Matter with Liberals?" *New York Review of Books* 52, no. 8, May 12, 2005. To be fair, incumbent presidents like George Bush whose party has held the

White House for only one term do even better. In the past century, ten of eleven such first-term presidents have been reelected; the only failure was Jimmy Carter in 1980. Viewed in this context, Bush's performance was the worst of any successful incumbent during this time, as he received the smallest share of both the popular and electoral votes of any reelected first-term incumbent since 1900. See Alan I. Abramowitz, "Explaining Bush's Victory in 2004 (It's Terrorism, Stupid!)," in *Get This Party Started*, ed. Matthew R. Kerbel (Lanham, Md.: Rowman & Littlefield, 2006), 11.

2. What Do Liberals Believe, Anyway?

1. Quoted in Barbara Kendall-Davies, *The Life and Work of Pauline Viardot Garcia*, vol. 1 (London: Cambridge Scholars Press, 2003), 358.

2. John Rawls, *A Theory of Justice* (Cambridge, Mass.: Belknap Press, Harvard University Press, 1971), 9.

3. Ibid., 538.

4. John H. Schaar, "Reflections on Rawls: A Theory of Justice" and "Equality of Opportunity and the Just Society," in *Legitimacy and the Modern State* (New Brunswick, N.J.: Transaction, 1981), 141–66, 211–30.

5. Michael Sandel, "Procedural Republican and the Unencumbered Self," in *The Self and the Political Order*, ed. Tracy Strong (New York: NYU Press, 1992), 89–92.

6. Ibid.

7. James T. Kloppenberg, *The Virtues of Liberalism* (New York: Oxford University Press, 1998), 5–7.

8. Quoted in Virgil Nemoianu, "The Church and the Secular Establishment: A Philosophical Dialogue between Joseph Ratzinger and Jürgen Habermas," *Logos* 9, no. 2 (Spring 2006): 17.

9. FDR quoted in Frances Perkins, *The Roosevelt I Knew* (New York: Harper and Row, 1964), 330.

10. Adam Smith, *An Inquiry into the Nature of the Wealth of Nations* (New York: Modern Library, 1937), 78–79.

11. Paul Starr, *Freedom's Power: The True Force of Liberalism* (New York: Basic Books: 2007), 149.

12. Trilling and Howe are quoted in Irving Howe, *Socialism and America* (New York: Harcourt Brace Jovanovich, 1985), 148–71.

13. Quoted in Andrew J. Bacevich, "The Realist Persuasion," *Boston Globe*, November 6, 2005.

3. What Does Liberalism Look Like?

1. Jonathan Cohn, "Great Danes: Neoliberal Utopia Awaits," *New Republic*, January 15, 2007, 13.

2. OECD data cited in Lawrence Mishel, Jared Bernstein, and John Schmitt, *The State of Working America, 2000–2001* (Ithaca, N.Y.: Cornell University Press, 2001), 373.

3. http://www.stateofworkingamerica.org/tabfig/08/SWA06_Tab8.3.jpg.

4. Income tax as a proportion of gross wages runs at 30.1 percent in Denmark, 19.3 percent in Finland, 19.3 percent in Sweden, and 18.7 percent in Norway, compared with 17.5 percent in Germany, 11.5 percent in Austria, and 11.7 percent in the Netherlands. Social security contributions, however, are lower than those in Germany, the Netherlands, and Austria by a very consid-

erable margin. "Taxing Wages 2005/2006: 2006 Edition," OECD report, February 28, 2007, www.oecd.org/ctp/taxingwages.

5. Trade union coverage of the workforce is 95.6 percent for Finland, 89.9 percent for Denmark, 86.4 for Sweden, and 71.3 percent for Norway. See Trade Unions Congress Task Force on Promoting Trade Unionism, *Reaching the Missing Millions* (London: TUC, 2001), 17.

6. Pal Eitrheim and Stein Kuhnle, *The Scandinavian Model: Trends and Perspectives*, EU working paper 99/7 (San Domenico, Italy: European University Institute, 1999); and Nelson Lichtenstein, *State of the Union: A Century of American Labor* (Princeton, N.J.: Princeton University Press, 2002), 14.

7. "In the Shadow of Prosperity," *Economist*, January 20, 2007, 32–34.

8. Cohn, "Great Danes," 13.

9. "Education at a Glance 2004," OECD report, September 9, 2004, http://www.oecd.org/document/7/0,3343,en_2649_34515_33712135_1_1_1_1,00.html#press.

10. Tony Pugh, "U.S. Economy Leaving Record Numbers in Severe Poverty," *McClatchy Newspapers*, February 22, 2007, http://www.mcclatchydc.com/staff/tony_pugh/story/15657.html.

11. U.S. Census Bureau, "Income in the United States 2002," September 2003; Office for National Statistics, *Social Trends 33* (London: HMSO, 2003), 106.

12. Timothy Smeeding, *Financial Poverty in Developed Countries: The Evidence from the Luxembourg Income Study* (Luxembourg: United Nations Development Program, 1997).

13. Will Hutton, *A Declaration of Interdependence: Why America Should Join the World* (New York: W. W. Norton, 2003), 254.

14. See "Snakes and Ladders; Charlemagne," *Economist*, May 27, 2006. See also Markus Jäntti, Bernt Bratsberg, Knut Røed, Oddbjørn Raaum, Robin Naylor, Eva Österbacka, Anders Björklund, and Tor Eriksson, "American Exceptionalism in a New Light: A Comparison of Intergenerational Earnings Mobility in the Nordic Countries, the United Kingdom and the United States," Institute for the Study of Labor Paper no. 1938, January 2006.

15. Rebecca Ray and John Schmitt, "No-Vacation Nation," Center for Economic and Policy Research, May 2007, http://www.cepr.net/documents/publications/working_time_2007_05.pdf.

16. John Micklethwait and Adrian Wooldridge, *The Right Nation: Conservative Power in America* (New York: Penguin Press, 2004), 7.

17. Nicholas Kristof, "The Larger Shame," *New York Times*, September 6, 2005.

18. Anna Bernasek, "Health Care Problem? Check the American Psyche," *New York Times*, December 31, 2006.

19. Malcolm Gladwell, "The Moral-Hazard Myth," *New Yorker*, August 29, 2005, http://www.newyorker.com/archive/2005/08/29/050829fa_fact.

20. Robert G. Kaiser, "In Finland's Footsteps: If We're So Rich and Smart, Why Aren't We More Like Them?" *Washington Post*, August 7, 2005. See also Erick Eckholm, "In Turnabout, Infant Deaths Climb in South," *New York Times*, April 22, 2007.

21. Associated Press, "U.S. Ranks Just 42nd in Life Expectancy: Lack of Insurance, Obesity, Racial Disparities to Blame, Experts Say," August 11, 2007, http://www.msnbc.msn.com/id/20228552/.

22. Kristof, "Larger Shame."

23. See Jonathan Cohn, "The Swedish Solution," *New Republic Online*, July 27, 2007, http://www.tnr.com/doc.mhtml?i=w072307&s=cohn72707.

24. Jeremy Rifkin, *The European Dream: How Europe's Vision of the Future Is Quietly Eclipsing the American Dream* (New York: Jeremy P. Tarcher/Penguin, 2004), 80.

25. Ibid.

26. Pew Research Center for the People and the Press, "Beyond Red vs. Blue," May 10, 2005, http://people-press.org/reports/display.php3?ReportID=242.

27. Adam Nagourney, "Social Issues That Bolster Bush Fail the Hapless British Tories," *New York Times*, April 27, 2005, 1.

28. Francis Fukuyama, "The History at the End of History," *Comment Is Free*, April 3, 2007, http://commentisfree.guardian.co.uk/francis_fukuyama/2007/04/the_history_at_the_end_of_hist.html.

29. Under current federal standards, any sex education program receiving federal funds must be "abstinence only," mentioning contraception only to discuss its failures and teaching, among other things, that "sexual activity outside of the context of marriage is likely to have harmful psychological and physical effects." But when a 2003 Kaiser/NPR/Harvard survey asked people whether they thought "the federal government should fund sex education programs that have 'abstaining from sexual activity' as their only purpose," or if "the money should be used to fund more comprehensive sex education programs that include information on how to obtain and use condoms and other contraceptives," 67 percent chose the latter. Only 12 percent said that "how to use and where to get contraceptives" was not an appropriate topic for sex education, though the federal standards prohibit such discussion. An evaluation of ten state abstinence-only programs concluded, "Abstinence-only programs show little evidence of sustained (long-term) impact on attitudes and intentions. Worse, they show some negative impacts on youth's willingness to use contraception, including condoms, to prevent negative sexual health outcomes related to sexual intercourse. Importantly, only in one state did any program demonstrate short-term success in delaying the initiation of sex; none of these programs demonstrates evidence of long-term success in delaying sexual initiation among youth exposed to the programs or any evidence of success in reducing other sexual risk-taking behaviors among participants." See Debra Hauser, *Five Years of Abstinence-Only-Until-Marriage Education: Assessing the Impact* (Washington, D.C.: Advocates for Youth, 2004).

30. Garry Wills, "Jimmy Carter and the Culture of Death," *New York Review of Books* 53, no. 2 (February 9, 2006), http://www.nybooks.com/articles/article-preview?article_id=18670.

31. Starr, *Freedom's Power*, 7.

4. So What's the Problem?

1. Edsall, *Building Red America*, 18.

2. Pew Research Center, "Trends in Political Values."

3. Edsall, *Building Red America*, 236.

4. Gregory Rodriguez, "The Democrats' Unreligious Fringe," *Los Angeles Times*, July 16, 2006.

5. Mark Schmitt, "A Last Few Words on Connecticut," *Decembrist*, August 7, 2006, http://markschmitt.typepad.com/decembrist/2006/08/a_last_few_word.html.

6. E. J. Dionne Jr., "A Gap in Their Armor," *Washington Post*, August 15, 2006.

7. Gitlin, *Bulldozer and the Big Tent*.

8. Paul Krugman, "Centrism Is for Suckers," *New York Times*, August 4, 2006.

9. John Dewey, "Renascent Liberalism," from *Liberalism and Social Action* (1935), reprinted in *John Dewey: The Political Writings*, ed. Debra Morris (Indianapolis: Hackett, 1993), 151.

10. American Political Science Association Task Force on Inequality and American Democracy, *American Democracy in an Age of Rising Inequality* (Washington, D.C.: American Political Science Association, 2004), 8, http://www.apsanet.org/imgtest/taskforcereport.pdf.

11. U.S. Census Bureau, *Statistical Abstract of the United States, 2004–2005* (Washington, D.C.: U.S. Government Printing Office, 2004), 419.

12. Hacker and Pierson, *Off Center,* 114–18.

13. Edsall, *Building Red America,* 228.

14. Ibid.

15. Todd Gitlin, "Democratic Dilemmas: The Party and the Movements," *Dissent,* Fall 2006.

16. Edsall, *Building Red America,* 52.

17. Ibid.

18. In the 2004 election, the top Bush fund-raisers—the elite "Rangers," who raised a minimum of $200,000 apiece—were largely CEOs and chairmen of large Wall Street firms. They included, for instance: E. Stanley O'Neal, chairman, CEO, and president of Merrill Lynch & Co.; Joseph J. Grano, chairman and CEO, UBS Wealth Management USE; John Mack, CEO, Credit Suisse First Boston; and Philip J. Purcell, CEO, Morgan Stanley. Five times as many corporate CEOs, presidents, and chairmen gave to Bush as to Kerry: 17,770 to 3,393. Conversely, the number of professors who gave to Kerry is eleven times the number of those who gave to Bush, 3,508 to 322. Actors split 212 for Kerry, 12 for Bush; authors, 110 to 3; librarians, 223 to 1; journalists, 93 to 1; social workers, 415 to 32. See Edsall, *Building Red America,* 115, 150.

19. Edsall, *Building Red America,* 235.

20. Media Matters for America, "Letter to Wash. Post Ombudsman Re: Solomon Article," January 25, 2007, http://mediamatters.org/items/200701250011.

21. Leslie Wayne, "Edwards Talks Tough on Hedge Funds," *New York Times,* July 11, 2007, http://thecaucus.blogs.nytimes.com/2007/07/11/edwards-talks-tough-on-hedge-funds/. See also Greg Sargent, "*New York Times*' Leslie Wayne Continues Twisted Jihad against Edwards," Election Central, http://electioncentral.tpmcafe.com/blog/electioncentral/2007/jul/12/new_york_times_leslie_wayne_continues_twisted_jihad_against_edwards.

22. Jamison Foser, "Media Matters," Media Matters for America, May 11, 2007, http://mediamatters.org/items/200705120002; and David D. Kirkpatrick, "Reports Show Wealth as a Common Factor among 2008 Contenders," *New York Times,* May 17, 2007.

23. For instance, the elimination of the estate tax, a major Republican priority during the Bush presidency, promises to provide the beneficiaries of each of the 830 estates annually valued at $20 million or more an average of $11.7 million in excess of what they would have gotten under the law as of 2004. Similarly, the administration's income tax cuts will result, by 2010, in an annual average savings of $166,264 for those in the top 0.5 percent of the income distribution. For those in the bottom 20 percent, the annual break will amount to $23; for those in the second quintile, $364; for those in the middle quintile, $1,079; and the top quintile, $3,623. Edsall, *Building Red America,* 47–48.

24. Ibid.

25. Dana R. Fisher, *Activism, Inc.: The Outsourcing of Grassroots Campaigns Is Strangling Progressive Politics in America* (Stanford, Calif.: Stanford University Press, 2006).

26. Edsall, *Building Red America,* 160.

27. Nicholas Mills, "The E Word," *American Prospect,* March 2004, http://www.prospect.org/cs/articles?article=the_eword.

28. Edsall, *Building Red America,* 161.

29. Nicholas Confessore, "Welcome to the Machine," *Washington Monthly,* July–August 2003, http://www.washingtonmonthly.com/features/2003/0307.confessore.html.

30. American Political Science Association Task Force, *American Democracy.*

31. National Public Radio/Kaiser Family Foundation/Kennedy School of Government, *National Survey of Americans' Views on Taxes,* April 2003, http://www.npr.org/news/specials/polls/taxes2003/20030415_taxes_survey.pdf.

32. Paul Farhi, "Talk Radio, Top Volume on the Right," *Washington Post,* May 8, 2002.

33. Jay Dixit, "The Ideological Animal," *Psychology Today,* January–February 2007, http://psychologytoday.com/articles/index.php?term=pto-20061222–000001&print=1.

34. Denise Gellene, "Study Finds Left-Wing Brain, Right-Wing Brain: Even in Humdrum Nonpolitical Decisions, Liberals and Conservatives Literally Think Differently, Researchers Show," *Los Angeles Times,* September 10, 2007.

35. Jeffrey Scheuer, *The Sound Bite Society: Television and the American Mind* (New York: Four Walls Eight Windows, 1999), 32–40. See also Scheuer, "The Television Thing," *Dissent,* Summer 1995, http://www.jscheuer.com/dissent.htm.

36. Tim Rutten, "Regarding Media: Enron's Press Pass," *Los Angeles Times,* May 27, 2006.

37. Barack Obama, "Tone, Truth, and the Democratic Party," Daily Kos, September 30, 2005, http://www.dailykos.com/story/2005/9/30/102745/165.

38. George Will, "Conservatives, Liberals and Reality," *New Hampshire Union Leader,* May 31, 2007.

39. See Eric Alterman, "The Hollywood Campaign," *Atlantic Monthly,* September 2004, http://www.theatlantic.com/doe/200409/alterman.

40. Edsall, *Building Red America,* 170.

41. Ann Hulbert, "Trading Family Values: How the Old Conservative/Liberal Stereotypes Break Down When It Comes to Parenting," *Slate,* October 22, 2004, http://www.slate.com/id/2108556/.

42. House Ethics Commitee, *Investigation of Allegations Related to Improper Conduct Involving Members and Current or Former House Pages,* 109th Cong. 2d sess., 2006, http://www.house.gov/ethics/Page_Report_Cover.htm.

43. Bill Adair, "Congress Sees through Party-Colored Glasses," *St. Petersburg Times,* September 12, 1998, http://www.sptimes.com/Worldandnation/91298/Congress_sees_through.html.

44. See Sheryl Gay Stolberg, "A Scandal-Scarred G.O.P. Asks, 'What Next?'" *New York Times,* August 29, 2007. For Craig's comments on Clinton, see http://archpundit.com/blog/2007/08/27/unfortunate-moments-in-eating-your-own-words/trackback/. For Allen, see Gail Collins, "Men's Room Chronicles," *New York Times,* August 30, 2007.

45. CNN, "Senate Set to Reject Gay Marriage," CNN.com, June 6, 2006, http://www.cnn.com/2006/POLITICS/06/06/same.sex.marriage/index.html.

46. Douglas Daniel, "Louisiana Sen. Vitter Apologizes after Number Appears on Escort Service Phone List," Associated Press, July 10, 2007. See also David Corn, "A Blast from Vitter's Past," July 10, 2007, http://www.davidcorn.com/archives/2007/07/a_blast_from_vi.php.

47. Ann Gerhart, "Settled . . . but Not Over: The Gingrich Divorce and Its Repercussions on the Right," *Washington Post,* December 18, 1999; and Scoobie Davis, "Sean Hannity Confronted about Republican Sexual Hypocrisy: Exclusive Transcript," October 21, 2002, http://scoobiedavis.blogspot.com/2002_10_01_scoobiedavis_archive.html.

48. James Wolcott, "Rush to Judgment," *Vanity Fair,* May 2007.

49. "Dossier: Red-State Values," *American Prospect,* December 20, 2004, http://www.prospect.org/cs/articles?article=dossier_redstate_values.

50. Curtis S. Dubay, "Federal Tax Burdens and Expenditures by State," Tax Foundation, Special Report no. 139, March 2006, http://www.taxfoundation.org/research/show/62.html.

51. See Jonathan Kastellec, Andrew Gelman, and Jamiee P. Chandler, "Seeking 50% of the Seats, Needing More Than 50% of the Votes; Predicting the Seats/Votes Curve in the 2006 Election," abstract, October 14, 2006, http://www.stat.columbia.edu/~gelman/research/unpublished/house2006.pdf.

52. Figures calculated on the basis of election results published at "America Votes," CNN.com, http://www.cnn.com/ELECTION/2006; and Jacob S. Hacker and Paul Pierson, "Enter Center: GOP RIP?" *New Republic*, December 25, 2006.

53. Paul Krugman, "The Straight and Not Narrow," *Conscience of a Liberal*, September 19, 2007, http://krugman.blogs.nytimes.com/2007/09/19/the-straight-and-not-narrow/. The 1994 *Time* cover can be viewed at http://www.time.com/time/covers/0,16641,19941121,00.html. The 2006 cover can be viewed at http://www.time.com/time/covers/0,16641,20061120,00.html.

54. Hacker and Pierson, *Off Center*, 35.

55. Edsall, *Building Red America*, 227.

56. David Epstein, "Democratic Dilemmas: The Conversation No One Is Having about the Voting Rights Act," *American Prospect*, August 4, 2006, http://www.prospect.org/cs/articles?articleId=11805.

57. Alterman, *What Liberal Media?*

58. Comment posted on Go Ahead and Shoot Me, June 11, 2007, http://time-blog.com/swampland/2007/06/go_ahead_and_shoot_at_me.html.

59. Media Matters for America, "If It's Sunday, It's Still Conservative. Special Report: How the Right Continues to Dominate the Sunday Talk Shows," http://mediamatters.org/sundayshowreport/online_version/. To be fair, the study's authors note that ABC's program *This Week* did show some improvement on the fairness front.

60. Steve Rendall and Julie Hollar, "Are You on the *NewsHour*'s Guestlist?" Fairness & Accuacy in Reporting, September–October 2006, http://www.fair.org/index.php?page=2967.

61. John Amato, "Rupert Murdoch Admits Manipulating the Media . . . Surprise . . . Surprise," Crooks and Liars, February 4, 2007, http://www.crooksandliars.com/2007/02/04/rupert-murdoch-admits-manipulating-the-mediasurprisesurprise/? media.

62. Huffington Post, "Fox News Internal Memo: 'Be on the Lookout for Any Statements from the Iraqi Insurgents . . . Thrilled at the Prospect of a Dem Controlled Congress,'" November 14, 2006, http://www.huffingtonpost.com/2006/11/14/fox-news-internal-memo-_n_34128.html.

63. International Institute for Strategic Studies, *Strategic Study 2003/2004* (New York: Routledge, 2004).

64. Eric Boehlert, "Fox News Can't Take a Punch," Media Matters for America, March 13, 2007, http://mediamatters.org/columns/200703130004.

65. Ronald Brownstein, "Fox Hounded: How the Democrats Are Turning on Fox News," *Los Angeles Times*, March 16, 2007.

66. Boehlert, "Fox News."

67. Alex Koppelman, "The Real Fox News Democrats," *Salon*, April 3, 2007, http://www.salon.com/opinion/feature/2007/04/03/fox_news_democrats/index.html.

68. Here are Couric's words: "Hi everyone. Is America ready to elect a president who grew up praying in a mosque? Barack Obama has arguably the most diverse religious background of any candidate, ever. He was raised in Indonesia by a Christian mother and Muslim stepfather, and attended a Catholic school, but while growing up, also studied

Islam. That background sparked rumors that he had studied in a radical madrassa, or Koranic school—rumors his campaign denied, declaring that Obama is now a practicing Christian." *CBS Evening News*, April 11, 2007. The wording was later changed on the CBS Web site. See also Rachel Sklar, "More Katie Couric Trouble: Updates Notebook *Again* after Spreading Debunked Obama Rumor," *Huffington Post*, April 14, 2007, http://www.huffingtonpost.com/eat-the-press/2007/04/14/more-katie-couric-trouble_e_45836.html.

69. Media Matters for America, "Most Outrageous Comments of 2006," December 22, 2006, http://mediamatters.org/items/200612220013; and Media Matters for America, "Only on Fox: 'Are Congressional Democrats Killing Spirit of Bipartisanship?'" January 3, 2007, http://mediamatters.org/items/200701030016.

70. Media Matters for America, "O'Donnell Asked Congresswoman to Go 'on the Record' with 'Promise' That Dems Won't 'Make the President's Final Two Years in Office a Living Hell,'" October 18, 2006, http://mediamatters.org/items/200610180015. For a series of examples along these lines, see Media Matters for America, "Media Election Coverage Wall of Shame," November 8, 2006, http://mediamatters.org/items/200611080005.

71. Eric Boehlert, "Can *The Note* Save Itself?" Media Matters for America, April 3, 2007, http://mediamatters.org/columns/200704030007.

72. Fairness & Accuracy in Reporting, "Too Many Liberals? Olbermann Says MSNBC Bosses Upset by Liberal Guests," October 27, 2005, http://www.fair.org/index.php?page=2707; *Countdown with Keith Olbermann*, transcript, October 25, 2007, http://www.msnbc.msn.com/id/9827774/; Rick Ellis, "The Surrender of MSNBC," *All Your TV*, February 25, 2003, http://www.allyourtv.com/0203season/news/02252003donahue.html; Media Matters for America, "Phil Donahue on His 2003 MSNBC Firing," October 29, 2004, http://mediamatters.org/items/200410290004.

73. Media Matters for America, "Exposed: Glenn Beck's Climate of Distortion," May 8, 2007, http://mediamatters.org/items/200705080009; and Eric Boehlert, "CNN's Rodeo Clown," Media Matters for America, May 8, 2007, http://mediamatters.org/columns/200705080004.

74. Associated Press, "No Timetable on Emissions," *New York Times* Web site, April 25, 2007, http://www.nytimes.com/2007/04/25/washington/25brfs-epa.html?ei=5070&en=d4e437064da22108&ex=1178769600.

75. David Leonhardt, "Truth, Fiction and Lou Dobbs," *New York Times*, May 30, 2007.

76. John Halpin, James Heidbreder, Mark Lloyd, Paul Woodhull, Ben Scott, Josh Silver, and S. Derek Turner, "The Structural Imbalance of Political Talk Radio," Center for American Progress and Free Press, June 11, 2007, http://www.americanprogress.org/issues/2007/06/talk_radio.html.

77. Josh Silver and Robert McChesney, "Air America's ABC Blacklist: The Real Story," *Huffington Post*, November 2, 2006, http://www.huffingtonpost.com/josh-silver/airamericas-abc-blackli_b_33123.html.

78. Jim Naureckas, "Why Progressive TV Is DOA," Fairness & Accuracy in Reporting, November–December 2003, http://www.fair.org/index.php?page=2595.

79. Media Matters for America, "*Wash. Times*' Pierce Reprinted GOP Talking Points (Literally)," February 23, 2007, http://mediamatters.org/items/200702230006.

80. "Kerry Gets His Man," *Wall Street Journal*, March 29, 2007, http://online.wsj.com/article/SB117513218882352729.

81. Matt Stoller, "Obey Smacks the *Washington Post* Editorial Board," MyDD, March 23, 2007, http://www.mydd.com/story/2007/3/23/112919/906.

82. David Brock, *The Republican Noise Machine: Right-Wing Media and How It Corrupts Democracy* (New York: Crown, 2004), 133.

83. See Paul Waldman, "Black and White and Re(a)d All Over: The Conservative Advantage in Syndicated Op-Ed Columns," Media Matters for America, September, 2007, http://mediamatters.org/reports/oped/report.

84. Christopher DeMuth, "Think-Tank Confidential," *Wall Street Journal*, October 11, 2007, http://online.wsj.com/article/SB119206742349355601.html?mod=opinion_main_commentaries.

85. Media Matters for America, "Right-Wing Pundits Play Doctor; Diagnose Gore as 'Insane,'" May 28, 2004, http://mediamatters.org/items/200405280001.

86. Charles Krauthammer, "Limousine Liberal Hypocrisy," *Time*, March 16, 2007, http://www.time.com/time/printout/0,8816,1599714,00.html.

87. Media Matters for America, "Attacks on Democrats and 'Liberals' a Common Thread among *Time* Columnists," April 12, 2006, http://mediamatters.org/items/200604120012; and Media Matters for America, "*Time*'s Klein at It Again: Liberals 'Hate America,'" April 11, 2006, http://mediamatters.org/items/200604110008.

88. Media Matters for America, "*Time*'s Joe Klein Claimed GOP Candidates with Multiple Marriages 'Live Like Liberals,'" March 19, 2007, http://mediamatters.org/items/2007031 90004; transcript, discussion with Joe Klein, *Washington Post Book World*, May 26, 2006, http://www.washingtonpost.com/wp-dyn/content/discussion/2006/04/28/DI2006042801217.html; Joe Klein, "The Crucial Difference between Liberals and Leftists," *Huffington Post*, April 14, 2006, http://www.huffingtonpost.com/joe-klein/the-crucial-difference-be_b_19124.html.

89. Media Matters for America, "Attacks on Democrats." See also Andrew Sullivan, "The Unbearable Wrongness of Galbraith," *Daily Dish*, May 14, 2005, http://andrewsullivan.theatlantic.com/the_daily_dish/2006/05/the_unbearable_.html.

90. Kathryn Jean Lopez, "Closing In: A Conversation with Lawrence Kaplan and Bill Kristol on Iraq," *National Review Online*, February 24, 2003, http://www.nationalreview.com/interrogatory/interrogatory022403.asp.

91. Eric Alterman, "Kristolizing the (Neoconservative) Moment," *Nation*, February 12, 2007, http://www.thenation.com/doc/20070212/alterman.

92. Eric Boehlert, "Mark Halperin's Flip-Flop at ABC News," Media Matters for America, November 6, 2006, http://mediamatters.org/columns/200611060008.

93. Eric Alterman, "*Time* Is on *Their* Side," *Nation*, June 12, 2006, http://www.thenation.com/doc/20060612/alterman.

94. Josh Benson, "Gore's TV War: He Lobs Salvo at Fox News," *New York Observer*, December 2, 2002.

95. Lloyd Grove, "Media to the Left! Media to the Right! The GOP, Shooting the Messengers," *Washington Post*, August 20, 1992.

96. Mark Hertsgaard, *On Bended Knee: The Press and the Reagan Presidency* (New York: Farrar, Straus and Giroux, 1988), 4.

97. Jim Naureckas, "Dole's Debt to the Press," Fairness & Accuracy in Reporting, January–February 1997, http://www.fair.org/index.php?page=1375.

98. Ibid.

99. The June 21, 2007, edition of *The O'Reilly Factor* is quoted in Susy Buchanan and David Holthouse, "The Oh-Really Factor: Fox News' Bill O'Reilly Offers Up an 'Expert' to Claim That Pink Pistol-Packing Lesbian Gangs Are Terrorizing the Nation," Southern Poverty Law Center, http://www.splcenter.org/intel/news/item.jsp?site_area=1&aid=274.

100. *The No-Spin Zone with Bill O'Reilly*, Fox News, July 26, 2005.

101. Bruce Bartlett, "Partisan Press Parity? The New Media World," *National Review Online*, March 13, 2007, http://article.nationalreview.com/?q=YTN1NGNhMT1kYzA3YTU3MWZiYTMxMWFiNzg0MWEzN2Q=.

102. Jamison Foser, "Media Matters," Media Matters for America, February 9, 2007, http://mediamatters.org/items/200702100007.

103. Alan Wolfe, "Why Conservatives Can't Govern," *Washington Monthly*, July 2006.

104. Ron Suskind, "Why Are These Men Laughing?" *Esquire*, January 1, 2003, 96–105.

105. Norman Ornstein, "GOP's Approach to Continuity: Not Just Unfortunate. Stupid," *Roll Call*, June 9, 2004.

106. Edsall, *Building Red America*, 129.

107. Ibid., 131.

108. "Agency Report Shows Secretary Personally Blocked Contracts to Democrats," *Think Progress*, September 22, 2006, http://www.thinkprogress.org.

109. Marisa Taylor and Kevin G. Hall, "Commerce, Treasury Funds Helped Boost GOP Campaigns," McClatchy Newspapers, August 10, 2007, http://www.mcclatchydc.com/227/story/19034.html; John Solomon, Alec MacGillis, and Sarah Cohen, "How Rove Harnessed Government for GOP Gains: Bush Adviser's Effort to Promote the President and His Allies Was Unprecedented in Its Reach," *Washington Post*, August 19, 2007.

110. General Accounting Office, "Department of Health and Human Services—Chief Actuary's Communications with Congress," September 7, 2004, http://www.gao.gov/decisions/appro/302911.pdf.

111. Ceci Connolly and Mike Allen, "Medicare Drug Benefit May Cost $1.2 Trillion, Estimate Dwarfs Bush's Original Price Tag," *Washington Post*, February 9, 2006.

112. Bruce Bartlett, *Imposter: How George W. Bush Bankrupted America and Betrayed the Reagan Legacy* (New York: Doubleday, 2006), 71.

113. David Blumenthal and Roger Herdman, eds., *Description and Analysis of the VA National Formulary* (Washington, D.C.: National Academies Press, 2000). Available at http://books.nap.edu/openbook.php?record_id=9879&page=R1.

114. Alan Wolfe, "Why Conservatives Can't Govern," *Washington Monthly*, July 2006.

115. Connolly and Allen, "Medicare Drug Benefit."

116. Edward Epstein, "Democrats Decry Republican Tactics in Marathon Vote," *San Francisco Chronicle*, December 9, 2003.

117. Timothy Noah, "Defendant DeLay? Nick Smith's Bribery Accusations Land in the Majority Leader's Lap," *Slate*, October 1, 2004, http://www.slate.com/id/2107623/.

118. Bartlett, *Imposter*, 78.

119. Edsall, *Building Red America*, 66.

120. Reinhold Niebuhr, *The Children of Light and the Children of Darkness: A Vindication of Democracy and a Critique of Its Traditional Defense* (New York: Charles Scribner's Sons, 1944), 140–44; Reinhold Niebuhr, "Christian Faith and the Race Problem," *Christianity and Society*, Spring 1945, 21–24.

121. Drew Westen, "Gut Instincts," *American Prospect*, November 19, 2006, http://www.prospect.org/web/page.ww?section=root&name=ViewPrint&articleId=12242.

122. See Michael Lind, *Up from Conservatism: Why the Right Is Wrong for America* (New York: Free Press, 1996), 201.

123. U.S. Census Bureau, *Statistical Abstract of the United States, 2004–2005*, 419.

124. AFL-CIO, "AFL Facts and Stats," July 24, 2006, http://www.aflcio.org/issues/factsstats/.

125. American Political Science Association Task Force, *American Democracy*.

126. Alan Brinkley, "Liberalism and Belief," in *Liberalism for a New Century*, ed. Neil Jumonville and Kevin Mattson (Berkeley and Los Angeles: University of California Press, 2007), 75–76.

127. James Bryce, *American Commonwealth* (London: Macmillan, 1889), 360–63.

128. Geoffrey Nunberg, "Words Failed the GOP; Will Dems Get the Message?" *Los Angeles Times*, November 19, 2006.

129. Rich Lowry, "Be Careful What You Believe: The Myths of '06," *National Review Online*, November 14, 2006, http://article.nationalreview.com/?q=M2UwMj1hNjY1ZT MwNzc5OWM1ZDQ5YTIwOGJiZDM5MDg=.

5. Why Do Liberals Hate Patriotism?

1. Thomas Frank, *What's the Matter with Kansas? How Conservatives Won the Heart of America* (New York: Metropolitan Books, 2004), 13.

2. Pew Research Center, "Trends in Political Values"; and Michael E. Ross, "Poll: U.S. Patriotism Continues to Soar," MSNBC, July 5, 2005, http://www.msnbc.msn.com/id/8410977/.

3. Andrew Sullivan, "America at War: America Wakes Up to a World of Fear," *Sunday Times* (London), September 16, 2001.

4. Nashville/Davidson County, 2004—Kerry: 132,362 (55 percent), Bush: 107,618 (45 percent); Austin/Travis County, 2004—Kerry: 196,780 (56 percent), Bush: 147,625 (42 percent). "Tennessee Presidential Results by County," *Washington Post* Web site, November 3, 2004, http://www.washingtonpost.com/wp-srv/elections/2004/tn/prescounties/; "Texas Presidential Results by County," *Washington Post* Web site, November 3, 2004, http://www. washingtonpost.com/wp-srv/elections/2004/tx/prescounties/.

5. David S. Broder, "The Other Democrats Weigh In," *Washington Post*, February 6, 2007, http://www.washingtonpost.com/wp-dyn/content/article/2007/02/05/AR2007020501250. html.

6. Media Matters for America, "Limbaugh: Half of Kerry's Political Base 'Hates the Military, Hates America,'" September 21, 2004, http://mediamatters.org/items/200409210005.

7. Pew Research Center, "Trends in Political Values."

8. Associated Press, "White House Defends Rove over 9/11 Remarks; Bush Adviser Said Liberals Urge 'Understanding' for Attackers," MSNBC, June 24, 2005, http://www.msnbc.msn. com/id/8324598/.

9. Quoted, among other places, in Conn Hallinan, "Shafting the Vets," *Foreign Policy in Focus Commentary*, November 10, 2006, http://fpif.org/pdf/gac/0611vets.pdf.

10. "Who Served in the Military?" AWOLBush.com, http://www.awolbush.com/ whoserved.html (accessed July 2007).

11. Dean Barnet, "In the 1960s, History Called the Baby Boomers. They Didn't Answer the Phone," *Weekly Standard*, July 30, 2007, http://weeklystandard.com/Utilities/printer_ preview.asp?idArticle=13904&R=114431688C.

12. Rush Limbaugh, "Democrats Flip Wigs over President Bush's Al-Qaeda in Iraq Speech," *Rush Limbaugh Show* Web site, July 25, 2007, http://www.rushlimbaugh.com/ home/daily/site_072507/content/01125109.guest.html.

13. Anthony Zinni interviewed by Steve Croft on *60 Minutes*, CBS, May 23, 2004.

14. Eyal Press, "Even Conservatives Are Wondering: Is Bush One of Us?" *Nation*, May 31, 2004, http://www.thenation.com/doc/20040531/press.

15. Fred Kaplan, "Delusions of Empire," *Slate*, June 25, 2003, http://www.slate.com/id/2084881/.

16. In late 2002, seventy national security experts and Mideast scholars met at the National Defense University to discuss the forthcoming war and concluded that the ensuing occupation would likely represent "the most daunting and complex task the U.S. and the international community will have undertaken since the end of World War II" (Michiko Kakutani, "From Planning to Warfare to Occupation: How Iraq Went Wrong," *New York Times*, July 25, 2006).

A prewar study by the Carnegie Endowment for International Peace found a meager 25 percent success rate for the United States during the past century in sixteen tries. And in each of these—Germany, Grenada, Japan, and Panama—the barriers to success were nowhere near as formidable as in Iraq, whose people have no experience whatever with democracy and few of what most political scientists consider its necessary preconditions. See Andrew Moravsik, "Striking a New Transatlantic Bargain," *Foreign Affairs* 82, no. 4 (July–August 2003): 85.

A study by several World Bank economists noted before the war that developing nations with significant natural resources often experience intensely violent internal conflict, as we have seen in Angola, Congo, Indonesia, Nigeria, and Sierra Leone—and now Iraq. See John Cassidy, "Letter from Iraq: Beneath the Sand," *New Yorker*, July 16 and 21, 2003, 73.

17. Bryan Bender, "Democracy Might Be Impossible, U.S. Was Told," *Boston Globe*, August 14, 2003.

18. Greg Miller, "Democracy Domino Theory 'Not Credible,'" *Los Angeles Times*, March 14, 2003.

19. Jason Vest, "The War after the War," *Village Voice*, March 19–25, 2003, http://www.villagevoice.com/news/0312,vest,42682,1.html.

20. Fred Kaplan, "Delusions of Empire."

21. Seymour M. Hersh, "Get Out the Vote," *New Yorker*, July 25, 2005, http://www.newyorker.com/fact/content/articles/050725fa_fact.

22. Robin Wright and Ellen Knickmeyer, "U.S. Lowers Sights on What Can Be Achieved in Iraq; Administration Is Shedding 'Unreality' That Dominated Invasion, Official Says," *Washington Post*, August 14, 2005.

23. Rajiv Chandrasekaran, "Ties to GOP Trumped Skill on Iraq Team," MSNBC, September 16, 2006, http://www.msnbc.msn.com/id/14868608/.

24. Michael Desch, "Bush and the Generals," *Foreign Affairs*, May–June 2007, http://www.foreignaffairs.org/20070501 faessay86309/michael-c-desch/bush-and-the-generals.html.

25. Peter Eisler, Blake Morrison, and Tom Vanden Brook, "Pentagon Balked at Pleas from Officers in Field for Safer Vehicles; Iraqi Troops Got MRAPs; Americans Waited," *USA Today*, July 16, 2007.

26. Michael Moss, "Pentagon Study Links Fatalities to Body Armor," *New York Times*, January 7, 2006.

27. Mark Thompson, "America's Broken-Down Army," *Time*, April 5, 2007, http://www.time.com/time/nation/article/0,8599,1606888,00.html.

28. Michael Moss, "Many Missteps Tied to Delay of Armor to Protect Soldiers," *New York Times*, March 7, 2005.

29. Paul Krugman, "Thanks for the M.R.E.'s," *New York Times*, August 12, 2003.

30. Ray Suarez, "Under Armored," PBS, *NewsHour with Jim Lehrer*, December 9, 2004, http://www.pbs.org/newshour/bb/military/july-dec04/armor_12–9.html.

31. Michael O'Hanlon, "Breaking the Army," *Washington Post*, July 3, 2003; Dan Ephron and Sarah Childress, "How U.S. Is Failing Its War Veterans," *Newsweek*, March 5, 2007.

32. Mark Benjamin, "The Pentagon's Chronic Neglect of Iraq Vets," *Salon*, April 25, 2007, http://www.salon.com/news/feature/2007/04/25/walter_reed_groups/.

33. Anne Hull and Dana Priest, "Hospital Officials Knew of Neglect; Complaints about Walter Reed Were Voiced for Years," *Washington Post*, March 1, 2007; Kelly Kennedy, "Walter Reed Patients Told to Keep Quiet," *Army Times*, February 28, 2007, http://www.armytimes.com/news/2007/02/TNSreedinspect070227/; Associated Press, "Walter Reed Medical Chief Relieved; General's Dismissal Follows Reports on Poor Treatment of Wounded Soldiers," MSNBC, March 1, 2007, http://www.msnbc.msn.com/id/17402872/.

34. Frank Rich, "A Profile in Cowardice," *New York Times*, July 8, 2007.

35. Fred Kaplan, "He Saw It Coming," *Slate*, August 5, 2003, http://www.slate.com/id/2086636/.

36. Barbara Slavin and Dave Moniz, "How Peace in Iraq Became So Elusive," *USA Today*, July 22, 2003.

37. Peter Slevin and Dana Priest, "Wolfowitz Concedes Iraq Errors," *Washington Post*, July 24, 2003.

38. Michelle Goldberg, "From Heroes to Targets," *Salon*, July 18, 2003, http://dir.salon.com/story/news/feature/2003/07/18/pre_war/index_np.html.

39. Kaplan, "He Saw It Coming."

40. Romesh Ratnesar with Simon Robinson, "Life under Fire," *Time*, July 5, 2003, http://www.time.com/time/magazine/article/0,9171,1005196,00.html.

41. Slavin and Moniz, "Peace in Iraq."

42. Larry Diamond, "Has America Failed in Iraq?" *Slate*, July 20, 2005, http://www.slate.com/id/2123079/entry/2123087/.

43. Slavin and Moniz, "Peace in Iraq."

44. Goldberg, "From Heroes to Targets."

45. George Packer, "No Blame, No Shame," *New Yorker*, Comment, May 14, 2007, http://www.newyorker.com/talk/comment/2007/05/14/070514taco_talk_packer.

46. Eliot A. Cohen, "A Hawk Questions Himself as His Son Goes to War," *Washington Post*, July 10, 2005.

47. Robert Schlesinger, "At the Breaking Point," *Salon*, April 29, 2004, http://dir.salon.com/story/news/feature/2004/04/29/military/index.html.

48. Eric Schmitt and David S. Cloud, "Part-Time Forces on Active Duty Decline Steeply," *New York Times*, July 11, 2005.

49. David Moniz, "Soldiers Re-enlist beyond U.S. Goal; Troops Help Offset Recruiting Shortfall," *USA Today*, July 18, 2005; Ann Scott Tyson, "Army Boosts Benefits for Recruits Taking High-Demand Jobs," *Washington Post*, July 22, 2005; Damien Cave, "Pentagon May Consider Older Recruits," *New York Times*, July 22, 2005.

50. Fred Kaplan, "GI Schmo: How Low Can Army Recruiters Go?" *Slate*, January 9, 2006, http://www.slate.com/id/2133908/nav/tap1/. Note: The army, and indeed all the services, has always allowed some small percentage of citizens with criminal records to enlist, but previously the number of "moral waivers" granted was minuscule. It has now doubled, of necessity, in the army.

51. Thom Shanker, "Young Officers Leaving Army at a High Rate," *New York Times,* April 10, 2006.

52. Ann Scott Tyson, "Shortages Threaten Guard's Capability; 88 Percent of Units Rated 'Not Ready,'" *Washington Post,* March 2, 2007.

53. Jonathan Chait, "Sucker Punch: How Bush Fooled the NeoCons," *New Republic,* December 25, 2006, http://www.tnr.com/doc.mhtml?i=w061225&s=chait122506.

54. Peter Baker and Dana Milbank, "Bush Says War Is Worth Sacrifice; Address Urges Public to Back His Iraq Policy," *Washington Post,* June 29, 2005.

55. Frank Rich, "Why Libby's Pardon Is a Slam Dunk," *New York Times,* March 11, 2007.

56. The *Today* show, NBC, April 25, 2007. The segment can be viewed at http://www.youtube.com/watch?v=f99k3KtD3g0.

57. Secretary of Defense Donald Rumsfeld, "Defense Department Regular Briefing," U.S. Department of Defense, Office of the Assistant Secretary of Defense (Public Affairs), August 23, 2005, http://www.defenselink.mil/transcripts/transcript.aspx?transcriptid=3110.

58. Associated Press, "Poll: 90 Percent Support Right to Protest War," MSNBC, August 26, 2005, http://www.msnbc.msn.com/id/9084651/.

59. Quoted in Sidney Blumenthal, "Operation Iraqi Betrayal," *Salon,* July 26, 2007, http://www.salon.com/opinion/blumenthal/2007/07/26/cheney/index.html.

60. Associated Press, "Democratic Senators Join Clinton in Pressing Pentagon about End-of-Iraq War Planning," *International Herald Tribune,* July 23, 2007. http://www.iht.com/articles/ap/2007/07/23/america/NA-POL-US-Clinton-White-House.php.

61. Michael R. Gordon, "U.S. Is Seen in Iraq Until at Least '09," *New York Times,* July 24, 2007.

62. Quoted in Blumenthal, "Operation Iraqi Betrayal."

63. Media Matters for America, "Limbaugh Lied about Republicans Undermining the Kosovo War," April 30, 2004, http://mediamatters.org/items/200405030001.

64. *Rush Limbaugh Radio Show,* May 5, 2004; Media Matters for America, "Limbaugh on Torture of Iraqis: U.S. Guards Were 'Having a Good Time,' 'Blow[ing] Some Steam Off,'" May 5, 2004, http://mediamatters.org/items/200405050003; Media Matters for America, "*Washington Times:* Limbaugh 'an Important Conservative Voice,'" May 10, 2004, http://mediamatters.org/items/200405100001.

65. *Rush Limbaugh Radio Show,* May 6, 2004; Media Matters for America, "Limbaugh: Prisoner Abuse 'Brilliant,'" May 6, 2004, http://mediamatters.org/items/200405070002.

66. Media Matters for America, "Limbaugh Touted 'Club G'itmo, the Muslim Resort,'" June 17, 2005, http://mediamatters.org/items/200506170004.

67. Media Matters for America, "Limbaugh: Service Members Who Support U.S. Withdrawal Are 'Phony Soldiers,'" September 27, 2007, http://mediamatters.org/items/200709270010.

68. Media Matters for America, "Limbaugh: VoteVets Lied to Soldier in Ad, 'Strapp[ed] Those Lies to His Belt,' Then Sent Him Out 'to Walk into as Many People' as He Can," October 2, 2007, http://mediamatters.org/items/200710020014.

69. Media Matters for America, "Oliver North: Iraqi Prisoner Abuse 'the Kind of Thing That You Might Find on Any College Campus Nowadays,'" May 12, 2004, http://mediamatters.org/items/200405120005.

70. Media Matters for America, "Severin on Abused Prisoners at Abu Ghraib: '[W]e Treated Them Essentially to a Week in Las Vegas," June 1, 2006, http://mediamatters.org/items/200606010011.

71. Robert Bateman, "Think Again: On Officers and Control," Center for American Progress, May 20, 2004, http://www.americanprogress.org/issues/2004/05/b80273.html.

72. Spencer Ackerman, "Silent Treatment," *New Republic Online*, July 27, 2005, http://www.tnr.com/doc.mhtml?i=w050725&s=ackerman072705.

73. Neil A. Lewis, "Military's Opposition to Harsh Interrogation Is Outlined," *New York Times*, July 27, 2005.

74. "Defense Department News Briefing on Detainee Policies," CQ transcripts wire, *Washington Post*, September 6, 2006, http://www.washingtonpost.com/wp-dyn/content/article/2006/09/06/AR2006090601442.html.

75. Josh White and R. Jeffrey Smith, "White House Aims to Block Legislation on Detainees," *Washington Post*, July 23, 2005.

76. Kurt M. Campbell and Michael O'Hanlon, "The Democrat Armed," *The National Interest*, Summer 2005, 93–101.

77. Sixty-four percent of the officers identified with the Republicans, whereas only about 8 percent claimed to be Democrats. In contrast, civilian respondents gave the two parties roughly even support. See Peter D. Feaver and Richard H. Kohn, "Digest of Findings and Studies: Project on the Gap between the Military and Civilian Society," Triangle Institute for Security Studies, October 28–29, 1999, 2. See also Colonel Lance Betros, "Political Partisanship and the Military Ethic in America," *Armed Forces and Society* 27, no. 4 (Summer 2001).

78. Rosa Brooks, "Weaning the Military from the GOP," *Los Angeles Times*, January 5, 2007, http://www.latimes.com/news/opinion/la-oe-brooks5jan05,0,3406790.column?coll=la-opinion-columnists.

79. Todd Gitlin, *The Intellectuals and the Flag* (New York: Columbia University Press, 2006), 131.

80. William A. Hammond, *Reporting Vietnam: Media and Military at War* (Lawrence: University Press of Kansas, 1998; originally published by the U.S. Army War College, Carlisle Barracks, Pa.).

81. Jerry Lembcke, *Spitting Image: Myth, Memory, and the Legacy of Vietnam*, 2nd ed., (New York: NYU Press, 2000).

82. Heather Hurlburt, "War Torn: Why Democrats Can't Think Straight about National Security," *Washington Monthly*, November 1, 2002, http://www.washingtonmonthly.com/features/2001/0211.hurlburt.html.

83. William A. Galston and Elaine C. Kamarck, "The Politics of Polarization," *Third Way*, October 6, 2005.

6. Why Do Liberals Always Blame America First?

1. Jeane Kirkpatrick, speech, 1984 Republican Convention, http://www.cnn.com/ALLPOLITICS/1996/conventions/san.diego/facts/GOP.speeches.pa st/84.kirkpatrick.shtml.

2. Fred Barnes, "They Still Blame America First: The Democrats Fall into the National Security Trap Again," *Weekly Standard*, July 4–11, 2005, http://www.weeklystandard.com/Content/Public/Articles/000/000/005/774oqxhi.asp.

3. CBS/*New York Times* poll, Mystery Pollster, September 20–23, 2001, http://www.mysterypollster.com/main/files/CBSNYT_ideology.pdf. For further analysis, see Mark

Blumenthal, "How Did Liberals React to 9/11?" Mystery Pollster, June 24, 2005, http://www.mysterypollster.com/main/2005/week25/index.html.

4. After withstanding a couple of days of tremendous public denunciations, Falwell was ultimately forced to issue a nonapology. He tried his best to defuse the situation without actually backing down: "I would never blame any human being except the terrorists, and if I left that impression with gays or lesbians or anyone else, I apologize." "Falwell Apologizes to Gays, Feminists, Lesbians," CNN.com, September 14, 2001, http://archives.cnn.com/2001/US/09/14/Falwell.apology/.

5. "Someone from the White House called me yesterday, asking for any input I might have"—Jerry Falwell, quoted in Carl Hulse and Richard W. Stevenson, "Senators Advise Bush on Picking Court Nominee," New York Times, July 12, 2005.

6. Inhofe is quoted in Shelley Lewis, Naked Republicans (New York: Villard, 2006), 12.

7. Media Matters for America, "Citing More Sex-Change Operations, Increased Lesbian Fertility Clinics, Savage Said of 9–11: 'That Was God Speaking,'" March 30, 2007, http://mediamatters.org/items/200703300007.

8. Ibid.

9. Dinesh D'Souza, The Enemy at Home: The Cultural Left and Its Responsibility for 9/11 (New York: Doubleday, 2007), 21.

10. Ibid., 16.

7. But Aren't Liberals Awfully Cavalier about Protecting Our National Security?

1. Mark Townsend and Paul Harris, "Now the Pentagon Tells Bush: Climate Change Will Destroy U.S.," Observer, February 22, 2004, http://observer.guardian.co.uk/international/story/0,6903,1153513,00.html.

2. Richard A. Clarke, "While You Were at War . . . ," Washington Post, December 31, 2006.

3. Deborah Solomon, "Questions for Drew Shindell," New York Times Magazine, February 18, 2007.

4. Union of Concerned Scientists, "Atmosphere of Pressure: Political Interference in Federal Climate Science," January 30, 2007. http://www.ucsusa.org/scientific_integrity/interference/atmosphere-of-pressure.html.

5. H. Josef Hebert, "Former White House Official Defends Editing of Climate Papers," Huffington Post/Associated Press, March 19, 2007, http://www.huffingtonpost.com/huffwires/20070319/na-gen-us-scientists-warming/; Andrew C. Revkin, "Climate Expert Says NASA Tried to Silence Him," New York Times, January 29, 2006.

6. See Elisabeth Rosenthal and Andrew C. Revkin, "Science Panel Calls Global Warming 'Unequivocal,'" New York Times, February 3, 2007; Ian Sample, "Scientists Offered Cash to Dispute Climate Study," Guardian, February 2, 2007, http://environment.guardian.co.uk/climatechange/story/0,2004397,00.html.

7. Juliet Eilpern, "U.S. Aims to Weaken G-8 Climate Change Statement," Washington Post, May 13, 2007.

8. Mark Mazzetti, "Bill Proposes Climate Study Focused on U.S. Defense," New York Times, May 3, 2007.

9. Mark Mazzetti, "Spy Chief Backs Study of Impact of Warming," New York Times, May 11, 2007.

10. Beverly Keel, "Gore Says Media Miss Climate Message; Journalists Have Leaned toward Balance at Expense of Consensus Data, He Says," *Nashville Tennessean,* February 28, 2007.

11. Jonah Goldberg, "I Wanna Know: Who'll Stop the Rain?" *National Review Online,* The Corner, April 2, 2007, http://corner.nationalreview.com/post/?q=NzBkMmU1MTAzMDc5 ZmEyM2Rh NjAzM mJmZjllZTgwYTY=.

12. Clarke, "While You Were at War."

13. Alan Berlow, "The Texas Clemency Memos," *Atlantic Monthly,* July–August 2003, http://www.theatlantic.com/doc/200307/berlow.

14. Adam Liptak, "Libby, Bush Seemed to Alter His Texas Policy," *New York Times,* July 8, 2007.

15. "Transcript: President Bush on Iraq," *New York Times,* July 12, 2007, http://www.nytimes.com/2007/07/12/washington/12bush_transcript.html?r=1&adxnnl=1&oref = slogin&adxnnlx=1184265025-p4bjRo55EpQoc2tDc519sw.

16. Walter Pincus and Jim VandeHei, "Prosecutor in CIA Leak Case Casting a Wide Net; White House Effort to Discredit Critic Examined in Detail," *Washington Post,* July 27, 2005.

17. Faiz Shakir, "Video: Bush I Calls Leakers 'Most Insidious of Traitors,'" *Think Progress,* July 28, 2005, http://thinkprogress.org/2005/07/28/video-bush-i/.

18. Secretary of Defense Donald Rumsfeld, September 13, 2003, quoted in *Congressional Record* ISO (January 27, 2004): S265.

19. Tom Mooney, "The President Is Religious and Resolute, Woodward Attests," *Providence Journal,* April 10, 2002, http://www.projo.com/news/content/projo_20020410_wood10.438f65c3.html.

20. E. J. Dionne Jr., "What the 'Shield' Covered Up," *Washington Post,* November 1, 2005.

21. "The Clare Luce Democrats," *Wall Street Journal,* November 3, 2005, and Jeffrey Bell and William Kristol, "Criminalizing Conservatives," *Weekly Standard,* January 24, 2005, http://www.weeklystandard.com/Content/Public/Articles/000/000/006/211eywgm.asp? pg=2.

22. Frank Rich, "Why Dick Cheney Cracked Up," *New York Times,* February 4, 2007.

8. Why Are Liberals So Damn Elitist?

1. Dewey, "Renascent Liberalism," 143.

2. John Judis, *The Paradox of American Democracy Elites, Special Interests and the Betrayal of the Republic* (New York: Pantheon, 2000), 169.

3. Bill Maher, "Say It Loud: I'm Elite and Proud!" *Salon,* April 13, 2007, http://www.salon.com/opinion/feature/2007/04/13/pat_robertson/.

4. Eric Lipton, "Colleagues Cite Partisan Focus by Justice Official," *New York Times,* May 12, 2007.

5. Chris Suellentrop, "Douglas Feith: What Has the Pentagon's Third Man Done Wrong? Everything," *Slate,* May 20, 2004, http://www.slate.com/id/2100899/.

6. Sarah Weber, "With Press under Attack Again, Agnew's Words Are Often Cited—but What Did He Actually Say?" *Editor & Publisher,* July 17, 2006.

7. Andrew Rosenthal, "Quayle Attacks a 'Cultural Elite,' Saying It Mocks Nation's Values," *New York Times,* June 10, 1992.

8. Christopher Connell, "Quayle Returns to Attack on 'Cultural Elite' over Abortion," Associated Press, June 11, 1992.

9. Michael Kinsley, "Class Warfare? Tell Me about It," *Time,* February 6, 1995, http://www.time.com/time/magazine/article/0,9171,982433-1,00.html.

10. David Brooks: David Brooks, *Bobos in Paradise: The Upper Class and How They Got There* (New York: Simon & Schuster, 2000), 14. Limbaugh: David Brooks, ed., *Backward and Upward: The New Conservative Writing* (New York: Vintage, 1996), 308.

11. G. Gordon Libby, *When I Was a Kid, This Was a Free Country* (Washington, D.C.: Regnery, 2002), 26–47.

12. Nunberg, *Talking Right,* 77.

13. Judis, *Paradox of American Democracy,* 169, 172.

14. Sidney Hook, "The New Failure of Nerve," *Partisan Review* 10, no. 1 (1943): 2.

15. Cathy Young, "Jesus Christ beyond the Thunderdome," *Reason Online,* August 19, 2003, http://www.reason.com/news/show/31956.html.

16. George Gurley, "Coultergeist," *New York Observer,* August 26, 2002.

17. Kate Zernike, "An Evening Out with Ann Coulter," *New York Times,* August 11, 2002.

18. Ann Coulter, *Slander: Liberal Lies about the American Right* (New York: Crown, 2002), 29, 27.

19. The first couple would have to be Irving Kristol and Gertrude Himmelfarb, both of whom are more accomplished in their respective worlds than Decter and Podhoretz; to say nothing of their son William Kristol.

20. Thomas Frank, *What's the Matter with Kansas? How Conservatives Won the Heart of America* (New York: Metropolitan, 2004), 20.

21. Carl Sullivan, "Everyone Loves a List," *Newsweek,* August 5, 2005, http://www.msnbc.msn.com/id/8765687/site/newsweek/.

22. See Michael Ledeen, "Flyover Country," *The Corner,* September 17, 2007, http://corner.nationalreview.com/post/?q=MTk3OTBiY2M5NTMxOGQ5MzQ3MzE5MWJIZDMwZjQ1ZmY=. See also Matthew Duss, "Redneck Chic," *Tapped,* September 8, 2007, http://blog.prospect.org/cgi-bin/mt/mt-tb.cgi/1593.

23. David Brooks, "One Nation, Slightly Divisible," *Atlantic Monthly,* December 2001.

24. Noam Scheiber, "Merit Scholars," *New Republic,* October 17, 2005.

25. Harold Meyerson, "Dissing His Own," *American Prospect,* October 6, 2005, http://www.prospect.org/cs/articles?article=dissing_his_own.

26. Ben Smith, "The Trouble with Harriet; Revolting Right Wing Recalls Manhattan 12; Intellectuals in Snit Resent Bush's Lawyer; Bork: 'Slap in Face to Conservative Movement,'" *New York Observer,* October 17, 2005.

27. Thomas Ricks, "Officers with PhDs Advising War Effort," *Washington Post,* February 5, 2007.

28. Nunberg, *Talking Right,* 70.

9. Why Do Liberals Love Hollywood Smut Peddlers?

1. Tim Goodman, "Couch Potatoes, It's Time to Drop the Remote," *San Francisco Chronicle,* December 13, 2004, http://sfgate.com/cgi-bin/article.cgi?f=/c/a/2004/12/13/DDG79AA71B1.DTL.

2. Eric Alterman, "The Hollywood Campaign," *Atlantic Monthly,* September 2004; Eric Alterman, "Money for Nothing," *Nation,* December 13, 2004, http://www.thenation.com/doc.mhtml?i=20041213&s=alterman.

3. Leroy Ashby, *With Amusement for All: A History of American Popular Culture since 1930* (Lexington: University Press of Kentucky, 2006), 480.

4. "The Moral Minority," *Wall Street Journal,* November 4, 2004.

5. Scott Lehigh, "Dems to Hollywood: The End," *Boston Globe,* December 15, 2004, http://www.boston.com/news/globe/editorial_opinion/oped/articles/2004/12/15/dems_to_hollywood_the_end.

6. Alterman, "Hollywood Campaign."

7. While the entertainment industry does have corporate PACs that do the business's bidding and spread their wealth accordingly, most of the money handed out by the entertainment industry is ideologically motivated and buys its giver nothing.

8. Edsall, *Building Red America,* 66.

9. Alterman, "Money for Nothing."

10. Frank, *What's the Matter with Kansas?,* 240.

10. When Will Liberals Stop Undermining America's Values and Poisoning the Minds of Its Youth?

1. Frank Rich, "The Great Indecency Hoax," *New York Times,* November 28, 2004.

2. John Borland, "Google Knows, We Like Janet Jackson Best," CNET NewsBlog, December 20, 2005, http://news.com/8301–10784_3–6003310–7.html.

3. Federal Communications Commission, "Indecency Complaints and NALs: 1993–2004," March 4, 2005, http://www.fcc.gov/eb/broadcast/ichart.pdf.

4. Susan Jones, "Bunny Flap: PBS Yanks Cartoon Featuring Lesbian Couples," *Cybercast News,* January 27, 2005, http://www.cnsnews.com/ViewCulture.asp?Page=%5CCulture%5Carchive%5C200501%5CCUL20050127b.html.

5. Frank Rich, "The Year of Living Indecently," *New York Times,* February 6, 2005.

6. Media Matters for America, "O'Reilly Compared Lesbian Parents on PBS' Buster Cartoon to 'a Bigamy Situation in Utah' or 'an S&M Thing in the East Village,'" February 17, 2005, http://mediamatters.org/items/200502170007.

7. Karen Everhart, "*Frontline* Tests FCC's 'Indecency,'" *Current,* February 28, 2005, http://www.current.org/fcc/fcc0504indecency.shtml.

8. Frank Rich, "On 'Moral Values,' It's Blue in a Landslide," *New York Times,* November 14, 2004.

9. Rich, "Year of Living Indecently."

10. Elizabeth Jensen, "PBS Firing of the Host on a Show for Children Draws Protest," *New York Times,* August 5, 2006.

11. Frank Rich, "The God Racket, from DeMille to DeLay," *New York Times,* March 27, 2005.

12. Nicholas Wapshott, "The Darwin Exhibition Frightening Off Corporate Sponsors," *Telegraph* (London), November 19, 2005, http://www.telegraph.co.uk/news/main.jhtml?xml=/news/2005/11/20/wdarwin20.xml&sSheet=/portal/2005/11/20/ixportal.html.

13. Eric Alterman, "Think Again: The New Content Commissars," Center for American Progress, March 10, 2005, http://www.americanprogress.org/site/pp.asp?c=biJRJ8OVF&b=446251.

14. James Poniewozik, "The Decency Police," *Time,* March 20, 2005, http://www.time.com/time/magazine/article/0,9171,1039672,00.html.

15. Ibid.

16. Quoted in "'Temptation Island'—the Complete Guide," *Salon,* http://archive.salon.com/ent/tv/temptation/.

17. Burt Kearns, *Tabloid Baby: An Uncensored Account of the Revolution That Gave Birth to 21st Century News Broadcasting* (New York: Celebrity Books, 1999), 55–60.

18. Marshall Sella, "The Red-State Network: How Fox News Conquered Bush Country—and Toppled CNN," *New York Times Magazine,* June 24, 2001, 26.

19. See Ashby, *With Amusement for All,* 466.

20. Howard Kurtz, "Doing Something Right; Fox News Sees Ratings Soar, Critics Sore," *Washington Post,* February 5, 2001.

21. Howard Kurtz, "Limbaugh, Post-Clinton: Dining Happily on What's Left," *Washington Post,* May 7, 2001.

22. Seth Ackerman, "A Special FAIR Report: The Most Biased Name in News, Fox News Channel's Extraordinary Right-Wing Tilt," Fairness & Accuracy in Reporting, August 2001, http://www.fair.org/index.php?page=137.

23. "Mmmm . . . Right Wing Porn," Blog Against the Right, November 3, 2005, http://www.rageagainsttheright.com/2005/11/mmmmright-wing-porn.html.

11. Why Do Liberals Deny That America Was Founded as a Christian Nation?

1. Pew Forum on Religion and Public Life, "Many Americans Uneasy with Mix of Religion and Politics; 69% Say Liberals Too Secular, 49% Say Conservatives Too Assertive," August 24, 2006, http://pewforum.org/docs/index.php?DocID=153.

2. Newt Gingrich, "It Is Impossible to Miss the Discrimination against . . . Believers," *Salon,* May 21, 2007, http://www.salon.com/news/primary_sources/2007/05/21/gingrich_liberty/print.htm.

3. Steven Waldman, "Separated?" *Newsweek,* September 11, 2006, 9.

4. Isaac Kramnick and R. Lawrence Moore, *The Godless Constitution: The Case against Religious Correctness* (New York: W. W. Norton, 1996), 143. See also Susan Jacoby, "Original Intent," *Mother Jones,* December–January 2006, http://www.motherjones.com/news/feature/2005/12/original_intent.html.

5. Brooke Allen, "Our Godless Constitution," *Nation,* February 21, 2005, http://www.thenation.com/doc/20050221/allen.

6. Rick Shenkman, "An Interview with Jon Butler . . . Was America Founded as a Christian Nation?" History News Network, December 20, 2004, http://hnn.us/articles/9144.html.

7. David L. Holmes, *Faiths of the Founding Fathers* (New York: Oxford University Press, 2006). See also Gordon S. Wood, "American Religion: The Great Retreat," *New York Review of Books* 53, no. 10 (June 8, 2006); Steven Waldman, "What George Washington Really Believed," Beliefnet, http://www.beliefnet.com/story/212/story_21221_1.html (accessed July 2007).

8. James Madison, "To the Honorable General Assembly of the Commonwealth of Virginia. A Memorial and Remonstrance," October 1785, available at http://www.founding.com/library/lbody.cfm?id=175&parent=58.

9. Wood, "American Religion."

10. Lambert is cited in Steven Waldman, "The Framers and the Faithful: How Modern Evangelicals Are Ignoring Their Own History," *Washington Monthly,* April 2006, http://www.washingtonmonthly.com/features/2006/0604.waldman.html.

11. Waldman, "The Framers and the Faithful."

12. Why Won't Liberals Admit That America Is Suffering from a Crisis in Moral Values?

1. Wayne Baker, *America's Crisis of Values: Reality and Perception* (Princeton, N.J.: Princeton University Press, 2005), 4.

2. Robert Bork, *Slouching towards Gomorrah: Modern Liberalism and American Decline* (New York: Regan Books, 1996), 1–5, 331.

3. "The End of Democracy? Introduction," *First Things* 67 (November 1996): 18.

4. Damon Linker, *The Theocons: Secular America under Siege* (New York: Basic Books, 2006), 97–109.

5. Thomas Sowell, "Don't Get Weak," *National Review Online*, May 1, 2007, http://article.nationalreview.com/?q=YmU0NGQ0ZTQzZTU4Zjk4MjdjZWMzYTM4Nzk2MzQ0 MGI=.

6. Bill Moyers, "9/11 and God's Sport," speech, Union Theological Seminary 170th Convocation, September 7, 2005, http://www.crosscurrents.org/moyers2006.htm.

7. Frances Fitzgerald, "Holy Toledo," *New Yorker*, July 31, 2006, 26; http://www.newyorker.com/fact/content/articles/060731fa_fact1.

8. Moyers, "9/11 and God's Sport."

9. Fitzgerald, "Holy Toledo."

10. Joe Conason, *Big Lies: The Right-Wing Propaganda Machine and How It Distorts the Truth* (New York: Thomas Dunne, 2003), 99.

11. Paul Krugman, *The Great Unraveling: Losing Our Way in the New Century* (New York: W. W. Norton, 2003), 7.

12. "A Nation Transformed: Clinton-Gore Administration Accomplishments, 1993–2000," Welcome to the White House, http://clinton3.nara.gov/WH/Accomplishments/summary.html.

13. See, for instance, Paul Dimaggio, John Evans, and Bethany Bryson, "Have Americans' Social Attitudes Become More Polarized?" *American Journal of Sociology* 102, no. 3 (1996): 690–755; Morris P. Fiorina, Samuel J. Abrams, and Jeremy C. Pope, *Culture War! The Myth of a Polarized America*, 2nd ed. (New York: Longman, 2006), 33–57; Alan Wolfe, *One Nation, After All* (New York: Penguin, 1998).

14. The Barna Group describes its mission this way: "The ultimate aim of the firm is to partner with Christian ministries and individuals to be a catalyst in moral and spiritual transformation in the United States." Barna Group, "About the Barna Group, Ltd.," http://www.barna.org/FlexPage.aspx?Page=AboutBarna (accessed July 2007).

The biblical worldview is defined as believing "that absolute moral truth exists; that the source of moral truth is the Bible; that the Bible is accurate in all of the principles it teaches; that eternal spiritual salvation cannot be earned; that Jesus lived a sinless life on earth; that every person has a responsibility to share their religious beliefs with others; that Satan is a living force, not just a symbol of evil; and that God is the all-knowing, all-powerful maker of the universe who still rules that creation today." Barna Group, "Most Adults Feel Accepted by God, but Lack a Biblical Worldview," August 9, 2005, http://www.barna.org/FlexPage.aspx?Page=Barna1 Update & Barna UpdateID =194.

15. Wolfe, *One Nation*, 55.

16. Farhad Manjoo, "Here Comes the Scalias," *Salon*, April 11, 2005, http://dir.salon.com/story/news/feature/2005/04/11/judges/index.html.

17. Borosage, "Rejecting the Right."

18. Ronald Asmus, Philip P. Everts, and Pierangelo Isernia, "Across the Atlantic and the Political Aisle: The Double Divide in U.S.-European Relations," *Transatlantic Trends Report*, German Marshall Fund, 2004.

19. Quoted in Daniel Bell, "Passion and Politics in America," *Encounter*, May–June 1956, 54–61.

20. Barry Goldwater, "Excerpts from Goldwater Remarks," *New York Times*, September 16, 1981.

21. James Madison, "The Federalist No. 10: The Utility of the Union as a Safeguard Against Domestic Faction and Insurrection (continued)," *Daily Advertiser*, November 22, 1787, http://www.constitution.org/fed/federa10.htm.

22. Edited transcript of May 26, 2005, White House meeting, quoted in Linker, *The Theocons*, 2.

23. Tom Hamburger and Peter Wallsten, *One Party Country: The Republican Plan for Dominance in the 21st Century* (New York: Wiley, 2006), 129.

24. David Martin, "The Holy Warrior: General Called a Religious Fanatic Finally Speaks Out," CBS News, September 15, 2005, http://www.cbsnews.com/stories/2004/09/15/60II/main643650.shtml.

25. Richard Leiby, "Christian Soldier," *Washington Post*, November 6, 2003. See also Esther Kaplan, *With God on Their Side* (New York: New Press, 2004).

26. Gary Wills, "A Country Ruled by Faith," *New York Review of Books* 53, no. 18 (November 16, 2006).

27. Hayes is quoted in Al Gore, *The Assault on Reason* (New York: Penguin Press, 2007), 58.

28. Kenneth Baer, "Faith Healing: The Air Force Scandal, Democrats and Religion," *New Republic Online*, July 24, 2005, http://www.tnr.com/doc.mhtml?i=w050620&s=baer062405.

29. Michelle Goldberg, "One Nation, Divisible," *Salon*, July 23, 2005, http://dir.salon.com/story/books/review/2005/07/23/feldman/index.html.

30. Judd Legum, Faiz Shakir, Nico Pitney, Amanda Terkel, Payson Schwin, and Christy Harvey, "Supreme Court: The Exploitation of Faith," *Progress Report*, October 13, 2005, Center for American Progress, http://www.americanprogressaction.org/progressreport/2005/10/pr_2005-10-13.html.

31. Susan Jacoby, "Original Intent," *Mother Jones*, December–January 2006, http://www.motherjones.com/news/feature/2005/12/original_intent.html.

32. CNN's "Inside Politics," April 8, 2005. Media Matters for America, "Wolf Blitzer 'Not So Sure' Liberal CNN Host Begala Is 'a Good Catholic,'" posted April 8, 2005, http://mediamatters.org/items/200504090001.

33. Pery Bacon Jr., "Trying Out a More Soulful Tone," *Time*, February 7, 2005, 32.

34. Media Matters for America, "In Tucker Discussion, *Weekly Standard*'s Ferguson on Clinton and Liberal Protestants: '[T]hey Believe in Everything but God,'" posted June 17, 2007, http://mediamatters.org/items/200706170001.

35. Media Matters for America, "Left Behind: The Skewed Representation of Religion in Major News Media," May 2007, http://mediamatters.org/leftbehind/online_version/.

36. Robert Jones and David Cox, "American Values Survey: Initial Report," Center for American Values in Public Life, September 20, 2006, http://media.pfaw.org/CAV/CAV_Memo.pdf.

37. Media Matters for America, "Robertson Affirmed His Belief That Democratic Judges Are a Greater Threat to the U.S. Than Al Qaeda, Nazi Germany or Civil War," May 2, 2007, http://mediamatters.org/items/200505020003.

38. "James Dobson," Media Transparency Person Profile, http://www.mediatransparency.org/personprofile.php?personID=19 (accessed July 2007).

39. Howard Fineman, "The Preacher Primary: GOP Leaders Battle for Support from the Three Kingmakers," MSNBC, February 14, 2007, http://www.msnbc.msn.com/id/17149388/.

40. Debra Rosenberg and Rebecca Sinderbrand, "Of Prayer and Payback," *Newsweek*, November 22, 2004, http://www.msnbc.msn.com/id/6479271/site/newsweek/.

41. Media Matters for America, "NPR Presented Vice President of Conservative Think Tank as Sole Expert on Democrats' Appeal to Religious Voters," February 21, 2007, http://mediamatters.org/items/200702220002?src=other.

42. See Michael Ruse, "Liberalism, Science and Evolution," in *Liberalism for a New Century*, Jumonville and Mattson, eds., 131–44.

43. Ben Adler, "Evolutionary War: Conservatives and Evolution," *New Republic Online*, July 7, 2007, http://www.tnr.com/doc.mhtml?i=w050704&s=adler070705.

44. Jake Tapper and Kendall Evans, "Ex-Bush Aide: White House Officials Called Evangelicals 'Ridiculous,'" ABC News, October 16, 2006, http://abcnews.go.com/GMA/story?id=2570947.

45. David Kuo, "Why a Christian in the White House Felt Betrayed," *Time*, October 16, 2006, http://www.time.com/time/magazine/article/0,9171,1546580,00.html.

46. Richard Wolffe, "'Seduction of Christians,'" *Newsweek*, October 16, 2006, http://www.msnbc.msn.com/id/15292065/site/newsweek/.

47. Neela Banerjee, "Liberal Denomination Fires Salvos at Right," *New York Times*, April 7, 2006.

48. Laurie Goodstein, "Disowning Conservative Politics, Evangelical Pastor Rattles Flock," *New York Times*, July 30, 2006.

13. If Liberals Are So Peace-Loving, Why Do They Want to Murder the Unborn?

1. Michael Kinsley, "The Right's Kind of Activism," *Washington Post*, November 14, 2004.

2. Judy Lundstrom Thomas, "Protest Sets Tiller Off on GOP," *Wichita Eagle*, August 20, 1992. In a story published a month later, Thomas reported that 83 percent of the new precinct committee people were "abortion foes and members of the religious right." Cited in Thomas Frank, *What's the Matter with Kansas?* (New York: Metropolitan Books, 2004), 95–96.

3. Jim Wallis, "Make Room for Pro-Life Democrats," *Sojourners Magazine* 33, no. 6 (June 2004): 5.

4. Atul Gawande, "Let's Talk about Sex," *New York Times*, May 19, 2007; and Rob Stein, "Teen Sex Rates Stop Falling, Data Show," *Washington Post*, July 22, 2007.

5. Jim Wallis, "The Message Thing," *New York Times*, August 4, 2005.

6. Hillary Clinton, "Remarks by Senator Hillary Rodham Clinton to the NYS Family Planning Providers," speech, January 24, 2005, http://clinton.senate.gov/~clinton/speeches/2005125A05.html.

7. Sarah Blustain, "Choice Language: Abortion Is a Right That Ends in Sorrow," *American Prospect*, November 21, 2004, http://www.prospect.org/cs/articles?articleId=8888.

8. Carla K. Johnson, "Study Doesn't Back Abortion-Cancer Link," Associated Press, April 24, 2007; National Cancer Institute, "Summary Report: Early Reproductive Events Breast Cancer Workshop," updated March 25, 2003, http://www.nci.nih.gov/cancerinfo/ere-workshop-report.

9. Ana Quindlen, "Connecting Up the Dots," *Newsweek*, January 24, 2005, 76.

10. Americans United for Life, "Defending Life, State-by-State Rankings, 2006," March 30, 2006, 300, www.aul.org.

11. Eric Lichtblau, "Ashcroft Defends Subpoenas," *New York Times*, February 13, 2004; Dorothy Samuels, "Talking Points: The Waning Power of Roe vs. Wade," *Times*, November 29, 2005, http://select.nytimes.com/2005/11/29/opinion/30talkingpoints.main.html?pagewante.

12. Michael Kinsley, "The Right's Kind of Activism," *Washington Post*, November 14, 2004; Jeffrey Toobin, "Still Standing: The Resilience of Roe v. Wade," *New Yorker*, November 18, 2005, 70–81; George F. Will, "What Voters Want: Competence," *Washington Post*, June 3, 2007.

14. Why Do Liberals Believe in Marriage Only for Homosexuals?

1. Edsall, *Building Red America*, 58–60.

2. Ibid., 87–88.

3. Ibid., 90.

4. Ibid., 91.

5. While only 35 percent of Americans favor marriage between same-sex couples, a Pew poll found that a 54 percent majority now favors allowing gay and lesbian couples to enter into legal agreements giving them many of the same rights as married couples—a figure nine percentage points higher than in October 2003. Only 30 percent of the public supports a constitutional amendment to ban marriages between gay and lesbian couples. Nor was there much evidence that this was an overriding concern for most voters. See Jodie T. Allen and Carroll Doherty, "What Was—and Wasn't—on the Public's Mind . . . and How Opinions Changed during 2006," Pew Research Center for the People and the Press, December 20, 2006, http://pewresearch.org/pubs/110/what-was-and-wasnt-on-the-publics-mind.

6. Pew Research Center for the People and the Press, "Pragmatic Americans Liberal and Conservative on Social Issues," polling summary, August 3, 2006, http://pewforum.org/publications/surveys/socialissues-06.pdf.

7. On gay marriage, almost half of "Gen Nexters" approve of gay marriage, compared with under a third of those over twenty-five. See Ann Hulbert, "Beyond the Pleasure Principle," *New York Times Magazine*, March 11, 2007, 15; Pew Research Center for the People and the Press, "A Portrait of 'Generation Next': How Young People View Their Lives, Futures and Politics," January 9, 2007, http://people-press.org/reports/display.php3?ReportID=300.

8. Thomas Edsall, "Party Boy: Why the GOP's Future Belongs to Rudy," *New Republic*, May 21, 2007, http://www.tnr.com/doc.mhtml?i=20070521&s=edsall052107.

9. Edsall, *Building Red America*, 60.

10. Coburn is quoted in Lewis, *Naked Republicans*, 8–9.

11. Alan Cooperman, "Santorum Angers Gay Rights Groups," *Washington Post*, April 22, 2003.

12. *Lawrence v. Texas*, 539 U.S. 558 (2003), decided June 26, 2003.

13. CNN.com, "Senate Set to Reject Gay Marriage Ban," June 6, 2006, http://www.cnn.com/2006/POLITICS/06/06/same.sex.marriage/index.html.

14. Borosage, "Rejecting the Right."

15. Why Are Liberals Educating Our Children to Be Perverts?

1. Janice Hopkins Tanne, "Abstinence Only Programmes Do Not Change Sexual Behaviour, Texas Study Shows," *British Medical Journal*, February 12, 2005, http://www.bmj.com/cgi/content/full/330/7487/326-b.

2. Ceci Connolly, "Some Abstinence Programs Mislead Teens, Report Says," *Washington Post*, December 2, 2004.

3. Tony Perkins, "Mathematic Study Doesn't Add Up to the End of Abstinence," Tony Perkins' Washington Update, Family Research Council, April 16, 2007, http://www.frc.org/get.cfm?i=WU07D09.

4. "The Abstinence-Only Delusion," *New York Times*, April 28, 2007.

5. See Hendrik Hertzberg, "It's His Biparty," *New Yorker*, December 24, 2006, http://www.newyorker.com/archive/2006/12/04/061204ta_talk_hertzberg.; Moiv, "'Stealth' Bush Appointee Worries about Wayward Wives," Alternet, November 16, 2006, http://www.alternet.org/story/44411/.

6. Ayelish McGarvey, "Dr. Hager's Family Values," *Nation*, May 30, 2005, http://www.thenation.com/doc/20050530/mcgarvey.

7. James W. Holsinger Jr., M.D., "Pathophysiology of Male Homosexuality," prepared for the Committee to Study Homosexuality of the United Methodist Church, January 14, 1991, http://abcnews.go.com/images/Politics/Holsinger_on_Homosexuality.pdf; Jake Tapper, "Homosexuality Isn't Natural or Healthy," ABC News, June 7, 2007, http://abcnews.go.com/Politics/story?id=3251663&page=1.

8. Christopher Lee, "Ex–Surgeon General Says White House Hushed Him," *Washington Post*, July 11, 2007.

9. Christopher Lee and Marc Kaufman, "Bush Aide Blocked Report; Global Health Draft in 2006 Rejected for Not Being Political," *Washington Post*, July 29, 2007.

10. "No Guardrails," *Wall Street Journal*, March 18, 1993.

11. Sharon Jayson, "Most Americans Have Had Premarital Sex, Study Finds," *USA Today*, December 19, 2006, http://www.usatoday.com/news/health/2006-12-19-premarital-sex_x.htm.

12. Laurie Garrett, "Sex and Foreign Aid," *Los Angeles Times*, May 2, 2007.

13. Ronald J. Snider, "The Scandal of the Evangelical Conscience," *Christianity Today*, January 1, 2005, http://www.ctlibrary.com/bc/2005/janfeb/3.8.html.

16. Why Do Liberals Hate Religion?

1. Pew Forum on Religion and Public Life, "Religion and the 2006 Elections," http://pewforum.org/docs/index.php?DocID=174.

2. Pew Forum, "Many Americans Uneasy with Mix."

3. Center for American Progress, "Voters Deeply Concerned about Rising Materialism and Self-interest in American Society; Desire Government Focused on the Common Good and Basic Decency and Dignity of All," poll, June 5, 2006, http://www.americanprogress.org/kf/familyvaluesreport.pdf.

4. Ross Douthat, "Crises of Faith," *Atlantic Monthly*, July–August 2007, http://www.theatlantic.com/doc/prem/200707/religion.

5. Wood, "American Religion."

6. Asmus, Everts, and Isernia, "Across the Atlantic."

7. Barack Obama, "'Call to Renewal' Keynote Address," speech, Washington, D.C., June 28, 2006, http://obama.senate.gov/speech/060628-call_to_renewal/index.php.

8. E. J. Dionne Jr., "Is God's Work Our Work? Religion and American Liberals," speech, Columbia University, New York, February 10, 2006, http://www.centerforamericanvalues.org/site/c.ggLRI4OCK1F/b.2009089/k.6745/American_VoicesEJ_Dionne.htm.

9. Michael Kazin, "A Difficult Marriage: American Protestants and American Politics," *Dissent*, Winter 2006, www.dissentmagazine.org.

10. Lew Daly, "In Search of the Common Good: The Catholic Roots of American Liberalism," *Boston Review*, May–June, 2007, http://bostonreview.net/BR32.3/daly.html.

11. Jeff Jacoby, "In the Footsteps of FDR, Truman, JFK," *Boston Globe*, December 26, 2004, http://www.boston.com/news/globe/editorial_opinion/oped/articles/2004/12/26/in_the_footsteps_of_fdr_truman_jfk/.

12. Kloppenberg, *Virtues of Liberalism*, 5–6.

13. Kazin, "A Difficult Marriage."

14. Robert Wright, "Why Americans Hate Democrats," *Slate*, November 4, 2004, http://www.slate.com/id/2109164/.

15. Matthew Barakat, "XM suspends Opie and Anthony for 30 Days for Crude On-Air Sex Comments and Lack of Contrition," Associated Press, May 15, 2007.

16. The group NWA, for instance, which stands for "Niggaz with Attitude," explains to their fans that the next time a girl says she doesn't want to "suck a dick," you should "punch her in the eye." When you've knocked "the ho" down, then get on top of her, "open up her mouth," put your cock in it, and begin humping her face so that she can realize that, the entire time, she wished to be "doin' it on her own." Quoted in Neil Jumonville, "Liberal Tolerance at Middle Age," in *Liberalism for a New Century*, Jumonville and Mattson, eds., 93.

17. Mill quoted in Richard Reeves, "John Stuart Mill," *Salmagundi* 153–54 (Winter–Spring 2007): 47–59.

18. Melody Barnes, "How Character Counted: Perspectives on the 2004 Election," panel, Center for American Progress, November 15, 2004, transcript at http://www.americanprogress.org/kf/how_character_counted_panel.pdf.

19. Dionne, "Is God's Work Our Work?"

20. Pew Forum, "Many Americans Uneasy with Mix."

21. Jim Wallis, "Life of the Party," *Salon*, May 6, 2005, http://dir.salon.com/story/news/lotp/2005/05/02/jim_wallis/index.html.

22. Michael Luo and Laurie Goodstein, "Emphasis Shifts for New Breed of Evangelicals," *New York Times*, May 21, 2007.

23. Frances FitzGerald, "The Evangelical Surprise," *New York Review of Books* 54, no. 7 (April 26, 2007), http://www.nybooks.com/articles/20131.

24. Darryl Hart, "Leftward Christian Soldiers," *American Conservative*, January 29, 2007.

25. Pew Forum, "Many Americans Uneasy with Mix."

17. Why Do Liberals Hate the Jews?

1. Jamie Glazov, "Symposium: Anti-Semitism—the New Call of the Left," *Front Page Magazine*, March 14, 2003, http://www.frontpagemagazine.com/Articles/ReadArticle.asp?ID=6651.

2. Marshall Wittmann, "Liberalism of Fools," posted on the Bull Moose blog, September 5, 2006, http://bullmooseblogger.blogspot.com/2006/09/liberalism-of-fools.html; William Kristol, "Anti-Judaism," *Weekly Standard*, September 11, 2006, http://www.weeklystandard.com/Content/Public/Articles/000/000/012/685aslgc.asp; Robert Goldberg, "Donkey See, Monkey Do," *Washington Times*, August 29, 2006; Winged Hussar, "MoveOn.Org Anti-Semitism Scandal Spreading," Free Republic, September 14, 2006, http://www.freerepublic.com/focus/f-news/1701700/posts.

3. Jennifer Medina, "On Lieberman, Some Jews Are Torn on 2 Wars," *New York Times*, July 27, 2006. See also Jamison Foser, "Media Matters," August 11, 2006, http://mediamatters.org/items/200608120001.

4. MSNBC's *Scarborough Country*, December 8, 2004, transcript at http://www.msnbc.msn.com/id/6685898/.

5. Quoted in Peter J. Boyer, "The Jesus War: Mel Gibson's Obsession," *New Yorker*, September 15, 2003, 58, http://www.newyorker.com/archive/2003/09/15/030915fa_fact_boyer.

6. Ibid.

7. Katha Pollitt, "The Protocols of Mel Gibson," *Nation*, March 29, 2004, http://www.thenation.com/doc/20040329/pollitt.

8. Charles Krauthammer, "Gibson's Blood Libel," *Washington Post*, March 5, 2004.

9. Lawrence Donegan, "Christ in the Crossfire," *Observer*, September 28, 2003, http://observer.guardian.co.uk/review/story/0,6903,1050963,00.html.

10. Michelle Goldberg, "How the Secular Humanist Grinch Didn't Steal Christmas," *Salon*, November 21, 2005, http://dir.salon.com/story/news/feature/2005/11/21/christmas/index.html.

11. Hugh Hewitt, "The Passion of the Christ," *WorldNetDaily*, posted January 29, 2004, http://worldnetdaily.com/news/article.asp?ARTICLE_ID=36832.

12. Michael Medved, "Live from the Headlines, Interview with Michael Medved, William Donohue," CNN.com, August 4, 2003, http://transcripts.cnn.com/TRANSCRIPTS/0308/04/se.21.html.

13. Quoted in Andrew Sullivan, "Gibson and the Right," Daily Dish, July 31, 2006, http://andrewsullivan.theatlantic.com/the_daily_dish/2006/07/gibson_and_the_.html.

14. Media Matters for America, "Conservative Media Figures Jumping to Mel Gibson's Defense," August 2, 2006, http://mediamatters.org/items/200608030002.

15. Cathy Young, "One Man's Culture War," *Reason Online*, January 2007, http://www.reason.com/news/show/117092.html.

16. J. Hoberman, "With God, and the Constitution, on His Side," *Forward*, February 20, 2004, http://www.forward.com/articles/with-god-and-the-constitution-on-his-side/.

17. Ibid.

18. Media Matters for America, "Limbaugh Claimed Ahmadinejad Letter to Bush Contained 'Liberal Hollywood Jewish People Talking Point,'" May 11, 2006, http://mediamatters.org/items/ 200605110002.

19. Media Matters for America, "Savage: Journalists 'with Curly Hair and Large Glasses' Won't Cover Shooting without 'a Christian to Crucify,'" February 16, 2007, http://mediamatters.org/items/200702160008.

20. Steve Rendall, "The Mainstreaming of Anti-Semitism; Few Raise Alarms When Media Bigs Attack Jews," Fairness & Accuracy in Reporting, May–June 2005, http://www.fair.org/index.php?page=2535.

21. Media Matters for America, "O'Reilly Attacked Media Matters: 'The Most Vile, Despicable Human Beings in the Country'; Called ADL President 'a Nut,'" December 9, 2004, http://mediamatters.org/items/200412100002.

22. For more, see Adam Cohen, "Times Select: The So-Called War on Christmas," *New York Times,* December 14, 2005, http://select.nytimes.com/2005/12/14/opinion/14talking points.main.html?pagewanted.

23. Nunberg, *Talking Right,* 254.

24. Goldberg, "One Nation, Divisible."

25. Burt Prelutsky, "The Jewish Grinch Who Stole Christmas," *WorldNetDaily,* December 7, 2005, http://www.worldnetdaily.com/news/article.asp?ARTICLE_ID=47775.

26. Michelle Goldberg, "How the Secular Humanist Grinch Didn't Steal Christmas," *Salon,* November 21, 2005, http://dir.salon.com/story/news/feature/2005/11/21/christmas/index.html.

27. Alan Cooperman, "'War' on Christians Is Alleged; Conference Depicts a Culture Hostile to Evangelical Beliefs," *Washington Post,* March 29, 2006.

28. People for the American Way, "Right-Wing Religious McCarthyism," *Right Wing Watch,* September 25, 2003, http://www.pfaw.org/pfaw/general/default.aspx?oid=12268.

29. "Frist's Attack on Civil Rights," *Think Progress,* April 15, 2005, http://thinkprogress.org/index.php?p=658.

30. Nunberg, *Talking Right,* 161.

31. Eric Alterman, "The Soros Slander Campaign Continues," *Nation,* July 5, 2004, http://www.thenation.com/doc.mhtml?i=20040705&s=alterman. For Soros's place in the all-time standings, see "Top 10 U.S. Philanthropists," MSNBC.com, November 27, 2006, http://www.msnbc.msn.com/id/15735533/.

32. "*NewsMax Magazine* Reveals: George Soros' Coup Attempt against George Bush," NewsMax.com, http://www.newsmax.com/adv/soros/.

33. Eric Alterman, "Target: George Soros," *Nation,* December 29, 2003, http://www.thenation.com/doc/20031229/alterman.

34. Alterman, "Soros Slander Campaign."

35. Michael Kaufman, *Soros: The Life and Times of a Messianic Billionaire* (New York: Alfred A. Knopf, 2002), 36–38.

36. Media Matters for America, "Echoing Lyndon LaRouche, Horowitz and Poe Smear 14-Year-Old George Soros as Nazi 'Collaborator,'" August 2, 2006, http://mediamatters.org/items/200608020003. See also David Horowitz and Richard Poe, *The Shadow Party: How George Soros, Hillary Clinton and Sixties Radicals Seized Control of the Democratic Party* (Nashville: Nelson Current, 2006). Peretz's comments appeared in the magazine ("Tyran-a-Soros: The Madness of King George," *New Republic,* February 7, 2007, https://ssl.tnr.com/p/docsub.mhtml?i=20070212&s=peretz021207; "George Soros vs. Martin Peretz," *TNR Online,* February 9, 2007, https://ssl.tnr.com/p/docsub.mhtml?i=w070205&s=peretzsoros020907, and, obsessively, on his *New Republic* weblog, which can be found at http://www.tnr.com/blog/spine. The "ruthless Jewish banker" quote appeared on February 12, 2007, and can be found at http://www.tnr.com/blog/spine?pid=80338.

37. Media Matters for America, "O'Reilly: 'They Ought to Hang This Soros Guy,'" posted January 3, 2006, http://mediamatters.org/items/200601030007.

38. For instance, Heather MacDonald writes on *National Review*'s blog, The Corner, "Plenty of conservatives have arrived at those core values through close observation of human society and history, by plumbing the wisdom of philosophers and poets, or simply through a

sound upbringing. It is just not the case that only Bible study could lead people to conservative, disciplined lives." Heather MacDonald, "Responding to Ramesh," *National Review Online*, The Corner, August 14, 2006, http://corner.nationalreview.com/post/?q=YWM3NmQ4YmQ4ZDUzNzFjMzFkOTU0NTAwMzM5ZDQ2Y2U=.

39. Media Matters for America, "On CNBC's *The Big Idea*, Coulter Said That 'We' Christians 'Just Want Jews to Be Perfected,'" October 10, 2007, http://mediamatters.org/items/200710100008?f=h_top.

18. Why Are Liberals So Contemptuous of Individual Freedom?

1. "Liberal," in *Conservapedia*, http://www.conservapedia.com/Liberals.

2. Institute for Humane Studies, "What Is a Libertarian?" quoted from Kenneth Janda, Jeffrey Berry, and Jerry Goldman, *The Challenge of Democracy* (New York: Houghton Mifflin, 1999), http://www.theihs.org/about/id.1084/default.asp.

3. William Bennett and Brian T. Kennedy, "The Right to Life," *National Review*, March 24, 2005, http://www.nationalreview.com/comment/bennet_kennedy/200503240814.asp.

4. Gary Wills, "Fringe Government," *New York Review of Books* 52, no. 15 (October 6, 2005), http://www.nybooks.com/articles/article-preview?article_id=18308.

5. Brink Lindsey, "Liberaltarians: A Progressive Manifesto," *New Republic*, December 11, 2006, http://www.tnr.com/doc.mhtml?i=20061211&s=lindsey121106.

6. Charlie Savage, "Disaffected Conservatives Set a Litmus Test for '08," *Boston Globe*, June 12, 2007.

19. Why Do Liberals Love "Activist Judges"?

1. Michiko Kakutani, "Does Tomorrow Belong to Gingrich's 'Popular Majority'?" *New York Times*, February 1, 2005.

2. Robert H. Bork, "Our Judicial Oligarchy," *First Things* 67 (November 1996): 21–24.

3. Michelle Goldberg, "In Theocracy They Trust," *Salon*, April 11, 2005, http://dir.salon.com/story/news/feature/2005/04/11/judicial_conference/index.html.

4. Max Blumenthal, "Justice Sunday Preachers," *Nation*, Web only, April 26, 2005, http://www.thenation.com/doc.mhtml?i=20050509&s=blumenthal.

5. Manjoo, "Here Come the Scalias."

6. Quoted in Stephen Pizzo, "Tom DeLay in His Own Words," Alternet, May 16, 2002, http://www.alternet.org/story/13152.

7. Christine Stansell, "Partial Law: A Lost History of Abortion," *New Republic*, May 21, 2007, http://www.tnr.com/doc.mhtml?i=20070521&s=stansell052107.

8. Richard Briffault, "A Fickle Federalism," *American Prospect* 14, no. 3 (March 1, 2003), http://www.prospect.org/cs/articles?article=a_fickle_federalism.

9. Just about the only conservative criticism that appeared in the wake of the Court's decision was that offered in the *Weekly Standard* by then–University of Pennsylvania professor John DiIulio, later an extremely disillusioned member of the Bush administration. John J. DiIulio Jr., "Equal Protection Run Amok," *Weekly Standard*, December 25, 2000.

10. The tally is as follows: Thomas, 65.63 percent; Kennedy, 64.06 percent; Scalia, 56.25 percent; Rehnquist, 46.88 percent; O'Connor, 46.77 percent; Souter, 42.19 percent; Stevens, 39.34 percent; Ginsburg, 39.06 percent; and Breyer, 28.13 percent. See Paul Gewirtz and Chad Golder, "So Who Are the Activists?" *New York Times*, July 6, 2005.

11. Thomas J. Miles and Cass R. Sunstein, "The Real Judicial Activists," *American Prospect*, December 17, 2006, http://www.prospect.org/cs/articles?article=the_real_judicial_activists.

20. When Will Liberals Stop Crying "Racism" at Every Opportunity?

1. E. J. Dionne Jr., "Race Bait and Switch," *Washington Post*, February 8, 2005.

2. Hilzoy, "Going Down in Flames," Obsidian Wings, April 20, 2007, http://obsidian wings.blogs.com/obsidian_wings/2007/04/going_down_in_f.html.

3. Neil A. Lewis, "Justice Dept. Reshapes Its Civil Rights Mission," *New York Times*, June 13, 2007.

4. Michael Barone, "The New Status Quo," *Jewish World Review*, December 27, 2004, http://www.jewishworldreview.com/michael/barone122704.asp.

5. Richard Rothstein, "Must Schools Fail?" *New York Review of Books* 51, no. 19 (December 2, 2004), http://www.nybooks.com/articles/17598.

6. Douglas S. Massey, *Return of the "L" Word: A Liberal Vision for the New Century* (Princeton, N.J.: Princeton University Press, 2005), 70.

7. Media Matters for America, "O'Reilly Denied Being 'Prejudice[d] in Any Way Shape or Form,'" November 16, 2006, http://mediamatters.org/items/200611160003.

8. Massey, *Return of the "L" Word*, 70.

9. Rothstein, "Must Schools Fail?" See also Alec Klein, "A Tenuous Hold on the Middle Class; African Americans on Shifting Ground," *Washington Post*, December 18, 2004.

10. Sam Dillon, "Evictions at Sorority Raise Issue of Bias," *New York Times*, February 25, 2007.

11. See Rick Perlstein, "Black High School Students in Louisiana Threatened with Lynching," CommonSense.com, June 28, 2007, http://commonsense.ourfuture.org/black_high_school_students_louisiana_threatened_lynching .

12. Sam Dillon, "Schools Slow in Closing Gaps between Races," *New York Times*, November 20, 2006.

13. Klein, "A Tenuous Hold on the Middle Class."

14. Genaro C. Armas, "Study Says Wealth Gap Widened for Blacks, Hispanics after Recession," Associated Press, October 17, 2004.

15. Clark quoted in William Julius Wilson, "Race-Neutral Policies and the Democratic Coalition," *American Prospect*, November 2002, http://www.prospect.org/cs/articles?article=raceneutral_policies_and_the_democratic_coalition.

16. Richard D. Kahlenberg, "Time for a New Strategy," Inside Higher Ed, November 10, 2006, http://insidehighered.com/views/2006/11/10/kahlenberg.

17. Suzanne W. Model and Gene A. Fisher, "Polarization and Progress in the Black Community: Earnings and Status Gains for Young Black Males in the Era of Affirmative Action," *Sociological Forum* 4 (Winter 1989): 323; Christopher Jencks, "Is the American Underclass Growing?" in *The Urban Underclass*, eds. Christopher Jencks and Paul E. Peterson (Washington, D.C.: Brookings Institution, 1991), 53–55.

18. William Julius Wilson, "Race-Neutral Policies and the Democratic Coalition," *American Prospect*, November 2002, http://www.prospect.org/cs/articles?article=raceneutral_policies_and_the_democratic_coalition.

19. See Linda Greenhouse, "Justices Reject Diversity Plans in Two Districts," *New York Times*, June 28, 2007.

20. Kahlenberg, "Time for a New Strategy."

21. Richard Morin, "Misperceptions Cloud Whites' View of Blacks," *Washington Post*, July 11, 2001.

22. Robert M. Entman and Andrew Rojecki, *The Black Image in the White Mind: Media and Race in America* (Chicago: University of Chicago Press, 2000), 64–66.

23. Earl Black and Merle Black, *Divided America: The Ferocious Power Struggle in American Politics* (New York: Simon & Schuster, 2007), 9.

24. Wilson, "Race-Neutral Policies."

25. Richard D. Kahlenberg, "Stay Classy: The New Integration," *New Republic*, December 18, 2006, http://www.tnr.com/doc.mhtml?i=20061218&s=kahlenberg121806.

26. Kahlenberg, "Time for a New Strategy." Richard D. Kahlen, "Back to Class," *American Prospect*, December 17, 2006, http://www.prospect.org/cs/articles?article=back_to_class.

27. When Charles Murray and the late William Hernstein published *The Bell Curve: Intelligence and Class Structure in American Life* (New York: Free Press, 1994), it received a tidal wave of media attention. But when those with expertise weighed in on the topic, the authors were revealed to have relied on racist pseudo-science to make their case.

According to the book's bibliography and to back issues of the *Mankind Quarterly*, the seventeen racist experts are W. J. Andrews, Cyril Burt, Raymond B. Cattell (eight citations), Hans J. Eysenck, Seymour Itzkoff, Arthur Jensen (twenty-three citations), Richard Lynn (twenty-four citations), Robert E. Kuttner, Frank C. J. McGurk (six citations), C. E. Noble, R. Travis Osborne (three citations), Roger Pearson, J. Philippe Rushton (eleven citations), William Shockley, Audrey Shuey, Daniel Vining (three citations), and Nathaniel Weyl. The ten who are or were either editors or members of the editorial board are: Cattell, Eysenck, Itzkoff, Kuttner, Lynn, McGurk, Noble, Pearson, Shuey, and Vining. See Leon J. Kamin, "Lies, Damned Lies and Statistics," in *The Bell Curve Debate: History, Documents, Opinions*, eds. R. Jacoby and N. Glauberman. (New York: Times Books, 1995), 81–105; Jared Diamond, *Guns, Germs and Steel: The Fates of Human Societies* (New York: W. W. Norton, 1997), 20; Nicholas Lemann, "The Bell Curve Flattened," *Slate*, January 18, 1997; and Charles Lane, "The Tainted Sources of the Bell Curve," *New York Review of Books*, December 1, 1994; *New Scientist*, July 22, 1995, 44.

28. According to the *Economist*, it's 1.1 million. See Lexington, "Black Power," *Economist*, February 3, 2007, 36.

29. Richard D. Kahlenberg, "Invisible Men," *Washington Monthly*, March 2007, http://www.washingtonmonthly.com/features/2007/0703.kahlenberg.html.

30. William H. Chafee, *Private Lives/Public Consequences: Personality and Politics in Modern America* (Cambridge, Mass.: Harvard University Press, 2005), 83–84.

31. Ibid., 86.

32. Esther Kaplan, "A Hundred Peace Movements Bloom," *Nation*, January 6, 2003, http://www.thenation.com/doc/20030106/kaplan.

21. Why Are Liberals So Soft on America's Enemies?

1. James Traub, "The Things They Carry," *New York Times Magazine*, January 4, 2004.

2. Robert Dallek, *Flawed Giant: Lyndon Johnson and His Times, 1961–1973* (New York: Oxford University Press, 1998), 491.

3. Media Matters for America, "Mission Accomplished: A Look Back at the Media's Fawning Coverage of Bush's Premature Declaration of Victory in Iraq," April 27, 2006, http://mediamatters.org/items/200604270005. See also Craig Lambert, "Reviewing 'Reality': New York Times Columnist Frank Rich Views Political Life through a Theatrical Lens," *Harvard Magazine*, March–April 2007, http://www.harvardmagazine.com/2007/03/reviewing-reality.html.

4. Media Matters for America, "After Saying Obama Seems Like 'Kind of a Wuss' Carlson Called Obama 'Rhetoric' 'Kind of Wimpy,'" July 11, 2007, http://mediamatters.org/

items/200707110003; and Media Matters for America, "Still More Carlson on Obama: '[W]hy Has Barack Obama Suddenly Turned into Oprah?'" July 13, 2007, http://mediamatters.org/items/200707130009.

5. Media Matters for America, "Tucker Carlson on Clinton: '[W]hen She Comes on Television, I Involuntarily Cross My Legs,'" July 18, 2007, http://mediamatters.org/items/200707180009.

6. Jamison Foser, "Media Matters: The Coulter-Matthews-Dowd Continuum," Media Matters for America, March 9, 2007, http://mediamatters.org/items/200703100003.

7. The story was actually picked up by CNN, MSNBC, National Public Radio, Fox News, *Time*, *U.S. News & World Report*, *Newsweek*, the Associated Press, the *Arizona Republic*, the *Boston Globe*, the *Boston Herald*, the *Charlotte Observer*, the *Chicago Sun-Times*, the *Chicago Tribune*, the *Dallas Morning News*, the *Denver Post*, the *Des Moines Register*, the *Detroit Free Press*, the *Indianapolis Star*, the *Kansas City Star*, the *Los Angeles Times*, the *New York Post*, the *New York Times*, the (Newark) *Star-Ledger*, the *Pittsburgh Post-Gazette*, the *San Francisco Chronicle*, the *Washington Post*, the *Washington Times*, the *Seattle Times*, the *Oregonian*, and the *San Antonio Express-News*. See Eric Boehlert, "What Haircut Stories Tell Us about the Press," Media Matters for America, May 1, 2007, http://mediamatters.org/columns/200705010001.

8. Media Matters for America, "Media Heaped Praise on Huckabee's 'Sexual Dig' at Edwards," May 16, 2007, http://mediamatters.org/items/200705160005.

9. Media Matters for America, "Hannity Suggested Edwards' 'Primping' Is Evidence That He Does Not 'Understand the Nature of the Battle in the War That's Being Waged Against Us,'" May 25, 2007, http://mediamatters.org/items/200705250008.

10. John Solomon, "Splitting Hairs, Edwards's Stylist Tells His Side of Story," *Washington Post*, July 5, 2007.

11. Ron Fournier, "Analysis: Is Edwards Real or a Phony?" Associated Press, September 18, 2007, available at http://ap.google.com/article/ALeqM5iDfwCkPNPJXxP18CddCFjgHkoHpQ.

12. Jamison Foser, "Media Matters," Media Matters for America, July 13, 2007, http://mediamatters.org/items/200707140001.

13. Jonah Goldberg, "Baghdad Delenda Est, Part Two," *National Review*, April 23, 2002, http://www.nationalreview.com/goldberg/goldberg042302.asp.

14. Office of the Director of National Intelligence, "Declassified Key Judgments of the National Intelligence Estimate 'Trends in Global Terrorism: Implications for the United States,'" April 2006, http://www.dni.gov/press_releases/Declassified_NIE_Key_Judgments.pdf.

15. Media Matters for America, "*LA Times* Suggested Opposing Iraq War and Being Tough on Terrorism Are Contradictory," April 30, 2007, http://mediamatters.org/items/200704300001.

16. Vic Fingerhut, "Iraq Is a Loser for Dems, Too," *Washington Post*, October 8, 2006.

17. William Kristol, "The War for Liberalism: American Liberalism Is in a Dangerous Predicament," *Weekly Standard*, March 7, 2003, http://www.weeklystandard.com/Content/Public/Articles/000/000/002/452kblzf.asp.

18. William Hamilton, "Book Says Top Aide Urged Bush to Fire Rumsfeld," *Washington Post*, September 30, 2006.

19. Exit polling from ABC News Polling Unit and Stanford Institute for Research in the Social Sciences at Stanford University, November 9, 2004.

20. Quoted in Jonathan Weiler and Marc J. Hetherington, "Authoritarianism and the American Political Divide," *Democratic Strategist*, 2006, http://www.thedemocraticstrategist.org/0609/weilera.php.

21. Frank Luntz, "The Environment: A Cleaner, Safer, Healthier America," *Straight Talk* 132, http://www.politicalstrategy.org/archives/001330.php.

22. Charles Krauthammer, "To Hell with Sympathy," *Time*, November 17, 2003, http://www.time.com/time/magazine/article/0,9171,1006162,00.html.

23. "Iraq and the Media: A Critical Timeline," Fairness & Accuracy in Reporting, March 19, 2007, http://www.fair.org/index.php?page=3062.

24. Peter Beinart, "Distant Shores," *New Republic*, January 17, 2005, 6.

25. E. J. Dionne Jr., "Progressives' French Lesson," *Washington Post*, May 8, 2007.

22. Why Do Liberals Love to Tax and Spend?

1. Robert L. Bartley, "The Collapse of Liberalism," *Wall Street Journal*, October 14, 1968; republished January 2, 2004.

2. Paul Krugman, "A Failed Revolution," *New York Times*, December 29, 2006.

3. Patrick J. Buchanan, "An American Who Can't Say No," *WorldNetDaily*, January 24, 2005, http://www.wnd.com/news/article.asp?ARTICLE_ID=42518.

4. Dennis Cauchon, "Rules 'Hiding' Trillions in Debt; Liability $516,348 per U.S. household," *USA Today*, May 29, 2007.

5. Jonathan Weisman and Peter Baker, "After Bush Leaves Office, His Budget's Costs Balloon," *Washington Post*, February 14, 2005.

6. "The Not-So-Incredible Shrinking Deficit," *Economist*, August 16, 2005, http://www.economist.com/agenda/displayStory.cfm?story_id=4289485.

7. Jonathan Weisman, "In Congress, the GOP Embraces Its Spending Side," *Washington Post*, August 4, 2005.

8. "Big-Government Conservatives," *Washington Post*, August 15, 2005.

9. The study was eventually published by the American Enterprise Institute. Mark Gongloff, "The $44 Trillion Hole?" CNN Money, May 29, 2003, http://money.cnn.com/2003/05/29/news/economy/social_security_pain/; Niall Ferguson and Laurence J. Kotlikoff, "The New New Deal: Benefits without Bankruptcy," *New Republic*, August 15, 2005, 18.

10. George Will, "Conservatives, Liberals and Reality."

11. Eyal Press, "Even Conservatives Are Wondering: Is Bush One of Us?" *Nation*, May 31, 2004, http://www.thenation.com/doc/20040531/press.

12. "Tax Lunacy: The US Administration Throws Prudence Out of the Window," *Financial Times*, May 23, 2000.

13. Media Matters for America, "Juan Williams on Public Telling Pollsters It Favors Democrats on Taxes: '[T]o Me, That's Crazy,'" November 5, 2006, http://mediamatters.org/items/200611050004. See also Frank Luntz, "Stuck in the Mud: How Can the GOP Get Moving Again? Drop the Dirty Politics and Get Real," *Washington Post*, February 25, 2007.

14. Media Matters, "Juan Williams on Public."

15. Deborah Solomon, "Fighting Words: Questions for Chuck Hagel," *New York Times Magazine*, July 3, 2005, 17.

16. Quoted in Shari Berman, *The Primacy of Politics: Social Democracy and the Making of Europe's Twentieth Century* (New York: Cambridge University Press, 2006), 212.

17. Jeff Faux, "Crashing the Party of Davos," *Democracy: A Journal of Ideas* 3 (Winter 2007).

18. Jonathan Chait, "Freakoutonomics," *New Republic*, November 6, 2006.

19. Greg Ip, "Income-Inequality Gap Widens: Boom in Financial Markets Parallels Rise in Share for Wealthiest Americans," *Wall Street Journal*, October 12, 2007.

20. Clay Risen, "Trading Stories," *New Republic*, September 19, 2006, http://www.tnr.com/doc.mhtml?i=w060918&s=risen091906.

21. Figure is based on U.S. Census statistics. "Harper's Index," *Harper's*, June 2007, 13.

22. *The Corporate Library's 2006 CEO Pay Survey*, Corporate Library, September 29, 2006.

23. The CEOs of America's largest corporations (the Fortune 100) make an average of $17.6 million per year. That is $67,692 per day, or approximately $8,461 per hour. The federal minimum wage was, until 2007, $5.15 per hour, or $10,712 per year (for a 40-hour work week). It takes the average CEO 2 hours and 2 minutes to earn $10,712. The CEOs of Fortune 100 companies can earn $10,712 in an average of 1 hour and 16 minutes. "Research Report: The Minimum Wage, CEO Pay and the Gap in Achieving the American Dream," Americans United for Change, January 2, 2007, http://cancampaign.3cdn.net/413f158867745fd117_6wm6bxi3r.pdf; David Cay Johnston, "Income Gap Is Widening, Data Shows," *New York Times*, March 29, 2007.

24. Michael Walzer, "In Defense of Equality," *Dissent*, 1973; reprinted in *The New York Intellectuals Reader*, ed. Neil Jumonville (New York: Routledge, 2007), 355–69.

25. Chait, "Freakoutonomics," 16.

26. Quoted in Eric Foner, *The Story of American Freedom* (New York: W. W. Norton, 1999), 269.

27. Quoted in Louis Uchitelle, "The Richest of the Rich, Proud of a New Gilded Age," *New York Times*, July 15, 2007.

28. Evan Thomas and Daniel Gross, "Private-Equity Billionaires and Lower Taxes," *Newsweek*, July 23, 2007, http://www.msnbc.msn.com/id/19762041/site/newsweek/.

29. See Raymond Hernandez and Stephen Labaton, "In Opposing Tax Plan, Schumer Breaks with Party," *New York Times*, July 30, 2007.

30. Bradford Plumer, "Purchasing Power: How Rich People Control Politics," *New Republic Online*, January 30, 2007, http://www.tnr.com/doc.mhtml?i=w070129&s=plumer013007.

31. Bradford DeLong, "What Kinds of Inequality Should We Worry About?" Grasping Reality with Both Hands: Brad DeLong's Semi-Daily Journal, January 31, 2007, http://econ161.berkeley.edu/movable_type/.

32. Barack Obama, *The Audacity of Hope* (New York: Crown, 2006), 114.

33. See Larry Bartels, "Political Parties and Economic Inequality," Princeton Working Group on Inequality 2005, http://www.princeton.edu/~bartels/economic.pdf.

34. Quoted in Peter Novick, *That Noble Dream: The "Objectivity Question" and the American Historical Profession* (New York: Cambridge University Press, 1988), 64.

35. David Cay Johnston, "At the Very Top, a Surge in Income in 03," *New York Times*, October 5, 2005.

36. Ibid.

37. Ramesh Ponnuru, "The Full McCain: An Interview," *National Review Online*, March 5, 2007, http://article.nationalreview.com/print/?q=MTMxOWRkYjgyNDhjOTU5ZTY2OWU2ZTg 2ZmUxMzQ1NjQ=.

38. Richard Kogan and Aiva Aron-Dine, "Claim That Tax Cuts 'Pay for Themselves' Is Too Good to Be True: Data Show No 'Free Lunch' Here," Center on Budget and Policy Priorities, revised July 27, 2006, http://www.cbpp.org/3-8-06tax.htm.

39. Lori Montgomery, "Lower Deficit Sparks Debate over Tax Cuts' Role," *Washington Post*, October 17, 2006.

40. Clay Risen, "Trading Stories," *New Republic Online*, September 19, 2006, http://www.tnr.com/doc.mhtm1?i=w060918&s=risen091906; Alan Blinder, "Free Trade's Great, but Offshoring Rattles Me," *Washington Post*, May 6, 2007.

41. Steven R. Weisman, "Bush in Accord with Democrats on Trade Deals," *New York Times*, May 11, 2007.

42. William Greider, "The Education of David Stockman," *Atlantic Monthly*, December 1981, http://www.theatlantic.com/doc/198112/david-stockman.

43. Media Matters for America, "Fox's Barnes: It's 'a Theological Issue' for Democrats 'to Raise Taxes'," November 20, 2006, http://mediamatters.org/items/200611200009.

23. Don't Conservatives Do a Better Job of Promoting Economic Growth Than Liberals?

1. C. Bradley Thompson, "The Decline and Fall of American Conservatism," *Objective Standard* 1, no. 3 (Fall 2006), http://www.theobjectivestandard.com/issues/2006-fall/decline-fall-american-conservatism.asp; John J. DiIulio Jr., "Are Conservative Republicans Now America's Permanent Ruling Class?" *Chronicle Review*, January 20, 2006; Chris Edwards and John Samples, eds., *The Republican Revolution 10 Years Later: Smaller Government or Business as Usual?* (Washington, D.C.: Cato Institute, 2005).

2. Thompson, "Decline and Fall."

3. See William Niskanen, "'Starve the Beast' Just Does Not Work," Cato at Liberty, the Cato Institute, May 11, 2006, http://www.cato-at-liberty.org/2006/05/11/starve-the-beast-just-does-not- work/.

4. Michael Kinsley, "More GOP Than the GOP," *Los Angeles Times*, April 3, 2005.

24. But Why Are Liberals So Nasty?

1. Peggy Noonan, "That's Not Nice," *Wall Street Journal*, March 10, 2007.

2. Brian C. Anderson, "Illiberal Liberalism," *City Journal*, Spring 2001, http://www.city-journal.org/html/11_2_illiberal.html.

3. Peter Wood, "The Liberalitarian Dust-Up," *National Review*, January 4, 2007, http://article.nationalreview.com/?q=NTYyOTM0NGY1YWY2YWUxMzM4ZWZmNTA4Y2F1Yzg2OTI=.

4. I should add that my own name has come up in this context. In conversation, right-wing talk-show hosts Laura Ingraham and Bill O'Reilly complained of myself, *Nation* editor in chief Katrina vanden Heuvel, and *Nation* Washington editor David Corn, "I won't put any of them on this program . . . because I do not believe they want to have a conversation. . . . You can't have a reasonable discussion with them." O'Reilly also said, "I believe that they come on in here with a viciousness that . . . makes me uncomfortable." Media Matters for America, "O'Reilly Attacked Liberal Critics as 'Vicious' and '[Un]reasonable,'" June 20, 2006, http://mediamatters.org/items/200606190012. Here is the part that dealt with yours truly:

> Alterman's most recent on-air encounter with O'Reilly occurred on the February 11, 2003, edition of the *Factor*. The interview was contentious, as Alterman confronted O'Reilly with instances in which the host was "not very careful about . . . facts," challenged O'Reilly's assertion that he is politically "independent," and asserted that "everybody on earth" thinks Fox News is conservative "except you and [Fox News chairman] Roger Ailes." But Alterman was hardly "vicious" or "[un]reasonable." In contrast, O'Reilly repeatedly attacked Alterman, calling him an "ideologue," and asserting that Alterman had "left the building with Elvis."

Alterman also appeared on the February 28, 2003, edition of the *Factor* opposite Media Research Center director of media analysis Tim Graham, which was guest-hosted by nationally syndicated columnist Cal Thomas. Alterman and Graham were on the show to discuss the February 26, 2003, interview of Saddam Hussein by then–CBS News anchor Dan Rather. The most heated portion of Alterman and Graham's discussion occurred when Alterman contradicted Graham's assertion that Rather "yelled" at then–presidential candidate George H. W. Bush during a 1988 interview. Alterman called this assertion—which appears to be untrue based on the MRC's own video—"a lie." Again, Alterman exhibited no signs of "viciousness" and the discussion remained "reasonable" throughout. More than a year later, O'Reilly unleashed another unprovoked attack on Alterman, characterizing him as a "Fidel Castro confidante." Alterman threatened to sue O'Reilly for defamation unless he retracted the remark, but O'Reilly maintained that in comparing Alterman to Castro, he was only "mak[ing] fun." Center for American Progress president and former Clinton White House chief of staff John Podesta confronted O'Reilly about his remarks on the June 22, 2004, edition of the *Factor,* and O'Reilly conceded that Alterman was "anti-Castro." Alterman did not pursue litigation against O'Reilly.

5. D'Souza, *The Enemy at Home,* 60–61.

6. Roger Cohen, "Manifesto from the Left Too Sensible to Ignore," *International Herald Tribune,* December 30, 2006.

7. Media Matters for America, "Kurtz: 'Imus Made Fun of Blacks, Jews, Gays, Politicians,'" April 13, 2007, http://mediamatters.org/items/200704140001.

8. Media Matters for America, "Savage: Michael Richards' 'Tirade' Demonstrates 'What Liberalism Really Is,'" November 21, 2006, http://mediamatters.org/items/200611220003.

9. D'Souza, *The Enemy at Home,* 232–33.

10. Ibid., 276.

11. Dana Bash, "Bush Takes on Critics," CNN.com, February 24, 2004, http://www.cnn.com/2004/ALLPOLITICS/02/23/elec04.prez.bush/.

12. Jennifer Harper, "The Mean of Dean," *Washington Times,* December 3, 2003.

13. Mike Conway, Maria Elizabeth Grabe, and Kevin Grieves, "Villains, Victims and the Virtuous in Bill O'Reilly's 'No Spin Zone': Revisiting World War Propaganda Techniques," *Journalism Studies* 8, no. 2 (2007).

14. Media Matters for America, "O'Reilly on Soros: An 'Incredible Imbecile, with All Due Respect,'" August 17, 2006, http://mediamatters.org/items/200608170007.

15. Media Matters for America, "O'Reilly: *LA Times* Editorial Board Won't 'Get It' until Terrorists Cut Off Michael Kinsley's Head," May 19, 2005, http://mediamatters.org/items/200505190003.

16. Media Matters for America, "O'Reilly Advocated Profiling of All 'Muslims Between the Ages of 16 and 45,' but Not 'Racial Profiling,'" August 17, 2006, http://mediamatters.org/items/200608170006.

17. Paul Burgess, "Friends, Neighbors, and Countrymen of the Left: I Hate Your Lying Guts," *Fredricksburg Free Lance-Star,* October 28, 2006, http://www.fredericksburg.com/News/FLS/2006/102006/10282006/232595/index_html.

18. Rep. Dana Rohrabacher, House Foreign Affairs Subcommittee on International Organizations and Human Rights in Europe hearing, April 2007, http://youtube.com/watch?v=RYS6mp8G8VQ.

19. Media Matters for America, "CNN's, ABC's Beck on Clinton: '[S]he's the Stereotypical Bitch,'" March 15, 2007, http://mediamatters.org/items/200703150011.

20. Media Matters for America, "Tucker on Sen. Clinton: '[T]here's Just Something About Her That Feels Castrating, Overbearing, and Scary,'" March 20, 2007, http://mediamatters.org/items/200703200013.

21. David Remnick, "The Wilderness Campaign: Al Gore Lives on a Street in Nashville," New Yorker, September 13, 2004, http://www.newyorker.com/archive/2004/09/13/040913fa_fact.

22. John Podhoretz, New York Post, May 27, 2004; Media Matters for America, "Right-Wing Pundits Play Doctor; Diagnose Gore as 'Insane,'" May 28, 2004, http://mediamatters.org/items/200405280001.

23. Frank Rich, "The Swiftboating of Cindy Sheehan," New York Times, August 21, 2005.

24. Frank Gaffney, "Poster Child for Surrender," Jewish World Review, August 16, 2005, http://www.jewishworldreview.com/cols/gaffney081605.asp.

25. Media Matters for America, "Conservatives, Others in the Media Launch Smear Campaign against Cindy Sheehan," August 17, 2005, http://mediamatters.org/items/200508170008.

26. Media Matters for America, "Recent CNN Hire Beck on Cindy Sheehan: 'That's a Pretty Big Prostitute,'" posted January 19, 2006, http://mediamatters.org/items/200601190005.

27. Media Matters for America, "Horowitz: 'Cornel West Is a Black Airhead,'" June 2, 2006, http://mediamatters.org/items/200606020004.

28. Media Matters for America, "Savage on Sawyer: A 'Lying Whore' Who 'in Essence, Is Agreeing That the Holocaust Didn't Occur,'" February 21, 2007, http://mediamatters.org/items/200702210005.

29. Eric Alterman, "Think Again: Change the Tone," Center for American Progress, June 15, 2006, http://www.americanprogress.org/issues/2006/06/b1779655.html.

30. Media Matters for America, "Savage: CNN's Blitzer and King 'Would Have Pushed Jewish Children into the Oven'; 'Curry Favor with the Turbanned Hoodlums,'" August 8, 2006, http://mediamatters.org/items/200608080010.

31. Media Matters for America, "Glenn Beck Called Hurricane Survivors in New Orleans 'Scumbags,' Said He 'Hates' 9–11 Families," September 9, 2005, http://mediamatters.org/items/200509090003.

32. Ann Coulter, "They Shot the Wrong Lincoln," Human Events, August 30, 2006, http://www.humanevents.com/article.php?id=16796&c=1&tb=1&pb=1&gd=08312006.

33. George Gurley, "Coultergeist," New York Observer, January 10, 2002, http://users.rcn.com/skutsch/anticoulter/observer.html.

34. Media Matters for America, "White House Soirée, Part Deux: Beck, Bennett, Ingraham, Medved, and Others Met with Bush," August 2, 2007, http://mediamatters.org/items/200708030001?src=other.

25. Why Are Liberals Such Wimps?

1. Adam Liptak, "A Liberal Case for Gun Rights Helps Sway Federal Judiciary," New York Times, May 6, 2007.

2. Michael Kinsley, "In God, Distrust," New York Times Book Review, May 13, 2007.

3. From David Brock, *The Republican Noise Machine: Right-Wing Media and How It Corrupts Democracy* (New York: Crown, 2004), 132; Nicholas D. Kristof, "Washing Away the Mud," *New York Times*, September 22, 2004.

4. Nicholas D. Kristof, "The New Democratic Scapegoat," *New York Times*, July 26, 2007.

5. Patricia Cohen, "In Economics Departments, a Growing Will to Debate Fundamental Assumptions," *New York Times*, July 11, 2007.

6. Kristof, "New Democratic Scapegoat."

7. Nicholas D. Kristof, "I Have a Nightmare," *New York Times*, March 12, 2005.

8. Nicholas D. Kristof, "Social Security Poker: It's Time for Liberals to Ante Up," *New York Times*, February 5, 2005.

9. Nicholas D. Kristof, "Another Kind of Racism," *New York Times*, April 2, 2005.

10. Thomas L. Friedman, "Let's Talk about Iraq," *New York Times*, June 15, 2005.

11. Michael Tomasky, "Lib Liberation," *New York Magazine*, June 23, 2003, http://nymag.com/nymetro/news/politics/columns/citypolitic/n_8818.

12. Paul Glastris, "Why Can't the Democrats Get Tough?" *Washington Monthly*, March 2002, www.washingtonmonthly.com/features/2001/0203.glastris.html.

Conclusion

1. According to Rasmussen, "20 percent said they consider it a positive description to call a candidate politically liberal while 39 percent would view that description negatively. However, 35 percent would consider it a positive description to call a candidate politically progressive. Just 18 percent react negatively to that term." See "Labels Matter: Progressive Better Than Liberal, Reagan-Like Better Than Conservative," Rasmussen Reports, July 26, 2007, http://rasmussenreports.com/public_content/politics/labels_matter_progressive_better_than_liberal_reagan_like_better_than_conservative.

2. Starr, *Freedom's Power*, 7.

3. Kirk Johnson, "In Minnesota Shift, Case Study for National Political Shake-Up," *New York Times*, December 29, 2006.

4. Kristol quoted in E. J. Dionne Jr., foreword to *Liberalism for a New Century*, eds. Jumonville and Mattson, ix.

5. Dewey is quoted in Chappell, *A Stone of Hope*. The introduction, in which the quote appears, can be found at http://www.americanprogress.org/issues/2004/01/b100382.html.

6. Chris Bowers, "The Role of the Netroots in the Democratic Victories," *Democratic Strategist*, 2006, http://www.thedemocraticstrategist.org/0703/bowers.php.

7. Adam Nagourney and Megan Thee, "Young Americans Are Leaning Left, New Poll Finds," *New York Times*, June 27, 2007, A1; note also the public opinion issues graph produced by political scientist James Stimson, covering the past fifty-five years of data, available at http://www.unc.edu/~jstimson/. See also Ross Douthat, "Blue Period," *Atlantic Monthly*, September 2007, http://www.theatlantic.com/doc200709/realignment.

8. Alan Wolfe, "Why Conservatives Can't Govern," *Washington Monthly*, July 2006.

9. John Solomon and Spencer S. Hsu, "Most Katrina Aid from Overseas Went Unclaimed," *Washington Post*, April 29, 2007.

10. Peter G. Gosselin and Ricardo Alonso-Zaldivar, "Limiting Government's Role; Bush Favors One-Time Fixes over Boosting Existing Programs to Help Katrina Victims," *Los Angeles Times*, September 23, 2005.

11. Spencer S. Hsu, "FEMA Knew of Toxic Gas in Trailers; Hurricane Victims Reported Illnesses," *Washington Post*, July 20, 2007.

12. Smith, *Inquiry into the Nature of the Wealth of Nations*, 651.

13. Pew Research Center, "Trends in Political Values."

14. Sean Wilentz: "The Worst President in History?" *Rolling Stone*, April 21, 2006, http://www.rollingstone.com/news/profile/story/9961300/the_worst_president_in_history; Eric Foner, "He's the Worst Ever," *Washington Post*, December 3, 2006; Douglas Brinkley, "Move Over Hoover," *Washington Post*, December 3, 2006.

15. Reinhold Niebuhr, *The Irony of American History* (New York: Charles Scribner's Sons, 1952), 143.

Index

Matalin, Mary, 135
maternity leave, 63, 71
Matthews, Chris, 101, 106, 281–82, 283, 298
media
  conservative companies, 42, 83, 98
  conservative press as self-consciously conservative, 323
  conservative punditocracy, 98–117
  denigration of women in, 239–40
  establishment becomes cheerleader, 333
  and global warming, 164
  Hollywood liberals, 10, 179–85
  liberal bias attributed to, 8, 98, 116–17, 246
  religion in, 213–14
  smut in, 186–95
  spaces reserved for liberalism in, 98, 319–24
  and Vietnam War, 157
  See also Hollywood; talk radio; television
Media Matters for America, 98, 110, 329
Media Research Center, 179, 190
Medicare drug plan, 120–22, 181, 263, 296, 307
Medved, Michael, 135, 249
Meese, Michael J., 177
Meet the Press, 99–101, 153
mega-churches, 83, 86
Megan's Law, 205
Mehlman, Ken, 36
Mellencamp, John, 312
Meyerson, Harold, 100
Michaels, Walter Benn, 279
Micklethwaite, John, 51
Miers, Harriet, 176–77, 211
Miklaszewski, Jim, 285
Miles, Thomas J., 268
military, the
  "chickenhawk" issue, 133–37
  conservatives and, 132–56
  gays in, 158
  liberals' problem with, 156–58, 358n.77
Mill, John Stuart, 240
minimum wage, 12, 79, 303, 305
Miranda, Manuel, 8
Miranda v. Arizona, 39
moderates, 13, 339n.50
Moffit, Robert, 62
Mondale, Walter, 48, 136
Montagne, Renee, 215
Moon, Sun Myung, 9, 42, 175, 258
Moore, Michael, 180, 247
Moore, R. Lawrence, 197
morality. See values
mortality amenable to health care, 68
Moseley-Braun, Carol, 125

MoveOn.org, 3, 85, 245–46, 328
Moyers, Bill, 204
MSNBC, 98, 101, 104–6, 246–48, 298, 312–13
multiculturalism, 280
murder rate, 70
Murdoch, Rupert, 42, 102, 103, 108, 109, 175, 190–92, 193, 325
Murray, Charles, 274, 320, 374n.27
My Lai massacre, 152
Myrdal, Gunnar, 33

Nader, Ralph, 39, 54, 60
NAFTA, 299
Nagel, Thomas, 23
NARAL, 77, 79, 81
Nation, The, 100, 246, 378n.4
national debt, 309
National Guard, 148
National Review, 62, 151, 164, 175, 176, 203, 212, 215, 250, 286, 310, 323
National Rifle Association, 70
national security
  liberals seen as cavalier about, 162–67
  strong leadership and, 287, 293
  See also military, the
nation-building, 137–38
Neas, Ralph, 81
negative liberty, 27, 341n.12
neoconservatives, 43, 326
Neuhaus, Richard John, 203
New Criterion, 8
New Deal, 24–26
  collapse of coalition, 37, 73
  corporate militancy against, 29
  gradual expansion of, 28
  Kennedy and, 33
  liberals fail to go beyond, 30
  seen as socialist, 6, 41
  Stevenson on, 31
  working-class whites as beneficiaries of, 35
New Liberalism, 24
New Republic, 10, 29–30, 101, 103, 167, 310, 320
News Corporation, 83, 102, 190–93
newspapers, 108–12, 303
  op-ed pages, 110–11, 292
  See also New York Times; Wall Street Journal; Washington Post; Washington Times
Newsweek, 112, 320
newsweeklies, 112–15
New York Post, 108, 312
New York Times, 9, 84, 89–90, 109, 112, 178, 248, 250, 252, 310, 311–12, 318, 320–23

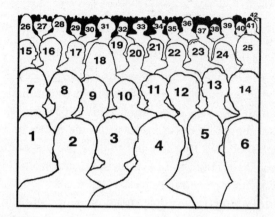

COVER KEY

1. Molly Ivins
2. Edward M. Kennedy
3. Nancy Pelosi
4. Franklin D. Roosevelt
5. Al Gore
6. Martin Luther King Jr.
7. Thomas Jefferson
8. Eleanor Roosevelt
9. Rosa Parks
10. Paul Wellstone
11. John Stuart Mill
12. Rachel Carson
13. Abraham Lincoln
14. Albert Einstein
15. Adam Smith
16. Robert F. Kennedy
17. Thurgood Marshall
18. Gloria Steinem
19. Harriet Tubman
20. The author
21. Walter Reuther
22. Cesar Chavez
23. Toni Morrison
24. Dolores Huerta
25. Thomas Paine
26. Jesus
27. Willie Nelson
28. Charles Darwin
29. John Kenneth Galbraith
30. I. F. Stone
31. Rabbi Abraham Joshua Heschel
32. Markos Moulitsas Zúniga
33. Robert Redford
34. Paul Newman
35. John Dewey
36. George McGovern
37. Jane Addams
38. Richard Rorty
39. John F. Kennedy
40. Arthur M. Schlesinger Jr.
41. Barney Frank
42. Russ Feingold

When Presidents Lie
A History of Official Deception and Its Consequences
One of the best-known left-of-center public intellectuals in America, Eric Alterman offers his devastating analysis of the costs of executive duplicity, arguing that those costs are not merely moral but practical. As examples, he uses four key lies told by presidents in the postwar era. From FDR at Yalta to LBJ in Vietnam, and from JFK in Cuba to Ronald Reagan in Central America, Alterman shows how attempts to mislead the American people ended up haunting their authors and dooming the very policies they were meant to advance. Closing with an examination of the Bush deceptions in Iraq, *When Presidents Lie* is history at its most compelling.

ISBN 978-0-14-303604-3

The Book on Bush
How George W. (Mis)leads America
When George W. Bush became president in January 2001, he took office with a familiar surname and the promise of calming a public shaken by the convulsions of a contested election. Then, after the tragedy of 9/11, both the country and the world looked to him for leadership that could unite people behind great common goals. Instead, George W. Bush squandered the good will felt toward America, turned allies into adversaries, and ran what may well be the most radical and divisive administration in the history of the presidency. Carefully documented and with vivid detail, *The Book on Bush* is an invaluable resource that exposes plutocracy posing as patriotism and, in area after area, the encroachment of radical right-wing ideology onto a moderate country.

ISBN 978-0-14-303442-1